Preconceptions of Policies, Strategies, and Challenges in Education 5.0

Ali Sorayyaei Azar
Management and Science University, Malaysia

Ahmad Albattat
Management and Science University, Malaysia

Marco Valeri
Niccolò Cusano University, Italy

Viana Hassan
University of Malta, Malta

A volume in the Advances in Educational Technologies and Instructional Design (AETID) Book Series

IGI Global
PUBLISHER of TIMELY KNOWLEDGE

Published in the United States of America by
IGI Global
Information Science Reference (an imprint of IGI Global)
701 E. Chocolate Avenue
Hershey PA, USA 17033
Tel: 717-533-8845
Fax: 717-533-8661
E-mail: cust@igi-global.com
Web site: http://www.igi-global.com

Library of Congress Cataloging-in-Publication Data

CIP Data in progress

British Cataloguing in Publication Data
A Cataloguing in Publication record for this book is available from the British Library.

For electronic access to this publication, please contact: eresources@igi-global.com.

Advances in Educational Technologies and Instructional Design (AETID) Book Series

Lawrence A. Tomei
Robert Morris University, USA

ISSN:2326-8905
EISSN:2326-8913

Mission

Education has undergone, and continues to undergo, immense changes in the way it is enacted and distributed to both child and adult learners. In modern education, the traditional classroom learning experience has evolved to include technological resources and to provide online classroom opportunities to students of all ages regardless of their geographical locations. From distance education, Massive-Open-Online-Courses (MOOCs), and electronic tablets in the classroom, technology is now an integral part of learning and is also affecting the way educators communicate information to students.

The **Advances in Educational Technologies & Instructional Design (AETID) Book Series** explores new research and theories for facilitating learning and improving educational performance utilizing technological processes and resources. The series examines technologies that can be integrated into K-12 classrooms to improve skills and learning abilities in all subjects including STEM education and language learning. Additionally, it studies the emergence of fully online classrooms for young and adult learners alike, and the communication and accountability challenges that can arise. Trending topics that are covered include adaptive learning, game-based learning, virtual school environments, and social media effects. School administrators, educators, academicians, researchers, and students will find this series to be an excellent resource for the effective design and implementation of learning technologies in their classes.

Coverage

- Bring-Your-Own-Device
- Curriculum Development
- Digital Divide in Education
- Game-Based Learning
- Hybrid Learning
- Online Media in Classrooms
- Social Media Effects on Education
- Virtual School Environments

IGI Global is currently accepting manuscripts for publication within this series. To submit a proposal for a volume in this series, please contact our Acquisition Editors at Acquisitions@igi-global.com or visit: http://www.igi-global.com/publish/.

The Advances in Educational Technologies and Instructional Design (AETID) Book Series (ISSN 2326-8905) is published by IGI Global, 701 E. Chocolate Avenue, Hershey, PA 17033-1240, USA, www.igi-global.com. This series is composed of titles available for purchase individually; each title is edited to be contextually exclusive from any other title within the series. For pricing and ordering information please visit http://www.igi-global.com/book-series/advances-educational-technologies-instructional-design/73678. Postmaster: Send all address changes to above address.

Titles in this Series

For a list of additional titles in this series, please visit: www.igi-global.com/book-series

Augmented Reality and the Future of Education Technology
Rashmi Aggarwal (Chitkara Business School, Chitkara University, India) Prachi Gupta (Chitkara Business School, Chitkara University, India) Satinder Singh (Chitkara Business School, Chitkara University, India) and Rajni Bala (Chitkara Business School, Chitkara University, India)
Information Science Reference • copyright 2024 • 297pp • H/C (ISBN: 9798369330159) • US $175.00 (our price)

Integrating Generative AI in Education to Achieve Sustainable Development Goals
Ruchi Doshi (Universidad Azteca, Mexico) Manish Dadhich (Sir Padampat Singhania University, India) Sandeep Poddar (Lincoln University College, Malaysia) and Kamal Kant Hiran (Sir Padampat Singhania University, India & Lincoln University College, Malaysia)
Information Science Reference • copyright 2024 • 532pp • H/C (ISBN: 9798369324400) • US $295.00 (our price)

Considerations and Techniques for Applied Linguistics and Language Education Research
Hung Phu Bui (University of Economics, Ho Chi Minh City, Vietnam)
Information Science Reference • copyright 2024 • 241pp • H/C (ISBN: 9798369364826) • US $245.00 (our price)

Comprehensive Sexuality Education for Gender-Based Violence Prevention
Mariana Buenestado-Fernández (University of Cantabria, Spain) Azahara Jiménez-Millán (University of Córdoba, Spain) and Francisco Javier Palacios-Hidalgo (University of Córdoba, Spain)
Information Science Reference • copyright 2024 • 342pp • H/C (ISBN: 9798369320532) • US $245.00 (our price)

Enhancing Curricula with Service Learning Models
Sharon Valarmathi (Christ University, India) Jacqueline Kareem (Christ University, India) Veerta Tantia (Christ University, India) Kishore Selva Babu (Christ University, India) and Patrick Jude Lucas (Christ University, India)
Information Science Reference • copyright 2024 • 328pp • H/C (ISBN: 9798369359334) • US $265.00 (our price)

Encouraging Transnational Learning Through Virtual Exchange in Global Teacher Education
Alina Slapac (University of Missouri-St. Louis, USA) and Cristina A. Huertas-Abril (University of Córdoba, Spain)
Information Science Reference • copyright 2024 • 424pp • H/C (ISBN: 9781668478134) • US $215.00 (our price)

IGI Global
PUBLISHER of TIMELY KNOWLEDGE

701 East Chocolate Avenue, Hershey, PA 17033, USA
Tel: 717-533-8845 x100 • Fax: 717-533-8661
E-Mail: cust@igi-global.com • www.igi-global.com

Table of Contents

Detailed Table of Contents

In this chapter, the authors investigate the transformative impact of cognitive computing, learning analytics, and game-based pedagogy in enhancing teachers' professional development within the dynamic societal context. Employing a comprehensive review of scholarly literature, explore how these technological advancements shape the educational landscape, paying particular attention to their implications for teachers' professional development. The discussion illustrates that through adopting cognitive computing, educators can access personalized insights and resources tailored to their needs, fostering continuous growth. Learning analytics provide valuable data-driven feedback, enabling educators to make informed decisions to optimize teaching strategies. Furthermore, gamification engages teachers in immersive learning experiences, enhancing motivation and collaboration. This research highlights the potential of innovative technologies in shaping a more responsive and effective educational system.

The aim of this study is to develop concept maps enriched with digital technologies to provide multimedia learning in science education. In the study, in which design and development research method was used, 6th and 8th grade students and science and technology teachers were considered as the common user group. In the process of developing concept maps enriched with digital technologies, the steps of applying instructional technology tools design methods and·introducing three designs obtained at the end of the process are included. It is expected that concept maps enriched with digital technologies in science education based on multimedia learning applications will support much more meaningful learning by enriching science lessons. With the concept maps enriched with digital technologies developed within the scope of the research, innovative technology applications were tried to be presented to our teachers and students in science and technology teaching.

In the realm of Education 5.0, individuals investing in English language learner (ELL) educator training recognize the imperative to equip students with an understanding of the challenges and possibilities emerging from the integration of technology into the English language classroom. Offering a comprehensive overview, this chapter delineates the utilization of an educational robotics approach in EFL education and contemplates potential outcomes for students studying English education.

This research assesses the effectiveness of Blended Learning (BL) in reducing English-speaking anxiety among STEM students. Language anxiety hinders engagement and knowledge acquisition in STEM, where English proficiency is crucial. The BL program combines traditional methods with digital resources to enhance language proficiency and confidence. The study uses a mixed-methods approach, measuring anxiety and performance, followed by a tailored behavior change intervention. Results show a significant reduction in anxiety levels, and a strong link between enhanced linguistic confidence and academic success in STEM. BL is identified as a valuable tool connecting language competency to academic excellence in STEM, with implications for educators, institutions, and policymakers. Further research is needed for a comprehensive understanding of its lasting impact.

Education is an essential component of human growth, equipping individuals with the skills and information required to tackle life's problems. Raising educational understanding is vital to providing equitable access for all. Education 5.0 aims to use modern technology to provide a more compassionate kind of education, emphasizing social and emotional development with creative solutions that improve societal well-being. Project-based learning (PBL) is a teaching strategy in which students investigate real-world challenges and topics via hands-on projects. This technique encourages the development of reasoning, problem-solving, and communication skills, all of which are crucial for success in today's professional world. PBL is an essential part of Education 5.0, a framework for personalized, collaborative, and technology-driven learning experiences. In conclusion, project-based learning systems in Education 5.0 are transforming education for the better, fostering meaningful learning experiences and practical skills that students can apply throughout their lives.

In the rapidly evolving landscape of education, the advent of Education 5.0 brings with it new challenges and opportunities for teachers. This chapter focuses on teacher professional development in the context of Education 5.0. It explores how teacher professional development has evolved with the integration of technology and new pedagogical approaches in education. The chapter discusses the importance of continuous professional development for teachers to keep up with the changing landscape of education and implement effective teaching practices. It also highlights the role of collaboration, personalized learning, and mentorship in enhancing teacher professional development in Education 5.0. Additionally, the chapter examines the challenges and barriers that teachers may face in adapting to the new demands of Education 5.0 and offers strategies for overcoming these challenges.

This chapter addresses the relevance of ICT to teacher professional development in the changing landscape of Education 5.0. It advocates a comprehensive strategy that harnesses ICT's numerous instruments to empower teachers, foster cooperation, and cultivate the necessary competencies for navigating the fast-expanding Education 5.0. Interviews and direct observations were employed. By addressing policies, competencies, strategies, directions, and problems, the book chapter gives a holistic vision of the transformative journey education must take to satisfy the needs of the 5.0 era. The involvement of ICT in teachers' professional development results in easier content delivery, collaboration, networking, and data-driven insights." This topical and thought-provoking compendium offers essential insights for educators, policymakers, researchers, practitioners, and postgraduate students negotiating the intricacies of contemporary education

Education 5.0 requires a fundamental change in the way assessments are conducted. To transcend the constraints of standardized examinations, it is essential to employ inventive approaches such as portfolios, projects, and digital badges, which play a vital role in fostering personalized learning and empowering students. The utilization of technology and data-driven methodologies such as big data and AI present exciting opportunities for adaptive learning and enhanced comprehension. Nevertheless, ethical concerns, safeguarding data privacy, and guaranteeing fairness in evaluation persist as significant obstacles. To enhance the abilities of students and bring about educational transformation, it is crucial to prioritize ongoing enhancement, international cooperation, and the use of innovative technologies. These factors are vital in determining the future of assessment and evaluation in Education 5.0.

The institutions which working in the educational field, are seeking to create an efficient educational process in proportion to technological changes. The success on the Educational approach, including Education 5.0, depends on the extent to which educational constraints and ethical considerations are taken into account as success requirements in the educational process such as feedback, discussions, and the teachers role, which are effects on the learners' understanding. Therefore, Institutions can work to develop the educational process without compromising educational quality through developing the ICT. So, In light of Education 5.0 endeavors achieving a smart society, and based on Perraton online education theory and other researches results, there is a need to focus on a group of necessary issues to ensure the success of the educational process and determining criteria for selecting appropriate online educational models that will overcome the educational constraints and help to keep up with the pace of acceleration and competition with other educational institutions.

"Steering Through Tomorrow's Educational Wave" provides a deep understanding of the areas of impact Education 5.0 is going to have within the learning environment of the future. This part is linked to the new technologies and evermore developing methods of educating, as well as newly appearing needs in society. Hence, this chapter concentrates on the changes the transformation of traditional educational strategies and tactics by Schooling 5.0 entails. Crucial topics include education that is customized to the relevant person, learning for life, the usage implementation of cutting-edge educational technology tools, the skills needed for the 21st-century skills, cooperation partnership cultures, equality and inclusion, and being able to change and adapt. As presented throughout the article in a complex form; this chapter is going to provide information based on sailing medical pills through the mazes of education as a student to get acquainted.

This chapter attempts to address the issue of freedom-responsibility nexus in the era of Education 5.0, defining and establishing the rationale between freedom and responsibility and their resilience in the educational realm through reviewing relevant literature from various respects steering towards education and particularly Education 5.0. This chapter also discusses the space of freedom anticipated and the extent of responsibility it places. It also discusses the opportunities and challenges that freedom-responsibility nexus in the era of Education 5.0 is prone to offer. The intersection between freedom, responsibility and education is further demonstrated with reference to historical and philosophical perspectives, and through analyzing three relevant case studies from different contexts to recommend a three-pillar method for introducing the change into education. Bearing in mind the impact of conceptualizing and reconceptualizing the nexus across freedom, responsibility and education alongside the massive new possibilities Education 5.0 offers.

Preface

The landscape of education is undergoing a profound transformation as we enter the 5.0 era, marked by rapid technological advancements, societal shifts, and unprecedented global connectivity. In response to these dynamic changes, we are pleased to present *Reconceptions of Policies, Strategies, and Challenges in Education 5.0*, an edited volume that provides a comprehensive exploration of the evolving educational environment.

This book addresses the pressing need for a paradigm shift in educational policies, recognizing the imperative to align frameworks with contemporary challenges and future directions. The contributors of this volume meticulously analyze the role of policies in adapting to the demands of the 5.0 era, emphasizing the critical importance of forward-thinking strategies in shaping educational systems that are resilient and responsive.

Central to our discussion are the competencies required for success in this new era. We delve into the essential skills and knowledge that learners need to navigate an increasingly complex and interconnected world. From digital literacy to critical thinking, the book identifies key competencies that will empower individuals to thrive. Our contributors offer in-depth analyses of how these competencies can be nurtured and developed within the educational ecosystem.

Strategies for the effective implementation of Education 5.0 are also a focal point of our volume. We explore innovative teaching methodologies, the integration of technology in classrooms, and collaborative approaches that redefine the learning experience. The insights provided herein aim to equip educators, institutions, and policymakers with the tools and knowledge to create dynamic and responsive learning environments.

Looking ahead, this book explores the future directions of education in the 5.0 era. Our contributors discuss emerging trends, potential disruptions, and novel approaches that are likely to shape the future of learning. This forward-looking perspective encourages readers to envision the trajectory of education and consider the possibilities that lie ahead.

However, the journey towards reconceptualizing education for the 5.0 era is not without its challenges. The book critically examines obstacles such as inclusivity and the digital divide, highlighting the need for equitable access and quality education for all. By addressing these challenges head-on, we hope to foster a more inclusive and equitable educational landscape.

Reconceptions of Policies, Strategies, and Challenges in Education 5.0 is a timely and thought-provoking compilation. It offers valuable insights for educators, policymakers, researchers, practitioners, and postgraduate students navigating the complexities of contemporary education. By addressing policies, competencies, strategies, directions, and challenges, this book provides a holistic view of the transformative journey that education must undertake to meet the demands of the 5.0 era.

We extend our deepest gratitude to the contributors for their insightful analyses and to our readers for engaging with this crucial discourse. Together, we embark on a journey towards a more innovative, inclusive, and future-ready educational system.

ORGANIZATION OF THE BOOK

Chapter 1: Globalization, Cultural Competence, and English Language Education 5.0 Policy Implications and Strategies

Dr. Haida Umiera Hashim

In this chapter, Dr. Haida Umiera Hashim examines the critical role of English Language Education (ELE) in a globalized world where cultural competence has become increasingly important. With globalization influencing cultural interactions and linguistic diversity, the chapter addresses the need for policy implications and strategies to enhance ELE 5.0. It scrutinizes existing policies, identifies challenges, and proposes strategies to improve cultural competence in ELE, emphasizing equitable access, inclusive practices, and effective teacher training. This comprehensive analysis highlights the intersection of globalization, cultural competence, and ELE, providing valuable insights for educators and policymakers.

Chapter 2: Data Security Knowledge Among Students of Public Universities: A Fundamental Competency for Success in The Education 5.0 Era

Hapini Awang, Abderrahmane Benlahcene, and Nur Suhaili Mansor

This chapter investigates the current understanding of data security among students in Malaysia's higher education system, with a focus on social media security and data protection measures. The findings reveal significant gaps in students' knowledge, underscoring the need for educational reforms. The authors advocate for incorporating data security education into the curriculum to cultivate a generation of digitally literate individuals. By evaluating existing challenges and proposing educational interventions, this chapter contributes to the broader discourse on preparing students for the digital era, with implications extending beyond Malaysia to a global context.

Chapter 3: Navigating through Education 5.0 Era Imperative Competencies for Success

Ram Singh

Ram Singh explores the competencies essential for thriving in the Education 5.0 era, characterized by rapid technological advancements and societal changes. The chapter emphasizes a shift from traditional academic achievements to holistic competencies, including critical thinking, adaptability, and collaboration. By providing practical insights and actionable strategies for both learners and educators, Singh offers a roadmap for navigating the dynamic landscape of Education 5.0. The development of these competencies is crucial for individuals to succeed and contribute meaningfully to a rapidly evolving global society.

Chapter 4: Educating to Innovate: Fostering Innovation through Interdisciplinary Collaboration between Design and Engineering Students

Elad Harison

Elad Harison examines the collaboration between design and engineering students in fostering innovation. Traditionally, research and development processes have been segmented, with engineers focusing on technical aspects and designers on aesthetics. This chapter highlights the benefits of interdisciplinary collaboration, using a workshop model involving students, practitioners, and researchers. Harison's findings provide insights into methods of enhancing innovation through joint design-engineering work, offering valuable recommendations for academia-industry partnerships that can drive innovative outputs.

Chapter 5: Rethinking Entrepreneurship Education (EE) in the Era of Education 5.0: Towards a Selective Approach

Aissa Mosbah and Abdelbaset Queiri

Aissa Mosbah and Abdelbaset Queiri critique the current approach to Entrepreneurship Education (EE), which is often inclusive but ineffective. They propose a selective approach to EE, targeting students who demonstrate a genuine interest and potential in entrepreneurship. The chapter discusses the limitations of teaching EE universally, citing resource constraints and varying levels of student engagement. By advocating for a more pragmatic, selective approach, the authors aim to enhance the effectiveness of EE and better align it with the demands of Education 5.0.

Chapter 6: Preparing Teachers and Students for the Challenges of Society 5.0: Integration of Cognitive Computing, Learning Analytics, and Gamification of Learning

Midya Yousefi, Jahirul Mullick, and Qiusu Wang

This chapter investigates the impact of cognitive computing, learning analytics, and gamification on teacher professional development. The authors review scholarly literature to explore how these technologies can enhance educational practices. Cognitive computing provides personalized insights for educators, learning analytics offer data-driven feedback, and gamification engages teachers in immersive learning experiences. The chapter highlights the potential of these innovations to create a more responsive and effective educational system, fostering continuous growth for both teachers and students.

Chapter 7: Multimedia Material for Science and Technology Teaching: Concept Maps Enriched with Digital Technologies

Canan Altundag and Rabia Elmas

Canan Altundag and Rabia Elmas focus on developing concept maps enriched with digital technologies to support multimedia learning in science education. Targeting 6th and 8th-grade students and teachers, the chapter details the design and development process of these enhanced concept maps. By integrating instructional technology tools, the authors aim to enrich science lessons and promote meaningful learning experiences. This innovative approach offers valuable resources for educators seeking to implement technology-driven teaching methods in science education.

Chapter 8: Navigating Education 5.0 Robotic Technique for Teaching Foreign Languages in Today's Classroom

Muthmainnah Muthmainnah, Eka Apriani, Abdul Marzuki, Ahmad Al Yakin, Nur Aeni, Ali Azar, and Mohd. Rafi Riyawi

This chapter explores the use of educational robotics in teaching English as a Foreign Language (EFL). The authors provide a comprehensive overview of how robotic techniques can enhance EFL education, highlighting the potential benefits for students. By integrating robotics into language learning, educators can create interactive and engaging learning environments. The chapter also discusses the challenges and opportunities associated with this innovative approach, offering practical recommendations for educators and policymakers.

Chapter 9: STEMvolution: Mastering English Language Confidence with Blended Learning in the Education

Soumya Sankar Ghosh

Soumya Sankar Ghosh assesses the effectiveness of Blended Learning (BL) in reducing English-speaking anxiety among STEM students. Combining traditional methods with digital resources, BL aims to enhance language proficiency and confidence. The chapter uses a mixed-methods approach to measure anxiety and performance, followed by a tailored behavior change intervention. Results show a significant reduction in anxiety levels and a strong link between enhanced linguistic confidence and academic success in STEM. The findings underscore the value of BL in improving language competency and academic outcomes.

Chapter 10: The Project-Based Learning Approach (PBL): Enthralling Students Through Project-Based Learning Approach (PBL) in Education 5.0

Arpita Nayak, Ipseeta Satpathy, and Vishal Jain

Arpita Nayak, Ipseeta Satpathy, and Vishal Jain discuss the role of Project-Based Learning (PBL) in Education 5.0. PBL involves students in hands-on projects that address real-world challenges, fostering critical thinking, problem-solving, and communication skills. The chapter emphasizes the importance of PBL in creating personalized, collaborative, and technology-driven learning experiences. By integrating PBL into the curriculum, educators can provide meaningful learning experiences that prepare students for the complexities of the modern world.

Chapter 11: Teacher Professional Development in Education 5.0

Nhat Truong Tran Minh

Nhat Truong Tran Minh explores the evolving landscape of teacher professional development in the context of Education 5.0. The chapter highlights the importance of continuous professional development to keep pace with technological advancements and new pedagogical approaches. It discusses the role of collaboration, personalized learning, and mentorship in enhancing teacher development. Additionally, the chapter addresses the challenges teachers face in adapting to Education 5.0 and offers strategies for overcoming these obstacles.

Chapter 12: The Contribution of ICT in Teacher Professional Development in Education 5.0

Titus Tossy

Titus Tossy addresses the relevance of Information and Communication Technology (ICT) in teacher professional development. The chapter advocates for a comprehensive strategy that leverages ICT tools to empower teachers, foster collaboration, and develop necessary competencies. Through interviews and observations, Tossy highlights the transformative potential of ICT in enhancing content delivery, collaboration, networking, and data-driven insights. This chapter provides valuable insights for educators, policymakers, and researchers on the integration of ICT in professional development.

Chapter 13: Assessment and Evaluation in Education 5.0

Maida Maqsood, Abeer Othman, Muhammad Ilyas, Rehan Mehmood Sabir, Isma Urooj, Tayyaba Zahra, and Obaid Muhammad Abdullah

This chapter examines the need for innovative assessment methods in Education 5.0. Moving beyond standardized examinations, the authors advocate for approaches such as portfolios, projects, and digital badges to support personalized learning. They discuss the opportunities presented by technology and data-driven methodologies like big data and AI. The chapter also addresses ethical concerns, data privacy, and fairness in evaluation, emphasizing the importance of continuous improvement and international cooperation in shaping the future of assessment.

Chapter 14: Ethical Considerations and Educational Constraints in 5.0 Education

Zaid Abu-Bajeh

Zaid Abu-Bajeh explores the ethical considerations and educational constraints inherent in Education 5.0. The chapter discusses the importance of addressing feedback, discussions, and the teacher's role in enhancing learners' understanding. Abu-Bajeh highlights the need for institutions to develop the educational process without compromising quality, focusing on ICT integration. By considering ethical issues and educational constraints, the chapter provides criteria for selecting appropriate online educational models to keep pace with technological advancements and competition.

Chapter 15: Education 5.0: Navigating the Future of Learning

Froilan Mobo

Froilan Mobo provides a comprehensive overview of the impact of Education 5.0 on the future learning environment. The chapter focuses on the transformation of traditional educational strategies, emphasizing personalized learning, lifelong education, and the use of advanced educational technology. Mobo discusses the skills needed for the 21st century, collaboration cultures, equality and inclusion, and adaptability. By navigating these changes, the chapter offers valuable insights into the future of education and the necessary steps to prepare for it.

Chapter 16: Freedom and Responsibility in Education 5.0

Mohammad Ali Al-Saggaf

This chapter attempts to address the issue of freedom-responsibility nexus in the era of Education 5.0, defining and establishing the rational between freedom and responsibility and their resilience in the educational realm through reviewing relevant literature from various respects steering towards education and particularly Education 5.0. This chapter also discusses the space of freedom anticipated and the extent of responsibility it places. It also discusses the opportunities and challenges that freedom-responsibility nexus in the era of Education 5.0 is prone to offer. The intersection between freedom, responsibility and education is further demonstrated with reference to historical and philosophical perspectives, and through analyzing three relevant case studies from different contexts to recommend a three-pillar method for introducing the change into education. Bearing in mind the impact of conceptualizing and reconceptualizing the nexus across freedom, responsibility and education alongside the massive new possibilities Education 5.0 offers.

IN CONCLUSION

As the editors of this comprehensive reference book on Education 5.0, we are delighted to present this collection of insightful chapters that collectively navigate the multifaceted landscape of contemporary education. Each chapter, contributed by esteemed scholars and practitioners from around the globe, illuminates critical aspects of Education 5.0, offering diverse perspectives and innovative approaches that reflect the dynamic nature of this transformative era.

The chapters in this book underscore the imperative to integrate technological advancements, cultural competence, and holistic educational strategies into our education systems. From exploring the intersection of globalization and English Language Education to addressing the significance of data security knowledge among university students, the contributions provide a nuanced understanding of the challenges and opportunities that characterize Education 5.0.

Our journey through the imperative competencies for success in this new era highlights the need for a shift towards holistic development, critical thinking, and collaboration. Interdisciplinary collaboration, as detailed in the examination of design and engineering education, showcases the potential of synergistic efforts in fostering innovation. The transformative power of formative evaluations and the Critical Incident Questionnaire exemplify how adaptive feedback mechanisms can enhance teaching effectiveness and student learning experiences.

The selective approach to Entrepreneurship Education, cognitive computing's role in professional development, and the integration of gamification and learning analytics demonstrate the evolving pedagogical methods that can empower both educators and students. The emphasis on blended learning and project-based learning further reinforces the importance of engaging, hands-on educational experiences that prepare learners for the complexities of the modern world.

Teacher professional development remains a cornerstone of Education 5.0, with ICT playing a pivotal role in enhancing content delivery, collaboration, and data-driven decision-making. The chapters dedicated to innovative assessment methods and ethical considerations in education provide critical insights into the evolving standards and practices necessary for ensuring fairness, privacy, and continuous improvement.

As we look towards the future, it is evident that Education 5.0 demands a paradigm shift that embraces personalization, inclusivity, and adaptability. This book serves as a valuable resource for educators, policymakers, researchers, and students, offering practical strategies and theoretical foundations to navigate the future of learning. By fostering collaboration, leveraging technology, and prioritizing holistic development, we can collectively shape an education system that meets the needs of our rapidly changing world.

We extend our deepest gratitude to the contributors for their invaluable insights and to the readers for engaging with this important discourse. It is our hope that this book will inspire continued innovation and progress in the field of education, ultimately contributing to the creation of a more equitable and effective learning environment for all.

Ali Sorayyaei Azar
Management and Science University, Malaysia

Ahmad Albattat
Management and Science University, Malaysia

Marco Valeri
Niccolò Cusano University, Italy

Viana Hassan
University of Malta, Malta

Chapter 1
Globalization, Cultural Competence, and English Language Education 5.0 Policy Implications and Strategies

Haida Umiera Hashim
English Language Department, Academy of Language Studies, Universiti Teknologi MARA (UiTM), Shah Alam, Malaysia

ABSTRACT

In this chapter, the author highlights how English language education (ELE) has become a crucial aspect of education systems worldwide. As globalization continues to impact cultural interactions and linguistic diversity, the importance of cultural competence in ELE has grown significantly. This chapter explores the policy implications and strategies necessary to address the intersection of globalization, cultural competence, and ELE 5.0. It examines existing policies, identifies challenges, and proposes strategies to enhance cultural competence in ELE, focusing on equitable access, inclusive practices, and effective teacher training.

BACKGROUND

Globalization has been a transformative force in shaping societies, economies, and cultures around the world (Pieterse, 2019). As communication technologies advance and international connections deepen, the need for effective cross-cultural communication becomes increasingly evident. Within the realm of education, globalization has significantly influenced language teaching and learning, particularly in the context of English Language Education (ELE) (Al-Issa, A., & Mirhosseini, 2019). English has emerged as a global lingua franca, facilitating communication and collaboration across borders. However, with linguistic diversity and cultural richness also comes the imperative for cultural competence in language education. According to Jackson (2019), cultural competence encompasses not only language proficiency but also the ability to navigate and understand diverse cultural perspectives, norms, and communication styles. In response to these complexities, Barrot (2022) believes that English Language Education 5.0 (ELE 5.0) has emerged as a holistic approach that integrates technology, cultural sensitivity, and inclusive

DOI: 10.4018/979-8-3693-3041-8.ch001

pedagogy. In conjunction to this, this chapter aims to venture into discussing the policy implications and strategies necessary to promote cultural competence in ELE 5.0, addressing the challenges and opportunities presented by globalization and cultural diversity in language education.

GLOBALIZATION AND ITS IMPACT ON ENGLISH LANGUAGE EDUCATION (ELE)

Globalization is a multifaceted phenomenon that encompasses the interconnectedness and interdependence of economies, cultures, technologies, and societies on a global scale (Zalli, 2024). At its core, globalization represents the integration and exchange of goods, services, ideas, and information across borders, transcending traditional barriers and reshaping the way the world operates. Economically, globalization has led to the emergence of a global market where goods and services flow freely, facilitated by advancements in transportation, communication, and digital technologies (Halder, 2023). Zohuri (2023) believes that this interconnectedness has spurred economic growth, created new opportunities for trade and investment, and interconnected economies in ways never seen before. Culturally, globalization has facilitated the exchange of cultural practices, values, and beliefs, leading to cultural hybridization and the emergence of a global culture characterized by shared experiences, influences, and trends. Technologically, globalization has accelerated innovation and knowledge-sharing, driving rapid advancements in science, technology, and communication that have revolutionized industries, transformed lifestyles, and connected people across the globe in real-time (Hennen & Van Est, 2023). Societally, globalization has brought people closer together, fostering greater awareness, understanding, and cooperation among individuals and communities from diverse backgrounds. However, according to Ahmed and Popova (2023), globalization also poses challenges, such as economic inequalities, cultural homogenization, environmental impacts, and geopolitical tensions, highlighting the complexities and nuances of this dynamic and evolving phenomenon.

Ruane (2022) mentioned that globalization has catalyzed a seismic shift in English Language Education (ELE), permeating its essence with multifaceted impacts. At its core, globalization has spurred an unprecedented demand for English proficiency, driven by the language's status as a global lingua franca (Alam, 2023). This demand transcends geographical boundaries, resonating in classrooms from bustling metropolises to remote villages, as individuals recognize the role of English in accessing international opportunities, forging global connections, and navigating the complexities of a rapidly evolving world. Moreover, globalization has engendered a mosaic of cultural diversity within ELE environments. Nazari, Karimpour & De Costa (2023) believed that students and educators from diverse linguistic and cultural backgrounds converge, creating vibrant ecosystems where languages, traditions, and perspectives intertwine. This diversity enriches the learning experience, fostering cross-cultural understanding, empathy, and collaboration—an essential aspect in cultivating global citizens adept at navigating intercultural communication nuances. Additionally, the digital revolution spurred by globalization has revolutionized language learning paradigms. Technological advancements have democratized access to ELE resources, unleashing a plethora of digital tools, online platforms, and immersive experiences that transcend physical boundaries, making language learning more interactive, personalized, and accessible (Kumbo, Mero & Hayuma, 2023). Furthermore, globalization has influenced language policies, curriculum design, and pedagogical approaches, propelling educators and institutions to adopt innovative strategies that resonate with the demands of a globalized society (Agarwal, 2018). In essence, globalization has become an intrinsic force shaping the landscape of ELE, heralding an era where linguistic proficiency, cultural competence, and technological fluency converge to equip learners with the skills and competencies needed to thrive in an interconnected world.

Globalization has had a profound impact on English Language Education (ELE) (Murray, 2020), shaping its evolution and redefining its role in an interconnected world. As globalization accelerates the flow of information, goods, and people across borders, English has emerged as a vital tool for communication, collaboration, and access to global opportunities (Rao, 2019). The demand for English proficiency has surged, driven by the language's status as a lingua franca in international business, diplomacy, academia, and digital communication. In response, English Language Education has undergone significant transformations, embracing innovative pedagogies, digital technologies, and cultural competencies to prepare learners for a globalized society (Barik, 2023). Globalization has also fostered cultural diversity within ELE environments, bringing together students and educators from diverse linguistic and cultural backgrounds. This diversity enriches the learning experience, promoting cross-cultural understanding, empathy, and communication skills essential for navigating intercultural interactions. Moreover, globalization has facilitated the exchange of educational resources, best practices, and collaborative initiatives among institutions worldwide, enhancing the quality and accessibility of English language education. However, Maqsood et al., (2023) also believes that globalization also presents challenges, such as ensuring equitable access to ELE resources, addressing linguistic inequalities, and navigating cultural sensitivities in language teaching and learning. Despite these challenges, globalization continues to shape and redefine English Language Education, emphasizing the importance of cultural competence, technological fluency, and inclusive practices in preparing learners for a globally interconnected future.

CULTURAL COMPETENCE IN ENGLISH LANGUAGE EDUCATION (ELE)

According to Eden, Chisom & Adeniyi (2024), cultural competence is a multifaceted concept that encompasses a range of skills, attitudes, and behaviors essential for effective communication and interaction in diverse cultural settings. At its core, cultural competence involves the ability to understand, respect, and navigate cultural differences, while also recognizing and valuing the inherent dignity and worth of individuals from different backgrounds (Barret, 2018). This includes developing awareness of one's own cultural biases and assumptions, actively seeking to learn about and appreciate other cultures, and adapting communication styles and behaviors to be inclusive and respectful of diverse perspectives. Cultural competence goes beyond mere tolerance; it involves empathy, curiosity, and a willingness to engage in meaningful dialogue and collaboration across cultural boundaries. In educational contexts, cultural competence is particularly important in fostering inclusive learning environments where students from diverse backgrounds feel valued, supported, and empowered to succeed. Educators play a critical role in promoting cultural competence by incorporating diverse perspectives into the curriculum, facilitating discussions on cultural topics, and creating opportunities for intercultural exchange and collaboration among students. Ultimately, cultural competence is a lifelong journey of learning, reflection, and growth, essential for building bridges across cultures, fostering mutual understanding, and promoting a more harmonious and inclusive global community.

Cultural competence in English Language Education (ELE) is a fundamental aspect that transcends mere language proficiency, encompassing a deep understanding and appreciation of diverse cultural backgrounds, beliefs, and communication styles. It entails fostering an inclusive learning environment where students from various cultural contexts feel respected, valued, and empowered to engage actively in the learning process. Cultural competence in ELE involves educators recognizing and addressing their own cultural biases, adapting teaching strategies to accommodate diverse learning styles, and incorporating multicultural perspectives into the curriculum. This includes exploring literature, media, and cultural artifacts from different cultures, facilitating discussions on global issues and perspectives, and promoting empathy, curiosity, and open-mindedness among students. Moreover, cultural competence in ELE extends to developing intercultural communication skills, such as navigating cross-cultural misunderstandings, using appropriate language and gestures in diverse settings, and promoting mutual respect and understanding in interactions with speakers of different languages. By fostering cultural competence in ELE, educators not only prepare students to communicate effectively in a globalized world but also contribute to building inclusive, respectful, and harmonious communities that celebrate diversity and promote cross-cultural collaboration and mutual respect.

POLICY FRAMEWORKS IN ENGLISH LANGUAGE EDUCATION 5.0 (ELE 5.0)

Policy frameworks in education play a crucial role in shaping the direction, priorities, and practices of educational systems at local, national, and international levels (Butler et al., 2018). These frameworks provide a structured and systematic approach to addressing key issues such as curriculum development, assessment practices, teacher training, resource allocation, and educational equity. Madani (2019) believes that the importance of policy frameworks in education lies in their ability to set clear objectives, standards, and guidelines that promote quality education, equitable access, and positive learning outcomes for all learners. They provide a framework for decision-making, planning, and implementation of educational initiatives, ensuring coherence, consistency, and accountability within educational systems. Policy frameworks also serve as a tool for promoting innovation, research, and evidence-based practices in education, driving continuous improvement and adaptation to changing societal needs and global trends (Gonzalez & Ramirez, 2022). Moreover, effective policy frameworks in education foster collaboration and partnership among stakeholders, including governments, educational institutions, teachers, parents, and communities, to work towards common goals and shared visions for educational excellence and student success. Overall, policy frameworks in education are essential for establishing a supportive and conducive environment for teaching and learning, promoting educational equity and inclusivity, and driving positive change and progress in education systems worldwide.

Policy frameworks in English Language Education 5.0 (ELE 5.0) are instrumental in navigating the complex landscape of language teaching and learning in the era of globalization and technological advancement. ELE 5.0 represents a transformative phase that integrates digital technologies, cultural competence, and inclusive pedagogical practices, necessitating robust and adaptive policy frameworks. These frameworks serve as guiding principles and strategic roadmaps for educational institutions, governments, and stakeholders to effectively implement and sustain innovative approaches in language education. They encompass a wide range of aspects, including curriculum development, teacher training, assessment methodologies, technology integration, linguistic diversity, and equitable access to educational resources.

One of the key focuses of policy frameworks in ELE 5.0 is promoting cultural competence and intercultural communication skills among educators and learners. This involves developing policies that encourage the inclusion of diverse cultural perspectives in the curriculum, fostering cross-cultural dialogue and understanding, and providing training and professional development opportunities for educators to enhance their cultural awareness and sensitivity. Additionally, policy frameworks in ELE 5.0 prioritize the integration of digital technologies into language teaching and learning processes. This includes establishing guidelines for the use of digital tools, online resources, and virtual platforms to enhance language acquisition, collaboration, and global connectivity. Furthermore, policy frameworks in ELE 5.0 address issues of linguistic diversity by promoting multilingual education approaches that value and support learners' native languages while fostering English proficiency. They also emphasize the importance of equitable access to quality language education for all learners, regardless of their socio-economic status, geographical location, or cultural background, thus promoting inclusivity and educational equity in ELE 5.0 initiatives.

In addition to promoting cultural competence and technological integration, policy frameworks in ELE 5.0 also emphasize the importance of continuous evaluation, research, and adaptation to ensure the relevance and effectiveness of language education strategies. They encourage data-driven decision-making, evidence-based practices, and collaboration with research institutions to monitor progress, identify areas for improvement, and incorporate emerging trends and best practices into ELE 5.0 policies. Moreover, policy frameworks in ELE 5.0 foster collaboration and partnerships among educational stakeholders, including governments, educational institutions, industry partners, non-governmental organizations, and communities, to collectively address challenges, share resources, and drive innovation in language education. By establishing clear objectives, standards, and guidelines, policy frameworks in ELE 5.0 promote accountability, coherence, and alignment with global trends and best practices, ultimately contributing to the enhancement of language learning outcomes and the development of culturally competent and globally engaged learners.

STRATEGIES FOR PROMOTING CULTURAL COMPETENCE

Promoting cultural competence in English Language Education (ELE) requires a multifaceted approach that encompasses curriculum design, teacher training, intercultural exchange programs, community engagement, and research-based assessment practices. Firstly, curriculum design plays a pivotal role in fostering cultural competence among learners. Gay (2018) believes that educators should integrate diverse perspectives, multicultural literature, and authentic cultural materials into the curriculum to expose students to a variety of cultural experiences, beliefs, and practices. This approach encourages students to develop empathy, respect, and curiosity towards different cultures, promoting a deeper understanding of cultural diversity and enhancing their ability to communicate effectively across cultural boundaries.

Secondly, teacher training and professional development are essential strategies for promoting cultural competence in ELE. Educators need training in cultural awareness, intercultural communication skills, and inclusive pedagogy to create inclusive learning environments and facilitate meaningful cross-cultural interactions. Professional development programs should provide educators with resources, workshops, and ongoing support to enhance their cultural competence and incorporate culturally responsive teaching practices into their classrooms. Moreover, Hands, Armstrong and Mitchell (2020) believe that mentorship programs and collaborative learning communities can facilitate knowledge-sharing and peer support among educators, fostering a culture of continuous learning and improvement in promoting cultural competence. On top of that, intercultural exchange programs and collaborative projects offer valuable opportunities for students to engage in cross-cultural interactions, build empathy, and develop intercultural communication skills. Virtual exchanges, cultural immersion experiences, and collaborative projects with students from diverse backgrounds promote dialogue, collaboration, and mutual understanding among learners. These programs provide real-world contexts for applying cultural competence skills, fostering empathy, respect, and appreciation for cultural diversity, and preparing students to navigate multicultural environments with confidence and sensitivity.

Alongside that, Lindsey et al., (2018) mention that community engagement initiatives play a crucial role in promoting cultural competence in ELE. Partnerships with local communities, cultural organizations, and language immersion programs provide students with opportunities to engage with authentic cultural experiences, interact with native speakers, and gain insights into diverse cultural perspectives. Community-based projects, cultural events, and service-learning activities encourage students to apply their cultural competence skills in real-world settings, fostering a deeper connection to global issues, promoting social responsibility, and preparing students to be active and engaged global citizens. Finally, research-based assessment practices are essential for measuring and promoting cultural competence in ELE. Assessment tools should go beyond traditional measures of language proficiency to include evaluations of intercultural communication skills, cultural awareness, and attitudes towards cultural diversity (Avgousti, 2018). Performance assessments, portfolios, reflective journals, and peer evaluations can provide valuable insights into students' cultural competence development and inform instructional practices. Moreover, ongoing research and evaluation studies on the effectiveness of cultural competence initiatives can contribute to evidence-based policy decisions, program improvements, and best practices in promoting cultural competence in ELE.

EQUITABLE ACCESS TO ENGLISH LANGUAGE EDUCATION (ELE)

Equitable access to English Language Education (ELE) is a fundamental principle that ensures all learners, regardless of their background, have fair and inclusive opportunities to access high-quality language education (Garcia & Kleifgen, 2018). One strategy for promoting equitable access is through the development of policies and initiatives that prioritize linguistic diversity and support multilingual education. This includes recognizing and valuing languages other than English, providing bilingual or multilingual education programs, and offering resources and support services for learners whose first language is not English. By promoting linguistic diversity and supporting students in maintaining their native languages while acquiring English proficiency, equitable access to ELE is enhanced, ensuring that all learners can thrive and succeed in language education.

Another strategy for promoting equitable access to ELE is addressing socio-economic barriers that may hinder access to educational resources and opportunities. This includes providing financial assistance, scholarships, and subsidies for language education programs, textbooks, and digital resources. Additionally, offering flexible learning options, such as online courses, distance learning, and evening classes, can accommodate learners with diverse schedules and responsibilities, promoting accessibility and inclusivity in ELE. Moreover, investing in infrastructure, technology, and digital literacy programs can bridge the digital divide and provide equal access to digital resources and online learning platforms for all learners, regardless of their socio-economic status (Chetty et al., 2018).

Furthermore, promoting inclusive practices in ELE is essential for ensuring equitable access and support for learners with diverse learning needs, abilities, and backgrounds. This includes adopting differentiated instruction strategies, providing accommodations and support services for students with disabilities or learning difficulties, and creating inclusive learning environments that celebrate diversity and foster a sense of belonging for all learners. Additionally, promoting culturally responsive teaching practices, incorporating diverse perspectives into the curriculum, and providing culturally relevant resources and materials can enhance engagement, motivation, and learning outcomes for students from diverse cultural backgrounds, promoting equity and inclusivity in ELE.

Moreover, community engagement and partnerships play a crucial role in promoting equitable access to ELE. Collaborating with community organizations, non-governmental organizations, cultural centers, and language immersion programs can provide additional support, resources, and opportunities for learners from marginalized communities, refugees, immigrants, and other underserved populations. Community-based initiatives, outreach programs, and mentorship opportunities can empower learners, build confidence, and promote educational equity by providing additional support and resources outside of the traditional classroom setting.

Finally, ongoing research, data collection, and evaluation are essential for monitoring progress, identifying barriers, and informing evidence-based policy decisions and interventions to promote equitable access to ELE. Collecting data on enrollment rates, retention rates, academic achievement, and student outcomes across diverse learner populations can provide insights into areas for improvement and inform targeted interventions and resources allocation to address disparities and promote equity in ELE. By adopting a comprehensive and holistic approach that addresses linguistic diversity, socio-economic barriers, inclusive practices, community engagement, and research-based strategies, equitable access to ELE can be promoted, ensuring that all learners have the opportunity to achieve their full potential and thrive in language education.

INCLUSIVE PRACTICES IN ENGLISH LANGUAGE EDUCATION (ELE)

According to Lau and Shea (2022), inclusive practices in English Language Education (ELE) are essential for creating supportive and empowering learning environments that embrace diversity, promote equity, and foster academic success for all learners. One strategy for promoting inclusive practices is adopting a differentiated instruction approach that recognizes and accommodates diverse learning needs, styles, and abilities. This includes providing flexible learning options, personalized learning pathways, and adaptive resources to meet the unique needs of each learner, promoting engagement, motivation, and learning outcomes in ELE. Additionally, incorporating Universal Design for Learning (UDL) principles into curriculum design and instructional strategies can further enhance inclusivity by ensuring that learning materials, activities, and assessments are accessible and beneficial for all learners, regardless of their background or abilities (Evmenova, 2018).

Promoting culturally responsive teaching practices is integral to creating inclusive ELE environments that honor and celebrate diversity. This involves incorporating diverse perspectives, cultural artifacts, and experiences into the curriculum, fostering dialogue, empathy, and mutual respect among students from different cultural backgrounds. Culturally responsive teaching also involves creating opportunities for students to share their cultural experiences, perspectives, and languages in the classroom, promoting a sense of belonging, identity affirmation, and cultural pride. Moreover, culturally responsive assessment practices, such as incorporating diverse assessment formats, providing multiple pathways for demonstrating learning, and valuing students' cultural assets and strengths, can enhance inclusivity and promote equitable assessment practices in ELE.

Additionally, Hymel & Katz (2019) mention that creating inclusive learning environments in ELE involves fostering a sense of community, collaboration, and belonging among students. This includes promoting positive classroom relationships, peer support networks, and collaborative learning experiences that encourage teamwork, communication, and social interaction among students from diverse backgrounds. Incorporating cooperative learning strategies, group projects, and interactive activities can facilitate peer learning, cultural exchange, and mutual support, promoting a sense of community and belonging for all learners. Furthermore, creating safe and inclusive spaces where students feel respected, valued, and empowered to express themselves, share their perspectives, and ask questions fosters a culture of inclusivity and openness in ELE.

Moreover, promoting inclusive practices in ELE involves providing additional support and accommodations for learners with diverse learning needs, abilities, and backgrounds (Villa & Thousand, 2021). This includes offering resources, assistive technologies, and support services for students with disabilities, learning difficulties, or language barriers to ensure equal access to educational opportunities and support their academic success. Additionally, providing differentiated instruction, individualized learning plans, and ongoing assessment and feedback can help identify and address learning gaps, promote personalized learning experiences, and empower students to reach their full potential in ELE. Moreover, fostering partnerships and collaboration with families, caregivers, and community stakeholders can further enhance inclusivity by involving families in the education process, understanding students' unique needs and strengths, and promoting a holistic and collaborative approach to supporting student learning and well-being in ELE.

Furthermore, promoting a culture of respect, empathy, and inclusion among educators, students, and stakeholders is essential for creating inclusive ELE environments. This includes providing professional development opportunities, resources, and support for educators to enhance their cultural competence, inclusive teaching practices, and understanding of diverse learner needs. Moreover, promoting dialogue, reflection, and continuous improvement through feedback mechanisms, collaborative learning communities, and ongoing assessment and evaluation can help identify areas for improvement, address challenges, and promote a culture of inclusivity and continuous learning in ELE. Ultimately, adopting a comprehensive and holistic approach that integrates differentiated instruction, culturally responsive teaching practices, collaborative learning experiences, support for diverse learners, and a culture of inclusivity and continuous improvement can create inclusive ELE environments that empower all learners to succeed and thrive in language education.

TEACHER TRAINING AND PROFESSIONAL DEVELOPMENT

Teacher training and professional development are critical components of English Language Education (ELE) as they equip educators with the knowledge, skills, and strategies necessary to effectively teach English language learners in diverse cultural contexts (Yoon, 2022). One key aspect of teacher training in ELE is developing cultural competence and intercultural communication skills. Educators undergo training to increase their awareness of cultural differences, biases, and assumptions, fostering empathy, understanding, and respect for diverse cultural perspectives (Warren, 2018). This includes learning strategies for promoting cross-cultural communication, adapting teaching practices to accommodate diverse learning styles, and incorporating multicultural perspectives into the curriculum. Moreover, teacher training in ELE emphasizes the importance of inclusive practices, equity, and social justice, providing educators with tools and resources to create inclusive learning environments, support diverse learners, and promote educational equity in language education.

Furthermore, teacher training in ELE encompasses language proficiency development, pedagogical training, and technological integration. Educators receive training to enhance their English language proficiency, fluency, and accuracy, ensuring that they can effectively model language use, provide clear instructions, and facilitate meaningful communication in the classroom. Additionally, teacher training focuses on pedagogical approaches and instructional strategies that promote language acquisition, critical thinking, and communication skills among English language learners. This includes learning how to design engaging and interactive lessons, provide meaningful feedback, and assess language proficiency using research-based assessment practices. Moreover, teacher training in ELE addresses the integration of digital technologies into language teaching and learning processes, providing educators with training on how to use digital tools, online resources, and virtual platforms to enhance language learning experiences, promote collaboration, and facilitate global connectivity among learners.

Zepeda (2019), believes that ongoing professional development is essential for educators to stay updated on best practices, research findings, and emerging trends in ELE. Professional development programs provide opportunities for educators to engage in collaborative learning communities, attend workshops and conferences, participate in online courses, and access resources and mentorship opportunities that support their continuous growth and improvement as language educators. Moreover, professional development in ELE emphasizes the importance of reflective practice, self-assessment, and continuous learning, encouraging educators to critically reflect on their teaching practices, identify areas for improvement, and implement evidence-based strategies to enhance student learning outcomes. Additionally, professional development fosters a culture of collaboration, innovation, and shared learning among educators, promoting knowledge-sharing, peer support, and collaborative problem-solving in addressing challenges and promoting excellence in language education.

Furthermore, teacher training and professional development in ELE involve ongoing assessment and evaluation to monitor progress, identify strengths and areas for improvement, and inform targeted interventions and support for educators. This includes collecting feedback from educators, students, and stakeholders, conducting self-assessments, and utilizing data and evidence to inform decision-making, program improvements, and policy development in ELE. By investing in teacher training and professional development, educators are equipped with the competencies, resources, and support they need to create engaging, inclusive, and effective learning experiences for English language learners, promoting their academic success, linguistic development, and cultural competence in a globalized world.

TECHNOLOGY INTEGRATION IN ENGLISH LANGUAGE EDUCATION (ELE)

Technology integration in education has become a transformative force, revolutionizing teaching and learning experiences across diverse educational settings. One of the key benefits of technology integration is its ability to enhance engagement and motivation among learners (Serrano et al., 2019). Interactive digital tools, multimedia resources, and educational apps offer dynamic and immersive learning experiences that cater to diverse learning styles, preferences, and abilities. For instance, virtual simulations, gamified learning platforms, and interactive multimedia content can make learning more engaging, interactive, and personalized, fostering deeper understanding, retention, and application of knowledge among students. Moreover, technology integration promotes active learning, collaboration, and creativity by providing opportunities for students to collaborate on projects, share ideas, and create multimedia presentations, fostering critical thinking, communication skills, and problem-solving abilities.

Furthermore, technology integration in education facilitates access to a wealth of educational resources and information, breaking down geographical barriers and expanding learning opportunities for students worldwide. Online libraries, digital repositories, open educational resources (OER), and virtual libraries provide students and educators with access to a vast array of educational content, research materials, and multimedia resources that support curriculum objectives, promote self-directed learning, and encourage lifelong learning. Additionally, technology integration enables personalized and adaptive learning experiences, as digital platforms and learning management systems (LMS) can track student progress, provide real-time feedback, and customize learning pathways based on individual learning needs, preferences, and performance data, enhancing the effectiveness and efficiency of teaching and learning processes.

Moreover, technology integration in education fosters collaboration, communication, and global connectivity among students, educators, and stakeholders. Online collaboration tools, video conferencing platforms, and virtual classrooms facilitate real-time communication, collaboration, and knowledge-sharing among learners from diverse cultural backgrounds and geographical locations, promoting intercultural understanding, empathy, and collaboration skills. Additionally, technology integration enables educators to connect with experts, guest speakers, and resources worldwide, enhancing professional development opportunities, promoting knowledge-sharing, and fostering a culture of continuous learning and innovation in education. Furthermore, technology integration supports inclusive education practices by providing accessibility features, assistive technologies, and digital tools that accommodate diverse learning needs, disabilities, and language barriers, ensuring equitable access to educational opportunities and promoting educational equity in a digital age.

Additionally, technology integration in education promotes data-driven decision-making, evidence-based practices, and continuous improvement in teaching and learning processes (Fernandes, 2019). Learning analytics, assessment tools, and data visualization platforms enable educators to collect, analyze, and interpret student performance data, track learning progress, identify learning gaps, and inform instructional strategies, interventions, and support services to support student learning outcomes and promote academic success. Moreover, Salimovna (2024) agrees that technology integration empowers educators to engage in reflective practice, self-assessment, and professional development opportunities, fostering a culture of lifelong learning, collaboration, and innovation in education. Ultimately, technology integration in education has the potential to transform education by enhancing engagement, access, collaboration, and learning outcomes for students, preparing them to thrive in a digital and globally connected world.

Technology integration in English Language Education (ELE) has revolutionized the way language teaching and learning are approached, offering a myriad of benefits and opportunities for both educators and students (Kohnke, 2024). One of the key advantages of technology integration in ELE is its ability to enhance language acquisition and proficiency. Digital tools, online platforms, and language learning apps provide interactive and immersive experiences that engage students, reinforce language skills, and facilitate self-paced learning. For example, language learning software with adaptive algorithms can customize learning pathways based on students' proficiency levels, preferences, and learning styles, providing targeted practice and feedback to enhance language acquisition. Moreover, digital resources such as multimedia content, virtual simulations, and interactive games can make language learning more engaging, contextualized, and relevant to students' interests and real-world contexts, promoting deeper understanding and retention of language concepts.

Technology integration in ELE promotes collaboration, communication, and global connectivity among students and educators. Online communication tools, video conferencing platforms, and virtual classrooms facilitate real-time interactions, discussions, and collaborative projects among learners from diverse cultural backgrounds and geographical locations, fostering intercultural understanding, empathy, and collaboration skills. Additionally, technology integration enables educators to incorporate authentic materials, cultural artifacts, and digital resources from global sources into the curriculum, providing students with exposure to diverse cultural perspectives, practices, and linguistic variations, enhancing their cultural competence and intercultural communication skills. Moreover, technology integration supports differentiated instruction and personalized learning experiences by providing adaptive learning platforms, digital assessments, and data analytics tools that track student progress, identify learning gaps, and tailor instruction to meet individual learning needs, promoting equitable access and support for diverse learners in ELE.

Moreover, technology integration in ELE facilitates access to a wealth of authentic language resources, digital libraries, and online learning materials that support language learning objectives, promote self-directed learning, and extend learning beyond the classroom. Language learning platforms, online dictionaries, language exchange forums, and multimedia resources provide students with opportunities to practice language skills, engage in authentic communication, and explore cultural content in a digital environment, enhancing their language proficiency, fluency, and confidence. Additionally, technology integration enables educators to leverage digital tools and resources for language assessment, feedback, and evaluation, providing timely and meaningful feedback to students, tracking their language development progress, and informing instructional decisions to support language learning outcomes and promote academic success in ELE.

Furthermore, technology integration in ELE supports inclusive education practices by providing accessibility features, assistive technologies, and digital tools that accommodate diverse learning needs, disabilities, and language barriers, ensuring equitable access to language learning opportunities and promoting educational equity in language education. For example, captioning, text-to-speech, and translation tools can support students with hearing impairments, visual impairments, or language difficulties, enabling them to access and engage with digital content and participate fully in language learning activities. Moreover, technology integration promotes culturally responsive teaching practices by incorporating diverse perspectives, cultural content, and multimedia resources that reflect students' linguistic and cultural backgrounds, fostering a sense of belonging, identity affirmation, and cultural pride among learners. Ultimately, technology integration in ELE has the potential to transform language education by enhancing engagement, access, collaboration, and learning outcomes for students, preparing them to thrive in a digital and globally connected world.

FUTURE RESEARCH DIRECTIONS

Future research directions in English Language Education (ELE) encompass a wide range of areas that can further enhance teaching practices, learning outcomes, and educational experiences for language learners. One key area of future research is exploring the effectiveness of technology-enhanced language learning environments, including virtual reality (VR), augmented reality (AR), and immersive digital simulations. Research can investigate how these technologies can be integrated into language instruction to enhance language acquisition, cultural understanding, and communication skills among learners. Additionally, research can focus on the impact of digital literacy skills development, online collaboration tools, and digital assessment practices on language learning outcomes and student engagement in ELE.

Furthermore, future research can delve into the intersection of language education and global citizenship education (GCE), exploring how language learning can promote intercultural competence, empathy, and global awareness among learners. Research can examine the role of language education in fostering global citizenship skills such as critical thinking, social responsibility, and cross-cultural communication, and how technology integration can support these goals. Additionally, research can explore innovative pedagogical approaches, curriculum design strategies, and assessment practices that promote global citizenship education in language learning contexts.

Another area of future research in ELE is addressing the needs of diverse learner populations, including learners with disabilities, language difficulties, and diverse cultural backgrounds. Research can focus on developing inclusive practices, adaptive technologies, and differentiated instruction strategies that support diverse learners in achieving language learning goals. Moreover, research can explore the impact of culturally responsive teaching practices, multicultural curriculum design, and community engagement initiatives on promoting equity, inclusion, and cultural competence in language education.

Additionally, future research can investigate the impact of policy frameworks, funding initiatives, and systemic supports on promoting excellence, innovation, and equity in English Language Education. Research can examine the role of government policies, educational leadership, and stakeholder collaborations in shaping the direction, priorities, and practices of language education systems. Moreover, research can explore effective models of professional development, teacher training programs, and mentorship opportunities that support educators in integrating technology, promoting cultural competence, and fostering inclusive practices in language education.

In conclusion, future research directions in English Language Education (ELE) hold immense potential for advancing knowledge, improving practices, and enhancing outcomes in language learning and teaching. By focusing on innovative technologies, global citizenship education, inclusive practices, and policy frameworks, researchers can contribute to the continued evolution and transformation of language education in a digital, multicultural, and interconnected world.

CONCLUSION

In conclusion, the integration of technology in English Language Education (ELE) has ushered in a new era of innovation, engagement, and accessibility for language learners and educators alike. Technology has revolutionized the way language skills are taught, practiced, and assessed, offering dynamic and immersive learning experiences that cater to diverse learning styles, preferences, and abilities. The use of digital tools, online platforms, language learning apps, and multimedia resources has enhanced language acquisition, proficiency, and fluency among learners, making language learning more engaging, interactive, and personalized. Moreover, technology integration has facilitated collaboration, communication, and global connectivity among students and educators, fostering intercultural understanding, empathy, and collaboration skills. Additionally, technology has expanded access to authentic language resources, digital libraries, and online learning materials, promoting self-directed learning, cultural exploration, and global citizenship in language education.

Looking ahead, there are several future recommendations and considerations for further enhancing technology integration in ELE. Firstly, there is a need for ongoing professional development and training for educators to stay updated on emerging technologies, best practices, and innovative pedagogies in language education. Providing educators with opportunities for continuous learning, collaboration, and mentorship can empower them to effectively integrate technology into their teaching practices, design engaging and interactive lessons, and support diverse learners in achieving language learning goals. Secondly, there is a need to address digital equity and accessibility issues to ensure that all students have equitable access to technology resources, digital tools, and online learning platforms. Investing in infrastructure, digital literacy programs, and assistive technologies can bridge the digital divide and promote inclusive education practices in language education.

Furthermore, there is a need to conduct research and evaluation studies to assess the impact of technology integration on language learning outcomes, student engagement, and educational equity in ELE. Collecting data, analyzing student performance, and gathering feedback from stakeholders can provide valuable insights into the effectiveness of technology-based interventions, identify areas for improvement, and inform evidence-based decision-making and policy development in language education. Moreover, fostering partnerships and collaborations with industry stakeholders, technology developers, and research institutions can promote knowledge-sharing, innovation, and collaboration in advancing technology integration in ELE.

In conclusion, technology integration holds immense potential for transforming language education, enhancing learning experiences, and preparing students for success in a digital and globally connected world. By embracing innovative technologies, promoting digital literacy, fostering collaboration and inclusivity, and conducting research-driven practices, we can continue to harness the power of technology to promote excellence, equity, and engagement in English Language Education.

REFERENCES

Agarwal, N. (2018). A study of innovations in instructional strategies and designs for quality enrichment in Higher Education. *Cosmos: An International Journal of Art & Higher Education*, 7(2), 1–12.

Ahmed, H., & Popova, N. (2023). Globalization and Its Socioeconomic Consequences: A Comprehensive Review. *The Critical Review of Social Sciences Studies*, 1(02), 87–97.

Al-Issa, A., & Mirhosseini, S. A. (2019). *Worldwide English Language Education Today*. Routledge. 10.4324/9780429485879

Alam, S. (2023). The conceptual relevance of English as lingua franca in non-English speaking countries: Revisiting history, policies and praxis. *Theory and Practice in Language Studies*, 13(9), 2398–2405. 10.17507/tpls.1309.28

Avgousti, M. I. (2018). Intercultural communicative competence and online exchanges: A systematic review. *Computer Assisted Language Learning*, 31(8), 819–853. 10.1080/09588221.2018.1455713

Barik, S. (2023). Embracing the transformative dynamics of English teaching and technology in higher education: A posthumanist perspective. *Smart Moves Journal IJELLH*, 17-31.

Barrett, M. (2018). How schools can promote the intercultural competence of young people. *European Psychologist*, 23(1), 93–104. 10.1027/1016-9040/a000308

Barrot, J. (2022). Language education. *International Encyclopedia of Education*, 216-223.

Butler, D., Leahy, M., Twining, P., Akoh, B., Chtouki, Y., Farshadnia, S., Moore, K., Nikolov, R., Pascual, C., Sherman, B., & Valtonen, T. (2018). Education systems in the digital age: The need for alignment. *Technology. Knowledge and Learning*, 23(3), 473–494. 10.1007/s10758-018-9388-6

Chetty, K., Qigui, L., Gcora, N., Josie, J., Wenwei, L., & Fang, C. (2018). Bridging the digital divide: Measuring digital literacy. *Economics*, 12(1), 20180023. 10.5018/economics-ejournal.ja.2018-23

Eden, C. A., Chisom, O. N., & Adeniyi, I. S. (2024). Cultural competence in education: Strategies for fostering inclusivity and diversity awareness. *International Journal of Applied Research in Social Sciences*, 6(3), 383–392. 10.51594/ijarss.v6i3.895

Evmenova, A. (2018). Preparing teachers to use universal design for learning to support diverse learners. *Journal of Online Learning Research*, 4(2), 147–171.

Fernandes, V. (2019). Investigating the role of data-driven decision-making within school improvement processes. In *Evidence-based initiatives for organizational change and development* (pp. 201–219). IGI Global. 10.4018/978-1-5225-6155-2.ch010

García, O., & Kleifgen, J. A. (2018). *Educating emergent bilinguals: Policies, programs, and practices for English learners*. Teachers College Press.

Gay, G. (2018). *Culturally responsive teaching: Theory, research, and practice*. teachers college press.

González-Pérez, L. I., & Ramírez-Montoya, M. S. (2022). Components of Education 4.0 in 21st century skills frameworks: Systematic review. *Sustainability (Basel)*, 14(3), 1493. 10.3390/su14031493

Halder, S. (2023). *Global Economic Integration-Challenges and Prospects*.

Hands, C. M., Armstrong, D. E., & Mitchell, C. (2020). Collaborative Learning and Knowledge-Sharing: The Potential of New Administrator Networks and Mentoring Programs. *The Wiley International Handbook of Mentoring: Paradigms, Practices, Programs, and Possibilities*, 205-222. Wiley.

Hennen, L., & Van Est, R. (2023). Globalisation as Reflexive Modernisation—Implications for S&T Governance. In *Technology Assessment in a Globalized World: Facing the Challenges of Transnational Technology Governance* (pp. 53–73). Springer International Publishing. 10.1007/978-3-031-10617-0_4

Hymel, S., & Katz, J. (2019). Designing classrooms for diversity: Fostering social inclusion. *Educational Psychologist*, 54(4), 331–339. 10.1080/00461520.2019.1652098

Jackson, J. (2019). *Introducing language and intercultural communication*. Routledge. 10.4324/9781351059275

Kohnke, L. (2024). *Navigating the digital turn: recent books on technological integration in ELT*.

Kumbo, L., Mero, R. F., & Hayuma, B. J. (2023). Navigating The Digital Frontier: Innovative Pedagogies for Effective Technology Integration in Education. *Journal of Informetrics*, 3(1).

Lau, W. S., & Shea, M. (2022). Empowering English learners in the classroom through culturally responsive social-emotional teaching practices. *Journal of Multilingual and Multicultural Development*, 1–18. 10.1080/01434632.2022.2078337

Lindsey, R. B., Nuri-Robins, K., Terrell, R. D., & Lindsey, D. B. (2018). *Cultural proficiency: A manual for school leaders*. Corwin Press.

Madani, R. A. (2019). Analysis of educational quality, a goal of education for all policy. *Higher Education Studies*, 9(1), 100–109. 10.5539/hes.v9n1p100

Maqsood, M., Sheikh, S., Shah, S. A., Haider, Z., Gul, S., & Gul, A. (2023). Sociolinguistic implications of online efl learning: an empirical study of language use and interaction in teacher education. *PalArch's Journal of Archaeology of Egypt/Egyptology, 20*(2), 1960-1980.

Murray, D. E. (2020). The world of English language teaching: Creating equity or inequity? *Language Teaching Research*, 24(1), 60–70. 10.1177/1362168818777529

Nazari, M., Karimpour, S., & De Costa, P. (2023). English language teachers' emotion-bearing situations in a professional development course: A critical-ecological perspective. *Journal of Multilingual and Multicultural Development*, 1–15. 10.1080/01434632.2023.2240750

Pieterse, J. N. (2019). *Globalization and culture: Global mélange*. Rowman & Littlefield.

Rao, P. S. (2019). The role of English as a global language. *Research journal of English, 4*(1), 65-79.

Ruane, C. (2022). *Global English, Global Identities, and the Global World: perceptions of a group of Korean English language users* [Doctoral dissertation, Macquarie University].

Salimovna, S. X. (2024). Enhancing the Pedagogical System for the Development of Professional Culture in General Urban Education Teachers. *Science Promotion*, 7(1), 210–216.

Serrano, D. R., Dea-Ayuela, M. A., Gonzalez-Burgos, E., Serrano-Gil, A., & Lalatsa, A. (2019). Technology-enhanced learning in higher education: How to enhance student engagement through blended learning. *European Journal of Education*, 54(2), 273–286. 10.1111/ejed.12330

Villa, R., & Thousand, J. (2021). *The Inclusive Education Checklist: A Checklist of Best Practices*. National Professional Resources, Inc.

Warren, C. A. (2018). Empathy, teacher dispositions, and preparation for culturally responsive pedagogy. *Journal of Teacher Education*, 69(2), 169–183. 10.1177/0022487117712487

Yoon, B. (2022). *Effective teacher collaboration for English language learners*. Routledge.

Zalli, E. (2024). Globalization and Education: Exploring the Exchange of Ideas, Values, and Traditions in Promoting Cultural Understanding and Global Citizenship. *Interdisciplinary Journal of Research and Development, 11*(1 S1), 55-55.

Zepeda, S. J. (2019). *Professional development: What works*. Routledge.

Zohuri, B. (2023). Navigating the Global Energy Landscape Balancing Growth, Demand, and Sustainability. *J Mat Sci Apl Eng 2*(4).

Chapter 2
Data Security Knowledge Among Students of Public Universities:
A Fundamental Competency for Success in the Education 5.0 Era

Hapini Awang
School of Computing, Universiti Utara Malaysia, Malaysia

Abderrahmane Benlahcene
http://orcid.org/0000-0003-1743-5679
College of Commerce and Business Administration, Dhofar University, Salalah, Oman

Nur Suhaili Mansor
School of Computing, Universiti Utara Malaysia, Malaysia

ABSTRACT

This chapter examines the current state of understanding of data security among students in Malaysia's higher education system, with a particular focus on knowledge regarding social media security and data security measures. The findings of revealed a widespread deficiency in respondents' knowledge regarding data security. These findings emphasise the pressing need for educational reforms. The findings also suggest incorporating data security education into the curriculum to nurture a generation of digitally literate individuals who are conscious of security. In line with the principles of Education 5.0, this chapter evaluates existing challenges and proposes educational interventions to address the identified gaps. These interventions align with the framework's emphasis on holistic development, critical thinking and technological literacy. This chapter makes a valuable contribution to the broader discourse on preparing students for the digital era and has implications for educational institutions not only in Malaysia but also on a global scale.

DOI: 10.4018/979-8-3693-3041-8.ch002

INTRODUCTION

In this era of digitalisation and the swift development of technology, data have transformed into a pivotal asset, propelling decision-making processes, innovation, and efficacy across various industries. The growing interest in data security and privacy has been spurred by the rapid advancement of technologies such as blockchain, the Internet of Things, and quantum computing. This has resulted in heightened expectations regarding the protection of data security and privacy (Yang et al., 2020). Data security, a key aspect of cybersecurity, is crucial for ensuring the integrity, confidentiality, and accessibility of the data. It encompasses a spectrum of practices, technologies, and policies to shield data from unauthorised entry, breaches, and cyber hazards. With the evolution of the digital sphere, the rise of social media platforms has further convoluted the domain of data security, presenting novel challenges and susceptibilities. Despite offering unparalleled communication and information dissemination avenues, social media platforms also act as potential channels for data misuse and privacy violations.

The repercussions of deficient knowledge in data security are profound, potentially resulting in financial setbacks, harm to reputation, and encroachment on personal privacy. Zwilling et al. (2022) stated that as Internet usage continues to surge due to advancements in information technology. However, numerous individuals who use the internet still lack sufficient understanding of the various perils that exist online. In fact, they frequently lack the essential knowledge required to safeguard their electronic devices (Zwilling et al., 2022). In higher education, students as digital natives are known for their extensive use of technology and social media. However, a lack of understanding and awareness of data security measures can pose significant risks, both personally and academically. This not only puts their data at risk but also threatens the security of institutional data, which could harm the overall integrity of the educational institution and its reputation. The research objectives of this investigation are twofold:

1. To evaluate the present state of comprehension and consciousness of data security among students in public universities in Malaysia, with a specific emphasis on knowledge of social media security and data safeguarding measures.
2. To scrutinise the prevailing challenges and deficiencies in data security knowledge among students and recommend educational interventions that follow the principles of Education 5.0, highlighting comprehensive development, critical thinking, and technological literacy.

The importance of this chapter lies in its capacity to shed light on the crucial issue of data security literacy among the younger generation, who are pioneers in the digital revolution. By pinpointing the gaps in the knowledge and understanding of data security among students in public universities in Malaysia, this study strives to advocate for educational reforms and the inclusion of data security education in the academic syllabus. This proactive stance is imperative for cultivating a cohort of digitally literate individuals adept at utilising technology and conscientiously safeguarding their data and privacy.

Furthermore, the findings of this study and proposed interventions have broader implications that surpass the Malaysian context and are relevant for educational institutions worldwide. As the globe transitions into Education 5.0 era, characterized by collaborative and customised learning experiences, there is a pressing need to equip students with the essential competencies and proficiencies to traverse the digital sphere securely and responsibly. Hence, this section provides a valuable contribution to the broader discussion on preparing students for the digital age, advocating a thorough and integrated approach to data security education in the higher education curriculum.

BACKGROUND OF THE STUDY

The rapid dissemination of social media in Malaysia has undeniably enhanced student connectivity, signifying a transformative shift in their modes of education, communication and information sharing (Rathakrishnan et al., 2023). Nevertheless, this upsurge in digital interaction has revealed a significant knowledge gap, particularly within the framework of Education 5.0. Despite the indisputable advantages of social media, such as its role in fostering creativity and facilitating communication, there is an urgent need to acknowledge and rectify the lack of awareness of the potential risks inherent in online activities (Kyza et al., 2020). In the ever-changing landscape of the Internet, where trust is often presumed, individuals, including students, become susceptible to cybersecurity threats encompassing phishing attacks and identity theft. The escalating prevalence of cybercrime underscores the critical necessity for educational interventions that adhere to the principles of Education 5.0.

The imperative to address this knowledge gap becomes even more pronounced within the Education 5.0 era, which advocates for holistic and adaptable learning. Educational institutions must proactively incorporate comprehensive cybersecurity education into their curricula to equip students with the skills to navigate the complexities of the online environment and instill a heightened sense of responsibility regarding their digital presence (AlDaajeh et al., 2022; Amankwa, 2023; Marquardson & L. Gomillion, 2018). Bridging this knowledge gap is not just a requisite for individual security but also a fundamental step toward cultivating a digitally literate and resilient generation capable of navigating the intricate landscape of the 21st century. Among the Asia-Pacific countries, Malaysia is one of the most active social media users (Irfan et al., 2018), and university students have been identified as enthusiastic social media users(Rathakrishnan et al., 2023). As these platforms, including TikTok, Facebook, Twitter, WhatsApp, and Instagram, are regarded as preferred online platforms that allow students to engage in social interactions, possession of data security knowledge has become imperative.

This chapter aims to address this pressing concern by exploring the issue of information disclosure on social networks among university students in Malaysia. Furthermore, this chapter seeks to formulate effective strategies to cope with challenges related to data security on social media, with a specific emphasis on password usage and phishing. The examination of online behaviour among university students in Malaysia within this context is of utmost importance, considering the potential risks associated with sharing sensitive information online. Despite the availability of privacy settings on social media platforms, the rapid global dissemination of information presents a significant threat, as hackers can intercept login credentials and personal details for fraudulent purposes (Jyothi et al., 2023). Hence, a critical analysis was conducted on the obtained data to provide valuable insights for devising proactive measures and enhancing data security awareness, stressing the crucial necessity of safeguarding individuals in the increasingly interconnected digital environment of Education 5.0 (Nair et al., 2021).

LITERATURE REVIEW

The rapid advancement of technology and the digital transformation of education have given rise to the concept of Education 5.0 (Carayannis & Morawska-Jancelewicz, 2022), which emphasises the integration of technology, critical thinking, and holistic development to prepare students for the challenges of the 21st century (Bates. Robert H., 2019). One critical aspect of this paradigm shift is the need for students to possess adequate knowledge and skills in data security, particularly in the context of the increasing prevalence of cyber threats and the critical role of data in the digital age (Selwyn & Aagaard, 2021). This literature review explores the existing body of research on data security knowledge among university students, focusing on the Malaysian higher education context in order to underscore its significance as a fundamental competency for success in Education 5.0 era.

Data Security Knowledge Among University Students

The increasing digitisation of every aspect of life, such as education, business, and healthcare, has resulted in the accumulation of various types of information, including sensitive data. The protection of digitised information from theft or damage while ensuring its confidentiality and availability is known as data security. However, with the rapid advancements in technology, the incidence of cybercrime is also on the rise, both in terms of frequency and complexity (Rajasekharaiah, Dule, & Sudarshan, 2020). In line with this, recent studies have highlighted a concerning lack of awareness and understanding of data security among university students globally, with many students exhibiting risky online behaviours and misconceptions regarding data protection (Feigin et al., 2019; Mohammed et al., 2020). Research indicates a similar trend in the Malaysian context, with public university students demonstrating limited knowledge and awareness of data security measures, particularly concerning social media platforms (Ismail et al., 2018). This deficiency in data security knowledge exposes students to potential cyber threats, and has significant implications for their academic and professional development in an increasingly interconnected and data-driven world (Behrens et al. 2018).

Challenges in Data Security Education

Several challenges contribute to the existing gaps in data security knowledge among university students. Firstly, the lack of comprehensive and standardised data security education in the higher education curriculum has been identified as a significant barrier (Rahman et al., 2020). Many educational institutions have yet to effectively integrate data security education into their programs, leading to a limited understanding of the importance of data protection and the adoption of safe online practices among students (Lee et al., 2017). Secondly, the rapid evolution of technology and the complexity of cyber threats require continuous updates and adaptations in data security education, which many institutions struggle to keep pace with (Tan et al., 2020). Lastly, the pervasive use of social media platforms among university students has exacerbated the risks associated with data security, necessitating targeted education and awareness initiatives to address these specific concerns (Abumalloh et al., 2021).

Education 5.0 and Data Security

Education 5.0 emphasizes the development of holistic competencies, critical thinking, and technological literacy among students to effectively navigate the complexities of the digital era (Bates. Robert H., 2019) Integrating data security education into the curriculum aligns seamlessly with the principles of Education 5.0, fostering a generation of digitally literate individuals who are conscious of security and capable of safeguarding their data and privacy online (Selwyn & Aagaard, 2021). Research suggests that incorporating data security education within the framework of Education 5.0 can enhance students' awareness, understanding, and adoption of safe online practices, thereby mitigating the risks associated with cyber threats and promoting responsible digital citizenship (Feigin et al., 2019; Rahman et al., 2020)

While the existing literature provides valuable insights into the current state of data security knowledge among university students in Malaysia, there is a notable lack of comprehensive studies that evaluate the effectiveness of educational interventions in addressing the identified gaps and enhancing students' data security awareness and practices. This chapter seeks to fill this research gap by evaluating the existing challenges and proposing targeted educational interventions aligned with the principles of Education 5.0. By doing so, this study aims to contribute to the broader discourse on preparing students for the digital era and to provide actionable recommendations for educational institutions to develop and implement effective data security education initiatives that foster a secure and responsible digital environment for students in Malaysia and beyond.

Thus, the current literature underscores the pressing need for enhanced data security education among university students, particularly in Malaysia's higher education system. The existing deficiencies in data security knowledge and the challenges associated with integrating effective data security education into the curriculum have significant implications for students' academic and professional success in Education 5.0 era. Addressing these gaps requires concerted efforts from educational institutions, policymakers, and stakeholders to develop and implement comprehensive and targeted data security education initiatives that align with the principles of Education 5.0, fostering a secure and responsible digital environment for students in Malaysia and beyond.

METHODOLOGY

This study was conducted in three distinct stages to achieve the stated objectives. In the initial phase, a structured survey instrument was developed. In the preliminary stage of this study, a meticulously designed questionnaire was developed to collect crucial information on the demographics of the participants, their social media usage patterns, and their perspectives on data security when using social media. The survey consisted of three main parts: collecting data on participants' age, gender, academic field, and year of study; exploring the frequency, duration, and types of social media platforms used; and evaluating their knowledge, awareness, and practices regarding data security on social media. A seven-point Likert scale was used for all survey items, with one symbolising "Strongly Disagree" and seven symbolising "Strongly Agree". A thorough content validation process was conducted involving six cybersecurity experts to ensure the validity of the survey tool. These experts, including four academic specialists in cybersecurity education, research, and curriculum development and two field experts with vast practical experience in cybersecurity (Allodi et al., 2018), assessed each survey item for relevance, clarity, and comprehensiveness using the Content Validity Index (CVI) suggested by (Polit et al., 2007).

Following content validation, a face validation process was conducted with 15 university students to evaluate the survey items' clarity, relevance, and accuracy. Furthermore, a pilot study was completed with 45 participants, similar to the target audience, to gauge the reliability of the survey items and overall consistency of the tool. Information from the pilot study was examined using statistical methods to assess the internal consistency and reliability of the survey items, resulting in necessary modifications to enhance the reliability and validity of the survey tool for primary research. By applying thorough design and validation strategies such as content validation, face validation, and a pilot study, this research assured the amassed robustness, accuracy, and dependability of the data, establishing a firm footing for the subsequent data collection and analysis phases.

In the second phase of the study, data collection implemented a quantitative approach using a convenience sampling method, as the sampling frame was not at one's disposal, making random sampling difficult. This method allowed for selection based on accessibility and willingness to participate, utilising the online environment to reach a diverse group of respondents. The survey was sent electronically to undergraduate students at various public universities in Malaysia, making the data collection process convenient and efficient. This enabled respondents to complete the questionnaire at their convenience and submit it electronically.

The survey was shared among Malaysian public university students through popular social media platforms, such as WhatsApp, Instagram, and Facebook, ensuring a broad reach. From the start, approximately 300 surveys were circulated online to undergraduate students from 20 public universities in Malaysia with the aim of achieving a representative sample. After five months, 150 completed surveys were obtained, with a 50% response rate. The sample included students from different academic majors, years of study, and demographic backgrounds, offering insight into data security knowledge among students. Descriptive and inferential statistical methods were used to analyse the collected data and identify patterns and relationships regarding data security. This study provides valuable insights into public university students' awareness of data security and guides future research phases. The study ensured a comprehensive dataset for analysing data security knowledge among undergraduate students in Malaysian public universities using convenience sampling, an online survey, and popular social media platforms.

In the final phase of this study, the collected responses were meticulously processed and analysed to derive meaningful insights into the landscape of data security knowledge on social media among university students in Malaysia. Upon completion of the data collection phase, all responses were systematically coded to facilitate efficient data management and analysis. Each survey was assigned a unique identifier in a Microsoft Excel spreadsheet, ensuring the anonymity and confidentiality of the respondents while enabling accurate data tracking and analysis. The primary method employed for data analysis was descriptive statistics, utilising Microsoft Excel to analyse the collected data based on frequencies and percentages, and summarising and presenting the respondents' attitudes, behaviours, and knowledge related to data security on social media platforms.

This statistical analysis provides a comprehensive overview of university students' current state of data security knowledge, highlighting prevalent trends, patterns, and areas of concern. The results of the descriptive analysis were meticulously organised and presented in tables and charts to enhance clarity and facilitate straightforward interpretation, offering a clear and concise understanding of respondents' data security practices, awareness, and attitudes toward data security on social media platforms. The findings derived from the data analysis were critically examined to identify existing gaps and challenges in data security knowledge among university students in Malaysia, based on which suitable interventions and recommendations were formulated to foster a secure environment for Education 5.0, emphasizing the importance of integrating data security education and awareness initiatives within the higher education curriculum. Figure 1 illustrates the comprehensive research process of this study, encompassing the instrument development, validation phases, data collection, and final data analysis and interpretation stages..

Figure 1. Research process

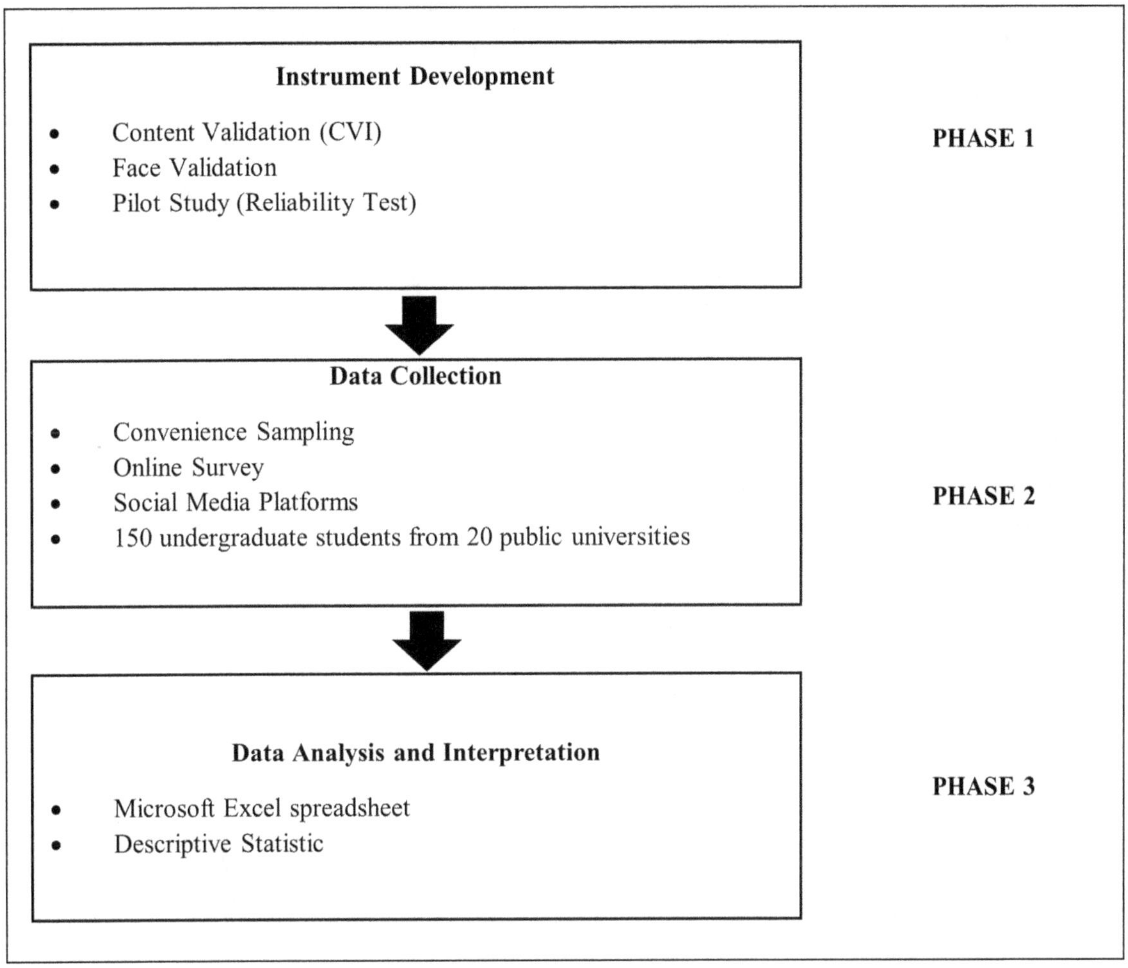

ANALYSIS AND FINDINGS

The respondents in this study were 59 male and 91 female students from 12 public universities across Malaysia. Most respondents are aged 19 to 24 years old, within their third to sixth semester of higher education programs. Table 1 illustrates the social media usage patterns of 150 respondents.

Table 1. Social media usage patterns among university students

No.	Item	Responses				
1.	Most popular social media platforms	Instagram (n=50, 33.3%)	WhatsApp (n=57, 38%)	TikTok (n=21, 14%)	Facebook (n=17, 11.3%)	Snapchat (n=3, 2.1%)
2.	Daily frequency of social media usage	Once (n=2, 1.3%)	2-3 times (n=27, 18%)	4-8 times (n=80, 53.3%)	9 times and above (n=41, 27.3%)	
3.	Average duration per session	1-5 minutes (n=19, 12.7%)	6-10 minutes (15.3%)	11-30 minutes (n=56, 37.3%)	More than 30 minutes (n=52, 34.7%)	
4.	Purpose of usage	Socializing and networking (n=79, 52.7%)	Business (n=20, 13.3%)	Education (n=41, 27.3%)	Others (n=10, 6.7%)	
5.	Number of active social media accounts	1 (n=0, 0%)	2 (n=28, 18.7%)	3 (n=42, 28%)	4 (n=50, 33.3%)	5 and more (n=30, 20%)
6.	Regularity of postings	Very often (n=28, 18.7%)	Occasionally (n=74, 49.3%)	Rarely (n=48, 32%)		

Note. N=150

Figure 2. Social media usage patterns among university students

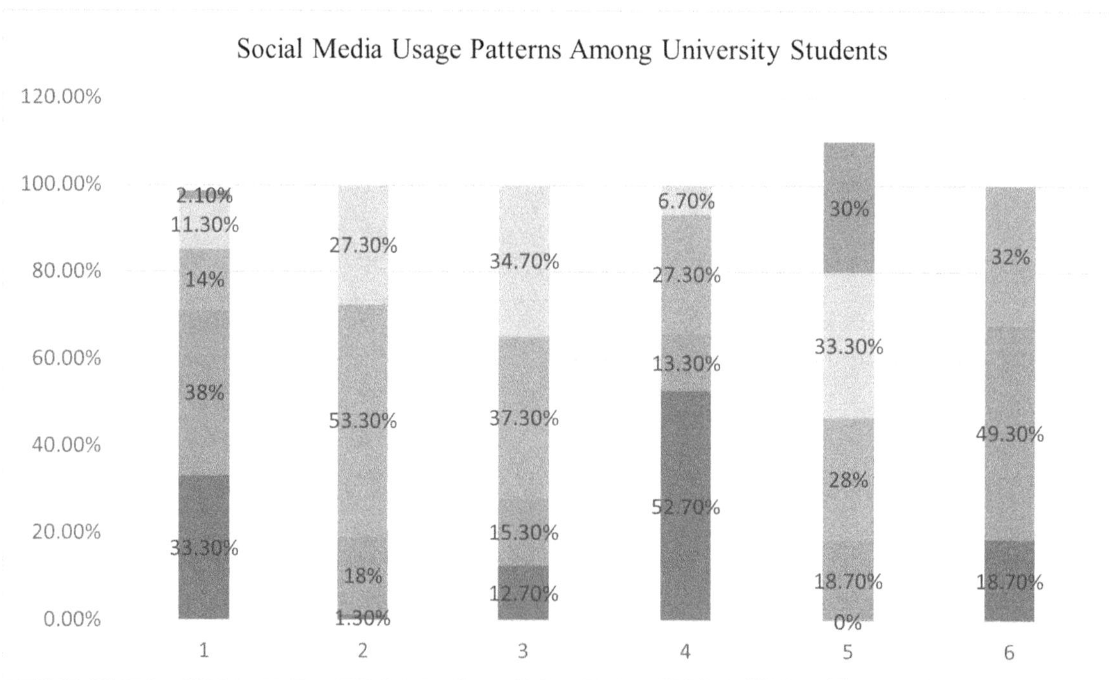

Based on Table 1 and Figure 2, it can be observed that students at the higher education level are indeed heavy Internet users who actively engage on various social media platforms. They are predominantly present on Instagram and WhatsApp, constituting 33.3% and 38%, respectively. Additionally, a significant portion utilizes TikTok, Facebook, and Snapchat, accounting for 27.4%. The extent of social media addiction was evident in their daily usage frequency and session duration. More than half of them (53.3%) access social media 4-8 times a day, with the most common session durations being 10-30 minutes (37.3%) and more than 30 minutes (34.7%). Only a small percentage (12.7%) rarely used social media, and their session times were limited to 1-5 minutes. When asked about their motivations for using social media, the majority cited networking and socialising (52.7%), followed by business-related activities (13.3%), educational purposes (27.3%), and other reasons (6.7%).

The subsequent question probes the extent of their social media usage, revealing that a substantial proportion of respondents (33.3%) actively participated in at least four social media platforms, highlighting their widespread engagement. Notably, none of the participants used only one platform, with each maintaining presence on at least two social media accounts. The final enquiry explored their posting habits, uncovering a notable lack of enthusiasm for frequent posting. Almost half of the respondents (49.3%) occasionally posted, 32% rarely posted, and only 18.7% expressed a keen interest in posting very often on social media. This indicates that most internet users in Malaysia, spanning all age groups, are ardent social networking enthusiasts. This study also affirms that students at higher education levels in Malaysia extensively utilise the internet for various purposes. Their data-security attitudes and behaviours while using social media are presented in Table 2.

Table 2. Students' data security attitudes and behaviours while browsing social media

No.	Items	Not Sure	Never	Rarely	Often	Always
1.	Before visiting a website, I will verify its credibility.	9 (6%)	52 (34.7%)	30 (20%)	25 (16.7%)	34 (22.7%)
2.	I constructed a password that includes my personal information (for example, last name and date of birth).	11 (7.3%)	27 (18%)	17 (11.3%)	35 (23.3%)	60 (40%)
3.	I am conscientious about the privacy settings on my social media accounts.	0 (0%)	1 (0.7%)	18 (12%)	40 (26.6%)	91 (60.7%)
4.	My personal information is safeguarded by social media platforms.	4 (2.7%)	8 (5.3%)	21 (14%)	33 (22%)	84 (56%)
5.	Before using any social media, I carefully read the terms and conditions.	34 (22.7%)	52 (34.7%)	18 (12%)	13 (8.7%)	33 (22%)
6.	I am cautious when it comes to clicking on links on social media posts.	4 (2.7%)	8 (5.3%)	16 (10.7%)	31 (20.7%)	91 (60.6%)
7.	I constantly update my social media passwords.	20 (13.3%)	63 (42%)	29 (19.3%)	12 (8%)	26 (17.3%)
8.	When I use public Wi-Fi, I feel safe.	12 (8%)	20 (13.3%)	29 (19.3%)	16 (10.7%)	73 (48.7%)
9.	I feel my social media has no value to hackers, and they do not target me.	6 (4%)	55 (36.7%)	27 (18%)	15 (10%)	47 (31.3%)

Note. N=150

Figure 3. Students' data security attitudes and behaviours while browsing social media

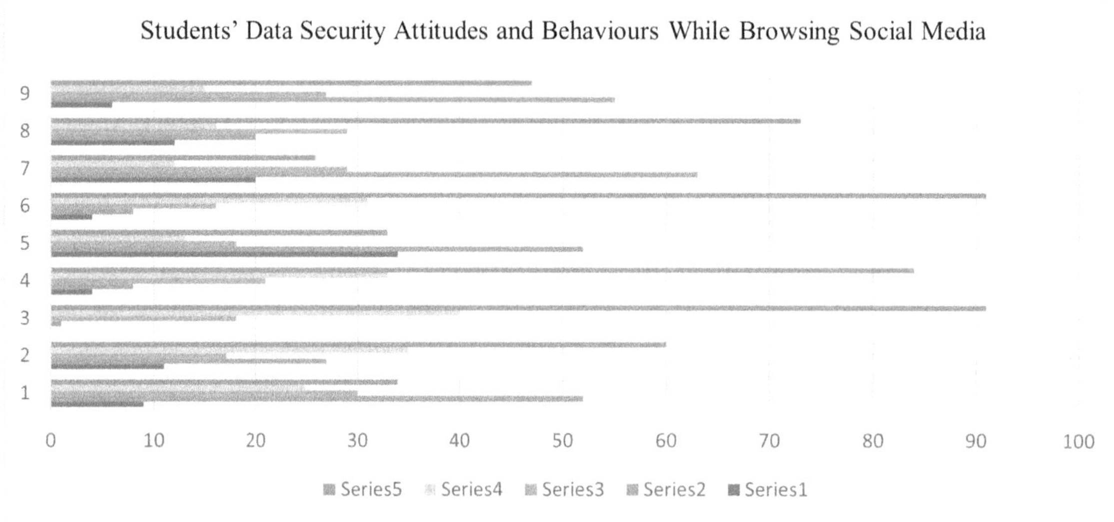

Table 2 and Figure 3 explicitly show the level of students' data security awareness when employing social media. The responses to the credibility of the platform exhibited a wide array of variations. A significant segment, amounting to 34.7%, indicated that they never authenticated the platforms' credibility while perusing the Internet, whereas less than half of the respondents appear to prioritise it. Regarding passwords, over 60% of individuals seem to include personal information, notwithstanding the risks it poses to their accounts. The responses to Question 3 indicate that virtually everyone is profoundly concerned about privacy on social media, yet their actions, as observed in Questions 1 and 2, do not align with this concern. Surprisingly, over 70% of participants believe that social media platforms protect their privacy, while only 5.3% were sceptical. The response to the subsequent question is relatively predictable, with 30.7% perusing the terms and conditions when utilising a social media platform, whereas the majority (69.3%) lack interest. Subsequent responses revealed that approximately 90% of individuals exercise caution when clicking on social media links, evincing awareness of potential phishing and malware threats.

With regard to password updates, a significant percentage of participants did not appear to be concerned. Approximately 48.7% consistently believe public Wi-Fi is safe, and only about 20% disagree. The ultimate question explored the perceptions of participants regarding hackers and their activities. Approximately half of them believed that hackers could target them because of the value of their social media accounts. By contrast, the other half are unconcerned, asserting that they possess nothing of value in their accounts. These figures illustrate that students lack substantial knowledge of the security of social media data. Many are negligent in this regard, notwithstanding the daily time dedicated to social media. Awareness often only arises when they become targets. However, not everyone is oblivious to their security on social media, and some individuals are notably cautious when utilising these platforms.

DISCUSSION

Based on the findings of this study, it can be concluded that data security attitudes and behaviours among Malaysian university students are contradictory and at an alarming level. Interestingly, Malaysian students exhibit the same pattern of social media usage when compared to previous studies conducted at an international level. Several previous studies have discovered that undergraduate students, despite claiming to know passwords, email, and data backup practices, engage in risky security practices (Awodiran et al., 2023; Chin et al., 2021). Previous studies have revealed that using passwords among college students also identified risky behaviours, such as infrequent password changes and the use of the same password for multiple applications (Kauthamy et al., 2017). In line with this, the respondents displayed a wide range of risky security behaviours.

In the context of Education 5.0, these findings emphasise the urgent need for an improved digital literacy curriculum that addresses cybersecurity awareness and practices among students. By including cybersecurity education as a fundamental component of the evolving educational paradigm, students can safely acquire the skills necessary to navigate the digital landscape (Simon et al., 2023). According to the 2015 ESET Asia Cyber Savviness Report, 93% of Asian Internet users know about online security issues, but only 40% can accurately answer basic cybersecurity questions (ESET, 2017). Despite this awareness, 38% of users in the region engage in risky online behaviour. ESET's research indicates that Indonesia and India rank at the bottom of the list of countries with the best cybersecurity awareness, while Malaysia is considered the most "cyber-savvy" nation.

Interestingly, countries with low cybersecurity awareness were more secure than Malaysia, which was ranked as the most 'cyber-savvy' country. In the context of Education 5.0, these findings underscore the importance of incorporating a comprehensive cybersecurity education framework that not only imparts theoretical knowledge but also fosters a culture of responsible online behaviour and security practices among students. Addressing these issues in the educational curriculum aligns with the principles of Education 5.0, promoting holistic development, and preparing students for the challenges of the digital age. The rapid surge in technology adoption, especially the heightened reliance on online platforms owing to COVID-19, has significantly elevated individuals' personal information vulnerability to data breaches (Mohd Yusof et al., 2022). The rise in cybercrime issues such as cyber harassment, cyberbullying, and cyber violence has disproportionately affected women as primary victims (Xiang & Hasbullah, 2023). Critically, Malaysia's existing cybercrime protection learning modules appear insufficient to address the comprehensive recognition, prevention, and cultivation of secure cyberculture amid growing cyber threats (Ramakrishnan et al., 2022).

Furthermore, empirical evidence indicates that university students exhibit low scores in cybersecurity awareness and cyberhuman values, with a significant correlation identified between these factors and incidents of cyberbullying. To address these trends, it is imperative to implement well-structured and standardised cybersecurity policies within higher learning institutions. These policies should go beyond the fundamental aspects of cybersecurity and encompass a holistic approach that integrates practical awareness, prevention strategies, and the cultivation of ethical cyber behaviour. To enhance the effectiveness of cybersecurity education, institutions should incorporate real-world case studies, interactive simulations, and regular updates to reflect the evolving cyber threat landscape. Collaborative efforts between academia, industry experts, and government agencies could also play a pivotal role in creating a dynamic and responsive cybersecurity curriculum. Additionally, promoting a culture of reporting and addressing cyber incidents within the academic community can contribute to the overall resilience against cyber threats. Ultimately, a multi-faceted and proactive approach is essential to fortify cybersecurity awareness and practices among university students in Malaysia.

CONCLUSION AND RECOMMENDATIONS

In conclusion, the findings of this chapter underscore the heightened connectivity among university students through social media, especially in challenging situations in which physical separation is prevalent. The investigation of various data security knowledge and threats revealed that respondents engaged in various risky security behaviours, aligning with the consistency observed in prior research. Despite being young and educated, these students exhibited a limited understanding of social media data security, reflecting a potential gap in their digital literacy. Considering the increasing reliance on social media in students' everyday lives, most students lack concerns about data security. To prepare students for challenges in Education 5.0, particularly regarding data security awareness when browsing social media, it is imperative to integrate comprehensive cybersecurity education into the curriculum (Alrobaian et al., 2023). This education should impart theoretical knowledge and foster a culture of responsible online behaviour and security practices among students.

Considering these findings, it is recommended that educational institutions implement proactive measures to enhance students' awareness of data security issues associated with social media. Initiatives may include workshops, seminars, and courses that specifically focus on cybersecurity in the broader digital literacy context. Additionally, promoting a cybersecurity culture and emphasising the importance of responsible online practices should be integral to the educational approach. Students should be equipped with the knowledge and skills necessary to defend themselves from the digital realm. This proactive approach aligns with the principles of Education 5.0, ensuring that students are academically prepared and possess the essential competencies to navigate the evolving digital landscape securely.

In addition, several other possible strategies for enhancing student awareness of data security within the framework of Education 5.0 could be implemented, for example, (i) encompassing the utilisation of gamified learning modules that replicate real-life situations; (ii) virtual reality simulations to facilitate practical comprehension; (iii) peer mentorship programs that foster collaboration; (iv) cybersecurity hackathons that encourage active participation; (v) the integration of educational content on social media platforms; (vi) campus-wide campaigns to promote cybersecurity awareness; (vii) interdisciplinary cooperation to address socio-technical aspects; (viii) a blockchain-based credentialing system for authentication; (ix) incident response simulations for hands-on experience; and (x) the integration of data security principles into extracurricular activities such as sports and arts. These methods strive to provide a dynamic and comprehensive educational milieu, preparing students academically and practically to navigate the intricacies of data security in the digital era. By fostering a culture of digital responsibility, educational institutions can empower students to make informed decisions and contribute positively to the digital society.

REFERENCES

Abumalloh, R. A., Asadi, S., Nilashi, M., Minaei-Bidgoli, B., Nayer, F. K., Samad, S., Mohd, S., & Ibrahim, O. (2021). The impact of coronavirus pandemic (COVID-19) on education: The role of virtual and remote laboratories in education. *Technology in Society*, 67, 101728. 10.1016/j.techsoc.2021.10172834538984

AlDaajeh, S., Saleous, H., Alrabaee, S., Barka, E., Breitinger, F., & Raymond Choo, K.-K. (2022). The role of national cybersecurity strategies on the improvement of cybersecurity education. *Computers & Security*, 119, 102754. 10.1016/j.cose.2022.102754

Allodi, L., Cremonini, M., Massacci, F., & Shim, W. (2018). The Effect of Security Education and Expertise on Security Assessments: The Case of Software Vulnerabilities. *Workshop of Economics of Information Security (WEIS'2018), May.*

Alrobaian, S., Alshahrani, S., & Almaleh, A. (2023). *Cybersecurity Awareness Assessment among Trainees of the Technical and Vocational Training Corporation.* Big Data and Cognitive Computing., 10.3390/bdcc7020073

Amankwa, E. (2023). Relevance of Cybersecurity Education at Pedagogy Levels in Schools. In *Research Highlights in Mathematics and Computer Science* (*Vol. 7*, pp. 21–37). 10.9734/bpi/rhmcs/v7/4624B

Awodiran, M. A., Ogundele, A. T., Idem, U. J., & Anwana, E. O. (2023). Cybercrime Consciousness Among Undergraduate Students. *2023 International Conference on Cyber Management and Engineering, CyMaEn 2023*, (pp. 301–306). IEEE. 10.1109/CyMaEn57228.2023.10050982

Bates. Robert, H. (2019; Vol. 1). Modernization, Ethnic Competition, and the Rationality of Politics in Contemporary Africa. In State Versus Ethnic Claims.

Behrens, A. W., Jones, M. H., & Lowery, R. S. (2018). Pediatric ocular injury secondary to a Burmese python bite. *Journal of AAPOS*, 22(5), 399–400.e1. 10.1016/j.jaapos.2018.03.00229574138

Berry, H. S. (2023). Survey of the Challenges and Solutions in Cybersecurity Awareness Among College Students. *ISDFS 2023 - 11th International Symposium on Digital Forensics and Security*. IEEE. 10.1109/ISDFS58141.2023.10131851

Carayannis, E. G., & Morawska-Jancelewicz, J. (2022). The Futures of Europe: Society 5.0 and Industry 5.0 as Driving Forces of Future Universities. *Journal of the Knowledge Economy*, 13(4), 3445–3471. 10.1007/s13132-021-00854-2

Chin, A., Jones, B., & Little, P. (2021). A Comparative Analysis of Smartphone Security Behaviors and Practices. [IJEDICT]. *International Journal of Education and Development Using Information and Communication Technology*, 17, 57–80.

ESET. (2017). *2015 ESET Asia Cyber Savviness Report.* ESET.

Feigin, V. L., Nichols, E., Alam, T., Bannick, M. S., Beghi, E., Blake, N., Culpepper, W. J., Dorsey, E. R., Elbaz, A., Ellenbogen, R. G., Fisher, J. L., Fitzmaurice, C., Giussani, G., Glennie, L., James, S. L., Johnson, C. O., Kassebaum, N. J., Logroscino, G., Marin, B., & Vos, T. (2019). Global, regional, and national burden of neurological disorders, 1990–2016: A systematic analysis for the Global Burden of Disease Study 2016. *Lancet Neurology*, 18(5), 459–480. 10.1016/S1474-4422(18)30499-X30879893

Irfan, A., Rasli, A., Sulaiman, Z., Sami, A., & Qureshi, M. I. (2018). Use of Social Media Sites by Malaysian Universities and its Impact on University Ranking. *International Journal of Engineering & Technology*. www.sciencepubco.com/index.php/IJET

Ismail, A. R., Nguyen, B., & Melewar, T. C. (2018). Impact of perceived social media marketing activities on brand and value consciousness: Roles of usage, materialism and conspicuous consumption. *International Journal of Internet Marketing and Advertising*, 12(3), 233. 10.1504/IJIMA.2018.093387

Jyothi, A. P., Badiger, V. N., & Shivakumar, V. (2023). Security in Social Networks and Media. *IEEE International Conference on Advances in Electronics, Communication, Computing and Intelligent Information Systems, ICAECIS 2023 - Proceedings*. IEEE. 10.1109/ICAECIS58353.2023.10170002

Kauthamy, K., Ashrafi, N., & Kuilboer, J. P. (2017). Mobile Devices and Cyber Security: An Exploratory Study on User's Response to Cyber Security Challenges. *WEBIST 2017 - Proceedings of the 13th International Conference on Web Information Systems and Technologies*, (pp. 306–311). Research Gate. 10.5220/0006298803060311

Kyza, E. A., Varda, C., Panos, D., Karageorgiou, M., Komendantova, N., Perfumi, S. C., Shah, S. I. H., & Hosseini, A. S. (2020). Combating misinformation online: Re-imagining social media for policy-making. *Internet Policy Review*, 9(4). Advance online publication. 10.14763/2020.4.1514

Lee, J., Lim, C., & Kim, H. (2017). Development of an instructional design model for flipped learning in higher education. *Educational Technology Research and Development*, 65(2), 427–453. 10.1007/s11423-016-9502-1

Marquardson, J., & Gomillion, L., D. (2018). Cyber Security Curriculum Development: Protecting Students and Institutions While Providing Hands-On Experience. [ISEDJ]. *Information Systems Education Journal*, 16(5).

Mohammed, S., Larsen-Reindorf, R. E., & Awal, I. (2020). Menstrual Hygiene Management and School Absenteeism among Adolescents in Ghana: Results from a School-Based Cross-Sectional Study in a Rural Community. *International Journal of Reproductive Medicine*, 2020, 1–9. 10.1155/2020/6872491 32411782

Mohd Yusof, S. B., Huda Sheikh Abdullah, S. N., Mohd, M., Adnan, N., Raja Yusof, R. J., Mokhtar, U. A., Norman, A. A., & Paizi Fauzi, W. F. (2022). The effectiveness of Women 4IR Cyber 3A #Aware, Avoid, Act Program in Malaysia. *International Conference on Cyber Resilience, ICCR 2022*. IEEE. 10.1109/ICCR56254.2022.9995864

Nair, M. M., Tyagi, A. K., & Sreenath, N. (2021). The Future with Industry 4.0 at the Core of Society 5.0: Open Issues, Future Opportunities and Challenges. *2021 International Conference on Computer Communication and Informatics (ICCCI)*, (pp. 1–7). IEEE. 10.1109/ICCCI50826.2021.9402498

Polit, D. F., Beck, C. T., & Owen, S. V. (2007). Focus on Research Methods: Is the CVI an Acceptable Indicator of Content Validity? Appraisal and Recommendations. *Research in Nursing & Health*, 30(4), 459–467. 10.1002/nur.2019917654487

Rahman, S. F. A., Yunus, M. M., & Hashim, H. (2020). The uniqueness of flipped learning approach. *International Journal of Education and Practice*, 8(3), 394–404. 10.18488/journal.61.2020.83.394.404

Rajasekharaiah, K., Dule, C. S., & Sudarshan, E. (2020). Cyber security challenges and its emerging trends on latest technologies. *Paper presented at the IOP Conference Series: Materials Science and Engineering*. IOP Science. 10.1088/1757-899X/981/2/022062

Ramakrishnan, K., Yasin, N. M., & Periasamy, J. (2022). Digital divide on cybersecurity awareness among the Malaysian higher learning institution students. *AIP Conference Proceedings*, 040022. 10.1063/5.0092796

Rathakrishnan, B., Singh, S. S. B., Yahaya, A., Kamaluddin, M. R., Mohamed, N. H., Krishnan, A. R., & Rahman, Z. A. (2023). *The Influence of Social Media Use on Social Connectedness Among University Students.*, 10.1007/978-3-031-16865-9_37

Selwyn, N., & Aagaard, J. (2021). Banning mobile phones from classrooms—An opportunity to advance understandings of technology addiction, distraction and cyberbullying. *British Journal of Educational Technology*, 52(1), 8–19. 10.1111/bjet.12943

Simon, N., Jiménez, J. L., & Strocchia, D. (2023). Reimaging Cybersecurity in Educational Practices: An International Case Study. In *Handbook of Research on Current Trends in Cybersecurity and Educational Technology*. 10.4018/978-1-6684-6092-4.ch001

Tan, Z., Beuran, R., Hasegawa, S., Jiang, W., Zhao, M., & Tan, Y. (2020). Adaptive security awareness training using linked open data datasets. *Education and Information Technologies*, 25(6), 5235–5259. 10.1007/s10639-020-10155-x

Xiang, C. S., & Hasbullah, M. (2023). Cybersecurity Awareness, Cyber Human Values and Cyberbullying Among University Students in Selangor, Malaysia. *International Journal of Advanced Research in Technology and Innovation*. 10.55057/ijarti.2023.5.2.1

Yang, P., Xiong, N., & Ren, J. (2020). Data security and privacy protection for cloud storage: A survey. *IEEE Access : Practical Innovations, Open Solutions*, 8, 131723–131740. 10.1109/ACCESS.2020.3009876

Zwilling, M., Klien, G., Lesjak, D., Wiechetek, Ł., Cetin, F., & Basim, H. N. (2022). Cyber security awareness, knowledge and behavior: A comparative study. *Journal of Computer Information Systems*, 62(1), 82–97. 10.1080/08874417.2020.1712269

KEY TERMS AND DEFINITIONS

Data Security: The various practices of safeguarding digital data from theft, unauthorised access, corruption, or any other malicious activities. This involves implementing different measures and protocols to make sure that sensitive information remains confidential, intact, and accessible only to authorised systems or individuals.

Digital Literacy: This relates to proficiency in effectively navigating, assessing, and utilising digital technologies and information in various contexts. This involves a spectrum of skills, such as but not limited to, employing digital devices and software, critically evaluating online information for authenticity and accuracy, preserving privacy and personal information online, engaging in communication and collaboration using digital platforms, and resolving problems with the aid of digital tools.

Education 5.0: Education 5.0 refers to the ongoing evolution of education that is influenced by technological progress and societal shifts. This concept promotes a comprehensive learning approach that incorporates state-of-the-art technologies such as artificial intelligence, virtual reality, and tailored learning tools to provide engaging and interactive educational experiences. Education 5.0 focuses on fostering crucial skills like creativity, critical thinking, communication, problem solving, and collaboration, equipping learners with the necessary abilities to succeed in the digital era.

Social Media: A term that encompasses various online platforms and tools that enable users to share, create, and interact with content in virtual networks and communities. These platforms facilitate numerous forms of communication and collaboration including text, images, videos, and audio, which are all examples of user-generated content.

Chapter 3
Navigating Through Education 5.0 Era:
Imperative Competencies for Success

Ram Singh
University of Lucknow, India

ABSTRACT

As we stand on the precipice of Education 5.0, characterized by unprecedented technological advancements and societal changes, the need for a transformative approach to education becomes paramount. This chapter delves into the imperative competencies that individuals must cultivate to thrive in this dynamic era. The chapter underscores the shift from conventional academic achievements to holistic competencies that encompass critical thinking, adaptability, and a collaborative mindset. The chapter provides a roadmap for navigating the Education 5.0 era, offering practical insights and actionable strategies for both learners and educators. By recognizing and developing these imperative competencies, individuals can not only succeed but also contribute meaningfully to a rapidly evolving global society.

INTRODUCTION

Education 5.0 signifies a transformative departure from conventional educational paradigms, embracing a holistic and interconnected approach to learning. This era extends education beyond the confines of physical classrooms, leveraging technology for immersive, personalized, and collaborative learning experiences. As we embark on this educational journey, the cultivation of competencies that transcend traditional academic prowess becomes crucial.

Education 5.0 signifies the utilization of emerging technologies to facilitate a more personalized and humanized approach to teaching, placing a distinct emphasis on the social and emotional development of students and implementing solutions that enhance societal well-being.

Education 5.0 is characterized by the seamless integration of technology into educational practices. Technologies such as artificial intelligence, augmented reality, and adaptive learning systems serve as enablers, reshaping the acquisition, dissemination, and application of knowledge. This integration necessitates a new skill set, emphasizing digital literacy, adaptability, and a proactive embrace of innovation for both educators and learners.

DOI: 10.4018/979-8-3693-3041-8.ch003

Economy 5.0 will require adaptive transformations in Education sector, focusing on flexibility, customization, cooperation, adaptability of teaching methods, and proactive teacher roles as mentors and trainers.(Sułkowski, et al., 2021)

Global interconnectedness demands an education that prepares individuals to be global citizens. Cultural competence becomes pivotal, encouraging an understanding and appreciation of diverse perspectives. In Education 5.0, learners transform from mere consumers of information into active participants in a global dialogue, contributing to the collective wisdom of humanity.

Education 5.0 envisions learning as a lifelong pursuit. The rapid evolution of knowledge requires a mindset of continuous learning, adaptability, and resilience. The ability to unlearn and relearn becomes paramount as the educational landscape evolves, ensuring individuals remain agile and equipped for the challenges of the future.

In recent decades, there has been a surge in digital transformation and the integration of new technologies into our daily lives. Artificial Intelligence, the Internet of Things, data processing, and various other tools have become essential parts of both personal and corporate spheres.

The onset of the Covid-19 pandemic further accelerated the shift towards digitalization, transforming online classes and distance learning from trends into everyday realities. Education 5.0 seeks to cultivate emotionally intelligent individuals who can harness digital transformation as a tool for societal progress, creating a symbiotic relationship between digital and technological knowledge.

Education 5.0 is an evolution of this concept. While not dismissing the principles of Education 4.0, it introduces a more human-centric perspective to learning. This includes the incorporation of social and emotional abilities to promote reduced environmental impact alongside enhanced health and safety considerations.

The previous generation focuses on the development of technological skills for professional development. Education5.0 integrate this perspective into the teaching philosophy and management processes that can cultivate, in addition to technical knowledge, skills viz. collaborative work, improved interpersonal relations, empathy, tolerance of diversity, creativity, conflict management, and more fluid communication.

Higher education should promote soft skills, including digital literacy, sustainability, and interculturality, to prepare students for professional and personal success in a super-smart society like Society 5.0.

This chapter explore the essential competencies that pave the way for moving ahead in the dynamic Education 5.0 era.

OVERVIEW OF KEY TECHNOLOGICAL, SOCIAL, AND ECONOMIC SHIFTS DEFINING THE EDUCATION 5.0 ERA

Education 5.0 transcends mere buzzword status; it embodies a transformative vision for the future of learning. Embracing these technological, social, and economic shifts leads to a future where education is personalized, engaging, and universally accessible. This empowerment enables individuals to embrace lifelong learning, becoming active contributors to a thriving world. The major Technological Social and Economic shifts in Education 5.0 are elaborate in this section

Technological Shift

- **AI-powered Personalization:** Picture an AI tutor tailoring your learning journey, suggesting resources, and customizing assignments based on your strengths and weaknesses. Education 5.0 harnesses the analytical capabilities of AI to personalize learning paths, ensuring optimal engagement and knowledge retention.
- **Immersive Reality Redefines Learning:** Step into virtual classrooms where ancient Rome springs to life or engage in frog dissections through augmented reality. Education 5.0 seamlessly integrates VR and AR to craft immersive learning experiences that transcend physical limitations and spark curiosity.
- **Big Data, Bigger Insights:** Learning analytics fuelled by big data offer educators' invaluable insights into student progress, enabling real-time identification of learning gaps and personalized interventions.

Societal Paradigm Shifts

- **Lifelong Learning Mindset:** Education 5.0 champions lifelong learning, departing from the traditional one-size-fits-all approach. Learners are empowered to continually acquire new skills and knowledge, adapting to an ever-changing world.
- **Global Collaboration:** With the advent of internet and Technology, Education 5.0 eliminate geographical barriers, fostering knowledge sharing and cross-cultural cooperation through peer connections worldwide. In engaging with peers globally, learners actively contribute to the promotion of global citizenship and intercultural awareness.
- **Focus on 21st-Century Skills:** Education 5.0 sidelines rote memorization, prioritizing critical thinking, problem-solving, creativity, communication, and collaboration – essential skills for navigating the complexities of the 21st century.

Economic Shifts

- **Future-proof Workforce Development:** Education 5.0 caters to evolving job market needs, 2equipping individuals with skills demanded by emerging technologies and industries, ensuring a future-proof workforce ready to thrive in a dynamic economic landscape.
- **Democratization of Education:** Leveraging technology and innovative learning models, Education 5.0 has the potential to bridge educational divides, making quality education accessible to all, irrespective of geographical location or socioeconomic background.
- **Nurturing Innovation and Entrepreneurship:** Education 5.0 cultivates a culture of innovation and entrepreneurship, encouraging learners to think beyond conventional boundaries and devise solutions to real-world challenges, thereby propelling economic growth and societal progress

ADAPTABILITY: THE LIFEBOAT OF EDUCATION 5.0 IN A SEA OF CHANGE

Adaptability is not merely a skill; it's a superpower for navigating the turbulent ocean of Education 5.0. By instilling learners with this essential trait, we empower them to become confident, resilient, and lifelong learners, ready to embrace the exciting uncertainties that the future holds. **Now the Question arises why adaptability so crucial in the era of Education 5.0. Let's have discussion on these aspects.**

Why is Adaptability so Crucial in Education 5.0?

- **The pace of change is dizzying:** Emerging technologies such as AI, VR, and AR are transforming the learning landscape at an astonishing pace. Skills valuable today might become obsolete tomorrow. Adaptable learners can embrace these changes, swiftly acquire new skills, and stay relevant in the job market.
- **Knowledge is constantly evolving:** New discoveries and innovations continually push the boundaries of what we know. Adaptable learners remain open to new information, can revise their understanding based on fresh evidence, and embrace lifelong learning.
- **Global interconnectedness:** In an interconnected world it is required that learners must collaborate with people from diverse backgrounds and cultures. Adaptability fosters empathy, cultural understanding, and the ability to navigate different perspectives.
- **Unforeseen challenges:** The future is inherently unpredictable. Pandemics, economic crises, and other unforeseen events can disrupt education systems and learning journeys. Adaptable learners can pivot their strategies, adjust their goals, and find creative solutions to overcome challenges.

Cultivating Adaptability in Education 5.0

It's a role of Academician how to cultivate the Adaptability skills among the present generations. Here are some strategies:

- **Embrace personalized learning:** With the help of education 5.0 platforms, students may customize their learning routes to fit their unique needs and learning preferences. This allows them to move at their own speed and modify their strategy as their comprehension grows.
- **Nurture a growth mindset:** Encourage learners to view challenges as opportunities for learning and growth. Developing a growth mindset makes them more resilient, persistent, and open to trying new things.
- **Micro-credentials and Personalized Learning Pathways:** Encourage students to shape their learning journeys with bite-sized modules and micro-credentials aligned with individual goals and interests.
- **Support Educators in Continuous Learning:** Invest in professional development programs to equip educators with skills to integrate new technologies, use adaptive learning strategies, and foster a culture of innovation.
- **Accessibility is Key:** Assure equitable access to resources and technology, bridging the digital gap with community projects and alternate teaching strategies.

- **Human Connection Matters:** While technology enhances learning, prioritize opportunities for meaningful human interaction, personalized guidance, and mentorship to provide emotional support and social-emotional learning.
- **Assessment for Growth, not Just Scores:** Shift focus from rote memorization to assessing critical thinking, collaboration, and problem-solving, providing actionable feedback to support continuous learning

DIGITAL LITERACY AND TECHNOLOGICAL PROFICIENCY IN EDUCATION 5.0

In the rapidly evolving landscape of education, the integration of digital literacy and technological proficiency has become an imperative aspect, marking the dawn of Education 5.0. This paradigm shift reflects a departure from traditional models of education towards a more dynamic and tech-centric approach. Digital literacy encompasses the ability to use and navigate digital tools and platforms effectively, while technological proficiency goes beyond mere usage, emphasizing a deeper understanding of the underlying technologies. In the context of Education 5.0, these competencies are indispensable, serving as the cornerstone for preparing students to thrive in a digital age.

Education 5.0 represents a transformative era where technology is seamlessly woven into the fabric of learning environments. Unlike its predecessors, this phase of education recognizes the pivotal role of digital literacy and technological proficiency in shaping the future workforce. Students are not merely consumers of information; they are active participants in a digital ecosystem that demands a nuanced understanding of technology. As industries undergo rapid digitalization, it is crucial for educational institutions to equip students with the skills needed to navigate the complexities of an interconnected, technologically-driven world.

Digital literacy, as a foundational component of Education 5.0, goes beyond basic computer skills. It encompasses the ability to critically evaluate information, discern digital sources' reliability, and ethically navigate the vast ocean of online content. Students are not only taught how to use software applications but are also instilled with a discerning eye to evaluate the credibility of digital information. In an era where misinformation proliferates, digital literacy serves as a shield, enabling students to navigate the digital landscape with resilience and discernment.

Technological proficiency, on the other hand, delves into the inner workings of technology. Education 5.0 recognizes that students need more than surface-level familiarity with devices; they need a deep understanding of the technologies that power these devices. Coding, data analytics, and an understanding of artificial intelligence are no longer niche skills but essential components of technological proficiency. As students gain insights into these areas, they not only become adept users but potential innovators, contributing to the ongoing digital revolution.

The integration of digital literacy and technological proficiency in Education 5.0 is not a one-size-fits-all approach. It acknowledges the diverse learning styles and paces of students. Adaptive learning technologies, personalized learning paths, and AI-driven assessments are employed to tailor educational experiences to individual needs. This customization ensures that students can progress at their own pace, focusing on areas where they need more attention, and advancing rapidly through familiar concepts. The result is a more inclusive and effective educational system that caters to the unique strengths and weaknesses of each learner.

In the landscape of Education 5.0, educators play a pivotal role as facilitators of learning rather than mere transmitters of knowledge. The traditional role of teachers as information providers is transformed into that of mentors and guides. They create learning environments that encourage exploration, collaboration, and critical thinking. The focus shifts from rote memorization to fostering a deep understanding of concepts, enabling students to apply their knowledge in real-world scenarios. Educators become co-learners, embracing the dynamic nature of technology and adapting their teaching methods to the ever-evolving educational landscape.

One of the key strengths of Education 5.0 is its emphasis on interdisciplinary learning. Digital literacy and technological proficiency are not confined to specific subjects but are integrated across the curriculum. Students are encouraged to draw connections between different disciplines, applying their digital skills in the context of diverse subjects. For instance, a history class may involve analyzing primary sources online, a biology class may incorporate virtual dissections, and a literature class may explore digital storytelling. This interdisciplinary approach prepares students for a future where problem-solving requires a synthesis of knowledge from various domains.

Furthermore, Education 5.0 promotes collaborative learning on a global scale. Technology enables students to connect with peers from different parts of the world, fostering a sense of global citizenship. Virtual classrooms, collaborative projects, and online forums become integral components of the learning experience. This not only enhances students' digital communication skills but also exposes them to diverse perspectives and ideas. The ability to collaborate across borders and time zones is a crucial skill in the interconnected world of the 21st century, and Education 5.0 recognizes and cultivates this competency.

However, the integration of digital literacy and technological proficiency in Education 5.0 comes with its own set of challenges. The digital divide, characterized by unequal access to technology, remains a significant barrier. While some students have access to state-of-the-art devices and high-speed internet, others may lack even basic connectivity. Bridging this gap requires concerted efforts from governments, educational institutions, and the private sector to ensure that all students have equal access to the tools and resources necessary for digital learning.

Moreover, the rapid pace of technological advancements poses a challenge in terms of keeping educational curricula up to date. Education 5.0 requires a flexible and adaptive approach to curriculum development, with regular updates to incorporate the latest technological trends. Professional development for educators is also crucial to ensure they are well-equipped to impart the latest knowledge and skills to students. Continuous learning becomes a cornerstone for both students and educators in this ever-evolving educational landscape.

The integration of digital literacy and technological proficiency in Education 5.0 represents a paradigm shift that aligns education with the demands of the digital age. As students navigate the complexities of a connected world, these competencies empower them to not only consume information critically but also to contribute meaningfully to the ongoing digital revolution. Education 5.0 is not just about preparing students for future jobs; it is about fostering a generation of thinkers, innovators, and responsible digital citizens who can navigate the complexities of the 21st century with confidence and competence.

The future of learning is being shaped by cutting-edge tools such as AI, VR, AR, and other emerging technologies. To fully profit from modern technologies, learners must comprehend how they operate and the various uses for which they might be put. In addition, there is a wealth of information available online, but not all of it is accurate or dependable. Digital literacy gives students the ability to analyse information critically, separate fact from fiction, and stay away from false information. Personalized learning and lifelong learning are key components of education 5.0. The ability to use technology. A student-centred science learning model, incorporating Social Inquiry and Creativity-Based Learning Skill Entrepreneurship, is essential for transforming teacher-cantered learning into Community 5.0-ready education. (Lantada, A. D., 2022; Saputro, et al., 2020)

Here are some of the skills required for ensuring digital literacy and technological proficiency in Education 5.0

- **Skill-based Assessment and Feedback:** Move beyond traditional assessments, utilizing AI tools to measure real-world skills, offer personalized feedback, and adjust learning paths based on progress.
- **Embrace Emerging Technologies:** Integrate VR/AR simulations, AI-powered tutors, and gamified learning to create immersive environments fostering problem-solving and critical thinking.
- **Integrate technology strategically:** One of the most effective tools for encouraging flexibility is technology. Virtual reality simulations transport students to a variety of settings, and AI-enabled tutors offer individualized feedback and recommend different courses of study. But it's important to keep in mind that technology should enhance human contact and critical thinking abilities, not replace them.
- **Flexible Learning Platforms:** Employ platforms accommodating diverse learning styles and paces, integrating asynchronous learning modules, gamification elements, and AI-driven adaptive features.
- **Incorporate project-based learning:** Real-world projects encourage learners to apply their knowledge to solve problems, think critically, and collaborate effectively—essential skills for adapting to new situations and challenges. Integrate real-world problem-solving scenarios, open-ended inquiries, and project-based learning to develop critical thinking, creativity, and effective communication skills.

CROSS-CULTURAL COMPETENCE IN EDUCATION 5.0

In the era of Education 5.0, the significance of cross-cultural competence in the educational landscape has gained unprecedented importance. This paradigm shift reflects a departure from traditional educational models towards a more interconnected and globally oriented approach. Cross-cultural competence, the ability to interact effectively with people from different cultural backgrounds, is recognized as a crucial skill in Education 5.0. As the world becomes increasingly interconnected, preparing students with the ability to navigate and thrive in diverse cultural contexts is imperative for their success in a globalized society.

Education 5.0 acknowledges that cross-cultural competence goes beyond traditional notions of cultural awareness. It involves a deep understanding and appreciation of diverse perspectives, values, and communication styles. Students are not only exposed to different cultures but are actively engaged in activities that foster cultural intelligence, enabling them to navigate and communicate effectively in multicultural environments.

One of the key pillars of cross-cultural competence in Education 5.0 is cultural awareness. Students are exposed to a rich tapestry of cultural experiences, both within and beyond their immediate surroundings. This exposure goes beyond superficial cultural stereotypes and encourages an exploration of the deeper cultural nuances that shape societies. By understanding the historical, social, and economic factors that influence different cultures, students develop a nuanced perspective that goes beyond surface-level observations.

Moreover, cross-cultural competence emphasizes effective communication across cultural boundaries. Education 5.0 recognizes the importance of language as a bridge between cultures and encourages the acquisition of multiple languages. Beyond linguistic skills, students are taught the art of non-verbal communication, understanding cultural norms, and adapting their communication styles to different contexts. This not only facilitates smoother interactions but also fosters a sense of empathy and respect for diverse ways of expression.

In the context of Education 5.0, cross-cultural competence is integrated into the curriculum across various subjects. For example, history classes may explore global events from multiple perspectives, literature classes may delve into works from different cultures, and science classes may examine how cultural factors influence scientific discoveries. This interdisciplinary approach ensures that cross-cultural competence is not treated as a standalone skill but as an integral part of a well-rounded education.

Furthermore, technology plays a pivotal role in facilitating cross-cultural competence in Education 5.0. Virtual exchange programs, online collaborations with students from different parts of the world, and digital platforms that showcase diverse cultural narratives become essential tools. Through these digital experiences, students not only learn about different cultures but also engage in meaningful dialogues, breaking down geographical barriers and fostering a sense of interconnectedness.

In Education 5.0, educators are instrumental in cultivating cross-cultural competence. They serve as cultural guides, creating inclusive learning environments that celebrate diversity. Professional development for educators includes training in cultural competency, ensuring that they are equipped to navigate the complexities of a multicultural classroom. Educators become facilitators of cross-cultural understanding, encouraging open discussions and providing students with the tools to critically analyze cultural phenomena.

Moreover, cross-cultural competence in Education 5.0 extends beyond the classroom. It encompasses experiential learning opportunities such as study abroad programs, cultural exchange initiatives, and community service projects that expose students to diverse perspectives. These real-world experiences enable students to apply their cross-cultural skills in practical settings, fostering a deeper understanding of global issues and instilling a sense of responsibility as global citizens.

The integration of cross-cultural competence in Education 5.0 aligns with the evolving needs of the workforce. In a globalized economy, employers value individuals who can work effectively in diverse teams and navigate international business environments. Cross-cultural competence becomes a competitive advantage, enhancing students' employability and preparing them for leadership roles in an interconnected world.

However, the integration of cross-cultural competence in Education 5.0 is not without its challenges. The potential for cultural misunderstandings and conflicts necessitates a thoughtful approach in curriculum design and pedagogy. Sensitivity to cultural differences and the ability to address potential biases are crucial aspects that educators must consider. Moreover, addressing the digital divide becomes essential to ensure that all students, regardless of their background, have access to the technological tools that facilitate cross-cultural learning experiences.

In conclusion, cross-cultural competence in Education 5.0 represents a transformative approach that recognizes the interconnected nature of the modern world. As students prepare for the challenges of a globalized society, the ability to navigate and thrive in diverse cultural contexts becomes a fundamental skill. Education 5.0 not only exposes students to different cultures but actively cultivates cross-cultural competence, ensuring that they graduate with the skills and perspectives needed to contribute meaningfully to an interconnected and diverse world. This holistic approach to education not only prepares students for future professional success but also fosters a sense of global citizenship and empathy, contributing to a more inclusive and harmonious global community.

Understanding diverse cultural perspectives is not just a box to tick; it's a continuous journey of learning, reflection, and growth. It's a journey that begins in the classroom but extends to every aspect of our lives, building a future where different cultures enrich and empower each other. Encountering different viewpoints and ways of knowing, students develop critical thinking skills, challenge their own assumptions, and understand the interconnectedness of our world. This is crucial for navigating complex global issues and collaborating effectively across cultures.

Diverse perspectives spark new ideas and innovative solutions. When students learn from and build upon diverse knowledge systems, they are better equipped to think creatively and address the challenges of the 21st century.

Learners in Education 5.0 will engage and work together with individuals from diverse cultural backgrounds more and more. Comprehending cultural distinctions facilitates empathy, proficient communication, and the capacity to handle intricate moral predicaments that emerge in globalized communities.

Indigenous and traditional knowledge systems provide insightful perspectives on human connections, problem-solving, and sustainability. With its embrace of these varied viewpoints, education 5.0 enhances learning and advances a more comprehensive view of the world. Through the intentional incorporation of varied cultural viewpoints into Education 5.0, we can establish a genuinely comprehensive and empowering educational setting that equips learners for triumph in a worldwide and interconnected society. Let's celebrate cultural variety and raise a new generation of scholars who are accountable, compassionate, and prepared to take on the issues of the future.

Here are some of the strategies for integrating cultural perspectives in Education 5.0:

- **Curriculum diversification**: Include diverse viewpoints and voices in textbooks, learning materials, and course content. Explore historical events and global issues from multiple perspectives.
- **Global collaboration:** Facilitate virtual exchange programs, international partnerships, and intercultural dialogue opportunities for students to learn from and interact with peers from different cultures.
- **Culturally responsive teaching:** Educators can adapt their teaching styles and strategies to cater to the diverse learning needs and cultural backgrounds of their students.
- **Community engagement:** Partner with local communities and cultural organizations to incorporate local knowledge and perspectives into the learning experience.
- **Technology as a bridge:** Utilize technology to explore diverse cultures virtually, connect with people from around the world, and foster intercultural understanding.
- **Nurture Intercultural Understanding and Global Collaboration:** Use online platforms and virtual exchange programs to connect students globally, fostering global citizenship and adaptability to diverse perspectives.

EMOTIONAL INTELLIGENCE AND SUCCESS IN EDUCATION 5.0

Emotional Intelligence (EQ) is a multifaceted skill set encompassing the understanding, utilization, and management of one's own emotions and those of others. In the context of Education 5.0, which places a strong emphasis on personalized learning, collaboration, and problem-solving, EQ emerges as a critical factor for student success.

Contributions of EQ in Education 5.0:

1. *Self-awareness:* Students with high EQ possess the ability to comprehend their strengths and weaknesses. This self-awareness empowers them to set realistic goals and make informed decisions about their learning journey.
2. *Social awareness:* High EQ enables students to understand the emotions of their peers, fostering the development of strong relationships and effective collaboration in a learning environment that emphasizes teamwork and interconnectedness.
3. *Relationship management:* EQ skills facilitate the building and maintenance of positive relationships, a crucial aspect of success not only in education but also in various professional fields.

Educator Strategies to Develop EQ:

1. ***Teaching about EQ***: Educators can explicitly teach students about the different facets of EQ and provide guidance on how to enhance their emotional intelligence.
2. ***Creating a supportive environment***: Establishing a safe and supportive learning environment encourages students to express their emotions freely, contributing to their emotional growth.
3. ***Social and emotional learning (SEL)***: Integrating SEL activities into the curriculum provides structured opportunities for students to develop and refine their EQ skills.
4. ***Modelling EQ skills***: Educators Can model EQ skills by demonstrating self-awareness, self-management, social awareness, and effective relationship management in their interactions with students.

The development of Emotional Intelligence in students goes beyond academic achievements, enhancing their ability to handle challenges, understand others, adapt to change, and maintain a genuine, intrinsic motivation for learning. These skills contribute not only to academic success but also to personal growth and well-rounded individuals. The integration of EQ into education not only enhances academic achievement but also nurtures well-rounded individuals equipped with the interpersonal and intrapersonal skills needed for success in the dynamic landscape of Education 5.0 and beyond.

ISSUES AND CHALLENGES IN ADOPTING EDUCATION5.0

The Education 5.0 era is characterised by the integration of advanced technologies that create immersive learning environments within classrooms. Additionally, It places a strong emphasis on fostering the development of 21st-century skills, which are deemed essential for thriving in the constantly evolving global society. Nevertheless, the aspiration for Education 5.0 encounters a harsh reality in developing nations such as India, where there exists a significant gap between the theoretical framework and the actual execution.

The concept of Education 5.0 proposes a transformative change in the field of education, which is marked by:

- **Personalised Learning:**

In this hypothetical scenario, we envision a classroom setting where artificial intelligence (AI) tutors are employed to accommodate the unique learning styles and paces of each student. These AI tutors would be responsible for creating and tailoring personalised learning journeys for each individual learner. When students encounter difficulties in understanding a concept, they are provided with specific and focused assistance to aid their comprehension. Conversely, students who quickly grasp the concept are given the opportunity to explore the topic in greater depth. The cultivation of a more profound comprehension and an affinity for acquiring knowledge is facilitated, surpassing the mere act of memorising information mechanically.

Technological Integration: The era of relying solely on dusty textbooks is now a thing of the past. Through the use of Virtual Reality (VR) and Augmented Reality (AR), the walls of classrooms are transformed into gateways that lead to immersive virtual worlds. The integration of gamification into educational settings introduces an enjoyable and competitive component, while the implementation of the Internet of Things (IoT) enables the collection of real-time data and provision of immediate feedback, resulting in the establishment of a dynamic and captivating learning environment.

Cultivation of 21st-century skills:

Going beyond the traditional focus on knowledge acquisition. The central tenets of critical thinking, problem-solving, creativity, collaboration, and communication are emphasised. It has been observed that students acquire the ability to engage in critical thinking, analyse information, and demonstrate creative problem-solving skills, thereby equipping themselves to effectively navigate the complexities and prospects of the information age.

The potential to transform education in India is immense with the advent of personalised, technology-driven learning. Consider the potential scenario in which students residing in rural areas are afforded the opportunity to partake in immersive experiences of the Great Barrier Reef via virtual reality technology. Additionally, envision these students engaging in collaborative problem-solving activities with their peers from various parts of the world. Education 5.0 has the potential to democratise access to high-quality education, which in turn can promote innovation and empower upcoming generations to make significant contributions on a global scale.

CHALLENGES IN IMPLEMENTATION OF EDUCATION 5.0

Nevertheless, the implementation of the theoretical framework in developing countries such as India poses notable obstacles:

- **Digital Divide:** The phenomenon known as the digital divide presents a significant challenge to the ideal vision of seamless technological integration. This divide represents the stark reality that not all individuals have equal access to and proficiency in digital technologies. The presence of unequal access to technology and reliable internet connectivity poses a substantial impediment. It is worth noting that a significant portion of the population, especially those residing in rural areas, face a dearth of fundamental infrastructure necessary to actively engage in the ongoing digital revolution. The phenomenon described gives rise to a dual-level educational structure, thereby amplifying pre-existing disparities.

- **Teacher Training:** Educators who were raised in an era dominated by traditional teaching tools such as chalkboards and textbooks may experience a sense of being inundated by the rapid introduction of new technologies. For the successful integration of these technologies into current curriculums and teaching methods, it is essential to establish a comprehensive system of teacher training and support. Insufficient training and limited access to resources can pose challenges for teachers in effectively harnessing the complete capabilities of Education 5.0, which in turn may impede student engagement and hinder the achievement of desired learning outcomes.
- **Infrastructure Limitations:** The educational institutions in developing economy like India face numerous challenges related to their infrastructure. One of the primary concerns is overcrowded classrooms, which hampers the learning environment. Additionally, these schools often have limited resources, making it difficult for students to access necessary materials and tools. Moreover, the physical infrastructure of many schools is inadequate, lacking proper facilities and amenities. These infrastructure limitations pose significant obstacles to the overall quality of education in India. Implementing personalised learning approaches within the given constraints necessitates the development of novel and creative solutions.
- **Socioeconomic disparity**: The phenomenon of socioeconomic disparity is a significant factor that contributes to the existing inequalities in access to quality education. It is worth noting that Education 5.0 has the potential to further exacerbate these disparities. Individuals hailing from socioeconomically disadvantaged backgrounds may encounter barriers in terms of accessing the requisite technology and support systems necessary to fully capitalise on these advancements.

In order to establish a connection between theoretical concepts and real-world application, it is imperative to adopt a comprehensive strategy that centres around the following key aspects:

- **Equity in access.**

Access to digital resources has emerged as a critical concern in contemporary society. The need to bridge the digital divide has become paramount in order to ensure equal opportunities for all individuals. Here Government initiatives and public-private partnerships have been identified as key factors in facilitating broader technology access and internet connectivity, especially in rural regions. These collaborative efforts can effectively address the digital divide by implementing policies and programmes that promote infrastructure development, affordability, and digital literacy. By leveraging the resources and expertise of both the public and private sectors, these initiatives can help bridge the gap and provide equal opportunities for individuals residing in remote areas to access technology and connect to the internet. One potential approach to address this issue is the establishment of community technology centres, which would serve as accessible hubs for individuals to access technology resources. Additionally, providing low-cost devices to individuals who may not have the means to purchase them could help bridge the digital divide. Furthermore, subsidising internet plans for those who cannot afford them may also play a crucial role in ensuring equitable access to the internet.

- **Teacher Empowerment:**

Teacher empowerment is a critical aspect of educational development. It is imperative to invest in teacher training programmes that focus on equipping educators with the necessary skills to effectively integrate technology and personalised learning strategies into their teaching practices. The design of these programmes should prioritise context specificity and offer continuous support to educators as they navigate the intricate landscape of Education 5.0.

- **Contextualised Solutions:** It is important to note that developing countries, such as India, face unique challenges that prevent them from simply adopting the Education 5.0 model implemented in developed nations. These challenges may include limited resources, infrastructure constraints, cultural differences, and varying educational needs. Therefore, it is crucial to develop solutions that are specifically tailored to the context of these countries, taking into account their specific circumstances and requirements. It is imperative to modify the existing framework in order to align it with the unique circumstances of the given context. One potential avenue of investigation could be the exploration of cost-effective and scalable technological solutions that make use of already available resources. The utilisation of open-source software and offline learning platforms has the potential to greatly contribute to the promotion of inclusivity. Furthermore, it is imperative that curriculum development takes into consideration the socio-cultural context in which students are situated.
- **Community Collaboration:** Collaboration between the education system, local communities, and non-profit organisations is a crucial aspect of fostering a supportive and inclusive learning environment. By working together, these stakeholders can leverage their unique strengths and resources to enhance educational opportunities and address the diverse needs of students. This collaborative approach promotes a sense of shared responsibility and empowers communities to actively contribute to the educational development of their members. Through effective communication, joint planning, and coordinated efforts, community collaboration can lead to improved educational outcomes and a more cohesive society.

LEARNING AND RESKILLING IN EDUCATION 5.0

Education 5.0 signifies a paradigm shift toward personalized, technology-driven learning that emphasizes adaptability and lifelong learning. In this transformative landscape, learning and reskilling become intertwined, forming the cornerstone of success.

The need for reskilling has become increasingly crucial due to the rapid evolution of job markets. The evolution of automation and technological advancements is causing disruptions in traditional industries, creating a demand for new skill sets and a persistent commitment to upskilling. In this dynamic landscape, individuals are required to adapt to evolving job roles and acquire fresh competencies to maintain competitiveness in the workforce. Furthermore, the dynamic nature of knowledge underscores the need for continuous learning, as information quickly becomes outdated, making ongoing education crucial for professional relevance.

In response to these challenges, Education 5.0 has emerged as a transformative approach. This educational paradigm recognizes the diversity of learners and advocates for individualized learning pathways. By addressing various needs and aspirations, Education 5.0 offers flexible reskilling opportunities, ensuring that individuals can customize their learning experiences to align with specific career objectives. This approach acknowledges the inadequacy of a one-size-fits-all model in the face of a rapidly changing job market

Reskilling for the future involves a strategic focus on essential skills. Individuals are encouraged to develop transferable skills such as critical thinking, problem-solving, communication, and digital literacy. Moreover, embracing emerging technologies is paramount. Familiarizing oneself with artificial intelligence, big data, cloud computing, and other relevant technologies positions individuals to navigate the evolving technological landscape. Nurturing creativity and innovation are equally important, fostering the ability to think outside the box and adapt to new challenges.

To navigate the complexities of the professional world, seeking mentorship and guidance is advised. Connecting with experienced individuals in one's field can provide valuable insights into career development and industry trends. This mentorship not only facilitates knowledge transfer but also offers support and perspective, enhancing an individual's ability to make informed decisions about their career trajectory.

Reskilling in Education 5.0 marks a transformative shift in the educational landscape, responding to the evolving needs of the 21st-century workforce. In this era of rapid technological advancements and global connectivity, traditional educational paradigms are becoming outdated, necessitating a fundamental rethinking of how we prepare individuals for the challenges of the future. Education 5.0 is characterized by a holistic approach that goes beyond mere skill acquisition, emphasizing adaptability, critical thinking, and lifelong learning. Reskilling, within this framework, takes center stage as a proactive response to the dynamic nature of the job market.

One of the key aspects of Reskilling in Education 5.0 is the recognition that job roles are continuously evolving due to automation, artificial intelligence, and other technological disruptions. As routine tasks become automated, there is a growing demand for skills that are uniquely human—such as creativity, emotional intelligence, and complex problem-solving. Reskilling initiatives aim to equip individuals with these sought-after skills, fostering a workforce that can thrive in the face of automation. This paradigm shift requires educators to move away from a one-size-fits-all approach to a more personalized and adaptive learning environment.

In the context of Reskilling, the traditional model of education, which often ends with formal degrees or certifications, is being redefined. Continuous learning throughout one's career is now seen as essential, challenging the notion of a fixed endpoint to education. Educational institutions, employers, and individuals alike are recognizing the importance of upskilling and reskilling to remain competitive in the rapidly changing job market. This paradigm shift has led to the emergence of flexible learning pathways, micro-credentials, and online platforms that enable individuals to acquire new skills incrementally, aligning education with the fluid demands of the modern workforce.

Moreover, Reskilling in Education 5.0 places a strong emphasis on interdisciplinary learning. Recognizing that real-world challenges often require a multifaceted approach, educational programs are designed to integrate knowledge and skills from various disciplines. This interdisciplinary approach not only prepares individuals for the complexity of modern problem-solving but also encourages a holistic understanding of the interconnectedness of different fields. It promotes creativity and innovation by fostering a mindset that transcends traditional disciplinary boundaries.

The role of technology in Reskilling cannot be overstated. Education 5.0 leverages cutting-edge technologies such as artificial intelligence, virtual reality, and augmented reality to create immersive and interactive learning experiences. These technologies not only enhance the effectiveness of reskilling programs but also enable remote and flexible learning, breaking down geographical barriers. The integration of technology in reskilling initiatives also allows for real-time feedback and adaptive learning experiences, tailoring education to the individual needs and pace of learners.

In addition to technological integration, Reskilling in Education 5.0 places a strong emphasis on soft skills development. As automation takes over routine tasks, the ability to communicate effectively, work collaboratively, and demonstrate emotional intelligence becomes increasingly valuable. Reskilling programs incorporate modules that focus on these essential soft skills, recognizing them as crucial components of a well-rounded and adaptable individual. This holistic approach aims to produce professionals who are not only technically proficient but also socially and emotionally intelligent.

Furthermore, Reskilling in Education 5.0 is characterized by a shift in assessment methodologies. Traditional exams and standardized testing are complemented by more dynamic and practical assessments that measure not only knowledge retention but also the application of skills in real-world scenarios. Project-based assessments, simulations, and portfolios play a significant role in evaluating the capabilities developed through reskilling programs. This shift towards outcome-based assessments reinforces the idea that education is not just about acquiring information but also about applying that knowledge in meaningful ways.

In conclusion, Reskilling in Education 5.0 represents a paradigm shift that acknowledges the dynamic nature of the modern workforce. It emphasizes continuous learning, adaptability, and the development of a diverse skill set that goes beyond technical expertise. The integration of technology, interdisciplinary learning, soft skills development, industry collaboration, and innovative assessment methodologies collectively contribute to a holistic approach that prepares individuals not just for a job but for a lifelong journey of learning and growth. As we navigate the challenges of the 21st century, Reskilling in Education 5.0 stands as a beacon of progress, shaping an educational landscape that is responsive, inclusive, and geared towards empowering individuals for success in an ever-evolving world.

DISCUSSIONS

Education 5.0 fosters learner autonomy in their learning journeys. A flexible and adaptable approach equips individuals to thrive in the ever-changing future. Lifelong learning, essential skill development, technology adoption, mentorship, and continuous upskilling empower individuals to navigate future challenges and opportunities. In these sections lets discuss some of the studies hightlighted the key skills requirement for the adoption of Education 5.0.

Studies by Ačimović et al. (2021)Fischer et al. (2020), and Sung et al. (2022) emphasize the importance of critical thinking, problem-solving, and collaborative learning in Education 5.0. Critical thinking skills are essential for evaluating information credibility and creative problem-solving. Collaborative learning equips students to work effectively in diverse teams. Faridi's (2020) study highlights the significance of clear communication, especially in a technologically advanced world. Hodges et al. (2021) emphasize lifelong learning as a crucial skill for navigating the rapidly evolving technological landscape. Adaptability and a willingness to continuously acquire new skills are essential for success. Andrews et al. (2020) advocate for cultivating a growth mindset, encouraging students to embrace challenges and view themselves as capable of continuous learning. Yasin et al. (2022) and Green and Baptise (2020) emphasize the importance of digital literacy skills, encompassing technology utilization, information evaluation, and responsible digital navigation. Rani et al. (2021) and Yong et al. (2020) highlight the growing demand for fostering creativity and innovation in students. Creativity is crucial for addressing complex problems and generating novel ideas in a technology-driven world. Luo et al. (2023) and Chen et al. (2021) emphasize the growing emphasis on self-directed learning and metacognition in Education

5.0. Students need to take ownership of their learning journeys, setting goals, tracking progress, and adapting strategies as needed. Metacognition, or awareness of one's thinking processes, equips students to effectively assess their learning and make necessary adjustments. Hwang and Lim (2022) and Akbulut and Ozcelik (2020) highlight the growing demand fzor data analysis proficiency and information literacy in Education 5.0. Students need to understand and derive insights from large data sets, and efficiently locate, evaluate, and utilize information in an information-saturated world. Chang et al. (2021) and Sun and Liu (2020) emphasize the importance of social and emotional intelligence (EQ) in Education 5.0. Strong interpersonal skills, empathy, and self-awareness are essential for navigating complex social situations and working effectively in teams. Cultivating EQ fosters student well-being and resilience in a rapidly changing environment.

Education 5.0 has the potential to revolutionise the learning experience, making it more personalised and enriching. However, its successful adoption necessitates a thorough examination of its socio-cultural implications. By focusing on matters of fairness, empowering educators, valuing cultural beliefs, and upholding ethical standards, we can leverage the potential of Education 5.0 to establish an all-encompassing and resilient learning environment. In addition, Education 5.0 has the potential to revolutionise education by providing tailored learning paths and greater accessibility through the use of technology. Nevertheless, a study conducted by Melluso et al. (2020) sheds light on the issues surrounding the digital divide. The disparity in access to technology and infrastructure can worsen educational disparities, especially in developing nations.

Education 5.0 advocates for a transition from a teacher-centered approach to a learner-centered approach in education. Research indicates that educators may benefit from additional training and support in order to effectively adapt to this evolving paradigm, as highlighted by the findings of Muzira & Bondai (2020). In addition, the growing focus on technology may lead to concerns regarding the diminishing value of educators' roles. It is crucial to strike a balance between the emphasis on technology in Education 5.0 and the significance of cultural values and human interaction. It is widely acknowledged that social and emotional learning play a vital role in education.

Student data privacy and the potential for algorithmic bias are significant concerns that arise from the widespread integration of technology in Education 5.0. It is crucial to prioritise responsible data collection and utilisation. Education 5.0 strives to provide learners with the necessary skills to thrive in the future job market. Nevertheless, the ever-increasing speed of technological advancements requires individuals to be adaptable and committed to continuous learning. Education systems need to evolve in order to foster adaptability, critical thinking, and problem-solving abilities in addition to technical expertise.

REFERENCES

Ačimović, S., Jovanović, M., & Jovanović, V. (2021). Critical thinking skills in the age of artificial intelligence. In *International Conference on New Trends in Education and Their Impact* (pp. 45-52). Springer, Cham.

Akbulut, Y., & Ozcelik, M. (2020). Information literacy in the digital age. *International Journal of Technology and Learning*, 16(2), 145–158.

Alharbi, A. M. (2023). Implementation of Education 5.0 in Developed and Developing Countries: A Comparative Study. *Creative Education*, 14(5), 914–942. 10.4236/ce.2023.145059

Andrews, T., Sayer, P., & Cameron, C. (2020). Developing a growth mindset in students: A review of growth mindset interventions in school settings. *Educational Research Review*, 31, 100322.

Chang, Y., Chen, Y., & Lin, Y. (2021). The importance of social and emotional learning (SEL) in Education 5.0. *International Journal of Learning and Development*, 11(2), 213–222.

Chen, P., Liu, X., & Li, Y. (2021). Promoting metacognition in the era of Education 5.0: A review of literature. *Studies in Educational Sciences*, 11(12), 1183–1192.

Faridi, A. (2020). The importance of communication skills in the digital age. *Journal of Applied Communication Research*, 48(3), 232–248.

Fischer, L., Nistor, A., & Morar, A. (2020). Problem-solving skills in the digital age: A theoretical framework. *Journal of Information Technology Education*, 19(1), 187–202.

. Green, B., & Baptise, D. (2020). *Technological fluency: A critical skill for the 21st century workforce.*

Hodges, C., Smith, M., Hayes, D., & Watson, J. (2021). Lifelong learning and the future of higher education. *Teaching & Learning Inquiry*, 10(1), 104–121.

Hwang, G., & Lim, S. (2022). Data analysis skills in the era of Education 5.0: A review of literature. [JETDE]. *Journal of Educational Technology Development and Exchange*, 16(3), 221–234.

. Lantada, A. D. (2022). Engineering education 5.0: Strategies for a successful transformative project-based learning. *Insights Into Global Engineering Education After the Birth of Industry 5.0*, 19.

Luo, Y., Liu, Y., & Liu, X. (2023). Self-directed learning in the era of Education 5.0: A literature review. [IJETL]. *International Journal of Emerging Technologies in Learning*, 18(1), 52–65.

Melluso, D., Pappano, L., & Anelli, F. (2020). *Implementation of Education 5.0 in Developed and Developing Countries: A Comparative Study.* Scientific Research Publishing. https://www.sydle.com/blog/education-5-0-61e71a99edf3b9259714e25a

Mitchell, J., & Guile, D. (2022). Fusion skills and industry 5.0: conceptions and challenges. In Bouezzeddine, M. (Ed.), *Insights into Global Engineering Education After the Birth of Industry 5.0.* IntechOpen. 10.5772/intechopen.100096

Mokhtar, S., Alshboul, J. A., & Shahin, G. O. (2019, December). Towards data-driven education with learning analytics for educator 4.0. [). IOP Publishing.]. *Journal of Physics: Conference Series*, 1339(1), 012079. 10.1088/1742-6596/1339/1/012079

. Muzira, D. R., & Bondai, M. (2020). *Perception of Educators towards the Adoption of Education 5.0: A Case of a State University in Zimbabwe*.

Rahim, M. N. (2021). Post-pandemic of Covid-19 and the need for transforming education 5.0 in Afghanistan higher education. *Utamax: Journal of Ultimate Research and Trends in Education*, 3(1), 29–39. 10.31849/utamax.v3i1.6166

Rusman, A., Mas'udi, M. M., Hermoyo, R. P., Yarno, Y., Yunianti, S., & Rafsanjani, H. (2023, June). Education transformation in 5.0 society development era. In *AIP Conference Proceedings* (*Vol. 2727*, No. 1). AIP Publishing.

. Sá, M., & Serpa, S. (2022). Higher Education as a Promoter of Soft Skills in a Sustainable Society 5.0. *Journal of Curriculum and Teaching*. .10.5430/jct.v11n4p1

Saputro, S., Perdana, R., Atmojo, I., & Nugraha, D. (2020). Development of Science Learning Model towards Society 5.0: A Conceptual Model. *Journal of Physics: Conference Series*, 1511(1), 012124. Advance online publication. 10.1088/1742-6596/1511/1/012124

Skitsko, V., & Osypova, O. (2022, September). Education 5.0 Maturity Index: Concept and Prospects for Development. In *International Conference on Electronic Governance with Emerging Technologies* (pp. 95-108). Cham: Springer Nature Switzerland. 10.1007/978-3-031-22950-3_8

Sułkowski, Ł., Kolasińska-Morawska, K., Seliga, R., & Morawski, P. (2021). Smart Learning Technologization in the Economy 5.0—The Polish Perspective. *Applied Sciences (Basel, Switzerland)*, 11(11), 5261. 10.3390/app11115261

Sun, P., & Liu, X. (2020). Fostering emotional intelligence in students for success in Education 5.0. *Journal of Educational Psychology*, 62(4), 521–532.

Sung, Y., Zheng, K., & Shao, A. (2022). Collaborative learning in the era of Education 5.0: A review of literature and a conceptual framework. [IJETL]. *International Journal of Emerging Technologies in Learning*, 17(2), 18–31.

Togo, M., & Gandidzanwa, C. P. (2021). The role of Education 5.0 in accelerating the implementation of SDGs and challenges encountered at the University of Zimbabwe. *International Journal of Sustainability in Higher Education*, 22(7), 1520–1535. 10.1108/IJSHE-05-2020-0158

Usmaedi, U. (2021). Education curriculum for society 5.0 in the next decade. *Jurnal Pendidikan Dasar Setiabudhi*, 4(2), 63–79.

Yasin, F. M., Rahman, M. S., & Hassan, A. (2022). Digital literacy in the era of Education 5.0: A conceptual framework for educators. *International Journal of Instruction*, 15(2), 133–152.

Chapter 4
Educating to Innovate:
Fostering Innovation Through Interdisciplinary Collaboration Between Design and Engineering Students

Elad Harison
https://orcid.org/0000-0002-8356-5626
Shenkar College of Engineering and Design, Israel

ABSTRACT

Until recently, research and development (R&D) of new technologies and products was broadly based on a division between engineering and design. Engineers were involved in different stages of the R&D processes that were either technical or functional in essence, while designers were mostly in charge of the visual, esthetic, and usability aspects of new products, prior to their production and introduction in the markets. The experiences and methodology described in this chapter has shed light on academia-industry collaboration. In this model, academia can be used as an innovation laboratory that facilitates broader and deeper research themes. This chapter assesses this form of collaboration by examining the education and innovation processes conducted in an interdisciplinary workshop that involved design and engineering students, practitioners, and researchers. The conclusions provide insights into methods of fostering the implementation of similar methodologies based on joint design-engineering work throughout the complete R&D process, as a vehicle for enhancing innovative output.

INTRODUCTION

Over an extended period, the landscape of research and development (R&D) in emerging technologies and product innovation predominantly adhered to a dichotomy between engineering and design. Engineers were typically engaged in facets of R&D processes characterized by technological or technical-functional dimensions. In parallel, designers assumed responsibility for the visual, aesthetic, and usability facets of products, along with managing the user experience and interfaces connecting users to products. Simultaneously, the assessment of product desirability for the market, involving the scrutiny of potential market

DOI: 10.4018/979-8-3693-3041-8.ch004

segments, their needs, profitability, and returns on investment in development processes and production operations, was typically delegated to managers, marketers, and industrial engineers.

Recent years, however, have witnessed the emergence of successful endeavors that incorporate methodologies from both business design and engineering design. This integration encompasses techniques and tools derived from both the engineering and design schools of thought. This approach underscores the advantages derived from fostering collaboration between designers and engineers, thereby enhancing innovative outcomes. Notably, Carmona Marques's (2017) exploration of stimulating ideation among doctoral engineering students through design methods exemplifies the potential of this interdisciplinary approach. The industry has embraced this as a beneficial practice, and it has been recognized as instrumental in the training of both designers and engineers. In an educational project reviewed by Bingham et al. (2015), this approach was implemented, leading to enhanced learning experience of the participating students. The study concludes that Product Design students received a more enriching and beneficial learning experience, better preparing them for the evolving expectations of the industry and product design employment. Further, their findings highlight the potential of integrated engineering-based learning in enhancing design education in a multiple stage methodology that can be applied by both design and engineering professors.

Exemplifying this collaborative ethos, Rompelman and De Graaff (2007) advocate for the infusion of design methods into the educational curriculum of engineering studies. Similarly, Moreira et al. (2016) propose that Amplified Mindset of Design clusters should incorporate integrative behaviors and social skills into the education of design students. In a parallel vein, Liem, Oritsland & Norstebo (2006) present insights into the potential of imbuing mechanical engineering students with fundamental design skills through a project-oriented course within their academic curriculum.

Their experience primarily revolves around equipping engineers with the ability to "think visually," advocating for the inclusion of basic design skills as an integral part of their academic training. The emphasis at the initial stages of training is on imparting "basic visualization skills" methodologically. This focus is driven by the recognition of the technical background and structured mindset of engineering students. The authors caution against the conventional approach of training engineering students in design-management methods, positing that failure in this context does not stem from a scarcity of innovative ideas and concepts. Instead, it results from challenges in selecting optimal product designs, which, in turn, arise from a deficiency in basic visualization skills.

In essence, the evolving landscape of R&D reflects a departure from the historically entrenched divisions between engineering and design. The amalgamation of methodologies from diverse design and engineering paradigms has proven to be not only feasible but also advantageous, fostering a collaborative environment that promotes innovation. The academic realm has begun to respond to this shift, with proposals to reshape curricula and instill essential design skills within engineering education. As these interdisciplinary approaches gain traction, they hold the potential to reshape the future of research and development, producing professionals equipped with a comprehensive skill set that transcends traditional disciplinary boundaries.

In the realm of new product development (NPD) processes, the interconnections between engineering and design play a pivotal role in the generation and depiction of innovative products, as posited by Chiva and Alegre (2009). These scholars underscore the indispensability of forging links between these two domains. Pei et al. (2011) further expound on this by contending that, within the design process industry, a scrutiny of various artifacts and outputs can give rise to 2D drawings that serve as amalgams of engineering and design. These drawings, according to Pei et al., function as visual representations that encapsulate both technical and engineering advancements.

Stewart and Claeys (2011) contribute to this discourse by emphasizing the significance of multidisciplinary and interdisciplinary teams in fostering innovation within firms. However, they critique prior studies for their failure to propose a methodology guiding the operation of such "mixed" teams, which have been in existence for over a decade. In lieu of this, Stewart and Claeys (2011) advocate for a deliberate suspension of disciplinary boundaries within mixed teams during certain phases of the process. This intentional disregard for disciplinary silos, they argue, enables team members to embrace novel methods and tools from other disciplines while melding them with the conventional approaches of their own field.

An alternative perspective is offered by Magee et al. (2012), who identify the potential of establishing joint academic frameworks tailored for the education of professionals in design and technology. Drawing upon the case study of the Singapore University of Technology and Design (SUTD), Magee et al. present a paradigmatic example of a collaborative institution where engineering and design faculties synergize to serve as a conduit for innovative ideas, concepts, and products. This collaborative model facilitates the initiation of cutting-edge technologies by engineering faculties, followed by the translation of these scientific and technical advances into marketable products by design faculties. As asserted by Magee et al., "design [acts] as translation of new research findings to useful products." Additionally, Asmawi et al. (2013) draw parallels between design and academic research, underscoring the risk-taking dimensions inherent in activities conducted within both realms of research and development.

Addressing a noticeable gap in the existing body of research pertaining to interdisciplinary research and development (R&D) teams comprising both designers and engineers, this chapter delves into the operational dynamics and outcomes of such teams through a comprehensive case study. The study is grounded in an academic workshop where interdisciplinary teams of students grappled with challenges presented by industry partners. This research endeavor seeks to illuminate the intricate workings and tangible outputs of teams that seamlessly integrate expertise from diverse disciplines, offering valuable insights into the collaborative processes that drive innovation at the intersection of design and engineering.

Some of the challenges of the collaboration between designers and engineers are portrayed by Pessôa and Becker (2020). The researchers suggest that communication barriers are often formed between engineers and designers due to use of different terminologies and professional languages. Thereby, bridging the communication gap and ensuring a shared understanding of project goals is both a major challenge as well as the key for the successful completion of joint projects. Quite often, engineers prioritize functionality and technical specifications, while designers may emphasize aesthetics and user experience. Balancing these priorities requires effective collaboration and compromise from both groups of professionals. As collaboration between engineers and designers requires the construction of common communication forms over long periods, in tight project timelines collaboration may be limited, leading to rushed decision-making and potential shortsighted results both in design or in technical aspects. The existence of traditional organizational structures and the lack of cross-organizational work and decision-making processes may lead to resistance to interdisciplinary collaboration. These are cultural barriers and overcoming them is essential for successful teamwork. Additionally, ensuring that designers and engineers can seamlessly integrate their tools and workflows can be a logistical challenge. Hence, adopting collaborative platforms that support both disciplines is crucial for effective cooperation.

Thereupon, despite the difficulties of carrying out this form of collaboration, the intricate relationship between engineering and design in the context of new product development processes is paramount for the creation of novel products. While the importance of multidisciplinary teams is acknowledged, the need for a methodological framework guiding the operation of these teams is emphasized. The establishment of joint academic frameworks for educating professionals in design and technology is presented as a promising avenue for fostering collaboration between engineering and design faculties. The case study approach adopted in this research provides a nuanced exploration of interdisciplinary teams' operations and outputs, shedding light on the practical aspects of collaboration between designers and engineers in the realm of research and development.

METHODOLOGY

This study was derived from a workshop organized within the scope of the TEMPUS IDEA project initiated by the European Commission (EC). The workshop served as a platform for the collaborative engagement of 45 students pursuing degrees in engineering and design across Bachelor's and Master's programs. The instructional guidance was facilitated by a cadre of educators drawn from diverse faculties. For a detailed breakdown of the participants, both students and staff, based on their professional affiliations, refer to Figure 1 and Table 1.

The composition of the workshop extended beyond local personnel, with the inclusion of five instructors hailing from German and Italian universities. These external instructors played a pivotal role, accompanying the student teams and offering supplementary guidance and perspectives throughout the workshop. To gain insights into the distribution of students and staff according to their professional backgrounds, consult Figure 1 and Table 1.

In adherence to a deliberate pedagogical approach, the local staff was tasked with adopting a minimally intrusive stance during the group discussions. The directive emphasized restraint, with staff members intervening only at the explicit request of the student groups. This approach aligns with the findings articulated by Gómez Puente et al. (2015), underscoring the significance of minimal intervention in nurturing the creative process. The emphasis on restrained involvement by the staff underscores a commitment to fostering an environment where students could independently explore and navigate their creative endeavors within the framework of the workshop. For a comprehensive exploration of the role of minimal intervention in the creative process, refer to the work of Gómez Puente et al. (2015).

Figure 1. The distribution of students by affiliation (N=45)

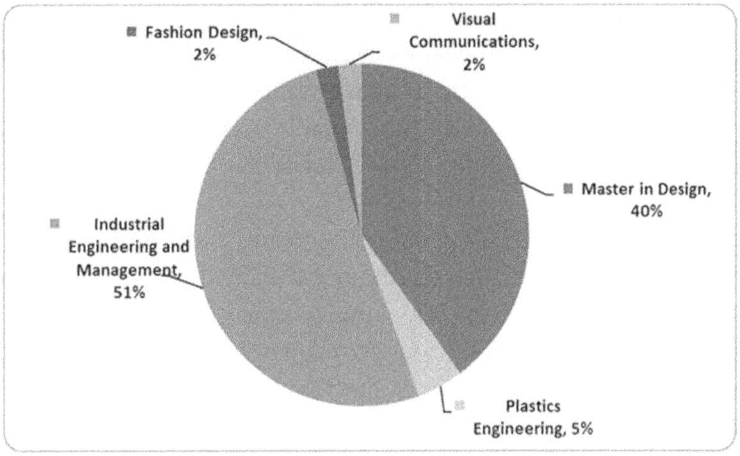

Table 1. Workshop instructors by affiliation

Academic Position	Affiliation
Head of the Master's program	Faculty of Design
Head of Department	Department of Software Engineering
Head of Department	Department of Industrial Engineering and Management
Lecturer	Master's program in Design and the Department of Software Engineering
Lecturer	Department of Textile Design
Lecturer	Department of Fashion Design

The student group was divided into four distinct groups, each tasked with addressing challenges delineated and submitted by the industrial collaborators involved in the project. These challenges were derived from a pool of 12 comprehensive company proposals, or briefs, which meticulously expounded upon the obstacles encountered by each company. Furthermore, these briefs outlined the specific types of support sought and provided directions for novel avenues in market development and research and development (R&D) that the students were expected to conceptualize and advance.

Preceding the commencement of the workshop, the local team of instructors strategically selected four briefs that could serve as the foundation for the students' endeavors. The selection process was guided by a comprehensive assessment of the requisite level of R&D, the innovative potential inherent in each challenge, and the feasibility of presenting preliminary solutions within the stipulated timeframe of one week.

The projects assigned to the student teams encompassed a diverse array of subjects, each intricately linked to the challenges articulated in the selected briefs. The students were thus presented with a multifaceted array of topics that demanded not only a nuanced understanding of the specific issues at hand but also the ability to devise innovative and feasible solutions within the constraints of the given time frame:

- New packaging and branding for a traditional, sugar-free sweetener;
- New directions for R&D for a manufacturer of plastic delivery boxes, utilizing its existing production technologies and facilities and its dominance in the B2B market (a similar R&D and design project for the food industry is described in Jiménez-Guerrero, Gázquez-Abad & Ceballos-Santamaría, 2015);
- Design of a disposable water purification apparatus for the Indian market, based on a groundbreaking chemical technology for economically accessible water treatment;
- Antiperspirant garments and clothing solutions for sports fashion.

In the culmination of the workshop, each of the four teams culminated their collaborative efforts by presenting comprehensive solutions and potential trajectories for research and development (R&D). These outcomes were intended for delivery to the respective companies and the instructional team overseeing the workshop. Impressively, three out of the four companies expressed satisfaction with the workshop's results, characterizing them as either groundbreaking innovations or as promising and unexplored avenues for future R&D endeavors. Regrettably, one company took a less optimistic stance, deeming the solution presented to them as mediocre. Their dissatisfaction extended to both the functional and aesthetic aspects of the proposed design. The company articulated that the proposal failed to align with the preferences, habits, and needs of their target market niches.

Subsequent to the workshop, participants engaged in a reflective analysis of their experiences through the lens of four focal dimensions. First, they assessed the extent to which interdisciplinary teamwork facilitated advancements in R&D projects. Second, participants evaluated the potential integration of interdisciplinary R&D teams, scrutinizing their methodologies, processes, and the likelihood of success in domestic firms and organizations. This evaluation was grounded in their collective experiences within the Israeli labor market. Third, attention was devoted to identifying the limitations and constraints inherent in the interdisciplinary approach to R&D, along with delineating the types of organizations expected to derive limited benefits from the application of this methodology. Lastly, the participants engaged in an evaluation of the contribution of foreign experts to the R&D process, alternatively considering the recommendation to involve teams of local professionals in the process.

To delve deeper into these reflections, twenty student assignments were meticulously collected and subjected to conventional qualitative and textual analysis methods. The ensuing section encapsulates the results gleaned from this analytical endeavor.

The overarching sentiment among the participating companies reflected a notable divergence in their reception of the workshop outcomes. While the majority perceived the solutions as revolutionary and conducive to future R&D trajectories, the dissenting company voiced dissatisfaction, primarily attributing it to a misalignment with their target market's preferences. This divergence in perspectives underscores the inherent challenges of interdisciplinary collaboration, as differing expectations and contexts among stakeholders can impede the universal applicability of proposed solutions.

The four focal dimensions of analysis provided a comprehensive framework for understanding the multifaceted impact of interdisciplinary collaboration on R&D. Participants' insights revealed not only the potential advantages of such collaboration but also shed light on the nuanced challenges and considerations that must be navigated to optimize its effectiveness. This analytical exploration serves as a precursor to the subsequent section, where the detailed findings of the qualitative and textual analysis are expounded upon.

RESULTS

The quantitative analysis of the student reports indicates a complete agreement of the participants (100% of the respondents) about the positive value of interdisciplinary teams involving both designers and engineers. The respondents suggest that the model of interdisciplinary teamwork introduced in the workshop should be applied in organizations performing R&D activities on a larger scale.

The vast majority of the students (90% of the respondents) indicated that from their work experience in organizations, firms can substantially benefit from the implementation of interdisciplinary teams on a project basis in R&D activities. 10% of the respondents agreed with this notion, but restricted this insight, mentioning that the advance of specialized projects in the fields of art or "pure" engineering may be hampered unless team members share a homogenous background in design or in engineering. In general, all the participants highlighted the importance of the work in interdisciplinary teams and its potential for generating substantial innovation and creative solutions when implemented as an integral part of R&D projects.

Similarly, all of the respondents responded positively to the question, "Would you recommend the application of interdisciplinary R&D teams in the companies that employ (or employed) you?" The explanations that they provided mentioned the following aspects of joint development teams of designers and engineers:

- A source for a broad spectrum of ideas and solutions (10% of the respondents);
- Expanding the opportunities for team members to "think outside the box" (15% of the respondents);
- A combination of creative thinking and identifying unique elements of products by designers and engineers, where solutions can be defined by applying proven scientific principles (15% of the respondents);
- Designers can better define the needs of customers and the message delivered by the product delivers, while engineers bring to the development process valuable know-how in terms of learning from past R&D projects and their faults, conducting market or SWOT analyses, and identifying business directions and challenges (10% of the respondents);
- Firms can use their engineers to develop advanced products, but can charge premium prices through the work of their designers (5% of the respondents).

Finally, one of the companies commissioned a follow-up research and implementation project that will be carried out by students at the Departments of Industrial Engineering and Management and Software Engineering.

DISCUSSION

The results of our study indicate a unanimous agreement among participants about the value of interdisciplinary teams involving both designers and engineers. These results correspond to the findings of Bingham et al. (2015) and Carmona Marques's (2017) that highlight the benefits of companies establishing collaboration between designers and engineers and offer training methodologies within the framework of academic education that provide a combined skillset and experience in both domains. This approach is also supported by Winberg et al. (2020) that advocate adoption of design education while training engineering students, such as the personal supervision of students.

The endorsement from the respondents suggests that the model of interdisciplinary teamwork introduced in the workshop holds significant potential and should be extended to organizations engaged in larger-scale research and development (R&D) activities. Specifically, Li et al. (2019) indicate that the incorporation of design and design thinking in science, technology, engineering, and mathematics (STEM) education is desirable in developing learning experiences and analytical skills that require multidisciplinary problem solving, knowledge and skills, rather than acquisition of these personal and professional merits in relatively limited areas of specialization.

Development of new methodologies that effectively enable both designers and engineers to provide novel and innovative solutions in contemporary and dynamic work environments is essential in light of the velocity and the volume that new technologies are introduced and are put into use. In particular, the need for collaboration across diverse disciplines in Industry 4.0 work environments is described as "a socio-technical transformation towards the Factory of the Future (cf. Factory 4.0 / Smart Factory) [that] will need a new design and engineering philosophy for 'human-centric' and 'cyber-physical' production systems." (Romero et al., 2020).

The respondents mentioned the expansion of the scope of the opportunities for team members to think in unconventional ways as a significant collaboration between designers and engineers. Micheli et al. (2019) and Retna (2019) suggest that the combination of designers, and through them design methodologies such as design thinking, in the engineering process can assist in the following dimensions:

1. Creativity and innovation: Design methodologies are associated with the generation of novel and useful ideas and the successful implementation of those ideas within an organization. They are considered as facilitators of ways of thinking that foster creativity and innovation in various aspects of businesses and organizations.
2. User-centeredness and involvement: Designers place a strong emphasis on understanding and empathizing with end-users. The process involves taking the perspective of users, identifying their needs, and incorporating user-driven insights into the design. Empathy is highlighted as a core value, enabling designers to shift their point of view to better imagine solutions.
3. Problem solving: Design methods are recognized as valuable approaches for solving complex and "wicked" problems that cannot be addressed through traditional analytical methods. They offer alternatives to linear problem-solving approaches and allow for the exploration of diverse solutions.
4. Iteration and experimentation: The design process is iterative, involving trial-and-error learning and testing possible solutions with end-users. Prototyping plays a crucial role, not for validation but for learning about the strengths and weaknesses of ideas, facilitating experimentation and concept development.
5. Interdisciplinary collaboration: Design promotes collaboration among individuals from different departments and disciplines. Multidisciplinary teams are seen as essential for addressing the complexity of problems, ensuring that technical, business, and human dimensions are considered.
6. Ability to visualize: Visualization is a fundamental aspect of design, involving the act of moving from abstract thinking to visualizing ideas. The ability to visualize concepts and ideas is crucial for guiding the inquiry process and fostering innovation.
7. Gestalt view: Many design methodologies adopt a holistic, gestalt approach to problem-solving, considering the total experience of various stakeholders. This perspective involves examining not only specific issues but also their relationships within the broader context.

8. Abductive reasoning: Design thinking incorporates abductive reasoning, which allows for the creation of new knowledge and insight. It involves imagining what might be and reframing and challenging existing practices and assumptions.
9. Tolerance of ambiguity and failure: Designers are encouraged to embrace ambiguity and accept failure as valuable for learning. The iterative nature of the design process involves continuous cycles of trial-and-error experiments and stakeholder feedback.
10. Blending analysis and intuition: Design thinking (and other design methodologies) blends analytical thinking with intuitive thinking. It combines research, analysis, intuition, and synthesis to address complex problems effectively.

CONCLUSION

The study underscores the critical role of interdisciplinary collaboration between designers and engineers to drive innovative outcomes. Examining a case study involving mixed student teams tackling real-world industry challenges, the analysis suggests that embracing interdisciplinary teams offers a valuable framework for R&D operations across companies, even within exclusively engineering-focused projects. In line with Harison and Warshavski's (2014) findings, incorporating designers into interdisciplinary R&D teams is linked to increased innovation, evident in patents and awards received for final products and technologies. Moreover, the inclusion of designers in post-disaster management teams, as highlighted by Boehm and Kopec (2016), enhances the value of solutions generated by these groups.

The study's findings reinforce previous research observations indicating that collaborative, interdisciplinary endeavors aimed at addressing practical issues—whether in engineering, design, or broader R&D contexts—have immense potential for fostering creativity. Creativity, seen as a product of connectivity, thrives within the collaborative and interdisciplinary sphere, providing an optimal environment for its emergence (Wilson and Zamberlan, 2017).

In particular, our study highlights the significance of interdisciplinary teams, integrating both designers and engineers. These findings resonate with prior research by Bingham et al. (2015), Carmona Marques (2017), and Winberg et al. (2020), emphasizing the advantageous outcomes of collaboration between these two domains and the necessity for combined skillsets within academic education frameworks.

The responses collected throughout the study suggest that the model of interdisciplinary teamwork introduced in our workshop holds substantial potential. Importantly, these results advocate for the extension of such collaborative approaches to organizations engaged in larger-scale research and development (R&D) activities. Aligning with the insights of Li et al. (2019), this interdisciplinary model is crucial in promoting multidisciplinary problem-solving, which is essential in contemporary work environments characterized by the rapid integration of new technologies.

The study affirms the importance of developing methodologies that empower both designers and engineers to provide innovative solutions in dynamic work environments. The expansion of the scope of opportunities for unconventional thinking, highlighted by respondents, is a key element of collaboration between designers and engineers. The combination of design methodologies in the engineering process contributes significantly to creativity, user-centeredness, problem-solving, iteration, interdisciplinary collaboration, visualization, gestalt view, abductive reasoning, tolerance of ambiguity and failure, and the blending of analysis and intuition.

These dimensions elucidate the broader benefits of incorporating design thinking into engineering processes, reinforcing its role in fostering creativity, innovation, and effective problem-solving. Furthermore, the findings advocate for the integration of design methodologies in STEM education, aligning with the evolving demands of Industry 4.0. In conclusion, our study supports the proposition that embracing interdisciplinary collaboration between designers and engineers, coupled with design methodologies, is pivotal for addressing the complexities of contemporary challenges and for fostering innovation in both academic and industrial settings.

Nonetheless, despite the consensus among students and instructors regarding the innovation-fostering potential of this model across diverse organizational realms, it is essential to acknowledge its susceptibility to shortcomings. Companies integrating similar models into their R&D strategies may encounter failures or only partial success. Nonetheless, these outcomes pave the way for further exploration into advanced studies focusing on evaluating the impact of mixed R&D team structures and governance mechanisms on their performance and innovative output.

REFERENCES

Asmawi, A., Zakaria, S., & Wei, C. C. (2013). Understanding transformational leadership and R&D culture in Malaysian universities. *Innovation (North Sydney, N.S.W.)*, 15(3), 287–304. 10.5172/impp.2013.15.3.287

Bingham, G. A., Southee, D. J., & Page, T. (2015). Meeting the expectation of industry: An integrated approach for the teaching of mechanics and electronics to design students. *European Journal of Engineering Education*, 40(4), 410–431. 10.1080/03043797.2014.1001813

Boehm, S., & Kopec, D. (2016). Interior design as a post-disaster team partner. *International Journal of Disaster Resilience in the Built Environment*, 7(3), 276–289. 10.1108/IJDRBE-10-2014-0075

Carmona Marques, P. (2017). Comparing Freshman and doctoral engineering students in design: Mapping with a descriptive framework. *European Journal of Engineering Education*, 42(6), 1097–1112. 10.1080/03043797.2016.1263277

Chiva, R., & Alegre, J. (2009). Investment in Design and Firm Performance: The Mediating Role of Design Management. *Journal of Product Innovation Management*, 26(4), 424–440. 10.1111/j.1540-5885.2009.00669.x

Furrer, O., Sudharshan, D., Tsiotsou, R., & Liu, B. S. (2016). A framework for innovative service design. *Service Industries Journal*, 36(9-10), 452–471. 10.1080/02642069.2016.1248420

Gómez Puente, S. M., van Eijck, M., & Jochems, V. (2015). Professional development for design-based learning in engineering education: A case study. *European Journal of Engineering Education*, 40(1), 14–31. 10.1080/03043797.2014.903228

Harison, E., & Warshavski, T. (2014). Exploring the links between design and innovation: evidence from Israeli firms, *UNU-MERIT Innovation & Governance in Development Conference*. Maastricht.

Jiménez-Guerrero, J. F., Gázquez-Abad, J. C., & Ceballos-Santamaría, G.Jiménez-Guerrero. (2015). Innovation in eco-packaging in private labels. *Innovation (North Sydney, N.S.W.)*, 17(1), 81–90. 10.1080/14479338.2015.1011055

Li, Y., Schoenfeld, A. H., diSessa, A. A., Graesser, A. C., Benson, L. C., English, L. D., & Duschl, R. A. (2019). Design and design thinking in STEM education. *Journal for STEM Education Research*, 2(2), 93–104. 10.1007/s41979-019-00020-z

Liem, A., Oritsland, T. A., & Norstebo, C. A. (2006). Introducing Form and User Sensitivity to Mechanical Engineering Students through Industrial Design Projects. In: Rodgers, P., Brodhurst, L. & Hepburn, D. (Eds.), *Crossing Design Boundaries:Proceedings of the 3rd Engineering & Product Design Education International Conference*, London: CRC Press.

Magee, C. L., Leong, P. K., Jin, C., Luo, J., & Frey, D. D. (2012). Beyond R&D: What design adds to a modern research university. *International Journal of Engineering Education*, 28(2).

Micheli, P., Wilner, S. J., Bhatti, S. H., Mura, M., & Beverland, M. B. (2019). Doing design thinking: Conceptual review, synthesis, and research agenda. *Journal of Product Innovation Management*, 36(2), 124–148. 10.1111/jpim.12466

Moreira, M., Murphy, E., & McAra-McWilliam, I. (2016). The Emergence of an Amplified Mindset of Design: Implications for Postgraduate Design Education. *International Journal of Art & Design Education*, 35(3), 356–368. 10.1111/jade.12118

Pahl, G., & Beitz, W. (2013). *Engineering Design: A Systematic Approach* (2nd ed.). Springer Verlag.

Pei, E., Campbell, I., & Evans, M. (2011). A taxonomic classification of visual design representations used by industrial designers and engineering designers. *Design Journal*, 14(1), 64–91. 10.2752/175630610X12877385838803

Pessôa, M. P., & Becker, J. J. (2020). Smart design engineering: A literature review of the impact of the 4th industrial revolution on product design and development. *Research in Engineering Design*, 31(2), 175–195. 10.1007/s00163-020-00330-z

Retna, K. S. (2019). Thinking about "design thinking": A study of teacher experiences. In *Teachers' perceptions, experience and learning* (pp. 4–18). Routledge. 10.4324/9781351173285-1

Romero, D., Stahre, J., & Taisch, M. (2020). The Operator 4.0: Towards socially sustainable factories of the future. *Computers & Industrial Engineering*, 139(106128), 106128. 10.1016/j.cie.2019.106128

Rompelman, O., & De Graaff, E. (2007). The engineering of engineering education: Curriculum development from a designer's point of view. *European Journal of Engineering Education*, 31(2), 215–226. 10.1080/03043790600567936

Seidel, V. P., & Fixson, S. K. (2013). Adopting Design Thinking in Novice Multidisciplinary Teams: The Application and Limits of Design Methods and Reflexive Practices. *Journal of Product Innovation Management*, 30(S1, No. S1), 19–33. 10.1111/jpim.12061

Stewart, J., & Claeys, L. (2011). Problems and Opportunities of Interdisciplinary Work Involving Users in Speculative Research for Innovation of Novel ICT Applications. In Pierson, J., Mante-Meijer, E., & Loos, E. (Eds.), *New Media Technologies and User Empowerment* (pp. 101–122). Peter Lang.

Wilson, E. W., & Zamberlan, L. (2017). Design Pedagogy for an Unknown Future: A View from the Expanding Field of Design Scholarship and Professional Practice. *International Journal of Art & Design Education*, 36(1), 106–117. 10.1111/jade.12076

Winberg, C., Bramhall, M., Greenfield, D., Johnson, P., Rowlett, P., Lewis, O., & Wolff, K. (2020). Developing employability in engineering education: A systematic review of the literature. *European Journal of Engineering Education*, 45(2), 165–180. 10.1080/03043797.2018.1534086

Chapter 5
Rethinking Entrepreneurship Education (EE) in the Era of Education 5.0:
Towards a Selective Approach

Aissa Mosbah
https://orcid.org/0000-0003-4092-8789
Dhofar University, Oman

Abdelbaset Queiri
Dhofar University, Oman

ABSTRACT

The educational landscape has been marked with a rapid growth of entrepreneurship education (EE) in the last decades. EE is spanning across different academic disciplines and taught inclusively as a university requirement across many universities/countries. However, while this inclusive approach is associated with many issues, its questionable effectiveness mixed with the challenging requirements of the current education 5.0 (educator wise) are sufficient reasons for scholars to rethink how and for whom entrepreneurship should be taught. In this chapter, the authors discussed and proposed a move to the more pragmatic student "selective approach" of EE after having laid the justification for such move. The chapter contends that teaching EE to every tertiary student is not a viable approach; not only does it drain the existing resources, but it requires additional ones which are beyond the capacity of many schools and universities around the world. Implications are discussed and aimed to assist policy makers and key education players to improve EE effectiveness.

INTRODUCTION

Entrepreneurship education (EE) can be traced back to 1947 (Katz, 2003). EE has emerged as arguably one of the most expanding courses across universities since the 1990s. This is evidenced in the curriculum and programs dedicated to entrepreneurship and the creation of new ventures (Kuratko, 2005). For example, the number of schools that offered entrepreneurship related courses in the United States has

DOI: 10.4018/979-8-3693-3041-8.ch005

grown from 263 schools in 1979 to 1400 in 1998 and over 1,600 in 2005 (Solomon et al., 1994; Kuratko, 2005). This number has increased tremendously with the development of entrepreneurship education across almost all countries because of policy makers' belief in the power of EE (Bager, 2011) to serve the aims of economic growth and development. The prevailing trends also point to a sharp growth in the number of trained educators and the number of academic institutions with centers of entrepreneurship (Bager, 2011). It should be noted that EE is offered at different levels of the educational system, not just at the tertiary level.

One apparent trend that has shaped EE practice in recent years is that many educational institutions worldwide are teaching entrepreneurship as a university requirement not a college (of business) requirement. We call this the "inclusive" or "one-size-fits-all" approach. As a matter of fact, assessment of EE effectiveness has triggered debate (Shih and Huang, 2017) and shown mixed results with some scholars praising it while others criticizing it EE (Nabi et al., 2019), and even though it imparts useful knowledge and abilities like financial management and business planning, there is evidence that it is not very effective at producing successful entrepreneurs (Chen et al., 2009). This is caused by a variety of profession-related factors, such as the diversity of entrepreneurial contexts, the significance of real-world experience, the complexity of entrepreneurship, and the extinction of intention over time. To add to this list, we believe that a major part of such ineffectiveness in producing successful entrepreneurs is attributed to the inclusive approach. Therefore, despite the advantages associated with EE, it might not be enough on its own -at least under the inclusive approach- to produce a sizable number of trainees who obtain the entrepreneurial intention, and subsequently discover and implement successful value-adding business ideas.

The inclusive approach does not work well with the emerging education 5.0 paradigm which has come with unique features and, therefore, requires numerous adjustments in terms of infrastructures, learners and, especially, educators to reach the desired learning outcomes. While targeting the holistic development of students with a human-centric approaches, education 5.0. places a strong emphasis on technological proficiency, collaborative environment, ethics and well-being, as well as sustainability and societal impact (Bonito-Osorio et al., 2012; Lantada, 2020; Broo et al., 2022; Aleixo et al. 2023). Given their central role under education 5.0, educators are required to have sufficient knowledge and a variety of skills to directly improve the teaching quality. In parallel, we contend that education 5.0 does not work well with the inclusive approach but it certainly does with the selective approach.

This chapter looks at this (student) selective approach within the lenses of education 5.0 and its requirements while paying close attention to preparedness of the educators since they assume key roles in the EE process. The chapter will first provide an overview of entrepreneurship education with its aims and challenges. It will then trace the journey of entrepreneurship education throughout the stages of education 5.0. The most compelling challenges of EE under the education 5.0 phase will be discussed in a subsequent section. Finally, in the last section there will be an explanation of the selective entrepreneurship education model.

ENTREPRENEURSHIP EDUCATION IN A NUTSHELL

Following the positive role played by entrepreneurship in boosting innovation and economic growth, creating jobs, solving social problems and fueling larger firms, governments across the globe have encouraged its incorporation in academic curriculums. This has led to the genesis of "entrepreneurship education" as an academic discipline, overwhelmingly present in most universities worldwide. Entrepreneurship Education (EE) refers to the process of providing individuals with the skills, knowledge, motivation, and entrepreneurial mindset needed for the creation and successful management of business ventures that add value to the society.

Entrepreneurship education *aims* to achieve two main goals. The first is to trigger the interest and desire of individuals for entrepreneurship. Research has generally shown a positive association between entrepreneurship education and students' intention to start their own business (see. e.g. Alharbi et al., Al-Jubari et al., 2019; 2018; Alshebami et al., 2020). The second goal is to draw the road for entrepreneurial success by empowering individuals with the skills and knowledge necessary not just to identify business opportunities and form viable business ideas, but to manage the business effectively and grow it as to ultimately yield socio-economic impact. Again here, numerous studies have reaches conclusions regarding the impact of entrepreneurship education on opportunity identification (Abuzhuri, 2017), formation of business ideas (Karimi et al., 2016), success of the business venture (Cruz et al., 2009), and economic sustainable business (Lindner, 2018).

Teaching students about entrepreneurship involves more than just focusing on how to launch a business venture. It fosters the entrepreneurial mindset by motivating people to spot opportunities, take risks, innovate, manage resources, create value, and withstand various challenges that face the entrepreneurial journey. This is in complete harmony with the fundamental ideas of Education 5.0, which places a strong emphasis on encouraging an innovative spirit and providing active learning opportunities.

However, teaching entrepreneurship has not always been a rosy path. Yet, several *challenges* have marked the way through which EE is taught and learnt. The extant literature demonstrates several issues and challenges that are associated with it; including the lack of definitional clarity, unclear aims, impeding academic structures, Lack of time and resources, unreliable assessment methods and techniques, teachers' fear of commercialism, limited contextual research (Rideout and Gray 2013; Blenker et al., 2014; Lackéus, 2015; Scott et al., 2016; Hägg and Kurczewska, 2022). For example, Rideout and Gray (2013, p-346) examined the extent to which EE really works and reported the following statement in their conclusion *"although some progress has been made, EE scholarship continues to be at a very early stage of development and we have a long way to go before we can confidently answer questions like, "Does EE work?", let alone "If it works, how does it work?"* Additionally. Despite the wide observed involvement of technology in education, the relevance and effectiveness of the use of technologies such as the internet-based and computer, especially in the context of distance learning, has not been examined properly (Fayolle, 2018). This limitation is of utmost importance in the context of education 5.0 where technology is a key feature.

EVOLUTION OF ENTREPRENEURIAL EDUCATION THROUGH THE EDUCATIONAL PARADIGMS

One of the main concerns in the constantly changing field of education has always been the development of an entrepreneurial mindset. The strategy for encouraging entrepreneurship has changed significantly as it moves through various stages of educational paradigms. Entrepreneurship education took place in the second half of the twentieth century and was shaped with the educational practices of education 2.0 and education 3.0. Education 2.0 was fueled by the transition from apprenticeship to universal schooling (Halverson and Collins, 2009), gradual inclusion of technology and a more interactive learning environment, whereas education 3.0 was marked by the educational reforms in the 1980s and 1990s (Goertz, 1995). However, while making use of the teacher-centered approach, entrepreneurial education began to include project-based learning, mentorship programs, and practical experience. An important part of developing an entrepreneurial mindset was to encourage students to be more creative, take calculated risks, and learn from their mistakes.

The education 4.0 phase, which has been in place for the past two decades, focused on integrating advanced and more accessible technologies like the Internet of Things (IoT), digitalization, Artificial intelligence and the analytics of data more deeply into the educational process. Modern technology has been used to improve learning results and get learners ready for the age of digitization. The focus of education 4.0 has been geared towards personalized learning experiences, in which instructional strategies and materials are adjusted to meet the needs and preferences of students. It encourages the use of digital infrastructure for online learning, remote access to educational materials, and collaborative learning. Its major goal is to arm students with the 21st-century skills such as critical creativity, thinking, digital mastery teamwork, and problem-solving. Furthermore, the accessibility of entrepreneurial resources has been made more democratic by the adoption online education, which has allowed aspirants from a variety of backgrounds to interact, work together, and share knowledge like never before. As such, the interconnectedness between entrepreneurship education and entrepreneurship has reached unprecedented levels (Neck and Greene, 2011). Under this era also, EE has moved towards the embracement of the action-based teaching approach which emphasizes learning by doing and gradually relinquishing traditional teaching approaches (Rasmussen and Sørheim, 2006).

The current education 5.0 has built upon the technological components of education 4.0 targeting the holistic development with a human-centric approaches. Together with technical skills, it acknowledges the significance of socio-emotional abilities, cultural competency, ethical reasoning, experiential leaning and values-based education. Therefore, entrepreneurship education aims to strike a balance between the advancement of technology and the welfare of students, teachers, and society at large. Students are showing inclination towards initiatives with greater social and environmental responsibility (see. e.g. pichaeats.com/en/). The current education paradigm promotes a change in perspective from a utilitarian one that takes workforce readiness into account to a more all-encompassing one that considers entrepreneurship students overall development and fulfillment.

Education 5.0 places a stronger emphasis on a more human-centered methodology that considers technological proficiency and holistic development, ethics, well-being, sustainability and societal impact; all in a collaborative environment (Bonito-Osorio et al., 2012; Lantada, 2020; Broo et al., 2022; Aleixo et al. 2023). The implication in the entrepreneurship field can be seen in perspectives like the transitional to experiential learning (Neck and Greene 2011), focus on technology (Kleine et al., 2019), holistic person (Jensen, 2014), ethics (Vázquez-Parra et al., 2022) and social responsibility (Maistry and Ramdhani 2010; Sánchez-Hernández et al., 2019).

CHALLENGES OF EE IN THE CURRENT EDUCATION 5.0

Teaching entrepreneurship has always been surrounded with challenges. Thes challenges continue to exist under education 5.0 with numerous obstacles and hurdles hindering EE in its trajectory for preparing students for the ongoingly complex world of affairs. The following challenges are either specific to education 5.0 or will exacerbate under it.

Prevalence of traditional curriculums: Traditional curriculum models which prioritize theoretical knowledge over real-world skills and practical experiences are still used in many entrepreneurship education programs. In the meanwhile, the focus of education 5.0 is on experiential and personalized learning, which may not be adequately incorporated into current programs that teach entrepreneurship. In fact, while developing viable content need times, rapid technological advancements, Covid-19 and post pandemic recovery seem to have slowed the move towards quality entrepreneurship programs. Yet, attempts to move into more innovative programs seem tedious. For example, Smith et al. (2006) studied how to inculcate new and innovative entrepreneurship education programs may be inculcated into UK higher education institutions and concluded that this is a difficult task due to: resource limitations; lack of training in synergistic methods; keeping the freshness alive; finding suitable entrepreneurs to take part in the program; finding the right space in academic timetable and curriculum.

Lack of resources (technology): the availability of human and technological resources is crucial to the success of EE in age of education 5.0. While technological resources are largely dependent upon financial resources, education providers need to ensure not only the access to available technologies but also a cadre of instructors who are tech-savvy and able to guide students towards the use of technology with a humanistic approach and ensure personalized teaching. Additional concerns relate to how would the emerging technologies such as the AI, IoT, blockchain, and robotics be integrated in course content? and at what cost? Developing countries seem to be in a disadvantageous position here as they are comparatively in a disadvantageous position, and are more likely to produce less innovative entrepreneurs, thus remaining less innovative economies. If Information Technology (IT) students are in a favorable position with regards to this event, then what about students from different programs and fields?

Transition to practical education: practicing entrepreneurship as part of its teaching is a major challenge and has always been a weakness. EE needs to go beyond theoretical concepts and emphasize real scenarios. For example, the large-scale study of Lima et al (2015) found the need of entrepreneurship students for practical applications and for larger and diversified educational offerings that extend beyond mere business planning. Other scholars have emphasized this reality and proposed practical approaches to overcome this weakness. This includes the creation of real businesses (Neck and Greene, 2011; Lackeus, 2015) and the challenge-based learning (Lindner, 2018) as an action-oriented approach through complex tasks in which learners are challenged not just with the development of ideas but their implementation too. This approach does not only require months or years to be implemented (Lackeus, 2015), but also needs collaboration among a group of students. However, the required duration may exceed the course duration, making it impractical. Furthermore, the implementation of this approach is nearly impossible, especially in developing countries given students' lack of financial resources as well as the possibly high number of students per class.

Transition to real innovation: This is perhaps the most dominant challenge given that entrepreneurship's impact on individuals, economies and societies can be best measured by the level of innovation embedded in the created ventures. However, while business educational institutions have been able to design good programs and deliver effective training for entrepreneurs, they failed to do so with innovative entrepreneurs (Summit Consulting, LLC (2009). In parallel, the vast majority of projects initiated by students are far from offering innovative products or services (Neck and Greene, 2011). Education 5.0, through its connection to technology, is expected to boost innovation among students. There is an apparent need for knowing how to use technology, existing models as well as teaching tools and approaches to push students to think out of the box and generate creative solutions. While technology is here to help, its impact on this remains contingent upon factors such as the attractiveness of educational environments, educator skills, passion for self-employment among others.

Measuring effectiveness: While evaluating EE effectiveness or how it affects students' entrepreneurial attitudes and abilities has lacked a standard framework and been insufficiently researched (Liu et al., 2021), measuring personal factors like risk taking and creativity, which are crucial to successful entrepreneurship, is challenging. Nonetheless, two main approaches have been used to measure EE effectiveness; the first is academic-based whereas the second is research-based. In the traditional/academic approach, course related methods and metrics - such as test scores- which aim to measure EE outcomes and serve as a standard to passing or failing the entrepreneurship course remain dominant. Therefore, the following questions need to be posed: Do students who pass the entrepreneurship course with high marks have higher intention for business than their peers with law marks? Are they more creative/innovative? and if they start their own businesses, they will be more successful? Future researchers may examine these issues comparatively by grouping students based on their grade score of the entrepreneurship course. Indeed, the learning outcomes are far more complicated and cannot be sufficiently captured by such traditional metrics.

The second approach takes place in the research sphere and attempts to assess changes in student intention to engage in their own ventures. Here, scholars have relied extensively on the Theory of Planned Behavior (TPB) to assess students' intention of students to start a business venture. However, three drawbacks are observed within this approach. First, intention does never guarantee action because it decays (Rideout and Gray, 2013), emerges and reemerges over time. Second, most studies are not longitudinal and fail to assess the "change" made by the course. Third, it fails to isolate the pre-existing tendencies related to intention because there might be among students those who already have a strong desire to launch a business by the time they enroll in the entrepreneurship program. For this reason, we argue that entrepreneurship education should enable students to overcome the hurdles of materializing their business ideas and entrepreneurial intentions. A detailed discussion of this idea will lead to us to the notion of action/experiential learning (leaning by doing), but again while the implementation of this approach is very difficult and demands extensive resources, it works best under the selective EE approach that we are defending in this chapter.

SHORTCOMINGS OF THE INCLUSIVE APPROACH

Making entrepreneurship education a prerequisite for all university students is deemed not effective, even though it can be beneficial for some students. Therefore, the inclusive approach is associated with many drawbacks. First, students tend to have dissimilar interests and career paths. Therefore, entrepreneurship is much more relevant for business and engineering students than for healthcare and education students. Second, the unique requirements of every discipline might not be met. For example, it will be challenging for social sciences and humanities students to relate fundamental business ideas to their subject of study. Third, it requires time and resources, and while it puts a strain on the existing resources, it takes focus away from other crucial subjects or support services.

Fourth, universities might not have the means or know-how to provide such a large audience with excellent entrepreneurship education. It might take extra training for educators with specialized training to teach these courses well. For instance, the poor engineering and medical background of entrepreneurship educators act as an impediment of quality at least when teaching natural and applied science students. There is a risk of devaluating student ideas and projects especially when they are so innovative or abnormal. Fifth, it affects quality as it may be difficult for teachers to modify the curriculum to fit the unique needs and interests of every program/discipline. Engineering students benefit more from technical coursework than from business plans. Finally, students who are disinterested in entrepreneurship may achieve low grades in entrepreneurship course which subsequently affects their GPA. This may not have alarming repercussions on their professional prospects but certainly affects their academic well-being, although with varying degrees.

TOWARDS A SELECTIVE ENTREPRENEURSHIP EDUCATION APPROACH (SEEA)

Because the inclusive approach of teaching entrepreneurship where entrepreneurship is a university requirement seems not very effective, we propose a move towards a Selective Entrepreneurship Education Approach (SEEA). SEEA refers to a more focused method of identifying and developing people who possess the aptitude and desire to succeed as business owners. This might entail evaluating candidates based on their commitment, skills, and entrepreneurial mindset before offering specialized training and support networks to develop their entrepreneurial aptitude. Selective entrepreneurship education seeks to optimize the effectiveness of entrepreneurial education initiatives by concentrating resources on individuals who are most likely to succeed as business owners. Our discussion focuses on students because they are key EE player but also pays attention to educators/instructors as whose action are crucial to the effectiveness of EE.

Students as a Basis of the Selective Approach

Some scholars argue that teaching entrepreneurship has worked well as an elective course in the tertiary level (Lackeus, 2015). Lackeus (2015, p-6) suggested a process that starts with assessing student motivation first then *"Those students that pick up strong interest and aptitude for value creation can then continue with elective courses and programs focusing on how to organize value creation processes by building new organizations"*

However, since students' fundamental reasons for choosing entrepreneurship course cannot be easily examined, the election decision that is solely decided by students does not change things nor it ensures effectiveness of the EE process. That is because of the absence of the mechanism permitting to assess whether students who choose entrepreneurship course do really have passion or interest for the entrepreneurship profession and to what extent they intend to start their own ventures somewhere in the future. Students may simply choose entrepreneurship course when its assessment is based on group projects instead of exams, to escape the pure technical or theoretical courses, or to align with some specific instructors with whom they have completed a different course satisfactorily in the past.

Thus, while we embrace the view of Lackeus (2015) on the "selective approach of EE" in this work, we link it to the current educational updates and extend it by proposing some techniques to ensure the right selection of the candidate students. However, for successful implementation of this new approach we recommend education providers to develop relevant procedures tools or approaches to ensure the selection of the most eligible students. Proper selection is the most important step in EE and a key determinant of its effectiveness. We suggest the following four tests be adopted in this process.

- *Expectation test:* It may include questions concerning the student's goals for becoming an entrepreneur, particular business ideas they have, what they aim to learn from the course, and how they think it will help them could fall under this category.
- *Traits inventory:* that lists the necessary personality traits (risk taking, creativity, critical thinking, problem-solving, etc.) of prosperous entrepreneurs. High scorers may be suitable candidates.
- *Skills test:* to let students report the extent of having (or not) specific skill necessary to success as entrepreneur.
- *Intention test*: should be created to gauge the level of students' interest in starting their own business.

Considered altogether, the overall score of these tests provides a good idea on the preparedness, willingness and seriousness of the candidates for entrepreneurship, which ultimately reflect possibilities of both the entrepreneurial success and EE effectiveness. EE providers are free to adjust these tests to suit their pedagogies, objectives and resources.

The Role of Educators

Because of the technological and humanistic circumstances that characterize entrepreneurship education in the current era, finding qualified educators with the necessary qualities is a challenging matter. Several educator-related challenges are prevailing in the current inclusive EE approach. This includes educators being incompatible with entrepreneurship training in cross-disciplinary settings due to specialization, they prefer to work with the transfer of available knowledge than creating new knowledge and avoid engaging in practical trainings (Scharmer 2007; Bager, 2011, Davidsen and Sorensen, 2017).

Fayolle (2013) argues that EE educators must possess scientific knowledge and rigor as well as research grounding. The availability of the following skills and qualities among entrepreneurship educators are very much needed in current times to improve the educational outcomes. However, many of these skills and qualities require institutional support (Tavakoli et al., 2019). Yet, resistance will prevail when such support implies additional costs. The following are qualities and characteristics of effective entrepreneurship educators in the current educational paradigm.

- Innovative/critical thinking: to help in the content delivered to students the evaluation guiding of student proposed ideas and solutions.
- Practical experience: to link theory to practice by bringing practical examples to class.
- Adaptability: to stay relevant by updating both curriculum and teaching techniques with the dynamic nature of entrepreneurship and technological advances.
- Tech-savviness: mastering the use of technological trends, tools, and platforms needed in the course teaching.

- Networking Skills: to facilitate collaboration with fellow entrepreneurs, mentors, government bodies and industry professionals to boost the practical engagement of students.
- Research power and continuous learning: to stay updated with research findings, best EE practices and industry trends.

CONCLUSION

Entrerpeneurship Educational (EE) has been growing at a fast pace in the last few decades, and increasingly taught across different programs, often as a university requirement. While the effectiveness has been questioned across different scholarly works, we further argue that the additional challenges imposed by education 5.0 undermine the effectiveness of EE. Subsequently we proposed a transition for a selective approach of entrepreneurship education to align with the current educational trends, maintain teaching quality, rationalize the use of the resources, and boost effectiveness. Our model focused on the crucial role of educator within the paradigm of education 5.0. Future researchers are urged to assess the SEEA from the perspective of the pedagogical components within the lenses of the current educational paradigm.

REFERENCES

Abuzhuri, N. M., & Hashim, N. B. (2017). Impact of entrepreneurship education on entrepreneurial opportunity recognition. *IOSR Journal of Business and Management*, 19(11), 74–79.

Al-Jubari, I., Mosbah, A., Talib, Z., Khalid, M. A., & Azman, N. (2019). How do entrepreneurship education and self-efficacy influence entrepreneurship intention. *International Journal of Innovation. Creativity and Change*, 5(2), 949–966.

Aleixo, C., Silva, S., & Godinho, T. (2023). Education 5.0 in the Context of Teaching Accounting. In *Internet of Behaviors Implementation in Organizational Contexts* (pp. 135-152). IGI Global.

Alharbi, J., Almahdi, H., & Mosbah, A. (2018). The impact of entrepreneurship education programs (EEPs) on the entrepreneurial attitudes among higher education students. *International Journal of Management, Economics and Social Sciences*, 7(3), 245–271. 10.32327/IJMESS.7.3.2018.16

Alshebami, A., Al-Jubari, I., Alyoussef, I., & Raza, M. (2020). Entrepreneurial education as a predicator of community college of Abqaiq students' entrepreneurial intention. *Management Science Letters*, 10(15), 3605–3612. 10.5267/j.msl.2020.6.033

Bager, T. (2011). Entrepreneurship Education and new venture creation: a comprehensive approach. In Hindle, K., & Klyver, K. (Eds.), *Handbook of Research on New Venture Creation*. Edward Elgar. 10.4337/9780857933065.00024

Benito-Osorio, D., Peris-Ortiz, M., Armengot, C. R., & Colino, A. (2013). Web 5.0: The future of emotional competences in higher education. *Global Business Perspectives*, 1(3), 274–287. 10.1007/s40196-013-0016-5

Blenker, P., Elmholdt, S. T., Frederiksen, S. H., Korsgaard, S., & Wagner, K. (2014). Methods in entrepreneurship education research: A review and integrative framework. *Education + Training*, 56(8/9), 697–715. 10.1108/ET-06-2014-0066

Broo, D. G., Kaynak, O., & Sait, S. M. (2022). Rethinking engineering education at the age of industry 5.0. *Journal of Industrial Information Integration*, 25, 100311. 10.1016/j.jii.2021.100311

Cheng, M. Y., Chan, W. S., & Mahmood, A. (2009). The effectiveness of entrepreneurship education in Malaysia. *Education + Training*, 51(7), 555–566. 10.1108/00400910910992754

Cruz, N. M., Rodriguez Escudero, A. I., Hernangomez Barahona, J., & Saboia Leitao, F. (2009). The effect of entrepreneurship education programmes on satisfaction with innovation behaviour and performance. *Journal of European Industrial Training*, 33(3), 198–214. 10.1108/03090590910950578

Davidsen, H. M., & Sørensen, K. B. (2017). A holistic design perspective on entrepreneurship education. *Universal Journal of Educational Research*, 5(10), 1818–1826. 10.13189/ujer.2017.051020

Fayolle, A. (2013). Personal views on the future of entrepreneurship education. *Entrepreneurship and Regional Development*, 25(7–8), 692–701. 10.1080/08985626.2013.821318

Fayolle, A. (2018). Personal views on the future of entrepreneurship education. In *A research agenda for entrepreneurship education* (pp. 127–138). Edward Elgar Publishing. 10.4337/9781786432919.00013

Goertz, M. E. (1996). *Studies of education reform: Systemic reform* (Vol. 1). Department of Education.

Hägg, G., & Kurczewska, A. (2022). *Entrepreneurship education: Scholarly progress and future challenges*. Taylor & Francis.

Halverson, A. C., & Collins, R. (2009). *Rethinking education in the age of technology*. Teachers College, Columbia University.

Jensen, T. L. (2014). A holistic person perspective in measuring entrepreneurship education impact–Social entrepreneurship education at the Humanities. *International Journal of Management Education*, 12(3), 349–364. 10.1016/j.ijme.2014.07.002

Karimi, S., Biemans, H. J., Lans, T., Aazami, M., & Mulder, M. (2016). Fostering students' competence in identifying business opportunities in entrepreneurship education. *Innovations in Education and Teaching International*, 53(2), 215–229. 10.1080/14703297.2014.993419

Katz, J. A. (2003). The chronology and intellectual trajectory of American entrepreneurship education: 1876–1999. *Journal of Business Venturing*, 18(2), 283–300. 10.1016/S0883-9026(02)00098-8

Kleine, K., Giones, F., & Tegtmeier, S. (2019). The learning process in technology entrepreneurship education—Insights from an Engineering Degree. *Journal of Small Business Management*, 57(sup1), 94–110. 10.1111/jsbm.12514

Kuratko, D. F. (2005). The emergence of entrepreneurship education: Development, trends, and challenges. *Entrepreneurship Theory and Practice*, 29(5), 577–597. 10.1111/j.1540-6520.2005.00099.x

Lackéus, M. (2015). *Entrepreneurship in education: What, why, when, how*. (OECD Working paper). OECD. https://www.vcplist.com/wp-content/uploads/2014/10/Lackeus-2014_WP_Entrepreneurship-in-Education-FINAL-for-OECD-141023.pdf

Lantada, A. D. (2020). Engineering education 5.0: Continuously evolving engineering education. *International Journal of Engineering Education*, 36(6), 1814–1832.

Lima, E., Lopes, R. M., Nassif, V., & Silva, D. (2015). Opportunities to improve entrepreneurship education: Contributions considering Brazilian challenges. *Journal of Small Business Management*, 53(4), 1033–1051. 10.1111/jsbm.12110

Lindner, J. (2018). Entrepreneurship education for a sustainable future. *Discourse and Communication for Sustainable Education*, 9(1), 115–127. 10.2478/dcse-2018-0009

Liu, H., Kulturel-Konak, S., & Konak, A. (2021). A measurement model of entrepreneurship education effectiveness based on methodological triangulation. *Studies in Educational Evaluation*, 70, 100987. 10.1016/j.stueduc.2021.100987

Maistry, S. M., & Ramdhani, J. (2010). Integrating Social Responsibility into an Entrepreneurship Education Program: A Case Study. *Online Submission*, 7(4), 23–29.

Nabi, G., Liñán, F., Fayolle, A., Krueger, N., & Walmsley, A. (2017). The impact of entrepreneurship education in higher education: A systematic review and research agenda. *Academy of Management Learning & Education*, 16(2), 277–299. 10.5465/amle.2015.0026

Neck, H. M., & Greene, P. G. (2011). Entrepreneurship education: Known worlds and new frontiers. *Journal of Small Business Management*, 49(1), 55–70. 10.1111/j.1540-627X.2010.00314.x

Rasmussen, E. A., & Sørheim, R. (2006). Action-based entrepreneurship education. *Technovation*, 26(2), 185–194. 10.1016/j.technovation.2005.06.012

Rideout, E. C., & Gray, D. O. (2013). Does entrepreneurship education really work? A review and methodological critique of the empirical literature on the effects of university-based entrepreneurship education. *Journal of Small Business Management*, 51(3), 329–351. 10.1111/jsbm.12021

Sánchez-Hernández, M. I., & Maldonado-Briegas, J. J. (2019). Sustainable entrepreneurial culture programs promoting social responsibility: A European regional experience. *Sustainability (Basel)*, 11(13), 3625. 10.3390/su11133625

Scharmer, C.O. (2007). *Theory U: Leading from the Future as It Emerges*. soL Press

Scott, J. M., Penaluna, A., & Thompson, J. L. (2016). A critical perspective on learning outcomes and the effectiveness of experiential approaches in entrepreneurship education: Do we innovate or implement? *Education + Training*, 58(1), 82–93. 10.1108/ET-06-2014-0063

Shih, T., & Huang, Y. Y. (2017). A case study on technology entrepreneurship education at a Taiwanese research university. *Asia pacific management review, 22*(4), 202-211.

Smith, A. J., Collins, L. A., & Hannon, P. D. (2006). Embedding new entrepreneurship programmes in UK higher education institutions: Challenges and considerations. *Education + Training*, 48(8/9), 555–567. 10.1108/00400910610710001

Solomon, G. T., Weaver, K. M., & Fernald, L. W.Jr. (1994). A historical examination of small business management and entrepreneurship pedagogy. *Simulation & Gaming*, 25(3), 338–352. 10.1177/1046878194253003

Summit Consulting, L. L. C. (2009). *Toward Effective Education of Innovative Entrepreneurs in Small Business: Initial Results from A Survey of College Students and Graduates*. SBA Office of Advocacy.

Tavakoli, M., Tixier, J., Baur, P., & Vincent-Lancrin, S. (2019). Hopes and challenges of entrepreneurship education: Dialogue between public civil servants and academics. *Entreprendre & innover*, (3), 12-21.

Vázquez-Parra, J. C., García-González, A., & Ramírez-Montoya, M. S. (2022). Ethical education and its impact on the perceived development of social entrepreneurship competency. *Higher Education. Skills and Work-Based Learning*, 12(2), 369–383. 10.1108/HESWBL-01-2021-0012

Chapter 6
Preparing Teachers and Students for the Challenges of Society 5.0:
Integration of Cognitive Computing, Learning Analytics, and Gamification of Learning

Midya Yousefi
https://orcid.org/0000-0001-8520-3576
Wenzhou-Kean University, China

Jahirul Mullick
Wenzhou-Kean University, China

Qiusu Wang
https://orcid.org/0000-0003-2460-2463
Wenzhou-Kean University, China

ABSTRACT

In this chapter, the authors investigate the transformative impact of cognitive computing, learning analytics, and game-based pedagogy in enhancing teachers' professional development within the dynamic societal context. Employing a comprehensive review of scholarly literature, explore how these technological advancements shape the educational landscape, paying particular attention to their implications for teachers' professional development. The discussion illustrates that through adopting cognitive computing, educators can access personalized insights and resources tailored to their needs, fostering continuous growth. Learning analytics provide valuable data-driven feedback, enabling educators to make informed decisions to optimize teaching strategies. Furthermore, gamification engages teachers in immersive learning experiences, enhancing motivation and collaboration. This research highlights the potential of innovative technologies in shaping a more responsive and effective educational system.

DOI: 10.4018/979-8-3693-3041-8.ch006

INTRODUCTION

As we navigate the era of Society 5.0, characterized by the seamless integration of the physical and digital territories (Kantipudi et al., 2022), the educational landscape undergoes a profound transformation. The traditional teaching and learning paradigms are challenged, and educators find themselves at the intersection of pedagogy and technological innovation. In this context, cognitive computing, learning analytics, and gamification emerge as critical change elements, offering unprecedented opportunities to enhance the educational experience (Kapp, 2012; Sousa et al., 2021). Cognitive computing, learning analytics, and gamification effectively equip teachers for student achievement by offering transformative tools and methodologies to enhance pedagogical practices. Cognitive computing enables personalized learning experiences tailored to individual student needs and preferences (Wang et al., 2018). By analyzing vast data, learning analytics provide valuable insights into student performance patterns and learning behaviors, empowering teachers to make informed instructional decisions and interventions (Siemens & Gasevic, 2012). Additionally, according to Hamari et al. (2016), gamification integrates game elements into educational activities, fostering student engagement and motivation, which are crucial ways for academic success. Therefore, by embracing these technological advancements, teachers can effectively address the diverse learning needs of their students and facilitate their journey toward achievement.

Therefore, society envisions a human-centric society empowered by cutting-edge technologies, and education stands as a critical arena where these technologies redefine the nature and scope of knowledge dissemination. By demonstrating the integration of these innovative interventions, below one by one, the research seeks to uncover their impact on improving teaching efficacy, fostering continuous growth, and adapting to the evolving needs of learners and institutions. Through comprehensive analysis, the study aims to provide insights into how these technologies can be effectively harnessed to empower educators, optimize teaching strategies, and ultimately contribute to the advancement of education in a rapidly changing world.

METHODOLOGY

Using a narrative review in your study can be beneficial for several reasons. Firstly, narrative reviews provide a comprehensive overview of existing literature on a particular topic, allowing you to synthesize and integrate findings from multiple studies (Green et al., 2006). Therefore, Scopus, Web of Science, Inspec database of systematic reviews, ERIC, ProQuest, and ERA were searched for studies to synthesize the transformative influence of cognitive computing, learning analytics, and game-based pedagogy in enhancing teachers' professional development within the dynamic societal context. The following data were received from each paper: authors, year, country, outcome level, type of study, purpose, material, methods, conclusion, and findings that supported each conclusion.

Concept of Learning Analytics

Learning analytics, as defined by the Society for Learning Analytics Research (SoLAR), is a growing field that centers on the measurement, collection, analysis, and reporting of data concerning learners, learning environments, and contexts (Kitto et al., 2020; Siemens et al., 2011). The core idea of learning analytics is to comprehend and optimize learning experiences in the virtual domain of learning environments because learners always leave behind a trail of data traces, ranging from test performance to content access frequency and engagement with supplementary materials, including downloadable files, PowerPoint presentations, and videos. Learning analytics proficiently gathers and meticulously analyzes these data, transforming it into actionable insights and visualizations tailored for educational stakeholders, including institutional managers, educators, and learners (Lang et al., 2022). By employing digital technologies such as Big Data and artificial intelligence, institutions can systematically harness and analyze educational data, fostering a more informed approach to educational decision-making.

Additionally, drawing upon methodologies from data mining, machine learning, and statistical analysis, learning analytics extracts invaluable insights from vast educational datasets (Lang et al., 2022). Its applications span diverse educational domains, encompassing formal education settings such as schools and universities, online learning platforms, corporate training programs, and informal learning environments. As institutions harness the potential of learning analytics, they endeavor to construct comprehensive databases that serve as essential resources for performance analysis and decision-making across various educational activities (Shah et al., 2017).

This transformative paradigm not only enhances the efficiency and efficacy of educational practices but also fosters a more personalized and optimized learning journey for students. Learning analytics tools fundamentally reshape the traditional relationship between educational institutions and students, paving the way for more tailored and effective educational pathways that cater to individual needs and optimize learning outcomes (Mougiakou et al., 2023). As institutions increasingly embrace learning analytics, they are poised to unlock new potentials for improving educational experiences and achieving better outcomes for learners in the digital age.

Learning analytics holds immense potential in transforming educational landscapes by harnessing the power of data to drive evidence-based decision-making and intervention strategies. Moreover, learning analytics facilitates continuous improvement cycles in educational practices, enabling institutions to adapt and evolve in response to changing student needs and societal demands. As learning analytics continues to mature, its role in enhancing the quality and equity of education is expected to expand, ultimately fostering a more inclusive, personalized, and effective learning ecosystem.

Application of Learning Analytics

Hantoobi et al. (2021) assert that "learning analytics has emerged as a new domain for identifying students' behaviors, academic performance, academic achievement, and other related learning issues" (p. 117). However, Siemens (2013) suggested that "analytics in education can also be viewed as existing at various levels, ranging from individual classroom, department, university, region, state/province, and international" (p. 1383). Learning analytics offers a broad range of practical applications. In a school setting where numerous students are enrolled across various classes taught by different instructors, manual analysis by teachers and learning managers can be slow and yield less-than-impressive results. Learning analytics addresses this challenge by closely monitoring student performance and providing automated solutions. Moreover, it is a valuable asset in experience management, enabling comprehensive assessments ranging from teaching methodologies to student interest levels in each subject.

Learning analytics essentially applies data analysis to the field of education. As educational institutions adapt to the changing demands of increasingly discerning audiences, understanding consumer behavior becomes crucial (Jayashanka et al., 2022; Susnjak et al., 2022). Learning analytics seeks to enhance instructional processes by leveraging data-driven insights. Despite its potential advantages, using learning analytics in schools remains relatively unexplored. While it could address challenges such as student dropout rates and the development of computational thinking abilities, its adoption across different institutions has been inconsistent. This inconsistency may stem from a lack of studies analyzing its potential in the school context and insufficient involvement of various stakeholders in the adoption process.

The Foundational Elements of Learning Analytics

Considering that learning analytics involves systematically analyzing learning and learning environment data, foundational elements are required to enhance educational processes and outcomes, improve learning experiences, and facilitate evidence-based educational decision-making (Mougiakou et al., 2023). At its core, learning analytics revolves around four foundational elements: data, people, learning, and management (Tsai, 2019). The subsequent section will explore each element in detail, providing relevant examples:

1. **Data**: Data are at the core of learning analytics. It includes various information collected from educational systems, such as student demographics, academic performance, engagement metrics, and learning activities (Mougiakou et al., 2023). These data can be structured (e.g., grades, attendance records) or unstructured (e.g., forum posts, essay submissions). Examples of data sources in learning analytics include the following:

    - *Learning Management Systems* (LMS): Tracking student logins, page views, time spent on tasks, and quiz scores.
    - *Student Information Systems* (SIS): Storing demographic information, enrollment status, and academic history.
    - *Online Learning Platforms*: Analyzing interactions in discussion forums, video views, and completion rates.

2. **People**: People refer to the stakeholders involved in the learning process, including students, instructors, administrators, and support staff. Learning analytics aims to understand how these individuals interact with each other and with educational technology to improve learning outcomes (Tsai, 2019). Examples include:

    - *Students*: Analyzing their engagement patterns, performance trends, and learning preferences to personalize learning experiences.
    - *Instructors*: Using data to monitor student progress, identify at-risk students, and tailor instructional strategies accordingly.
    - *Administrators*: Analytics assess program effectiveness, allocate resources efficiently, and make data-driven decisions.
    - *Support Staff*: Leveraging data to provide targeted interventions and support services for struggling students.

3. **Learning** refers to acquiring knowledge, skills, and competencies. Learning analytics focuses on understanding students' learning and identifying factors contributing to their success or challenges (Tsai, 2019). Examples of learning analytics applications include the following:

- *Predictive Analytics*: Forecasting student performance and identifying early warning signs of academic distress based on historical data.
- *Adaptive Learning Systems*: Personalizing learning pathways and content recommendations based on individual learner profiles and performance data.

Competency Mapping: Mapping learning outcomes to course objectives and assessing student proficiency levels to inform instructional planning and assessment strategies.

Figure 1. Four foundational elements of learning analytics

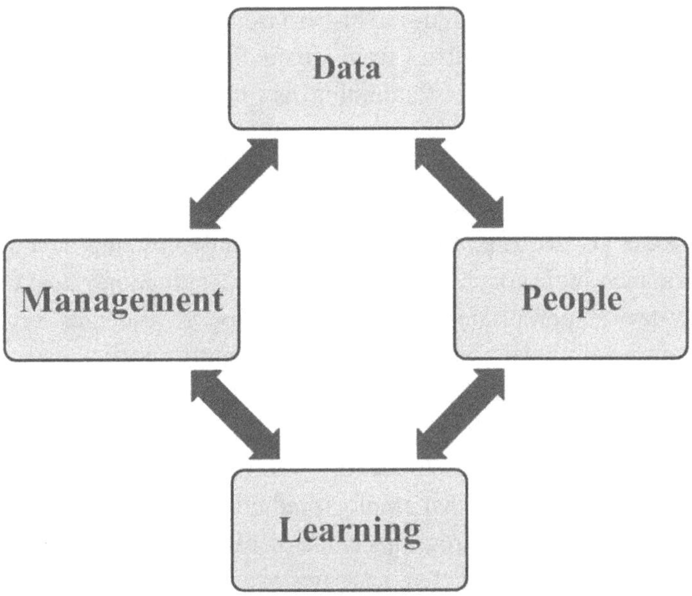

4. **Management**: Management uses data to inform decision-making and improve educational processes at various levels, including course design, curriculum development, and institutional policy. Mougiakou et al. (2023) call this "action," which "is the ultimate goal of any learning analytics process" (p. 133). Examples of management applications in learning analytics include the following:

    - *Curriculum Design*: Using data-driven insights to revise course content, assessments, and instructional methods to align with learning objectives and student needs.
    - *Resource Allocation*: Allocating resources such as faculty time, technology investments, and support services based on identified learning analytics priorities and goals.
    - *Quality Assurance*: Monitoring and evaluating the effectiveness of educational programs and interventions through ongoing data analysis and assessment practices.

Methodologies of Learning Analytics

Learning analytics methodologies encompass various approaches and techniques to analyze educational data to gain insights into learning processes and outcomes. These methodologies can be combined and tailored to specific educational contexts to provide valuable insights for enhancing teaching and learning practices. Paulsen and Lindsay (2024) asserted that there are four levels of analytics, refraining from categorizing them as methodologies, including descriptive, diagnostic, predictive, and prescriptive. The following section elaborates on these four methodologies (levels of analytics) alongside other common approaches in learning analytics, accompanied by examples:

Descriptive analytics entails examining historical data to gain insights into past occurrences. It employs data aggregation and mining techniques to discern trends and evaluate metrics over time (Susnjak et al., 2022). For instance, collecting feedback from satisfaction and graduate surveys offers insights into student experiences and satisfaction levels. Examining data at various stages of the student lifecycle, from admission to graduation, aids in recognizing patterns and trends in student behavior and performance.

***Diagnostic* analytics** seeks to comprehend the reasons behind past events or trends. It utilizes methods such as drill-down, data discovery, and correlations to address the question, "Why did a student fail an exam?" (Jayashanka et al., 2022, p. 153). Examples include utilizing data analysis to enhance key organizational performance indicators, such as retention or graduation rates. Patterns in student data should be detected to devise appropriate interventions or support strategies, such as identifying at-risk students who may require additional assistance, analyzing equity access data to grasp student outcome variations, and devising effective strategies to support underrepresented student populations.

Predictive Analytics utilizes historical data to predict future trends or outcomes. It integrates historical data with statistical models and algorithms to identify patterns and make forecasts (Susnjak et al., 2022). For example, creating staff dashboards that employ predictive models to anticipate student enrollment numbers and cohort mobility through programs can assist institutions in better resource planning and identifying areas for enhancement. Predictive analytics can identify students at risk of dropping out or failing a course, enabling early intervention and support.

Prescriptive analytics transcends mere prediction by recommending actions to achieve a desired outcome. It employs machine learning, algorithms, and computational modeling (Jayashanka et al., 2022). Examples include identifying specific subjects or courses where minor adjustments could significantly enhance student engagement, feedback, and outcomes. The use of data visualization tools to furnish program-level metrics on student enrollment, progress, results, and feedback empowers teaching staff to identify areas for improvement and customize their teaching strategies accordingly.

Social Network Analysis (SNA) examines the relationships and interactions among individuals or entities within a network to understand social structures, influence, and information flow. For example, in an online learning environment, SNA can be used to analyze communication patterns in discussion forums. By mapping connections between students based on their interactions (e.g., replies, mentions), educators can identify influential students who act as connectors or hubs within the network. Additionally, SNA can reveal communities of practice or subgroups within a larger learning community based on shared interests or collaboration patterns.

Text mining and natural language processing (NLP) involve analyzing textual data to extract meaningful insights, patterns, and sentiments. For example, educators can use NLP techniques to analyze student essays, forum posts, or feedback comments. Using sentiment analysis, they can determine students' overall tone or sentiment toward course materials or assignments. Text mining can also identify common themes or topics discussed in student reflections, allowing educators to gain insights into student perceptions, interests, and learning experiences.

Cluster analysis groups similar entities together based on shared characteristics or behaviors, aiming to identify meaningful patterns or segments within the data. For example, in higher education, cluster analysis can segment students into distinct groups based on their learning preferences, study habits, or engagement patterns. Educators can personalize interventions and support strategies by clustering students with similar characteristics. For instance, students who prefer visual learning methods may be grouped and provided with visual aids or resources tailored to their learning style.

Decision trees and machine learning algorithms are used to identify patterns in data and make predictions or classifications. For example, in the context of student course preferences, educators can utilize machine learning techniques to build predictive models. Decision tree models can predict which courses or subjects students will likely prefer by analyzing students' demographic and academic background features. This information can inform course scheduling, curriculum development, and personalized course recommendations for individual students.

Advantages of Learning Analytics

Learning analytics can revolutionize education by offering numerous benefits to *students*, *educators*, and *educational institutions*. Learning analytics provides personalized learning experiences tailored to students' needs, learning styles, and preferences. Through early intervention facilitated by learning analytics, students at risk of academic challenges or dropping out can receive timely support, enhancing engagement and motivation in their learning endeavors (Mougiakou et al., 2023). Moreover, personalized feedback and support provided through learning analytics contribute to improved academic performance and overall learning outcomes, fostering a more conducive learning environment for students.

Educators also stand to gain significantly from the adoption of learning analytics. By leveraging data-informed decision-making, educators can make informed choices regarding curriculum design, instructional strategies, and student support services. Learning analytics offers insights into the effectiveness of teaching methods and materials, enabling educators to refine their practices to better meet students' diverse needs.

For *educational institutions, learning analytics presents* a multitude of advantages. By identifying at-risk students early and providing tailored support, institutions can improve student retention rates and reduce dropout rates, ultimately enhancing the institution's reputation and attracting more students and faculty. Learning analytics also helps optimize the allocation of educational resources, such as time, personnel, and technology, by identifying areas where resources can be more effectively utilized.

Cognitive Computing in Education

In education, Cognitive computing uses advanced computing systems that mimic human cognitive functions to enhance learning experiences, teaching methods, and educational outcomes; the following sections illustrate this concept as a beneficial tool to be adopted by teachers toward class engagement.

Cognitive Computing Evolution

The widespread adoption of computer technology in the second half of the 20th century, along with advancements in linguistics, information theory, and data science, brought about a significant cognitive revolution (Chen et al., 2018). Cognitive science is an interdisciplinary study that analyzes how information is processed and manipulated in the human brain. Scientists in this field investigate human mental capacities by analyzing language, perception, memory, attention, reasoning, and emotion. Combined with the cognitive computing evolution shown in Figure 2, the researcher provides a more comprehensive explanation of knowledge discovery, cognitive science, big data, and cognitive computing.

- **Knowledge Discovery:** The procedure for extracting necessary information from the original data collection and transforming it into knowledge.
- **Cognitive Science:** The field of cognitive science investigates how the brain generates, stores, and processes information. It focuses on mental processes, including learning, thinking, and behavior.
- **Big Data:** Big data is commonly defined by the five V's: volume (comprising large-scale data), variety (encompassing a wide range of data formats), velocity (generated continuously, frequently in a "streaming" fashion), veracity (incorporating elements of uncertainty into the data), and value (extracting actionable intelligence). A wide range of technologies are applied to the analysis and exploration of data.
- **Cognitive Computing:** There are four stages in cognitive computing. First, observation is a crucial component of cognitive computing systems that perform data aggregation, integration, and inspection. Second, explanation aids in comprehending and resolving intricate issues, particularly in the presence of multiple sources of information. Third is evaluation, a component of the inherent human capacity to produce data. Fourth, decision-making features pertain to the cognitive computing system's capacity to make decisions using the examined data.

Figure 2. Cognitive computing evolution

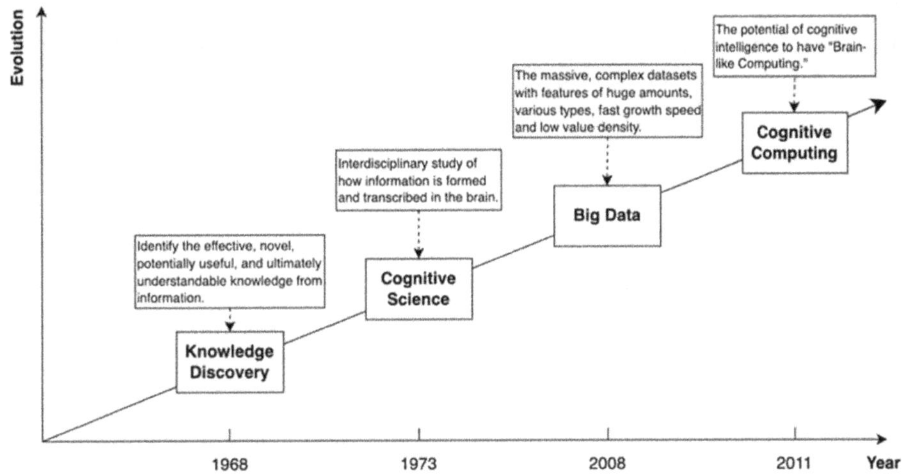

(adapted from Chen et al., 2018)

The Composition of Cognitive Computing

Cognitive computing is the convergence of neuroscience, nanotechnology, and supercomputing; IBM scientists are using this definition as the basis for the development of a novel computing architecture that emulates the efficiency, energy consumption, and compactness of the human brain (Aggarwal et al., 2020).

COGNITIVE COMPUTING = PRINCIPLES OF
(Neuroscience + Nanotechnology + Supercomputing)

- **Neuroscience:** the study of the mind and nervous system. Cognitive computing systems have a similar structure to the brain and consist of electronic neurons and synapses called synapse chips.
- **Nanotechnology:** the study of materials with dimensions of 10^-9 meters. Nanotechnology supports cognitive computing technically
- **Supercomputing:** involves the use of compelling computers that can execute millions of calculations every second.

Cognitive Computing Architecture

Cognitive computing architecture systems consist of network technologies such as the Internet of Things (IoT), analytical technologies such as deep learning and reinforcement learning, and cloud computing, including task scheduling systems (Chen et al., 2018). Figure 2 depicts a cognitive computing system structure. The IoT gathers essential data from physical items utilizing advanced computer technologies like cloud computing, machine learning, and data mining to analyze the data and make conclusions.

The IoT will enhance its data processing and transmission capabilities, becoming a crucial information source for cognitive computing as it progresses.

The emergence of artificial intelligence and the availability of cloud computing resources are boosting the advancement of cognitive computing. Combining IoT and cloud computing enables cognitive computing using software and hardware, while big data analytics offer new possibilities for data analysis. Real-life data is analyzed extensively on cloud computing platforms. This is followed by data mining; the results are applied in many fields using machine learning and other technologies (Matoori & Nourafza, 2021).

Figure 3. Cognitive computing architecture

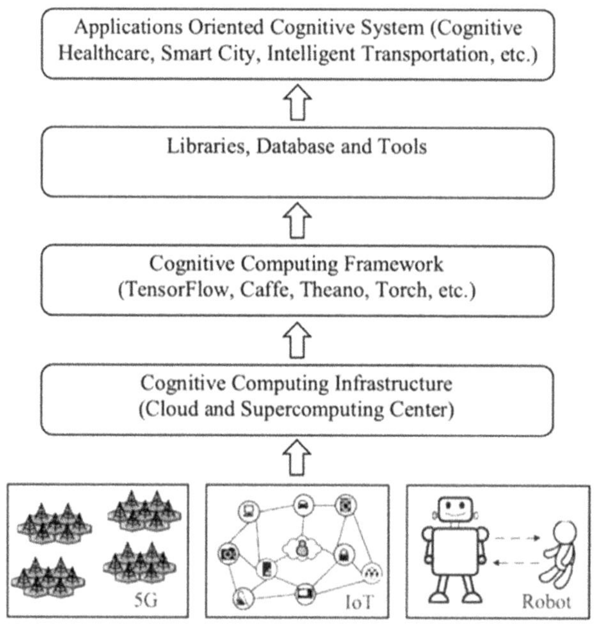

(adapted from Chen et al., 2018)

Cognitive Computing Model

Cognitive computing models aim to replicate the human brain's perceptions, behaviors, interactions, and cognitive capacities. The advancement of brain research and computing science will further improve the implementation of cognitive computing models in education. The state operator and result (SOAR) model and the Bayesian brain model are examples of traditional cognitive computing models.

SOAR Model

The SOAR model is a comprehensive problem-solving software model depicted in Figure 3. Working and long-term memory are partitioned into knowledge blocks following the knowledge block theory. Symbol-based working memory serves the dual purpose of storing the assessment of the present problem scenario and retrieving pertinent information from long-term memory

Figure 4. The SOAR cognitive computing model

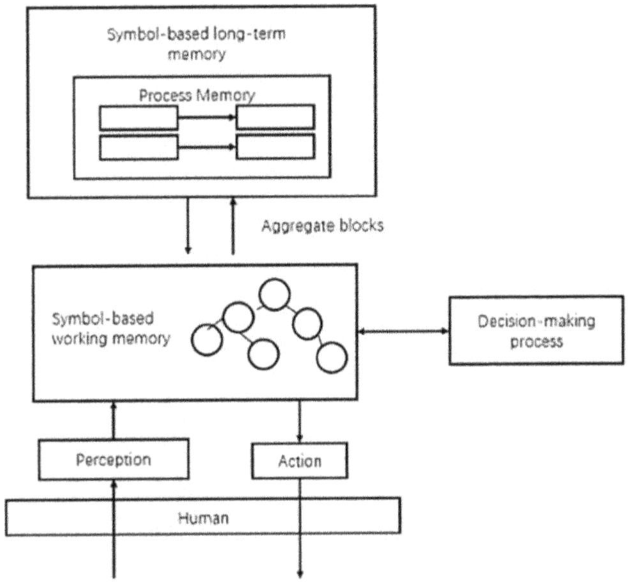

(adapted from Yang et al., 2023)

Bayesian Brain Model

The Bayes theorem explains combining or updating previous knowledge about a certain quantity with new observations to generate an updated posterior probability. Figure 5 shows its mathematical expression.

Figure 5. Bayes' theorem

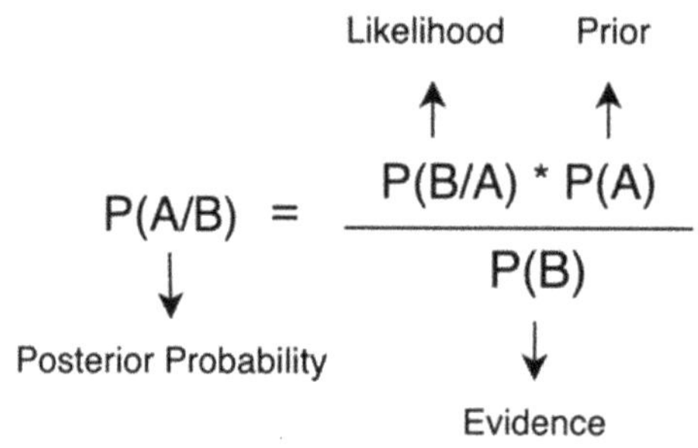

The brain includes an internal model with assumptions about the world, depicted in a schematic picture of a "Bayesian brain" (Figure 6).

Figure 6. Schematic of a "Bayesian brain"

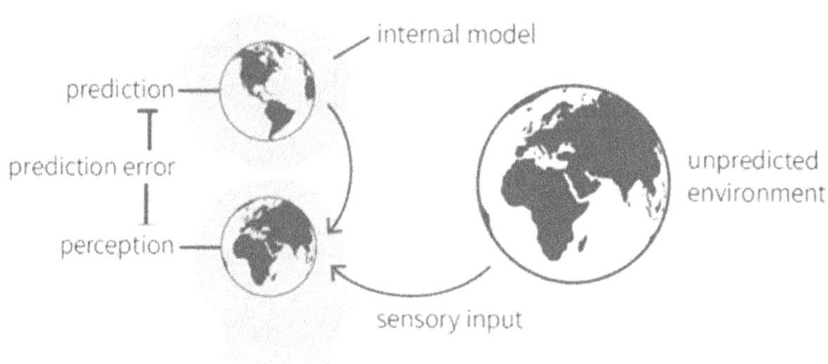

(adapted from Manjaly & Iglesias, 2020)

It then creates models at different cognitive levels to anticipate incoming information and forecast probable outcomes in a specific context. It compares predicted information with sensory input, interprets any discrepancies, and transmits this error to higher brain regions to update the prediction model and reduce future prediction errors.

Cognitive Computing Integrated Framework for Education Applications

Cognitive computing models conduct intelligent demonstrations to support personalized learning better and serve educational decision-making. It improves learning and teaching by providing customized learning support services and cognitive computing-driven educational strategies. We must consider two main aspects regarding the learning process: first, learners gain new knowledge through educational strategies and methods, and second, machines, systems, and platforms process information to support individual learning through cognitive services. Learner-centered cognitive computing models can leverage data from educational environments to enable human-computer interaction at a deep algorithmic level. The cognitive computing integrated framework in education (Figure 7) provides more intelligent data and services for learning and teaching.

Figure 7. Cognitive computing integrated framework

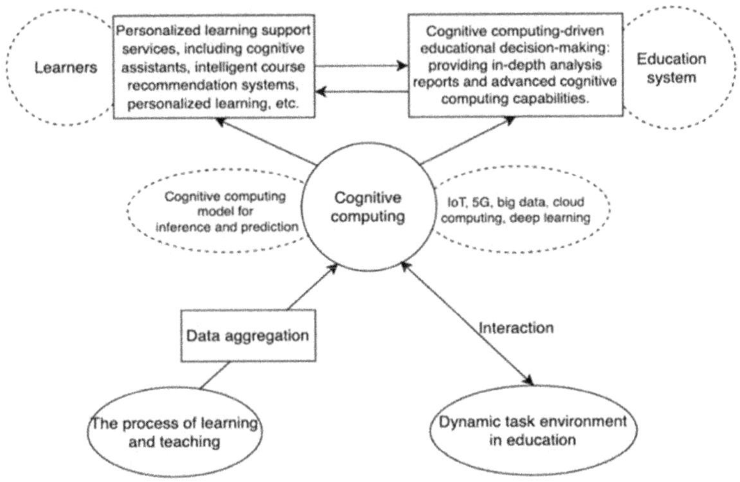

(adapted from Meixian et al., 2021)

Cognitive Computing Supporting Educators

Cognitive computing can be applied in education and is progressing alongside digital education's development. It also examines many data sources to assess the efficacy of practice-based learning. Improving the availability of data-gathering devices such as biometric data, speech recognition, and eye tracking would empower cognitive computing systems to offer fresh insights into skills presently challenging to evaluate, such as speech recognition and eye tracking. Cognitive computing can implement the spoken language interaction method, which has three steps, each corresponding to a specific cognitive process (Figure 8).

Figure 8. Three-step spoken language interaction method

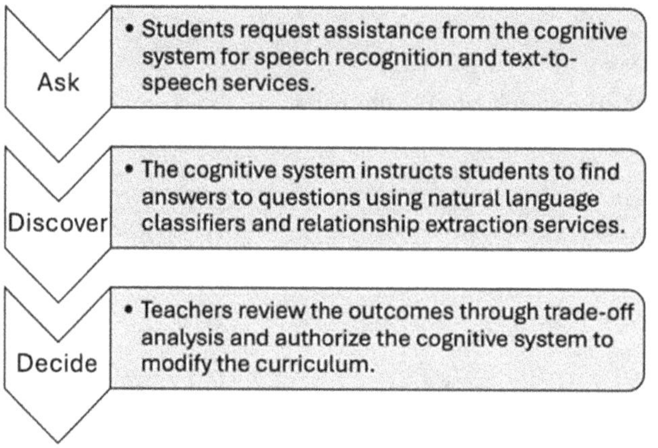

(adapted from Coccoli et al., 2016)

Teachers can implement cognitive computing-based systems to engage students in conversation through a recursive loop comprising six phases, as Coccoli et al. (2016) proposed.

- The cognitive system evaluates each student's strengths and limitations.
- The cognitive system recommends behaviors and content that match students' skills and learning styles.
- Educators choose suitable learning routes and develop individualized strategies for each student.
- Students use the content recommended in the program materials.
- Educators oversee student advancement and adjust strategies as necessary.
- Educators employ cognitive computing systems to assess student skill acquisition in alignment with established benchmarks.

Cognitive computing also helps refine situational aspects, including technology, teachers, and surroundings, to amplify the efficacy of a specific teaching approach. Cognitive computing-based systems can effectively support teachers by analyzing data (Aghav-Palwe & Gunjal, 2021).

Applications in the Classroom

- Personalized Learning and Evaluation Materials: Cognitive computing tutors can evaluate student learning and provide personalized learning materials and additional assessments based on the initial assessment results. The cognitive tutor lets students inquire about topic-specific questions linked to the study material and evaluation components. Cognitive tutors replicate a teacher's capacity to tutor, evaluate, and guide numerous students simultaneously, enabling them to offer consistent help to a large group of students in a course.
- Student Profile Search and Application for Courses: Relevant courses will be recommended to students based on their past student data. One way to accomplish this is by having a cognitive assistant that uses natural language processing for conversations and interactions. Students could start

conversing with the assistant by requesting help to select their courses. Courses can be tailored to better suit students' requirements by harnessing teaching expertise and closely monitoring students' progress and problem-solving skills.

Applications on Campus

- Digital Campus: Tailored campus news, announcements, and updates can improve student participation in campus activities, enabling students to understand campus functions better and work closely with school administration to address concerns.
- Virtual Library: To save time, offer students books and articles to assist with exam preparation instead of browsing through enormous libraries. The system can monitor pupils' reading habits and track the books they have read to improve productivity. Educational assistance systems can be strengthened by providing virtual tools to simplify and improve book availability.

Improving Teaching and Learning Practices

Educational data mining (EDM) is a developing field focusing on using cognitive computing in education and learning. Progress in data mining and machine learning has influenced EDM's development (Rahman, 2022); it offers crucial data and enhances learners' understanding and learning processes. The main objective is to assist teachers, students, and other involved parties in reaching their individual goals through applying big data in education (Irfan & Gudivada, 2016). Baker and Yacef (2009) suggested four primary areas where EDM might enrich education.

- Enhancement of Student Models
- Enhancing Domain Models
- Studying Pedagogical Support
- Seeking Empirical Evidence

Du et al. (2020) highlighted how EDM improves decision-making assistance for teachers and learners. EDM elevates the learning process by offering valuable information to education stakeholders, enabling them to make more informed decisions. It identifies and emphasizes information pertinent to educational tasks, offering feedback to both teachers and students. Various methodologies, such as descriptive statistics, data visualization, social network analysis, clustering, and rule mining, are used to search for feedbackThis aligns with Trung et al.'s (2023) research in Table 1. Cognitive computing applies cognitive science principles to create algorithms that enable machines to comprehend and perceive the world through a human-like thought process.

Table 1. Enhancing education with EDM

Application	Purpose	Examples
Predicting student characteristics	Each student's academic, demographic, and psychological data should be used to forecast indicators of their academic ability, achievements, teamwork skills, learning styles, and emotions. Teachers can guide students and focus on individuals who are facing difficulties.	Utilize algorithms like the k-nearest neighbor, decision tree, multilayer perceptron (MLP), genetic algorithms, or the Parzen window method to forecast student performance in network-based education systems on LON-CAPA (Minaei-Bidgoli et al., 2003).
Detecting student undesirable behavior	To identify behaviors or occurrences that adversely impact student academic advancement, such as dropouts, distractions, and academic setbacks, to alert instructors to intervene promptly.	Forecast dropout in online courses with feed-forward neural networks, support vector machines, and probabilistic ensemble simplified fuzzy ARTMAP (Lykourentzou et al., 2009).
Intelligent tutoring system	Learning assistance systems, such as interactive exercises and visual course manuals, are designed to facilitate instruction while minimizing teacher intervention. They also feature instant feedback and customization for various users.	Identify student misuse of intelligent tutoring software with a Bayesian knowledge tracing algorithm (Baker et al., 2004).
Student modeling	To develop a profile that encompasses a student's learning abilities, personality traits, and conduct. This profile can be utilized to create customized systems or suggestions.	Create a collaborative filtering model to automatically categorize learners based on their learning styles and educational preferences (Khribi et al., 2013).
Grouping students	This process is designed to group students based on common characteristics, such as learning ability, personality, and learning style.	Random forest, MLP, radial basis function networks, and K-Star are used to classify and forecast academic talents (Jantan et al., 2010).
Providing recommendations for student	To create a recommendation system that offers suggestions for specific courses or learning routes and helpful guidance while learning and searching for educational resources.	Collaborative filtering and content-based filtering techniques provide automated suggestions to personalize e-learning (Khribi et al., 2008).
Classroom monitoring	To identify and anticipate learners' attention levels or to analyze sentiment data during learning to develop adaptive systems.	OpenFace, support vector machines, and logistic regression forecast student classroom involvement based on facial expressions (Thomas & Jayagopi, 2017).
Providing feedback for supporting educators	To develop a feedback system for teachers, course developers, and course designers to promptly and effectively address issues related to students' classroom learning skills and styles.	Principal component analysis and the apriori algorithm build a framework to assist teachers in analyzing rule evaluation metrics (Ventura et al., 2008).
Designing curriculum/ developing course	To empower course creators and designers to streamline courseware creation and organization of learning resources through automated procedures. This allows them to improve and expand upon current information by incorporating new updates and repurposing past resources.	The Felder–Silverman learning styles model is used to develop a customized learning curriculum (Knauf et al., 2009).
Decision Support System	To encourage stakeholders in education to make decisions by supporting their efforts, with a primary focus on management duties. These support systems aid school administrators make more suitable and rational decisions about student learning.	Use the J48, k-means clustering, expectation-maximization, and apriori algorithms to build a knowledge-driven educational decision support system (Vo & Nguyen, 2012).

Game-Based Pedagogy

This section elucidates the emergence of gamification in educational paradigms as an innovative concept, synthesizing it with the previous section on the learning analytics niche of teachers towards gameful learning and pedagogical skills in deploying strategies to enrich students' learning experiences through immersive gamification techniques.

Technology integration into education has opened many opportunities to accelerate the learning experience in the last few years. The emergence of gamification as a thrilling trend in the educational arena is essential. According to Smith & Johnson (2019), gamification in the classroom can be a powerful tool for teacher development, engaging educators in interactive and enjoyable learning experiences. By adopting gamification techniques, teacher development can become more engaging, interactive, and practical, improving teaching practices, class engagement, and student outcomes. This analytical learning approach strengthens the inherent appeal of games to captivate learners' interest and promote active participation in the learning process. It should be highlighted here that gamification is not a game application; hence, Shahri et al. (2019) clarified that it uses game-based application components and game-based principles in a non-game environment and context to engage students and increase their retention with the system implemented. Primarily, it is used to increase involvement, engagement, and motivation due to the result-oriented game-based activities if demonstrated in the classroom context. Thus, the study by Gatautis et al. (2016) revealed that gamification, as might be expected, concerns users' behaviors since it focuses on the end-user's phase.

Game pedagogy is an alternative expression to classroom gamification. Also known as game-based pedagogy or metric- pedagogy, it refers to integrating elements of games and game design principles into educational settings to enhance learning outcomes. It involves using games, simulations, and other interactive activities as instructional tools to engage learners, promote active participation, and facilitate a deeper understanding of concepts and skills. Teachers adopt games' inherent motivational and immersive qualities in game-based learning to create engaging learning experiences catering to diverse learning styles and preferences. This approach encourages students to participate actively in their learning process, fostering critical thinking, problem-solving, collaboration, and creativity.

With increased digital tools and resources, educators provide technology to create dynamic, engaging, and personalized student learning experiences. Technology offers diverse classroom exploration and discovery methods, from interactive smartboards and educational apps to online platforms and virtual reality simulations.

Table 2. Learning analytics and gamification

Data-Driven Decision Making
Learning analytics can provide teachers with data from different rages on student performance, interaction patterns, and learning preferences. Also, by analyzing this data, which is one of the critical components of DDDM, teachers can identify areas where gamification elements can be integrated to enhance student engagement and motivation.

With increased digital tools and resources, educators provide technology to create dynamic, engaging, and personalized student learning experiences. Technology offers diverse classroom exploration and discovery methods, from interactive smartboards and educational apps to online platforms and virtual reality simulations. Impressive, integrating learning analytics with gamification offers a robust toolset for teachers to enhance student engagement and academic performance. Ultimately, as shown in Table

2 above, this symbiotic integration empowers teachers to create dynamic learning environments that motivate students while offering valuable insights into their academic journey.

Figure 9. Implementation of class gamification outcome

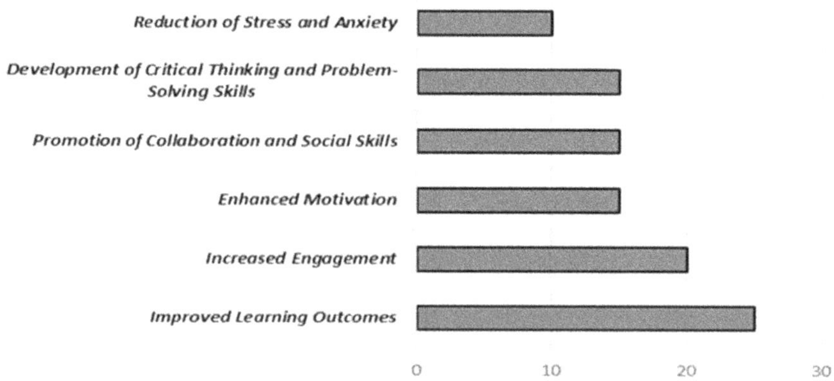

While technology is merging into education, as pointed out, and mobilized educational analytics in the -12 context, teachers should adopt creative teaching strategies and methods to engage students more in the teaching and learning process. Using gameful pedagogy tools, teaching and learning can become more collaborative and enjoyable. In addition, applying the gamification domain in education persuades students to participate in class and affects their academic achievement. Remarkably, the primary key of gamification should be on the students to make a positive and desirable change in their behavior since Gatautis et al. (2016) state that gamification's primary purpose is to guide learners/users' actions.

However, the findings of Calderon et al. (2018) do not parallel the above study and reveal that gamification goes beyond behavior orientation and is a non-gaming learning tool, specifically in academic, educational, teaching-learning, and, as well as, training contexts. Furthermore, Yıldırım (2017) notes that game-based learning positively impacts students' achievement and behaviors aligned with course-learning outcome goals. To add more clarifications of using gamification in the classroom and its importance are summarized previous studies based on play-based education representative studies that have been published since 2000, shown in Figure 1 above:

1. **Reduction of Stress and Anxiety**

According to Kapp (2012), gamification creates a low-stress learning environment where students feel comfortable taking risks and making mistakes, reducing anxiety and increasing confidence in their abilities. By providing a safe space for experimentation and exploration, gamification helps alleviate performance pressure and empowers students to take ownership of their learning journey.

2. **Development of Critical Thinking & Problem-Solving Skills**

Studies by Gee (2003) indicate that gamification promotes critical thinking and problem-solving skills by challenging students to think creatively, strategize, and adapt to changing situations within game-based environments. By presenting students with complex problems to solve and allowing them to experiment with different solutions, gamification fosters the development of higher-order thinking skills essential for success in academic and professional settings (Seaborn & Fels, 2015).

3. **Increased Social Skills**

Research by Deterding et al. (2011) suggests that gamification encourages collaboration and teamwork among students, fostering the development of social skills such as communication, cooperation, and empathy. Additionally, a study by Gee (2003) found that multiplayer gamified learning environments promote social interaction and peer learning, creating opportunities for students to share ideas, collaborate on projects, and learn from one another.

4. **Enhanced Motivation**

In addition to increased engagement, gamification enhances student motivation. Deci and Ryan's Self-Determination Theory (SDT) (2000) posits that gamification gives students a sense of autonomy, competence, and relatedness, enhancing their intrinsic motivation to learn. Furthermore, a study by Deterding et al. (2011) found that gamification taps into students' psychological needs for achievement and recognition, fostering a sense of accomplishment and motivating them to overcome challenges.

5. **Increased Engagement**

Based on Hamari et al. (2014) have shown that gamification increases student engagement by incorporating elements such as points, badges, and leaderboards, which make learning more interactive and enjoyable. Furthermore, a study by Werbach and Hunter (2012) found that gamified learning environments capture students' attention and maintain their focus longer than traditional instructional methods. Additionally, research by Landers (2014) suggests that the use of narrative and storytelling in gamification enhances emotional engagement, immersing students in the learning process and fostering a deeper connection to the content.

6. **Improved Learning Outcomes**

The incorporation of gamification in the classroom has been shown to lead to improved learning outcomes. A meta-analysis by Landers and Landers (2014) found that gamification positively impacts learning outcomes, including knowledge acquisition, retention, and transfer. By providing immediate feedback and creating a sense of progress, gamification promotes deeper learning and facilitates the application of knowledge to real-world contexts.

Outlining Classroom Game-Based Activities

Primary to high school teachers can effectively integrate gamification into the classroom by following a structured approach and synthesizing game elements to enhance student engagement and learning outcomes, as briefly demonstrated.

Figure 10. Class gamification activities

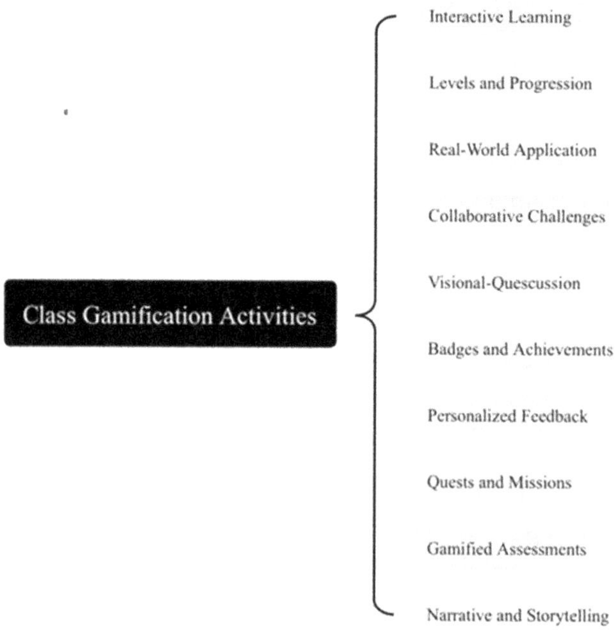

Effective Classroom Gamification and Teacher Skill Competencies

These significant research findings further emphasize the importance of increased engagement in the classroom facilitated by gamification, highlighting its positive impact on motivation, learning outcomes, social skills development, critical thinking, problem-solving, and emotional well-being, as mentioned above; however, there is a literature gap between game-based learning and teachers adoption behavior. It converts the principal content material and objectives in a fun way. In their study outcome, Hamari et al. (2016) suggest that the game challenge must keep up with learners' increasing performance. Teachers must communicate the rules, goals, and expectations of the gamified activities and provide timely and constructive feedback to students as they engage in them. In addition, skilled teachers can empower students to make choices and exercise autonomy within the gamified learning environment to impact positive behavior adoption.

Overcoming Difficulties With Gamified Education

Prevailing the challenges associated with integrating game-based activities in the teaching-learning process in the classroom is vital from the teacher's perspective to maximize student course achievement. By effectively addressing these challenges through professional development, collaboration, and ongoing support, teachers can utilize the potential of gamification to create dynamic and personalized learning experiences that cater to diverse student needs and learning styles. Moreover, this proactive approach empowers teachers to increase gameful learning as powerful instructional equipment to enhance deeper learning and academic success among their students.

To the point, gamification in education has many advantages, but it has drawbacks that among the most common roadblocks are summarized in this study:

1) Effective Course Design
2) Teacher Professional Development
3) Infrastructure & Resources
4) Engagement & Motivation
5) Assessment & Evaluation
6) Accessibility & Inclusivity
7) Research & Evaluation

CONCLUSION

In conclusion, integrating cognitive computing, learning analytics, and gamification represents a groundbreaking approach to enhancing teachers' professional development within the rapidly evolving societal landscape. Primarily using innovative technologies, teachers are empowered to continuously learn, adapt their teaching methodologies, and improve student outcomes. By implementing cognitive computing, as mentioned in this study, teachers gain access to personalized insights and resources that cater to their individual needs, nurturing a culture of lifelong learning. On the other hand, learning analytics provide valuable data-driven feedback, enabling them to make informed decisions and optimize their instructional strategies for maximum effectiveness in their classes. Additionally, game-based pedagogy elements that increase excitement and motivation in professional development activities and promote teacher collaboration and engagement have been explored here. As we move forward, it is essential to recognize the transformative potential of these interventions and ensure equitable access to such resources across diverse educational settings. Moreover, collaboration among principals, teachers, administrative school staff, policymakers, and technologists is crucial to navigating the ethical considerations, privacy concerns, and implementation challenges associated with integrating these technologies into professional development initiatives. By embracing the opportunities presented by cognitive computing, learning analytics, and gamification, we can prepare a dynamic educational ecosystem that empowers educators to improve and adapt to the ever-changing landscape of the teaching-learning process.

REFERENCES

Aggarwal, L., Chahal, D., & Kharb, L. (2020). Pruning deficiency of big data analytics using cognitive computing. *2020 International Conference on Emerging Trends in Communication, Control and Computing (ICONC3)*, (pp. 1–4). 10.1109/ICONC345789.2020.9117504

Aghav-Palwe, S., & Gunjal, A. (2021). Introduction to cognitive computing and its various applications. In *Cognitive Computing for Human-Robot Interaction* (pp. 1–18). Elsevier. 10.1016/B978-0-323-85769-7.00009-4

Baker, R. S., Corbett, A. T., & Koedinger, K. R. (2004). Detecting student misuse of intelligent tutoring systems. In *Intelligent Tutoring Systems* (pp. 531–540). Springer Berlin Heidelberg. 10.1007/978-3-540-30139-4_50

Baker, R. S. J. D., & Yacef, K. (2009). The state of Educational Data Mining in 2009: A review and future visions. *Journal of Educational Data Mining*, 1(1), 3–16. https://files.eric.ed.gov/fulltext/EJ1115366.pdf

Calderón, A., Boubeta-Puig, J., & Ruiz, M. (2018). MEdit4CEP-Gam: A model driven approach for user-friendly gamification design, monitoring and code generation in CEP-based systems. *Information and Software Technology*, 95, 238–264. 10.1016/j.infsof.2017.11.009

Chen, M., Herrera, F., & Hwang, K. (2018). Cognitive Computing: Architecture, Technologies and Intelligent Applications. *IEEE Access : Practical Innovations, Open Solutions*, 6, 19774–19783. 10.1109/ACCESS.2018.2791469

Coccoli, M., Maresca, P., & Stanganelli, L. (2016). Cognitive computing in education. *Journal of E-Learning and Knowledge Society*, 12(2), 55–69. 10.20368/1971-8829/1185

Deterding, S., Dixon, D., Khaled, R., & Nacke, L. (2011). From game design elements to gamefulness: Defining "gamification". In *Proceedings of the 15th International Academic MindTrek Conference: Envisioning Future Media Environments* (pp. 9-15). ACM. 10.1145/2181037.2181040

Du, X., Yang, J., Hung, J.-L., & Shelton, B. (2020). Educational data mining: A systematic review of research and emerging trends. *Information Discovery and Delivery*, 48(4), 225–236. 10.1108/IDD-09-2019-0070

Gee, J. P. (2003). What video games have to teach us about learning and literacy. [CIE]. *Computers in Entertainment*, 1(1), 20–20. 10.1145/950566.950595

Green, L. W., & Glasgow, R. E. (2006). Evaluating the relevance, generalization, and applicability of research: Issues in external validation and translation methodology. *Evaluation & the Health Professions*, 29(1), 126–153. 10.1177/0163278705284445165 10882

Hantoobi, S., Wahdan, A., Al-Emran, M., & Shaalan, K. (2021). A Review of Learning Analytics Studies. In Al-Emran, M., & Shaalan, K. (Eds.), *Recent advances in technology acceptance models and theories* (pp. 119–134). Springer Nature. 10.1007/978-3-030-64987-6_8

Irfan, M. T., & Gudivada, V. N. (2016). Cognitive computing applications in education and learning. In *Handbook of Statistics* (pp. 283–300). Elsevier.

Jantan, H., Hamdan, Gatautis, R., Dagiene, V., & Futschek, G. (2016). Gamification and education: A literature review. In Proceedings of the 11th European Conference on Game Based Learning (pp. 230-238). Academic Conferences International Limited.

Jayashanka, R., Hettiarachchi, E., & Hewagamage, K. P. (2022). Technology enhanced learning analytics dashboard in higher education. *Electronic Journal of e-Learning*, 20(2), 151–170. 10.34190/ejel.20.2.2189

Kantipudi, M. V. V. P., Aluvalu, R., Maheswari, U. V., & Raisinghani, M. S. (2022). Insights on implications of cognitive computing in leveraging online education systems. *International Journal of Online Pedagogy and Course Design*, 12(1), 1–16. 10.4018/IJOPCD.302082

Kapp, K. M. (2012). *The gamification of learning and instruction: Game-based methods and strategies for training and education.* John Wiley & Sons.

Khribi, M. K., Jemni, M., & Nasraoui, O. (2008). Automatic recommendations for E-learning personalization based on web usage mining techniques and information retrieval. *2008 Eighth IEEE International Conference on Advanced Learning Technologies*, (pp. 241–245). IEEE. 10.1109/ICALT.2008.198

Khribi, M. K. Jemni, M., Nasraoui, O., Graf, S., & Kinshuk. (2013). Toward a fully automatic learner modeling based on web usage mining with respect to educational preferences and learning styles. *2013 IEEE 13th International Conference on Advanced Learning Technologies*, 403–407.

Kitto, K., Whitmer, J., Silvers, A. E., & Webb, M. (2020). *Creating data for learning analytics ecosystems.* The Society for Learning Analytics Research (SoLAR). https://www.solaresearch.org/wp-content/uploads/2020/09/SoLAR_Position-Paper_2020_09.pdf

Knauf, R., Sakurai, Y., Tsuruta, S., Takada, K., & Dohi, S. (2009). Personalized curriculum composition by learner profile-driven data mining. *2009 IEEE International Conference on Systems, Man and Cybernetics*, (pp. 2068–2073). IEEE. 10.1109/ICSMC.2009.5346317

Landers, R. N., & Landers, A. K. (2014). An empirical test of the theory of gamified learning: The effect of leaderboards on time-on-task and academic performance. *Simulation & Gaming*, 45(6), 769–785. 10.1177/1046878114563662

Lang, C., Wise, A. F., Merceron, A., Gašević, D., & Siemens, G. (2022). What is learning analytics? In C. Lang, G. Siemens, A. F. Wise, D. Gašević, & A. Merceron (Eds.) *Handbook of Learning Analytics* (2nd. ed.) (pp. 8-18). SoLAR.

Lykourentzou, I., Giannoukos, I., Nikolopoulos, V., Mpardis, G., & Loumos, V. (2009). Dropout prediction in e-learning courses through the combination of machine learning techniques. *Computers & Education*, 53(3), 950–965. 10.1016/j.compedu.2009.05.010

Manjaly, Z.-M., & Iglesias, S. (2020). A computational theory of mindfulness based cognitive therapy from the "Bayesian brain" perspective. *Frontiers in Psychiatry*, 11, 1–16. 10.3389/fpsyt.2020.0040432499726

Matoori, S. S., & Nourafza, N. (2021). Big data analytics and cognitive computing: A review study. *Journal of Business Data Science Research*, 1(01), 23–32. http://jbdsr.com/index.php/home/article/view/4

Meixian, S., Ruiyang, Z., & Zhe, S. (2021). Research of Cognitive Computing and Educational Application from the Perspective of "Intelligence +" Education. *Journal of Distance Education*, 39(2), 21–33.

Minaei-Bidgoli, B., Kashy, D. A., Kortemeyer, G., & Punch, W. F. (2003). Predicting student performance: An application of data mining methods with an educational web-based system. *33rd Annual Frontiers in Education, 2003.FIE*, 2003, T2A_13–T2A_18. 10.1109/FIE.2003.1263284

Mougiakou, S., Vinatsella, D., Sampson, D., Papamitsiou, Z., Giannakos, M., & Ifenthaler, D. (2023). *Educational data analytics for teachers and school leaders*. Springer. 10.1007/978-3-031-15266-5

Paulsen, L., & Lindsay, E. (2024). Learning analytics dashboards are increasingly becoming about learning and not just analytics: A systematic review. *Education and Information Technologies*. Advance online publication. 10.1007/s10639-023-12401-4

Rahman, L. (2022). Cognitive Computing and Education and Learning. [IJASRD]. *International Journal of Advanced Scientific Research & Development*, 6(3), 1628–1632.

Seaborn, K., & Fels, D. I. (2015). Gamification in theory and action: A survey. *International Journal of Human-Computer Studies*, 74, 14–31. 10.1016/j.ijhcs.2014.09.006

Shah, M., Nair, C. S., & Richardson, J. T. E. (2017). *Measuring and enhancing the student experience*. Elsevier.

Shahri, A., Asadollahi, A., & Khoshraftar, E. (2019). Understanding the concept of gamification in education: A systematic literature review. *Computers & Education*, 142, 103641. 10.1016/j.compedu.2019.103641

Siemens, G. (2013). Learning analytics: The emergence of a discipline. *The American Behavioral Scientist*, 57(10), 1380–1400. 10.1177/0002764213498851

Siemens, G., & Gasevic, D. (2012). Guest Editorial - Learning and Knowledge Analytics. *Journal of Educational Technology & Society*, 15(3), 1–2. https://www.jstor.org/stable/jeductechsoci.15.3.1

Siemens, G., Gasevic, D., Haythornthwaite, C., Dawson, S., Shum, S. B., Ferguson, R., Duval, E., Verbert, K., & Baker, R. (2011). *Open Learning Analytics: an integrated & modularized platform*. The Society for Learning Analytics Research (SoLAR). https://solaresearch.org/wp-content/uploads/2011/12/OpenLearningAnalytics.pdf

Smith, A., & Johnson, B. (2019). The role of gamification in teacher development: Engaging educators through interactive learning experiences. *Journal of Educational Technology*, 42(3), 365–378.

Sousa, E. B. G., Alexandre, B., Mello, R. F., Falcão, T. P., Vesin, B., & Gašević, D. (2021). Applications of learning analytics in high schools: A systematic literature review. *Frontiers in Artificial Intelligence*, 4, 1–14. 10.3389/frai.2021.73789134647016

Susnjak, T., Ramaswami, G. S., & Mathrani, A. (2022). Learning analytics dashboard: A tool for providing actionable insights to learners. *International Journal of Educational Technology in Higher Education*, 19(12), 1–23. 10.1186/s41239-021-00313-735194560

Thomas, C., & Jayagopi, D. B. (2017). Predicting student engagement in classrooms using facial behavioral cues. *Proceedings of the 1st ACM SIGCHI International Workshop on Multimodal Interaction for Education*, (pp. 33–40). ACM. 10.1145/3139513.3139514

Trung, B. D., Son, N. T., Tung, N. D., Son, K. A., Anh, B. N., & Lam, P. T. (2023). Educational data mining: A systematic review on the applications of classical methods and deep learning until 2022. *2023 IEEE Symposium on Industrial Electronics & Applications (ISIEA)*, (pp. 1–15). ACM. 10.1109/ISIEA58478.2023.10212273

Tsai, Y. (2019, August 18). *Learning analytics in a nutshell* [Video]. YouTube. https://www.youtube.com/watch?v=XscUZ8dIa-8

Ventura, S., Romero, C., & Hervás, C. (2008). *Analyzing rule evaluation measures with educational datasets: A framework to help the teacher*. Educational Data Mining 2008.

Vo, T. N. C., & Nguyen, H. P. (2012). A knowledge-driven educational decision support system. *2012 IEEE RIVF International Conference on Computing & Communication Technologies, Research, Innovation, and Vision for the Future*, (pp. 1–6). IEEE.

Werbach, K., & Hunter, D. (2012). *For the win: How game thinking can revolutionize your business*. Wharton Digital Press.

Yang, Z., Fan, G., Pan, W., & Ren, Z. (2023). Research on educational cognitive computing model based on problem solving. *2023 IEEE 12th International Conference on Educational and Information Technology (ICEIT)*, (pp. 125–131). IEEE.

Yildirim, I. (2017). The effects of gamification-based teaching practices on student achievement and students' attitudes toward lessons. *The Internet and Higher Education*, 33, 86–92. 10.1016/j.iheduc.2017.02.002

Chapter 7
Multimedia Material for Science and Technology Teaching:
Concept Maps Enriched With Digital Technologies

Canan Koçak Altundağ
https://orcid.org/0009-0006-2844-473X
Hacettepe University, Turkey

Rabia Elmas
Hacettepe University, Turkey

ABSTRACT

The aim of this study is to develop concept maps enriched with digital technologies to provide multimedia learning in science education. In the study, in which design and development research method was used, 6th and 8th grade students and science and technology teachers were considered as the common user group. In the process of developing concept maps enriched with digital technologies, the steps of applying instructional technology tools design methods and introducing three designs obtained at the end of the process are included. It is expected that concept maps enriched with digital technologies in science education based on multimedia learning applications will support much more meaningful learning by enriching science lessons. With the concept maps enriched with digital technologies developed within the scope of the research, innovative technology applications were tried to be presented to our teachers and students in science and technology teaching.

INTRODUCTION

It is an undeniable fact that there are technological devices and applications at every point of our daily life in the 21st century, which is called the age of technology. Education should carry the latest innovations of the century in which it takes place and teaching should be designed according to these innovations. While these innovations brought by technology facilitate our daily lives, developing an understanding away from technological developments in the education systems that we try to direct our future is not an action suitable for the age. Science learning in schools should be complemented by science learning

DOI: 10.4018/979-8-3693-3041-8.ch007

that utilises the real world, the presented world and multimedia that are increasingly accessible through digital technologies (Braund & Reis 2006). The use of different resources in multimedia, such as smart boards in today's classrooms, gives the opportunity to have multiple resources in the classroom such as videos, documentaries, interactive presentations and experiments, digital games, songs and much more. Thanks to the materials such as smart boards that we can easily apply multimedia, interaction in the classroom increases (Sarı, 1993). This interaction can be between teacher and student as well as between student and student. Permanent learning increases in environments where peers learn from each other (Lever-Duffy, McDonald & Mizell, 2003). The digitalisation of multimedia causes the student to be involved in the process and to decide which source he/she wants to use. This situation will also help the student to choose the information he/she will learn and make permanent learning.

The first step to be taken in order to explain the place of concept maps in education, which are supported by the literature to support permanent learning, is to turn to the meaning of the word concept. While concepts constitute the basis of the educational process, lesson flow and planning are based on concepts (Kaptan, 1998). This situation maintains its validity in modern education models. Although concepts are sometimes universal, they sometimes take shape and gain meaning according to the society in which they find life. For this reason, concept maps also contain breezes from the imagination and perception world of the person who creates the concept map. The preparation of concept maps by teachers and students in education and training shows us how the concepts of the subject learnt form a scheme in the meaning world of the person. The concept map preparation technique, in which it is important to establish a connection between concepts, has a great place in concept learning in the learning-teaching process (Ülgen, 1996).

Constructivist Learning Approach and Multimedia Learning Cognitive Theory

Constructivist learning theory, as the name suggests, is a learning theory, not a teaching theory. At the centre of this theory should be the learner, the student. Constructivism, which has passed into our language from the English word 'constructivism', is used in the sense that the knowledge or the subject to be learnt is structured, constructed and created by the learner (Demirel, 2001, p.241). With the developing technology, it was known that classical education methods and atmosphere negatively affected the learning process of both teachers and students. Because in classical learning classrooms, the flow of information from the teacher to the student was generally one-way and limited. However, in the age of developing technology, students can quickly find any information they want to find or learn in the internet world, so classical classrooms harm the creativity of the student and even the teacher (Beevevino, et.al., 1999, p.276). For these reasons, the constructivist approach, in which the teacher takes on the role of a guide in modern educational environments, allows students to create their own knowledge, and the interaction between teacher and student is at a high level, has managed to become a very important theory in recent years (İşman et al., 2002). In addition, constructivism also supports meaningful learning in that the information to be learnt in constructivism is the concepts chosen by the student based on his/her own experience and world of meaning and is formed by himself/herself under the guidance of the teacher (Andaç & Gönen, 2009). This situation has been effective in the rise of the theory (Demirel et al., 2000). The classroom atmosphere in which the constructivist approach is used has an environment in which the student can clearly explain his/her own experiences, discuss the subject freely and respectfully with his/her friends, exchange ideas with the teacher, and share responsibility for learning (Jonassen, 1994). Students determine their own problems and solutions during the learning process and the theory always offers flexibility in favour of the student during learning (Özden, 2003). Due to these advantages, the rate of gaining intrinsic motivation, which is the biggest supporter of the student in learning, is quite high in this understanding (Tezci & Gürol, 2003). More than one technique can be used easily in lessons where we want to apply constructivist learning. If group work is to be done, the constructivist approach can easily be used in teaching methods such as cooperative learning techniques, problem-based learning, project/scenario-based learning, educational games (Yaşar, 1998). One point that should be taken into consideration in constructivist approach is that the way each student constructs knowledge and the concepts he/she uses and the meaning of these concepts in students vary from person to person. Therefore, under the guidance of the teacher in the evaluation phase, the student can easily evaluate his/her own construction. In summary, the constructivist approach tells us educators that students should bring their real life into the classroom (Hall, 2006).

Although the constructivist approach seems to be a new theory, its philosophy is quite old (Andaç & Gönen, 2009). Since some problems encountered in its implementation cause concern for teachers even in today's classrooms, the frequency of its implementation has gained momentum only in recent years. The curriculum that teachers must train causes not enough time to be allocated to the structuring of knowledge by students. In crowded classrooms, it is very difficult to control each student's construction process. Today's students have turned the seemingly unlimited freedom given in constructivism into undesirable behaviours in the classroom (Şimşek, 2004). If the opportunities of our learning environments will increase with the rapidly developing technology in the following years and the situations that make it difficult to apply constructivism will be eliminated, this theory, which brings a new generation of understanding to new generation students, will spread to wider learning areas in the world, especially in our country.

How the learning and teaching process should be organised has always been a subject open to discussion. In order for these processes to be prepared correctly, learning environments should also be made suitable for learning. The design of the classroom environment where the student, one of the elements of the learning process, spends the most time while performing the learning action is also very important for the good realisation of the action. In addition, the organisation of this environment is also very important for the teacher, who manages this environment or acts as a guide, to ensure the flow of the lesson and to transform the learning action into success. With the developing technology, the idea of adding technology to the environment to improve learning environments has started to grow rapidly. In addition, when different resources such as telephone, computer, internet, which the new generation can easily access at home, are not available at school, the act of learning could become ordinary or even unnecessary for this generation. With the introduction of different resources that appeal to different senses in the classrooms, education started to become more interesting and accessible for everyone, and the teaching process started to become more efficient (Akkoyunlu & Yılmaz, 2005). In addition, classroom environments shaped according to the needs of new generation students increased the motivation of the students and created permanent and successful learning (Yılmaz & Özgür Dinçol, 2012).

The fact that teaching environments reach resources that appeal to everyone with different applications has given birth to the concept of Multimedia Learning. There are different definitions of multimedia learning from many scientists in the literature. Multimedia comes from the English word 'multimedia' and can be translated into our language as having more than one media source. Newby et al. (2000) defines multimedia as an environment in which systems containing many tools (text, graphics, pictures, video, audio) are created by combining them in a computer environment, while Smith (2002) explains it as an information environment formed by fusing text, sound, and picture (graphics) into a digital environment (e.g. software). Mayer (2001), on the other hand, defined multimedia as the presentation of a material in more than one form, in other words, by supporting it with pictures and text (Akkoyunlu & Yılmaz, 2005). Based on all these definitions, since more than one media source is used in multimedia, more than one sensory organ of the learner can be addressed at the same time. The use of different sources and sensory organs has also contributed to the success of this theory in the learning process. Technologybased multimedia, especially suitable for the new generation, enables learning to be more successful due to its features such as its proximity to real life, increasing retention, containing remarkable elements, and providing flexible learning environments (Marmara University, 2003). The use of interactive resources such as computers in multimedia also enables students to be more active in the process. It also provides the teacher who designs multimedia with the opportunity to use effective materials and design more effective lessons (Najjar, 1996). For example, the teacher shows his/her creativity more easily and enjoys the process himself/herself in the classes where graphics are drawn, videos are watched, listening activities are carried out, interactive experiments are carried out rather than the classes where only books and notebooks are used. One of the purposes of using different resources is to try to create meaningful learning in learners. Therefore, Mayer developed the cognitive theory of multimedia learning based on meaningful learning (Sezgin & Aldağ, 2003). In this theory, it is interpreted that the processing centre of visual and auditory information in the brain is different, the capacities of information processing channels have a limited structure, and the information processing process is interpreted as the process of transforming information into correct symbols in different sources (Mayer, 2001). Again, according to Mayer, the learner does not have the capacity to process new information from a single channel and in an unlimited way. This theory focuses on how the learner understands and interprets the information (Bülbül, 2019). Like every learning theory, multimedia also has some disadvantages. Difficulties in the use of multimedia and inadequate technological facilities in classrooms, internal or professional difficulties experienced by teachers in using different resources constitute the technical problems of this theory. In addition, the flexibility offered by this theory may cause students and teachers to make wrong applications and experience classroom problems. The use of different media that are not properly planned in advance may cause confusion in the cognitive process of students (Cited in Demirbilek, 2004). Sometimes, correct links may not be established between the source used and the subject taught. If these issues are not taken into consideration, the theory cannot reach its success in the parts where it is ambitious in learning.

Metacognition-Based Learning-Teaching Models

Nowadays, when we live in the age of technology, we need to adapt our education standards to the present day in order to make it easier for our students to adapt to the life they live and to increase their life skills. For example, it is not right to expect today's students to have the same life anxiety as a student in the 1920s. Today's students should be the ones who shape their own lives, design their lives before they set off, and know how to be responsible for their own decisions. The equivalent of these concepts in the educational literature is known as metacognition.

The concept of metacognition was first put forward by Flavel in 1976 for the first time in history and has inspired many researches with the idea of knowing how to know, which continues with the question of whether it is possible for a person to control the act of thinking and its results in the process of conscious thinking (Brown, 1980; De Jager et al., 2005; Reeve & Brown, 1985; Schoenfeld, 2016). Flavel (1976) defined metacognition as the knowledge one has about one's own cognitive processes and products or anything related to these processes (Kalemkuş, 2021). Metacognition can also be defined as the knowledge that people have about their own thinking process, monitoring, and control of this process (Hacker & Dunlosky, 2003). Reeve and Brown (1985) define metacognition as the ability to manage one's own cognitive processes. Metacognition is thinking about thinking (Jimenez-Aleixandre, 2007). Metacognition can be divided into two parts: metacognitive knowledge and metacognitive control (Baker & Brown, 1980; Nietfeld et al., 2005; Pintrich, 2002; Schraw & Dennison, 1994; Schraw & Moshman, 1995; Vrugt & Oort, 2008). While metacognitive knowledge includes the knowledge and strategies, they have in the thinking process (Nietfeld et al., 2005), metacognitive control/regulation is defined as metacognitive activities that control one's thinking and learning (Schraw & Moshman, 1995).

The most important factor that will enable metacognitive thinking, that is, the student to be able to do the act of knowing to know or thinking to think on his/her own, is the quality of the education he/she has received. Learning and teaching models in which metacognitive learning is included will help the student to acquire this skill. According to Blakey and Spence (1990), when life creates situations that cannot be solved by learned responses, metacognitive behaviour comes into play. Metacognitive skills are needed when habitual responses are not successful. For this very reason, providing metacognitive skills to students (Kalemkuş, 2021) makes them individuals with high reasoning power who learn independently and think correctly. The use of metacognitive strategies in teaching will prepare students for the problems they may encounter in life, while enabling them to play an active role in the solution process of problems and transfer these solutions to other problems (Victor, 2004). Raising students with metacognition means raising individuals who think strategically and have a unique learning style (Telman, 1988. 29; Eggen & Kauchak, 2001:338,339; Davis & Davis, 2000:85). Metacognition helps students to use most of their mental resources (Fisher, 1998). The use of metacognition skills in education has been supported by academic studies. For example, Schraw (2002) reported that students with high metacognition skills are more determined and self-confident in the learning phase, have lower anxiety levels, use the strategies they have correctly and achieve more successful results. In other words, the use of metacognitive skills will increase success in education. It is also among the research results that successful students have higher levels of metacognition and self-control than low successful students (Sternberg, 1985; Garner, 1990; Hartman, 2002). Metacognitive skills, whose effect on student success has been proven by research, are not even known as a concept by today's students (Hartman, 2002).

It would not be a correct idea to expect students to directly acquire a concept that they are not even aware of. Therefore, this concept should be mentioned in our education systems and the difference between cognition and metacognition should be explained to students. After teaching this difference and concept, metacognition should be provided to students in accordance with metacognition skills. With the tasks to be given to the students before or after the lesson or during the lesson, the skills that the student has in himself/herself should be allowed to emerge. Students should discover and realise their own thinking skills and strategies (Kalemkuş, 2021). Only in this way can we raise individuals who are aware of their own learning process, use different strategies, and experience how knowing is a process of knowing. In this process, methods such as creating the right learning environment for students (Schraw, 1998), giving feedback on the strategies used (Cardelle-Elawar & Corno, 1985), problem solving (Schraw, 1997; Kramarski, Mevarech & Liebermann, 2001), asking thought-provoking questions (Schoenfeld, 1985; Mayer, 1998), and providing a discussion environment (Schraw, 1998) should be used (Özsoy, 2008). Metacognition increases student success in many courses and achievements such as science, mathematics, reading comprehension and interpretation (Fisher, 1998; Callan et al., 2016). Metacognitive thinking aims to provide individuals with abilities appropriate to the characteristics of the century we are in, such as daily life problem solving, critical thinking, being a leader, and taking responsibility for learning (Blakey & Spence, 1990). Metacognitive skills are becoming increasingly important in order to increase students' success not only in school lessons but also in coping with the difficulties they may encounter in life. Let us not forget that independent and strong societies will consist of individuals who can think independently, criticise their own thoughts and have high analytical power. In order to provide today's students, who will form the society of tomorrow, with these valuable characteristics, the concept of metacognition should be included more in our education system.

Concept Maps

Concepts are meaningful expressions that symbolise a certain object, object or events that emerge under the influence of people's feelings, thoughts and ways of living, gain meaning with words, and form the basis of knowledge, which is the essence of life (Senemoglu, 1997; Erden & Akman, 1998; Ülgen, 1988, 1994). Concepts can be made more understandable through concept maps. Concept maps are concrete teaching materials that place concepts in a certain order after determining the key words of an event, a long subject, or a unit, and show the relationships between concepts with arrows (Kaymak, 2005). While concepts are abstract words for the individual, they are integrated with many words in concept maps and become graphic, and they help the subject to gain meaning by becoming concrete in the minds of students (Martin, 1994). Concept maps were used for the first time in history in the 1970s by the researcher Joseph Novak and his team of students graduated from Cornell University for a research project (Kaptan, 1998). Concept maps can generally be analysed in 3 groups (Ebenezer & Haggerty, 1999).

1. Hierarchical Concept Maps,
2. Non-Hierarchical Concept Maps,
3. Chain Concept Maps

The most important difference that distinguishes concept maps from mind maps is that the relationship between concepts must include one-word expressions written on the arrows. Determining the concepts to be used before making the map will prevent chaos in the process. After the main concept is determined and placed in the centre, the concepts related to this concept in the first degree can be put in place and then the sub-concepts that support these concepts can be used. In concept maps, the word placed in the centre is explained with other words and a visual concrete diagram is created. The concepts placed in the concept map can sometimes be supported by visuals. Since concept maps supported by visual elements enrich the learning environment, they enable the person doing the learning work to keep the concepts in mind more easily and facilitate the transfer to memory during the learning process. Due to its visual use, it can be easily used in all educational units from preschool to university before the lesson, during the teaching process or in the evaluation process (Novak & Gowin, 1984).

The main purpose of concept maps is to understand how the subject turns into a diagram in the mind of the person who prepares it, and how the relationships between concepts are related to each other. Thanks to concept maps, students see the subject as a whole rather than memorising the concept, and when they go into details, they learn the relationship between concepts in a meaningful way (Ivie, 1998). Another advantage of the concept map is that the student connects the concepts that he/she chooses and takes from the important points of the subject with the correct relationship he/she designs in his/her mind, not with imposed concepts and words. While preparing a concept map, the person making the map is actually quite free. After the concepts are determined, it can easily go beyond the classical concept map by adding visuals, videos, graphics, tables instead of words. These maps, which are also suitable for today's digital age, support meaningful learning and multiple intelligence. Concept maps show the teacher how words that are likely to be confused with each other correspond in the eyes of the student. Maps prepared with students in classrooms are student-centred and help to create an active learning environment where students can express themselves, easily ask questions and get answers. In addition, the attitude of the student who sees that the concepts and the relationship between them are supported by the teacher will change positively (Toper, 2002; Barut, 2006). Since concept maps are based on vocabulary knowledge, they also contribute to the development of the student's vocabulary.

METHOD

This study provides a comprehensive overview of concept maps and its necessity on education by using it via smarts boards, with a particular focus on some educational methodology and theories. Students will be able to access concept applications enriched with digital technologies. Design-based research method was applied in the design, development and production of concept maps enriched with digital technologies developed to provide multimedia learning in science and technology teaching.

Table 1. Questions

Can concept maps enriched with digital technologies be developed to provide multimedia learning in science and technology teaching?	
Which concept maps enriched with digital technologies developed to provide multimedia learning in science and technology teaching,	Applicable for grade level?
	Applicable for the unit?
	Applicable for the subject?
	Applicable for the outcome?

The study was carried out with a research design that combines teaching methods and techniques with designed teaching materials and activities and produces products that meet the teaching needs. The decisions taken for concept maps enriched with digital technologies developed to provide multimedia learning in science and technology teaching are as follows:

1. Concept maps enriched with digital technologies developed to provide multimedia learning in science and technology teaching should create different forms and be suitable for new form combinations each time.
2. Concept maps enriched with digital technologies developed to provide multimedia learning in science and technology teaching should be suitable for group work or individual work.
3. Concept maps enriched with digital technologies developed to provide multimedia learning in science and technology teaching should be suitable for arousing new curiosities.
4. Concept maps enriched with digital technologies developed to provide multimedia learning in science and technology teaching should provide students with gains about some of the subjects in the science and technology curriculum.

5. Concept maps enriched with digital technologies developed to provide multimedia learning in science and technology teaching should be used as course materials in science and technology courses.
6. Concept maps enriched with digital technologies developed to provide multimedia learning in science and technology teaching should be suitable for use in the classroom, lesson or at home.
7. Concept maps enriched with digital technologies developed to provide multimedia learning in science and technology teaching should provide students with the opportunity of compatible use.
8. Concept maps enriched with digital technologies developed to provide multimedia learning in science and technology teaching should be used repeatedly.

Data Collection Process Published studies, articles, master's and doctoral theses, pilot application reports, published articles of the results of the pilot application reports in the field of concept maps applications enriched with digital technologies developed to provide multimedia learning in science and technology teaching; MEB reports on the subject, educational kit sales sites, MEB curriculum and sample activities were examined.

Table 2. Assumptions and limitations

Within the scope of the research, concept maps enriched with digital technologies developed to provide multimedia learning in science and technology teaching; determined.	**Class level**
	Unit
	Subject
	Gain for the following
Concept maps enriched with digital technologies developed to provide multimedia learning in science and technology teaching include some of the topics covered in	The curriculum
	the textbook
Concept maps enriched with digital technologies developed to provide multimedia learning in science and technology teaching will be suitable for students'	Cognitive characteristics
	psychomotor characteristics
	affective characteristics

Within the scope of the research, the development of concept maps enriched with digital technologies prepared to provide multimedia learning in science and technology teaching was carried out in 5 stages according to the opinions of 4 experts (Table 3).

Table 3. Experts

Expertise	Mission
Prof. Dr.	Faculty Member
Dr	Faculty Member
Teacher	Science
Teacher	Information Technology

Phase 1: In order to provide multimedia learning in science and technology teaching, 3 concept maps enriched with digital technologies were designed. Opinions were taken from 2 experts (lecturers) about the concept maps and the concept maps were renewed according to the feedback.

Phase 2: Opinions and suggestions about concept maps were received from 1 teacher in the field of science education and 1 teacher in the field of information technologies.

Phase 3: In line with the opinions, the concept maps were renewed, and it was decided that the materials were ready.

Phase 4: Concept maps enriched with digital technologies that can be used to provide multimedia learning in science and technology teaching developed from Lucidchart Programme for application in secondary schools were prepared in 3 sets.

FINDINGS

Concept maps enriched with digital technologies developed to provide multimedia learning in science and technology teaching were tried to be designed to be used as course materials based on the science and technology curriculum determined by the Ministry of National Education. Concept maps enriched with digital technologies are not limited to science and technology courses. Applications can also support students in extracurricular science and technology education studies and individual studies. The "meta-cognitive knowledge, metacognitive experiences, cognitive goals and cognitive strategies" components of Flavell's (1979) metacognitive model were also taken into consideration in concept maps enriched with digital technologies developed to provide multimedia learning in science and technology teaching. A teacher's guide was also prepared for the valid and reliable use of 3 concept maps enriched with digital technologies developed according to this model in the teaching process. The manual is presented in the appendix. Concept maps enriched with digital technologies developed to provide multimedia learning in science and technology teaching were made with Lucidchart software.

1. ***Design Proposal:*** The first of the concept maps enriched with digital technologies developed to provide multimedia learning in science and technology teaching is proposed with the name "Blood" for the 6th grade level, Systems in Our Body Unit, Circulatory System Subject.
2. ***Design Proposal:*** The second of the concept maps enriched with digital technologies developed to provide multimedia learning in science and technology teaching is proposed for the 8th grade level, DNA and Genetic Code Unit, Heredity Topic with the name "Heredity"
3. ***Design Proposal:*** The third of the concept maps enriched with digital technologies developed to provide multimedia learning in science and technology teaching is proposed with the name "Solar Eclipse" for the 6th grade level, Solar System and Eclipses Unit - Solar Eclipse Topic.

Below are the images of the interface of 3 concept maps enriched with digital technologies (Figure 1, 2,3).

Figure 1. Blood

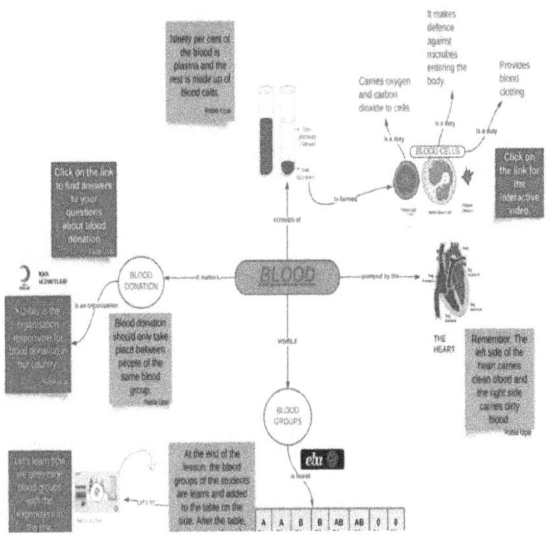

Figure 2. Heredity

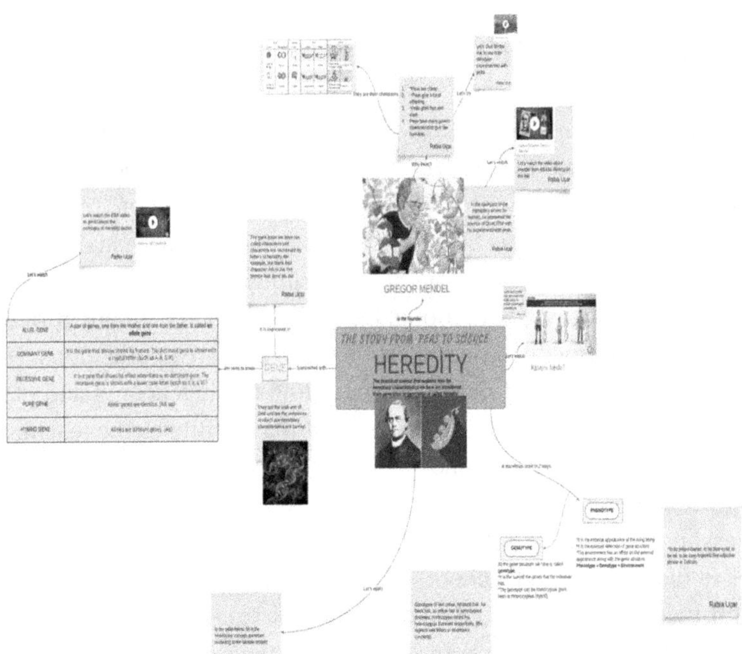

Figure 3. Solar eclipse

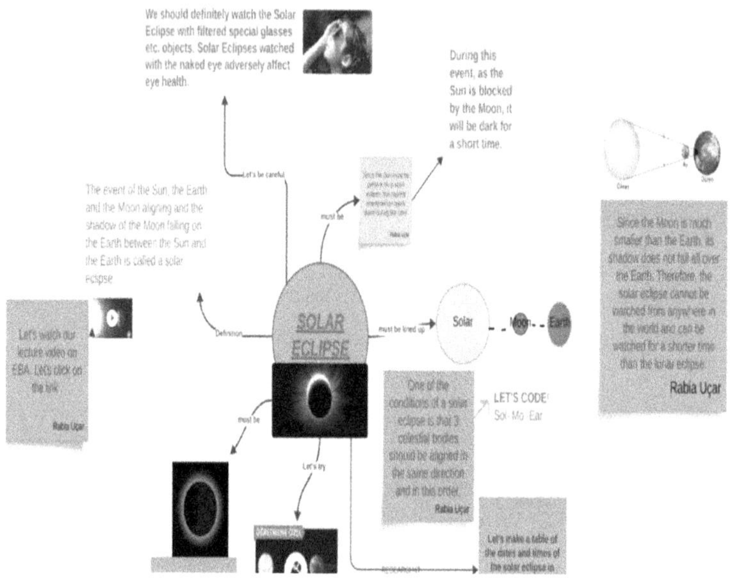

CONCLUSION AND DISCUSSION

In the 21st century, our students are faced with too many stimuli in daily life. The use of only textbooks in the classroom also causes the student to break away from the lesson. Science and technology are the branches of science that deal with abstract events, and these concrete representations can help students reduce their mental load. It has been observed in studies that visual representations have great importance in the description of abstract events in learning and teaching (Alkan & Altundağ, 2015; Yücel & Koçak, 2010). As of today, instructional technologies include many different members such as computers, video players, multimedia tools, smart boards, software applications. How and at what level instructional technologies will be used may vary according to the teaching and planning of the course. While some see instructional technologies as an element that facilitates the teaching of the lesson in the classroom and increases retention, some educators see these technologies as an innovative approach that takes the education and training process to another dimension (Ely, 1993). In both cases, the person who will use it in the lesson and start the interaction is the teacher. In order to increase the use of instructional technologies in the classroom, teachers should be ready to use technology and the process should be made suitable for the use of teachers (Becker, 1994; Christiansen, 2002; Hew & Brush, 2007). The issues to be considered in order to integrate instructional technologies into education and to increase the willingness of students and teachers to use these technologies are explained in the literature by Cradler (1993) as follows; factors such as students' needs, financial competences, attitudes towards technology, technical support and guidance studies for the use of technology are the points that should be arranged in advance for the use of instructional technologies (Adıgüzel, 2010).

In Turkey, many measures have been taken for the implementation of instructional technologies in classrooms (Yucel, 2006). One of the best examples of this is the Instructional Technology and Material Development (ITMD) course that prospective teachers take after the 5th semester of education faculties. In this course, it is aimed to teach both the use of technological tools in the lessons and to teach pre-service teachers to design technological teaching materials that they can use in their own lessons (Yapıcı & Karataş, 2006). Teachers who know how to use instructional technologies in lessons and how to design and use these applications will pave the way for technological transformations in education. In our world where technological developments are going further and further every day, directing our students to the correct use of technology, and using the integrated form of technology in our lessons are among the most important goals of contemporary societies that we want to catch. In classroom environments where multimedia is not used, the act of learning will remain limited and will not go beyond being a rote action. While the outside world sends multiple stimuli to our students and distracts their attention, it will not be easy to attract the attention of our students to the lesson in monotonous lessons. The first step to overcome this difficulty is to make our students experience the multiple learning environment by using it in our lessons as much as possible. For this reason, the study aimed to develop concept maps enriched with digital technologies in order to provide multimedia learning in science education. Concept maps are very important in the formation of schematic structures in the mind of the learner in making the words, which are very important in explaining scientific studies, meaningful and permanent. It is also possible to summarise large science and technology subjects easily and to place them easily in the mind with concept maps (Kendall, 1994). Therefore, it is important and necessary to use concept maps in science and technology teaching (Novak & Gowin, 1984). The increase of concepts in science will continue as long as science develops, even by expanding its meaning. Concept maps will be a successful guide in teaching concepts that do not contain narrow meanings to the students of the new generation and will not fit the classical expression. Concept maps are one of the most important tools to concretise the abstract concepts in science and technology sciences that seem to have no connection with real life and to strengthen the connection between them (Barenholz & Tamir, 199, Trowbridge & Wandersee, 1994). Since science and technology lesson is a process in which new discoveries are made, new generation enriched digital concept maps, which have the power of combining concepts, visuals and many other materials that enable this process to take place in the mind better, should take its place in science and technology teaching in order to strengthen the teacher-student relationship.

As a result of the research, concept maps enriched with digital technologies developed to provide multimedia learning in science and technology education.

- Firstly, "Blood" for the 6th grade level, Systems in Our Body Unit, Circulatory System Topic
- Secondly, 8th grade level, DNA and Genetic Code Unit, "Inheritance" for the topic of Inheritance.
- The third one was proposed for the 6th grade level, Solar System and Eclipses Unit - Solar Eclipse Topic with the name "Solar Eclipse".

Ausebel, who comes to mind when it comes to meaningful learning, stated that concept maps contribute to meaningful learning instead of students memorising concepts and that this contribution will also improve students' metacognitive thinking skills (Ivie, 1998). Novak also started from meaningful learning while developing concept maps, and as an alternative to the rote memorisation system, he brought us this technique that requires the learner to use his/her own mind. Since concept maps are the most important concrete outputs of how the concepts of the subject are synthesised in the mind and how personal skills in combining concepts emerge (Novak & Gowin, 1984; Kılıç & Sağlam, 2004), they are not a material that only the teacher can use. Concept maps prepared by students alone or in small groups can also be a guide for teachers (Şahin, 2001; Kaymak, 2005). Because maps are tools that show the student's strategy in determining the central concepts and the subconcepts that support these concepts. Thanks to this situation, important gains of the learning process such as misconceptions of the student, how much he/she has mastered the concepts of the subject, the accuracy of the relationship between the concepts can be easily measured and accurate feedback can be given to the student (Çetin & Sarıca, 2012). In some courses, joint concept maps can be prepared by student-teacher co-operation. This situation increases the student's interest and desire for the lesson and enables the creation of a meaningful learning environment more easily (Toper 2002; Barut, 2006). In addition, nowadays, concept maps take their place not only in learning but also in evaluation strategies due to these features. Since concept maps contain schemas from the mind of the person who prepared them, they also provide personalised evaluation and interpretation (Novak et.al, 1983).

REFERENCES

Adıgüzel, A. (2010). The Status of Instructional Technologies in Primary Schools and Classroom Teachers' Levels of Using These Technologies. *Dicle University Ziya Gökalp Education Faculty Journal*, (15), 1–17.

Akkoyunlu, B., & Yılmaz, M. (2005). Derivativist Multimedia Learning Theory. *Hacettepe University Journal of Faculty of Education*, 28, 9–18.

Aktürk, A. O., & Şahin, İ. (2011). Üstbiliş Ve Bilgisayar Öğretimi. *Selçuk Üniversitesi Ahmet Keleşoğlu Eğitim Fakültesi Dergisi*, 31, 383–407.

Aldağ, H.& Sezgin E. (2003). Dual Coding Theory and Cognitive Model in Multimedia Learning. *Çukurova University Journal of Institute of Social Sciences*, *11*(11).

Alexander, J. O. (1999). Colloborative design, constructivist learning, infor- mation technology immersion & electronic communities: A case study. *Interpersonal Computing and Technology: An Electronic Journal for the 21st Century*, *7*(1-2).

Alkan, F. & Altundağ (Koçak), C. (2015). the role of technology in science teaching activities: Web based teaching applications. *Journal for the Education of Gifted Young Scientists*, *3*(2),1-7.

Altundağ, C. (2023). *Teaching profession in the 100th year of the Republic, yesterday, today and tomorrow. Teacher training from the perspective of teaching 21st century skills in the 100th year of the Republic*. Nobel.

Baker, L., & Brown, A. L. (1980). Metacognitive skills and reading. In Pearson, P. D. (Ed.), *Handbook of Reading Research* (pp. 1–74). Longman.

Barenholz, H., & Tamir, P. (1992). A comprehensive use of concept mapping in design instruction and assesment. *Research in Science & Technological Education*, 10(1), 37–52. 10.1080/0263514920100104

Becker, H. J. (1994). How Exemplary Computer-Using Teachers Differ From Other Teachers: Implications For Realizing The Potential of Computers in Schools. *Journal of Research on Computing in Education*, 26(3), 291–321. 10.1080/08886504.1994.10782093

Beevevino, M. M., Dengel, J., & Adams, K. (1999). Costructivist Theory in The Classroom: Internalizing Concepts Through Inquiry Learning. *The Clearing House: A Journal of Educational Strategies, Issues and Ideas*, 72(5), 275–278. 10.1080/00098659909599406

Blakey, E., & Spence, S. (1990). *Developing metacognition*. Clearinghouse on Information Resources (ERIC Document Reproduction Service No. ED 327 218).

Brooks, G., & Books, M. G. (1993). *The case for constructivist classrooms*. ASCD Alexandria.

Brown, A. L. (1980). Metacognitive development and reading. In Spiro, R. J., Bruce, B. C., & Brewer, W. F. (Eds.), *Theoretical issues in reading comprehension* (pp. 453–481). Routledge.

Bülbül, A. H. (2019). *The Effect of Emotional Design in Multimedia Applications on Cognitive Load, Motivation, Subject Interest and Learning*. Anadolu University Graduate School of Educational Sciences.

Cakmak, E. K. (2007). Bottleneck in Multiple Environments: Cognitive Overload. *Gazi University Gazi Faculty of Education Journal*, 27(2), 1–24.

Callan, G. L., Marchant, G. J., Finch, W. H., & German, R. L. (2016). Metacognition, strategies, achievement, and demographics: Relationships across countries. *Educational Sciences: Theory & Practice*, 16, 1485–1502.

Christiensen, R. (2002). Effects of Technology Integration Education on the Attitudes of Teachers and Students. *Journal of Research on Technology in Education*, 34(4), 411–433. 10.1080/15391523.2002.10782359

De Jager, B., Jansen, M., & Reezigt, G. (2005). The development of metacognition in primary school learning environments. *School Effectiveness and School Improvement*, 16(2), 179–196. 10.1080/09243450500114181

Delil, A., & Güleş, S. (2007). Evaluation of Geometry and Measurement Learning Areas in the New Primary 6th Grade Mathematics Programme in terms of Constructivist Learning Approach. *Journal of Uludağ University Faculty of Education*, 20(1), 35.

Ellis, R. D., & Kurniawan, S. H. (2000). Increasing the usability of online information for older users: A case study in participatory design. *International Journal of Human-Computer Interaction*, 12(2), 263–276. 10.1207/S15327590IJHC1202_6

Ely, D. P. (1993). *The Field of Educational Technology: A Dozen Frequently Asked Questions*. ERIC Digest # ED366330.

Erdem, E., & Demirel, Ö. (2002). Constructivism Approach in Programme Development. *Hacettepe University Journal of Faculty of Education*, 23, 81–87.

Ferry, B., Herberg, S., & Harper, B. (1996). How Do Preserves Teachers Use Concept Maps to Organize Their Curriculum Concept Knowledge, *Research in Science Education*. *Cilt*, 26, 205–209.

Fisher, R. (1998). Thinking about thinking: Developing metacognition in children. *Early Child Development and Care*, 141(1), 1–15. 10.1080/0300443981410101

Flavell, J. H. (1976). Metacognitive aspects of problem solving. In Resnick, L. (Ed.), *The Nature of Intelligence* (pp. 231–236). Erlbaum.

Flavell, J. H. (1979). Metacognition and cognitive monitoring: A new area of cognitive–developmental inquiry. *The American Psychologist*, 34(10), 906–911. 10.1037/0003-066X.34.10.906

Forcier, C. R., & Descy, E. D. (2002). *The computer as an educational tool: productivity and problem solving*. Merrill Prentice Hall.

Greenlaw, R., & Hepp, E. (1999). *In-line / On-line: Fundamentals of the Internet and The World Wide Web*. McGraw-Hill.

Ivie, S. D. (1998). Ausubel's Learning Theory: An Approach To Teaching Higher Order Thinking Skills. (educational psychologist David Paul Ausubel). *High School Journal*, 82(1), 35.

Jimenez-Aleixandre, M. P. (2007). Designing argumentation learning enviroments. In Erduran, S., & Jimenez-Aleixandre, M. P. (Eds.), *Argumentation in Science Education: Perstectives from Classroom-Based Research* (pp. 3–27). Springer. 10.1007/978-1-4020-6670-2_5

Jonassen, D. H. (1994). Towards a Constructivist Design Model. *Educational Technology*, 34(4), 34–37.

Kalaycı, N., & Çakmak, M. (2000). Using Concept Maps in the Teaching Process. *Journal of Educational Administration in Theory and Practice.*, 24, 571–580.

Kalemkuş, J. (2021). Bilmeyi Bilme: Üstbiliş. *Atatürk Üniversitesi Kazım Karabekir Eğitim Fakültesi Dergisi*, (42), 471–495.

Kaptan, F. (1998). Using Concept Map Method in Science Teaching. *Hacettepe University Journal of Faculty of Education*, 14, 95–99.

Karadağ, E., Deniz, S., Korkmaz, T., & Deniz, G. (2008). Constructivist Learning Approach: A Research within the Scope of Classroom Teachers' Opinions. *Journal of Uludağ University Faculty of Education*, 21(2), 383–402.

Karataş, S., & Yapıcı, M. (2006). Öğretim Teknolojileri ve Materyal Geliştirme Dersinin İşlenişi ve Uygulama Örnekleri. *Afyon Kocatepe Üniversitesi Sosyal Bilimler Dergisi*, 8(2), 311–325.

Kaya, O. N. (2003). Concept Maps in Science Education. *Pamukkale University Journal of Faculty of Education*, 13, 70–79.

Kaymak, H. (2005). *The Effect of Concept Map Method on Students' Understanding of Periodic Table*. Pamukkale University Graduate School of Natural and Applied Sciences.

Klett, F. (2002). Visual communication in web-based learning environments. *Journal of Educational Technology & Society*, 5(4), 38–48.

Lever-Duffy, J., & McDonald, J. B. ve Mizell, A. P. (2003). *Teaching and Learning with Technology*. New York, USA: Allyn and Bacon.

Mayer, R. E. (2001). *Multimedia learning*. Cambridge University Press. 10.1017/CBO9781139164603

Mayer, R. E. (2009). *Multimedia Learning* (2nd ed.). Cambridge University Press. 10.1017/CBO9780511811678

Mene, J. M., & Mene, J. W. (1972). The relative efficiency of bimodal presentation as an aid to learning. *AV Communication Review*, 20(2), 170–180. 10.1007/BF02768415

Najjar, L. J. (1996). Multimedia information and learning. *Journal of Educational Multimedia and Hypermedia*, 5, 129–150.

Newby, T. J., Stepich, D. A., Lehman, J. D., & Rusell, J. D. (2000). *Instructional technology for teaching and learning desinging instruction, integrating computers and using media* (2nd ed.). Prentice-Hall Inc.

Nietfeld, J. L., Cao, L., & Osborne, J. W. (2005). Metacognitive motitoring accuracy and student performance in the postsecondary classroom. *Journal of Experimental Education*, 74(1), 7–28.

Novak, J. D. & ve Gowin, D. B. (1984). *Learning how to learn.* Newyork: Cambridge University Press.

Novak, J.D. (2010). Learning, creating, and using knowledge: Concept maps as facilitative tools in schools and corporations. *Journal of e-Learning and Knowledge Society*, *6*(3), 21-30.

Numanoğlu, G., & Şen, B. (2007). Learning Styles of Computer Education and Instructional Technology Department Students. *Journal of Ahi Evran University Kırşehir Faculty of Education*, 8(2), 129–148.

Özsoy, G. (2008). Üstbiliş. *Türk Eğitim Bilimleri Dergisi*, 6(4), 713–740.

Paas, F., Renkl, A., & Sweller, J. (2004). Cognitive load theory: Instructional implications of the interaction between information structures and cognitive architecture. *Instructional Science*, 32(1/2), 1–8. 10.1023/B:TRUC.0000021806.17516.d0

Pintrich, P. R. (2002). The role of metacognitive knowledge in learning, teaching and assessing. *Theory into Practice*, 41(4), 219–225. 10.1207/s15430421tip4104_3

Raupers, P. M. (2000). Effects of accommodating learning- style preferences on long-term retention of technology training content [Electronic Version]. *National Forum of Special Education Journal, 9E.*

Reeve, R. A., & Brown, A. L. (1985). Metacognition reconsidered: Implications for intervention research. *Journal of Abnormal Child Psychology*, 13(3), 343–356. 10.1007/BF009127214045006

Şahin, F. (2001). Prospective Teachers' Opinions on Making and Applying Concept Maps. *Pamukkale University Journal of Faculty of Education*, 10, 12–25.

Sarıca, R., & Çetin, B. (2012). The Effect of Using Concept Maps in Teaching on Students' Academic Achievement and Retention. *Primary Education Online Journal*, 11(2), 306–318.

Schoenfeld, A. H. (2016). Learning to think mathematically: Problem solving, metacognition, and sense-making in mathematics. *Journal of Education*, 196(2), 1–38. 10.1177/002205741619600202

Schraw, G., & Dennison, R. S. (1994). Assessing metacognitive awareness. Contemporary Educational Psychology, 19, 460-475.Schraw, G., & Moshman, D. (1995*). Metacognitive theories.Educational Psychology*, 7(4), 351–371.

Schwier, R. A. ve Misanchuk, E. R. (1994). *Interactive Multimedia Instruction*. Englewood Cliffs, New Jersey: Educational Technology Publications.

Shepherdson, E. (2001). *Teaching concepts utilizing active learning computer environments* [Doctoral dissertation, Massachusetts Institute of Technology].

Tenenbaum, G., Naidu, S., Jegede, O., & Austin, J. (2001). Constructivist pedagogy in conventional on-campus and distance learning practice: An exploratory investigation. *Learning and Instruction*, 11(2), 87–111. 10.1016/S0959-4752(00)00017-7

Trowbidge, J., & Ve Wandesee, J. (1994). Identifying Citical Junctures in Learning in a College Course on Evolution. *Journal of Research in Science Teaching*, 31(5), 459–473. 10.1002/tea.3660310504

Tsou, W., Wang, W., & Tzeng, Y. (2004). Applying a multimedia storytelling website in foreign language learning. *Computers & Education*, 47(1), 17–28. 10.1016/j.compedu.2004.08.013

Uğurlu, C. T. (2009). Primary School First Grade Teachers' Opinions on Constructivist Learning Approach and First Literacy Teaching. *Electronic Journal of Social Sciences*, 8(30), 103–114.

Vrugt, A., & Oort, F. J. (2008). Metacognition, achievement goals, study strategies and academic achievement: Pathways to achievement. *Metacognition and Learning*, 30(2), 123–146. 10.1007/s11409-008-9022-4

Wilson, B. G. (1995). *Maintaining the ties between learning theory and instructional design.*

Yucel, A. S. (2006). E-learning approach in teacher training. *Turkish Online Journal of Distance Education*, 7(4), 123–131.

Yücel, A. S., & Koçak, C. (2010). *Evaluation of the basic technology competency of the teacher's candidate according to the various variables. 2nd World Conference on Educational Sciences (WCES-2010)*, İstanbul, Turkey.

Yünkül, E. (2018). Learner Opinions on Multimedia Learning. *Balıkesir University Journal of Institute of Social Sciences*, 21(40), 255–269.

Yünkül, E. (2019). The Effect of Multimedia Learning Material on Academic Achievement and Retention Level. *Kastamonu Journal of Education*, 27(2), 727–736.

KEY TERMS AND DEFINITIONS

Blood: The red-coloured liquid circulating in our veins.

Concept: It is a variable that points to the common features of different objects and events or a group whose members are different.

Heredity: The science that explains how our genetic characteristics are transmitted from generation to generation.

Lucidchart Intelligent Diagramming: Lucidchart is a visual collaboration tool that makes drawing diagrams quick and easy.

ENDNOTE

1 Prepared from Hacettepe University Institute of Educational Sciences Graduate Project without Thesis.

Chapter 8
Navigating Education 5.0 Robotic Technique for Teaching Foreign Languages in Todays Classroom:
Unveiling the Potential of Virtual Pedagogical Agents

Muthmainnah Muthmainnah
Universitas Al Asyariah Mandar, Indonesia

Eka Apriani
IAIN, Curup, Indonesia

Abdul Gafur Marzuki
State Islamic University of Datokarama Palu, Indonesia

Ahmad Al Yakin
Universitas Al Asyariah Mandar, Indonesia

Nur Aeni
Universitas Negeri Makassar, Indonesia

Ali Sorayyaei Azar
https://orcid.org/0000-0003-3539-8250
Management and Science University, Malaysia

Mohd. Rafi Riyawi
https://orcid.org/0000-0001-7904-6084
STAI Hubbulwathan Duri, Indonesia

ABSTRACT

In the realm of Education 5.0, individuals investing in English language learner (ELL) educator training recognize the imperative to equip students with an understanding of the challenges and possibilities emerging from the integration of technology into the English language classroom. Offering a comprehensive overview, this chapter delineates the utilization of an educational robotics approach in EFL education and contemplates potential outcomes for students studying English education.

DOI: 10.4018/979-8-3693-3041-8.ch008

INTRODUCTION

Technological interventions in the teaching and learning process are increasingly preferred because they can be used to facilitate actual education. In the educational process, the use of technology turns out to have many benefits. Research shows that technology can improve students' academic performance, engagement, and independent learning (Kouser & Majid, 2021; Rosenbusch, 2020). Additionally, technology can help teachers improve the way they teach, reduce the cost of physical teaching materials, increase practice opportunities, and give students access to vast amounts of information. However, it is important to remember that technology must be used properly and teachers should not use it carelessly. Figuring out how to balance device use with traditional classroom interactions is also critical. It's also important to ensure that educational resources and online courses have a quality assurance system. The presence of technology places students in a more realistic learning environment, whether through media simulation or their real-life presence in an environment where the skills or knowledge are applied, which promotes retention and effective transfer of training. It is common knowledge that the development of computer robot technology can be a useful educational resource. Several studies (Hrastinski et al., 2019; Latif et al., 2023) have highlighted the potential of robotics to revolutionize teaching and learning in various situations, including in universities. According to (Al Omoush & Mehigan, 2023) the utilization of educational robots can enhance several student skills such as problem-solving, self-efficacy, creativity, teamwork and cooperative skills, and computational thinking.

Additionally, robots have been integrated into several fields, including language teaching. Teaching foreign languages with robot intervention is very effective in increasing motivation to learn languages that tend to be conventional and only reach the cognitive domain. A study of engagement in foreign language classes found that when robots were used in the classroom, students reported higher interaction-based conventional behavioral engagement and individual-based behavioral engagement (Guo et al., 2022). Studies have shown that due to internal factors related to one's culture and external factors related to the texture of the language, learning a foreign language can be challenging for students (Hadi, 2022). Cognitive linguistics can be useful in teaching and learning foreign languages. This can help in the creation of effective strategies, activities and educational materials (Wirag et al., 2022). A comprehensive analysis of the effects of foreign language learning on cognitive function in healthy adults found that foreign language learning improved or maintained cognitive abilities, regardless of age (Klimova & Pikhart, 2020). The use of models that incorporate robots in classroom activities is on the rise. Robots have made great progress in mastering foreign languages. (Vashisht et al., 2021) states that some of the causes of this phenomenon are increased awareness of the current and future importance of linguistic abilities, advances in speech recognition and text-to-speech (TTS) technology, the expansion of the field of commercial robotics, and advances in education. The study was conducted by (Al-Hakim et al., 2022; van den Berghe et al., 2018; Zhang & Zou, 2022) have demonstrated a significant correlation between early language development and later academic success. Additionally, there are advantages associated with acquiring second language proficiency regardless of age.

Social robotics interventions and human-robot interaction, or human-computer interaction (HCI), cover subfields that focus on robot-assisted learning or virtual robots. Although there are some overlapping goals between robots in teaching or teaching positions, such as the need for user acceptance, the desire for interpretable and safe interactions, and the building of relationships, robots are ultimately evaluated on their capacity to transfer knowledge playfully. Social robotics interventions have been studied as tools for teaching and learning. Social robots are pedagogical tools that can help students learn and demonstrate social aspects. They may serve as teachers, conversation partners, or tutors, providing individual attention in a way that can enhance a teacher's abilities in the overall classroom setting. Social robots can be used in lessons that require interaction with the real world, which is not possible with just a touch screen. They trigger more social behavior than screens, which helps learning. Studies of social robots in education have shown promising affective and cognitive outcomes. However, further field studies are needed to gain a further understanding of the possible use of social robots in the teaching and learning process and their benefits (Woo et al., 2021). Therefore, language and behavior must be designed with these domains in mind. Nonetheless, RALL considers the general findings of HCI and can build on previous research to inform new efforts.

The acquisition of a foreign language is intrinsically a social activity, making social robots a natural fit for the task (Konijn et al., 2022; Peura et al., 2023a; Zhang & Zou, 2022). It is more than just exposure to words; it is also about communicating meaning and carrying out social interactions that happen to use words to communicate in different and certainly interesting ways (Mezzenzana & Peluso, 2023; Urakami & Seaborn, 2023). Due to the embodiment of increasing the perception of agents as social partners, robots can become communication partners or practice foreign language communication either with the help of voice or chatting, which is very relevant compared to other technologies, especially because it can help students reduce anxiety and encourage their urge to learn (Almaiah et al., 2022; Feser et al., 2023). Many studies have been conducted regarding the use of RALL. Robots can be used to teach languages to humans, but the results vary depending on how the method is used. Robot-Assisted Language Learning (RALL) is a new field in language learning in which robots are used to teach native or non-native language skills, including sign language. Social robots have been developed to aid language learning, but their effectiveness as language teachers is still the subject of research. Previous research found that robots appeal to students and improve their performance, but previous research found that robots are not useful for teaching students native-like speaking skills. However, robots can play different roles in language learning situations, and more research is needed to determine how to use robots effectively in the language classroom (G. Huang & Moore, 2023). Because robots in RALL are usually meant to supplement or serve as learning media and technologies instead of replacing human teachers, they are often compared to 3D technologies like computers, smartphone tablets, and virtual agents to show what they can do. Some evidence suggests that robots can also assist undergraduate students in language production and task engagement in ways no other technology can. When used in conjunction with teacher training alone, they also appear to have a beneficial impact on self-esteem and anxiety (Psara & Christodoulidou, 2019) student motivation (Hong et al., 2014), and critical thinking skills (Muthmainnah et al., 2022). They do not appear to offer any significant benefit for vocabulary acquisition.

The objective of this study is to present a comprehensive overview of recent research discoveries about the use of robots in facilitating educational results. Additionally, this research aims to highlight specific components of the study that contribute to a more comprehensive comprehension of these findings.

THEORETICAL FRAMEWORK

From CALL to RALL in Foreign Language Teaching

Additionally, the CALL framework (Computer-assisted Foreign Language Learning) emphasizes the value of interaction in general (Dimulescu & Nechifor, 2022). As a result, while developing call-based lessons, researchers and content producers are beginning to consider it. Consequently, scientists working in the CALL sector began utilizing technologies associated with computation. Language learners can interact with technology through language in a variety of ways, such as chatbots (Klímová & Ibna Seraj, 2023), machine reading comprehension (Lin et al., 2023), and social robots (Pentina et al., 2023; Rudolph et al., 2023). These developments in technology hold considerable promise for using media to effectively engage language learners.

The presence of social robots is designed to interact and communicate with people (Fox & Gambino, 2021) by imitating typical human interactions using words, gestures, and facial expressions. The term social robot is quite evocative of the subject. First, the term social defines a certain category of robots. That is, social robots do not function like the common robots used to assemble cars in factories because of their ability to interact with humans. Second, animated characters or avatars are created for limited interaction with people via a computer screen, whereas robot refers to real robots that are in the same physical place as humans. Social robots have been extensively used for educational reasons, including language acquisition.

The utilization of robots for language acquisition is deemed more advantageous compared to software-based Computer-assisted Language acquisition (CALL) due to the potential for physical interactions facilitated by the robots. According to (Pennington & Rogerson-Revell, 2019; Tanaka et al., 2014; Wu et al., 2015), there is a consensus that the emphasis on the learner's physical environment in the context of language acquisition is a distinguishing characteristic of RALL. Other benefits of RALL are argued (Pennington & Rogerson-Revell, 2019) including repeatability, adaptability, humanoid appearance, and the ability to express emotions. (Geçkin, 2023) supports and claims that robots can facilitate L2 acquisition and looks at how robots can be used in the classroom to complement traditional teaching methods. Based on the findings of this experiment, we can conclude that robots can help students learn languages more efficiently than traditional exercises. (Ahtinen & Kaipainen, 2020) propose that robots can assume the roles of teachers or peers and engage in corresponding interactions throughout the presentation of educational content. This is due to the tendency of students to anthropomorphize robots, attributing human-like qualities to them based on their humanoid or animal-like appearance, as well as their verbal and non-verbal conduct.

RALL contains extensive documentation of the robot's vocabulary-teaching capabilities and the increase in vocabulary (Saud et al., 2022) in writing found by (Khang et al., 2023) showed students working in child-robot pairs stimulated greater learning compared to child-robot pairs, further proving the efficacy of robots in learning. It may come as no surprise to hear that robots can help students expand their vocabulary. The more interesting question is how well robots do this task compared to other technologies. Besides that, (Zinina et al., 2023) found that robots are as effective as iPads and even human teachers in teaching basic languages. Another scholar found that children prefer learning and interacting with robots to iPads and human teachers although this may be due to the novelty of the situation. Robots and computers were both found to increase productivity and English performance (Chiang et al., 2023).

Overall speaking skills, as measured by (Ersoy & Güneyli, 2016) as a combination of pronunciation, grammar, vocabulary, and communicative abilities, improved significantly when students used the robot for conversation practice. In addition, it was determined that robots were more successful than computers in improving language skills (Lynch et al., 2023). There may be more to learn from robots than just letting students talk to each other (Aeni et al., 2023).

Furthermore, the effect of RALL on grammar is known, although not much research has been done on how robots affect language use. One study to uncover these results found that the students' grammar skills had greatly improved (Aeni et al., 2023; Nacher et al., 2016). Gains are made by students at all levels of language study. However, it is not yet known how well the robot performs compared to other technologies in this regard. Along with improving vocabulary and grammar, RALL also improves pronunciation, which is only indirectly measured in a small number of RALL investigations carried out by Lee et al., which found considerable advantages in students' pronunciation (Belpaeme et al., 2018; Kennedy et al., 2017). (Peura et al., 2023b) also found that students improved their pronunciation to be understood by robot or virtual robot speech recognition modules. This applies to students of all skill levels.

Virtual Robots as Virtual Pedagogical Agents in English Education

For many years, virtual educators have been employed to offer instruction. A great deal of research has been done on the use of social robots in the classroom, with comparable positive outcomes anticipated for students (Khang et al., 2023). The use of social robots in educational settings is becoming more and more common, even though there have only been a few studies done in this field in the past (Zinina et al., 2023). One such survey focused on long-term human-robot interaction (HRI). Robotic social interaction improves human learning's cognitive and affective results (Hong et al., 2016; Zinina et al., 2023). Numerous investigations (Aeni et al., 2023; Nacher et al., 2016) have discovered that human-robot interactions are impacted by this tendency. While some robots aren't social and can teach children about technology, our review mostly focuses on robots made to enhance education through human-robot interaction.

The justification for incorporating robots in educational environments lies in the fact that virtual agents, which can be accessed through laptops, tablets, or smartphones, possess comparable capabilities to physical robots. This alternative approach eliminates the need for extra expenses on hardware, maintenance, and distribution, while also providing flexible accessibility and convenient installation. Physically embodied robots have three advantages over virtual agents: (1) they can be used in contexts where students need to interact with the real world; (2) students exhibit more pro-learning social behaviors when interacting with physical robots; and (3) students learn more when interacting with physical robots than with virtual agents.

In addition, (Tafazoli & and Gómez-Parra, 2017) have been recommended as potential recipients of robotic assistance. Utilizing robot tutors provides the advantages of consistency, adaptability, and scalability, while virtual tutors offer a simulated yet immersive environment to hone interview skills. However, it is important to recognize that implementing such technology comes with its own set of challenges, including ethical considerations, technological proficiency, and user acceptance.

There are various studies that have shown that educational robots, such as friendly robots, have made significant contributions to the topic of English. English According to lio et al., (2020), the use of Robovie has been proven to increase Japanese students' English-speaking skill. Alemi (2015) found that interacting with objects such as smart toys and robots facilitates the development of vocabulary. As stated by

Pandey et al., (2022) the Nao robot is a humanoid robot widely used in teaching as aid for acquire foreign language in the classroom. The study conducted by Louie, et al. 2021), say that second-ranked robots like Dragonbot have more functional diversity, which could lead to the development of zoomorphic and animal-like features in the game RALL. These social robots are considered more profitable, reliable, enlightening, and fun to interact with, thereby improving the learning environment in the 21st century.

A study conducted in Greece, found that students' motivation and learning outcomes increased significantly when they collaborated with a self-developed robot. This conclusion was reached through a comprehensive analysis of quantitative and qualitative data (Pampaliari, et al., 2023). Similarly, Huang and Moore (2023) conducted research on this topic The integration of robot in the formulation of design decisions for useful objects, tools, systems., interfaces, or software programmes has been shown to positively impact users for comprehensive language teaching robots that have proficiency in all four language skills, namely listening, speaking, reading, and writing, are still lacking. Despite its practical limitations, RALL has presented a variety of prospective approaches to transforming language teaching and acquisition, particularly in the context of Mandarin as a second language. Achieving a positive attitude among students towards robots is the desired outcome of RALL research, as this research aims to develop reliable robotic agents that improve students' mastery of foreign languages and increase the quality and diversity of their classroom activities.

According to Yang. (2021), educational programs that incorporate robotics encourage the utilisation of certain mental talents and focus, thereby improving cognitive function and influencing cognitive processes. In addition, there is often a correlation between logical thinking and creative thinking. González and Ramírez (2022) distinguish between educational robot activities, which focus on precise and formal solutions, and interdisciplinary activities, which emphasise collaborative approaches and cooperation, thus requiring cooperative problem-solving. According to Fakaruddin, et., (2024), the use of educational robots has the potential to significantly improve the learning environment for students and teachers, fostering an engaging atmosphere that effectively improves cognitive and creative skills. One of the advantages of utilising robot-environment interactions in educational settings is the rapid feedback students receive on their work and computationa thinking Akinci et al., (2024), and Pellas, (2024) . This allows students to revise their work and reflect on their actions.

Significant progress has been made since the birth of social robots. The technological advances available to researchers today significantly surpass those of the early pioneers in robotics. The use of learning robotics has increased significantly over the previous decade.

An increasing number of companies are producing commercial robots designed specifically for educational purposes. Recently, the world of education has reached a consensus that the integration of robots in classrooms must include all students and work together with teachers. Although most current educational interventions fail to meet these criteria, we strive to achieve this goal Al Yakin et al., (2024).

Research on adult Mandarin learners' engagement with online representation is somewhat scarce compared with research on robots Nomoto et al., (2022) and Wang (2024). The practical experiments carried out in this research regarding vocabulary learning formed the basis of the research. The group of ten students was divided into two different groups: one group collaborated with a tangible robot, while the other group collaborated with an instructor. In each group, three different modes of interaction were carried out in the presence of an instructor, namely translation, quizzes, and chat. According to Wang et al. (2024), the group exposed to physical agents showed reduced levels of demotivation and increased levels of engagement. Additionally, it also suggests other possible directions for RALL studies, including the feasibility of developing robots that can aid language acquisition and involving language instructors in the design stage.

METHOD

The utilized research methodology is a quantitative approach employing a pre-experimental study design, as outlined by (Klimova & Pikhart, 2020), the research strategy employed in this study is a quantitative approach aimed at examining the impact of a treatment on a specific group, without the inclusion of a control group. In this study, the pre-test instrument will be used, the treatment will use a virtual robot with certain learning steps, and the post-test will be administered. In addition, questionnaires and Likert scale observations will be used to collect data, as will data analysis using SPSS version 26 software. The chosen research design is pre-experimental, namely a research design carried out without a control group, so it is more suitable for use in conditions where controlling external variables that affect behavior is difficult. In this study, a pre-experimental research design will be used to measure the impact of treatment using virtual robots on the variable English skills of undergraduate students.

Research Participants

Participants in this study were students from an educational institution with a population of 350 people. The samples taken were from 24 undergraduate students who were purposefully selected based on certain criteria. The sample selection criteria were students enrolled in a class that uses virtual robots as a medium and technology for learning English in the 2022–2023 academic year, namely undergraduate students from the faculty of computer science of the informatics system study program.

Research Instruments

In this study, the following instruments will be used:

- The pretest instrument will be used before being given treatment to measure the variables studied at the beginning of the study. This test is a test of English skills by asking undergraduate students to answer the questions given, namely a multiple-choice test of 20 questions using the Quizalize application.

Figure 1. Pretest using Quizalize apps

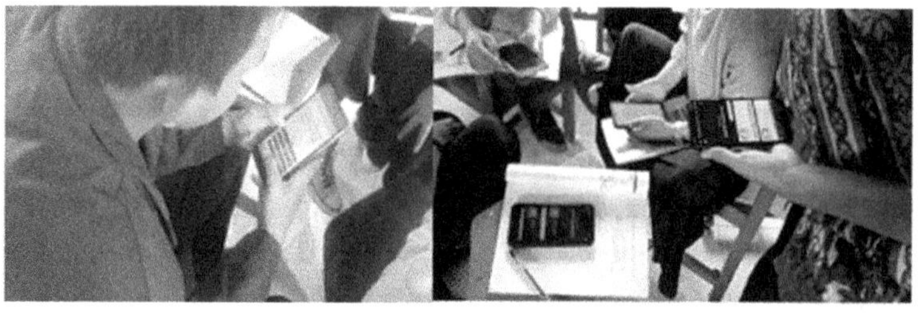

- Treatment using virtual robots. Virtual robots will be used as a treatment in this study. The learning steps include: (1) an introduction to virtual robots and how to operate them; (2) an explanation of learning objectives using virtual robots; and (3) a demonstration of the use of virtual robots. My virtual dream friends in learning contexts (d) Independent practice by research subjects using virtual robots; (e) Discussions, questions, and answers related to the subject's experiences using virtual robots.

Figure 2. Treatment with virtual robots (observation)

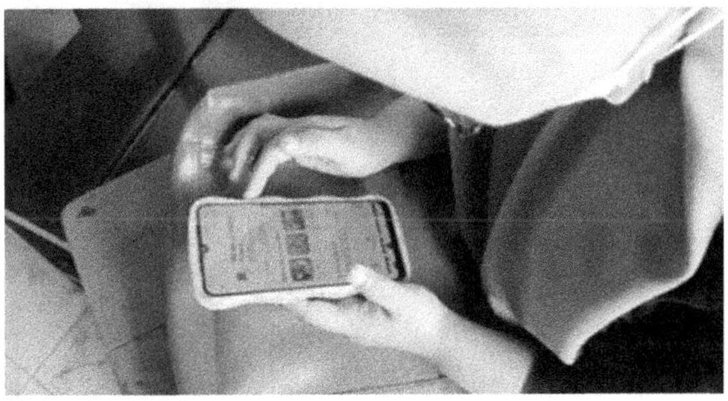

Figure 3. Students' performance after interaction with the robot

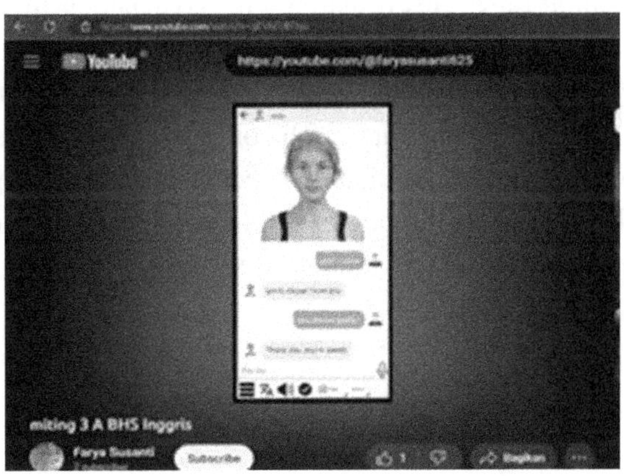

- Post-test. The post-test instrument will be used after being given treatment to measure changes that occur in the variables studied.

Figure 4. Post-test with Quizalize apps

Data Analysis

The data processing technique used in this study was carried out after all the data had been collected (Bogdan & Bilken, 1992). Data processing begins with analyzing all the data obtained from the results of student work. After carrying out the test, the next activity is correcting student work and assessing it by calculating the number of scores obtained by students from the pre-test and post-test results.

The data obtained from the pre-test, post-test, Likert scale questionnaire, and observation will be subjected to analysis using the statistical program SPSS version 26. Data analysis involves the use of calculating descriptive statistics such as standard deviation, median, and mean to indicate the characteristics of the data. Using a paired t-test, this research will test whether there is a statistically significant difference between the pre-test and post-test results. Hypothesis testing will be used. Frequency analysis, calculation of average scores, and hypothesis testing using the t test or ANOVA test will be carried out on data obtained from the Likert scale questionnaire. The purpose of this statistical analysis is to determine whether there are significant statistical differences between the various groups studied. This research aims to find out how effective the use of virtual robots is in learning. This was done using pre-experimental quantitative research methods and follow-up data analysis using SPSS version 26.

RESULTS AND DISCUSSION

Result

The Students' Pre-Test and Post-Test Score

Table 1. The pretest and post-post-test score

One-Sample Statistics				
	N	Mean	Std. Deviation	Std. Error Mean
Pretest	24	61.0417	9.08644	1.85476
Post-test	24	86.8750	4.12113	.84122

The data acquired from the pre-and post-tests was analyzed using the Statistical Package for the Social Sciences (SPSS) in this study. A pre-test is given to students before they start interacting with virtual robots. Table 3 describes the mean (average) value of students in this pre-test as 61.04. After the students receive the treatment (interact with the virtual robot), a post-test is given to measure their performance again. The average score of students in the post-test was 86.87.

Based on the provided data, it can be observed from Table 3 that the mean post-test score (86.87) surpasses the mean pre-test score (61.04). This elucidates how the performance of the typical student exhibits improvement after engaging with the virtual robot. The increase in the average score shows that the treatment, which in this case uses virtual robots in the English class, has a positive impact on students' English skills. Higher post-test scores imply that students learn and improve because of treatment. The findings of this study indicate a statistically significant improvement in the mean scores of students on the post-test in comparison to the pre-test after they engage with the RALL virtual robot during their English instructional sessions. The results showed that implementing this intervention had a positive effect on children's language abilities. These findings underscore the significance of ascertaining the statistical significance of the observed rise in score. This entails conducting a statistical analysis, such as a t-test, to evaluate whether the disparity in means is more plausibly attributable to the therapy rather than mere random variation.

Table 2. One sample t-test

One-Sample Test						
	Test Value = 0					
	t	df	Sig. (2-tailed)	Mean Difference	95% Confidence Interval of the Difference	
					Lower	Upper
Pretest	32.911	23	.000	61.04167	57.2048	64.8785
Postest	103.272	23	.000	86.87500	85.1348	88.6152

A one-sample t-test was conducted to compare the means of two different time points—pre-test and post-test—for the RALL variable. The results are presented in Table 4. The test results are the difference in test scores: for the pre-test, the average difference is 61.04167, and for the post-test, it is 86.87500. 95% confidence interval of difference This interval provides the range within which the actual difference in population means tends to fall with 95% confidence. For the pre-test, the confidence intervals were between 57.2048 and 64.8785, and for the post-test, between 85.1348 and 88.6152.

The p-values (sig. 2-tailed) for the pre-test and post-test were very close to 0 (specifically, 0.000), indicating that the differences in observed means were highly unlikely to have been due to chance alone. Typically, this outcome results in the null hypothesis being rejected, thereby signifying a substantial disparity between the means of the pre-test and post-test. Based on the available data, there is a notable disparity between the average scores obtained in the pre-test and post-test assessments. The post-test average exhibits a substantial increase, which can be attributed to the implementation of Reading and Language Learning (RALL) techniques inside the English classroom.

These results highlight the potential of the virtual robot as an effective tool for enhancing language learning experiences within the context of the RALL approach.

Discussion

The findings mentioned above can be discussed by considering the results of the pre-test and post-test as well as the survey results regarding the use of RALL in English classes, which were obtained from the results of the questionnaire. The results of statistical data show that the distribution between pre-test and post-test results in learning sessions using RALL affects their English ranking, and there are still differences in the accumulation of preference scores for the completion group (Table 3). In summary, we found that virtual-based RALL engagement is more suitable for English language teaching overall, and the use of virtual-based RALL generally has many benefits. First, virtual classrooms allow students to participate in real-time and access content whenever they want, which can increase student motivation and engagement. Additionally, virtual classrooms allow for flexibility, personalized learning opportunities, and automatic exercise creation, which can be beneficial for English language teaching. Virtual-based RALL engagement can be a suitable and effective method for English language teaching. This is even though traditional teaching may be effective for some specific subjects. Therefore, it is important to consider the learner's situation and needs when selecting the best engagement strategy. Researchers also found that there was a significant difference between pre-test and post-test learning outcomes. This shows that robot interaction strategies must be adapted to the appropriate teaching model, combining learning materials or content with the robot application that will be used.

Compared to previous research at RALL, we found that students felt more comfortable, more involved, and more motivated to practice with robots compared to teachers and human friends, but the assistance of robot practice turned out to provide comfort in discussing before practicing with humans. friends in class Figure 2 that they are interested in learning because it can help improve understanding of grammar, vocabulary, writing, and reading, as well as increase confidence in dialogue and sharing personal details with robotic friends Figure 3. Unlike other studies, this one involved a collaborative arrangement with four undergraduate students in a team (Figure 3). The use of robots in language learning has been proven to have several benefits, such as increasing student motivation and comfort. Research studies have shown that interactions between robots and humans not only increase teaching effectiveness but also increase students' motivation to learn as students become happier and less anxious (Hong et al., 2016). Motivation is also considered to be one of the most important components that influences the success and speed of learning a foreign language. Even though robots in language learning have shown positive results, it is important to consider the costs and difficulties associated with implementing such technology in educational settings.

When faced with challenges involving robots, we discovered that students depended on one another to get over them, beginning with the act of downloading, using, or generating words for their English speech. How to use robots as effective media and technology to step in and reduce the need for teachers to repeat and explain the information. This circumstance highlights how crucial it is to have a cooperative setting for practice English classes that include peer support via robots. More realistic figures must be incorporated into the appearance and behavior of robots intended to serve as educational tools for the latter. We concluded that using My Virtual Dream Friends to practice realistic discussions with L2 learners is appropriate. When engaging with others, it is important to employ more non-verbal cues, such as eye contact, glances, blinking, and visual-emotional presentation.

Combining elements from the perceptual, social, and cognitive dimensions, the learning robot setting has the potential to accommodate a variety of learner preferences during language acquisition in foreign language classes. This research shows that collaboration between robots and humans has different benefits than one-on-one interactions with robots that don't involve interaction with other robots. This is shown through an analysis of previous interactions and collaborations, (Saud et al., 2022). This interaction still involves the teacher controlling virtual robot-based classroom management, who benefits from the learner-lecturer-robot interaction. Collaborative efforts so that undergraduate students actively practice English and understand robots work better by building learner speech that is accessed by chat and voice applications during learning. This study is an example of RALL's potential to overcome the challenges of learning English, which are generally not liked by undergraduate students; they still think that English is a boring and uninteresting subject to follow and only teaches grammar. Linguistic barriers and technical limitations faced by students with the help of robots can be overcome with this teaching model.

The six sessions with the robot were successful in improving the cognitive, affective, and psychomotor skills of undergraduate students. However, this study does not cover all tenses; it only focuses on present, past, and future tenses. Grammatically, undergraduate students still found errors when interacting and mistakes in pronunciation, accuracy, and fluency when performing orally in front of the class. Even so, they still practice and are passionate about correcting mistakes that occur. A study shows that students make common grammatical errors when speaking English. These include the use of articles, question formation, plural noun forms, subject-verb agreement, and tenses (Ting et al., 2010). Automated pronunciation assessment tools can also help students improve their fluency and speaking skills by providing feedback on their pronunciation and encouraging them to do repeated pronunciation practice. To learn a language, it is also important to strike the right balance between clarity and precision. Fluency is the ability to speak fluently and confidently, regardless of mistakes, while accuracy refers to the correctness and correctness of language use, including pronunciation, grammar, and vocabulary. For effective communication, accuracy, and fluency are both important. Language learners should also see mistakes as opportunities to grow and learn (Ting et al., 2010). As a result, the use of robots in language learning can help improve grammatical accuracy and fluency.

In addition, this study shows that students who are involved in their learning are proven to increase test scores (Table 3), in line with (Chen Hsieh & Lee, 2023). However, our research found no relationship between how much a person invests in their activity or the robot and how much vocabulary, pronunciation, accuracy, and fluency they learn. Studies show that students can remember and acquire English vocabulary taught by robot tutors the same as that taught via tablet applications (Kanero et al., 2021). Other studies have looked at the use of robots in language learning for activities such as dialogic reading, vocabulary training, and digital storytelling. They found that robots helped in terms of teaching effectiveness, incentives for learning, and story outcomes (Hsieh & Lee, 2021)(Kory Westlund et al., 2017)(Hsu et al., 2023). However, it is unclear whether the use of robots will be effective for more complex language skills beyond vocabulary learning tasks. Learning outcomes can also be influenced by differences in a person's attitudes toward robots, anxiety in L2 learning, and personality characteristics (van den Berghe et al., 2021). Although the use of AI in education can make learning environments more engaging and increase student motivation, the use of robots for learning English may be ineffective due to complexity, cost, and pre-programmed interaction scenarios. When speaking, the practice still finds pronunciation errors and a lack of fluency. Because the My Virtual Dream Friends application in this study currently does not have a visual recognition system, an automatic speech recognition system, or a system for correcting dialogue or errors made by undergraduate students to help them communicate fluently in English, every second language learner will need a system for correcting dialogue or errors.

The increased interest and motivation of undergraduate students in assignments or robots is not only translated into acquiring grammatical vocabulary. The desire to correct mistakes, the awareness of mistakes in English, and the confidence in applying English in various situations are quite good. Consistent with previous research on improving English skills by interacting with robots, we found that the effect of HRI on learning appears to be very significant. The use of robots in language learning has been proven to have several benefits, such as increasing student motivation and comfort. Research studies have shown that interactions between robots and humans not only increase teaching effectiveness but also increase students' motivation to learn as students become happier and less anxious. Motivation is also considered to be one of the most important components that influences the success and speed of learning a foreign language. Even though robots in language learning have shown positive results, it is important to consider the costs and difficulties associated with implementing such technology in educational settings (Alnwairan et al., 2023; Y.-T. Huang et al., 2018; Vân & Hien, 2022). Additionally, it is proven that the use of inquiry and a personalized teaching approach contributes to increasing students' ability and confidence in English. Analysis of students' grammatical errors in spoken English has also shown that a good command of grammar is essential for communicating well (Hartanto, 2022). The results show that to support students' desire to correct mistakes and build confidence in using English, personalized teaching, feedback, and tailored approaches are essential.

The results of this research support how robots affect our cognitive, social, and emotional processes. It is shown that robot-assisted learning content aims to improve students' cognitive functions and has considerable potential to improve the emotional abilities necessary for learning (Ван, 2022). To get started, choose a robot application that can be downloaded via the Play Store and is free; the virtual robot must have an anthropomorphic appearance; the robot's voice must sound as human as possible; and the robot must be easy to operate. Since the robot's ability to perform in a variety of social roles has been shown to have a beneficial effect on the enjoyment of learning, playing the role of a peer or tutor is suggested. This is because the function of a teacher is generally seen as being unable to manage practical time in class, while students perceive the importance of communication practice. Meanwhile, robots accompany undergraduate students as they become more actively involved in expressing themselves. Undergraduate students are more confident in the role of robots in peer or tutor positions. Designing teaching materials and connecting with robots is very important, requiring teacher creativity by presenting challenging assignments that must also be adapted to each learner and change as their skills develop. Based on a short-term, single-session study with a small number of participants, this study has not yet evaluated the effectiveness of robots in facilitating language acquisition or having a lasting impact on cognitive filters. This study still needs to conduct a different type of evaluation.

CONCLUSION

The study's findings demonstrate that RALL provides important advantages for learning English that other technology-based language teaching approaches like CALL, Mobile-assisted Language Learning (MALL), and CMC do not. Nonetheless, these advantages could result in notable enhancements in undergraduate students exposed to HRI's learning outcomes. An additional advantage that shows promise is the embodied potential of robots to interact with students and classrooms, particularly in light of the growing demand for consistency and reliability in language learning robots. According to the questionnaire's results, learning motivation, engagement, and interest in learning English were all higher during the HRI intervention in the English course than they were before the use of RALL.

Students can participate in role-playing dialogues thanks to the integration of robotic devices, which offers a realistic and immersive language learning environment. Through this simulation, students' practical ability can be improved by bridging the gap between classroom instruction and language use in everyday situations.

ACKNOWLEDGMENTS

The researchers would like to extend their sincerest appreciation to the rector of Al Asyariah Mandar University and the rector of Makassar State University for their unwavering support during the entire process of planning, executing, and finalizing this research endeavor. We would like to extend our utmost gratitude to our colleagues who have made significant contributions to our scientific endeavor.

REFERENCES

Ван, Ш. (2022). Students' Cognitive And Cognitive Activity In The Process Of Learning A Foreign Language Using Learning Robots. *Вестник Тверского Государственного Университета. Серия: Педагогика и Психология*. https://api.semanticscholar.org/CorpusID:253616374

Aeni, N., & Nadya Nurhidayah, N. Hasriani, Ammade, S., & Dewi, A. C. (2023). How online learning materials developed: Need analysis in developing online materials for zoom platform teaching. *AIP Conference Proceedings, 2510*(1), 30043. 10.1063/5.0128844

Ahtinen, A., & Kaipainen, K. (2020). Learning and Teaching Experiences with a Persuasive Social Robot in Primary School – Findings and Implications from a 4-Month Field Study. *Lecture Notes in Computer Science (Including Subseries Lecture Notes in Artificial Intelligence and Lecture Notes in Bioinformatics), 12064 LNCS*, 73–84. Springer. 10.1007/978-3-030-45712-9_6

Akinci, M., Burak, M., Kasal, F. Z., Özaslan, E. A., Huri, M., & Kurtaran, Z. A. (2024). The Effects of Combined Virtual Reality Exercises and Robot Assisted Gait Training on Cognitive Functions, Daily Living Activities, and Quality of Life in High Functioning Individuals With Subacute Stroke. *Perceptual and Motor Skills*, 131(3), 00315125241235420. 10.1177/00315125241235420384l8444

Al Hakim, V. G., Yang, S.-H., Liyanawatta, M., Wang, J.-H., & Chen, G.-D. (2022). Robots in situated learning classrooms with immediate feedback mechanisms to improve students' learning performance. *Computers & Education*, 182, 104483. 10.1016/j.compedu.2022.104483

Al Omoush, M. H., & Mehigan, T. (2023). Leveraging Robotics to Enhance Accessibility and Engagement in Mathematics Education for Vision-Impaired Students. *HORA 2023 - 2023 5th International Congress on Human-Computer Interaction, Optimization and Robotic Applications, Proceedings*. IEEE. 10.1109/HORA58378.2023.10156748

Al Yakin, A., Khang, A., & Mukit, A. (2023). Personalized social-collaborative iot-symbiotic platforms in smart education ecosystem. In *Smart Cities* (pp. 204–230). CRC Press.

Alemi, M., Meghdari, A., & Ghazisaedy, M. (2015). The impact of social robotics on L2 learners' anxiety and attitude in English vocabulary acquisition. *International Journal of Social Robotics*, 7(4), 523–535. 10.1007/s12369-015-0286-y

Almaiah, M. A., Alfaisal, R., Salloum, S. A., Hajjej, F., Thabit, S., El-Qirem, F. A., Lutfi, A., Alrawad, M., Al Mulhem, A., Alkhdour, T., Awad, A. B., & Al-Maroof, R. S. (2022). Examining the Impact of Artificial Intelligence and Social and Computer Anxiety in E-Learning Settings: Students' Perceptions at the University Level. *Electronics (Basel)*, 11(22), 1–22. 10.3390/electronics11223662

Alnwairan, M., Al Harthy, S. R., Darwish, A. S., & Yacoub, M. A. (2023). To Correct or Not to Correct: The Impact of Written Corrective Feedback on Improving Students' Writing about Literature. *World Journal of English Language*. https://api.semanticscholar.org/CorpusID:260999444

Belpaeme, T., Vogt, P., van den Berghe, R., Bergmann, K., Göksun, T., de Haas, M., Kanero, J., Kennedy, J., Küntay, A. C., Oudgenoeg-Paz, O., Papadopoulos, F., Schodde, T., Verhagen, J., Wallbridge, C. D., Willemsen, B., de Wit, J., Geçkin, V., Hoffmann, L., Kopp, S., & Pandey, A. K. (2018). Guidelines for Designing Social Robots as Second Language Tutors. *International Journal of Social Robotics*, 10(3), 325–341. 10.1007/s12369-018-0467-630996752

Bogdan, B., & Bilken, S. K. (1992). Quality research for education: An introduction to theory and methods. *Qualitative Research For Education An Introduction to Theory and Methods : Allyn and Bacon.*, 106–156.

Chen Hsieh, J., & Lee, J. S. (2023). Digital storytelling outcomes, emotions, grit, and perceptions among EFL middle school learners: Robot-assisted versus PowerPoint-assisted presentations. *Computer Assisted Language Learning*, 36(5–6), 1088–1115. 10.1080/09588221.2021.1969410

Chiang, Y. hui V., Cheng, Y. W., & Chen, N. S. (2023). Improving Language Learning Activity Design through Identifying Learning Difficulties in a Platform Using Educational Robots and IoTbased Tangible Objects. *Journal of Educational Technology & Society*, 26(3), 84–100. 10.30191/ETS.202307_26(3).0007

Dimulescu, C., & Nechifor, A. (2022). Accommodating English for Specific Purposes to Computer Assisted Language Learning. *Bulletin of the Transilvania University of Brasov. Series IV: Philology and Cultural Studies, 14*(2), 5–18. 10.31926/but.pcs.2021.63.14.2.1

Ersoy, M., & Güneyli, A. (2016). Social networking as a tool for lifelong learning with orthopedically impaired learners. *Journal of Educational Technology & Society*, 19(1), 41–52.

Fakaruddin, F. J., Shahali, E. H. M., & Saat, R. M. (2024). Creative thinking patterns in primary school students' hands-on science activities involving robotic as learning tools. *Asia Pacific Education Review*, 25(1), 171–186. 10.1007/s12564-023-09825-5

Feser, M. S., Haak, I., & Rabe, T. (2023). *VeSP-Be – Vergleich von Studieneingangsphasen in Physik hinsichtlich des Sense of Belonging von Studierenden. Dokumentation der Erhebungsinstrumente und deren deskriptive, quantitative Ergebnisse. 9*. https://doi.org/10.25656/01

Fox, J., & Gambino, A. (2021). Relationship Development with Humanoid Social Robots: Applying Interpersonal Theories to Human-Robot Interaction. *Cyberpsychology, Behavior, and Social Networking*, 24(5), 294–299. 10.1089/cyber.2020.018133434097

Geçkin, V. (2023). Assessing the Learning Outcomes of Robot-Assisted Second Language Learning. In *Handbook of Research on Perspectives in Foreign Language Assessment* (p. 18). IGI Global. 10.4018/978-1-6684-5660-6.ch005

González-Pérez, L. I., & Ramírez-Montoya, M. S. (2022). Components of Education 4.0 in 21st century skills frameworks: Systematic review. *Sustainability (Basel)*, 14(3), 1493. 10.3390/su14031493

Guo, Y., Xu, J., & Chen, C. (2022). Measurement of engagement in the foreign language classroom and its effect on language achievement: the case of Chinese college EFL students. *International Review of Applied Linguistics in Language Teaching, 0*. https://api.semanticscholar.org/CorpusID:246362278

Hadi, S. A. (2022). Foreign Language Learning in Light of Cognitive Learning Theory. *Journal of English Language Teaching and Applied Linguistics*. https://api.semanticscholar.org/CorpusID:253755264

Hartanto, B. (2022). Grammatical Errors in English Study Made by UIB Students. *Issues in Applied Linguistics & Language Teaching*. https://api.semanticscholar.org/CorpusID:258850624

Hong, Z.-W., Chen, Y.-L., & Lan, C.-H. (2014). A courseware to script animated pedagogical agents in instructional material for elementary students in English education. *Computer Assisted Language Learning*, 27(5), 379–394. 10.1080/09588221.2012.733712

Hong, Z.-W., Huang, Y.-M., Hsu, M., & Shen, W.-W. (2016). Authoring Robot-Assisted Instructional Materials for Improving Learning Performance and Motivation in EFL Classrooms. *Journal of Educational Technology & Society*, 19, 337–349. https://api.semanticscholar.org/CorpusID:17667686

Hrastinski, S., Olofsson, A. D., Arkenback, C., Ekström, S., Ericsson, E., Fransson, G., Jaldemark, J., Ryberg, T., Öberg, L.-M., Fuentes, A., Gustafsson, U., Humble, N., Mozelius, P., Sundgren, M., & Utterberg, M. (2019). Critical Imaginaries and Reflections on Artificial Intelligence and Robots in Postdigital K-12 Education. *Postdigital Science and Education*, 1(2), 427–445. 10.1007/s42438-019-00046-x

Hsieh, J. C., & Lee, J. S. (2021). Digital storytelling outcomes, emotions, grit, and perceptions among EFL middle school learners: Robot-assisted versus PowerPoint-assisted presentations. *Computer Assisted Language Learning*, 36(5-6), 1088–1115. https://api.semanticscholar.org/CorpusID:239683847. 10.1080/09588221.2021.1969410

Hsu, T.-C., Chang, C., & Liang, Y. S. (2023). Sequential Behavior Analysis of Interdisciplinary Activities in Computational Thinking and EFL Learning With Game-Based Learning. *IEEE Transactions on Learning Technologies*, 16(2), 256–265. https://api.semanticscholar.org/CorpusID:257320094. 10.1109/TLT.2023.3249749

Huang, G., & Moore, R. K. (2023). Using social robots for language learning: Are we there yet? *Journal of China Computer-Assisted Language Learning*, 3(1), 208–230. 10.1515/jccall-2023-001338013743

Huang, Y.-T., Chen, M. C., & Sun, Y. S. (2018). *Development and Evaluation of a Personalized Computer-aided Question Generation for English Learners to Improve Proficiency and Correct Mistakes*. http://arxiv.org/abs/1808.09732

Iio, T., Maeda, R., Ogawa, K., Yoshikawa, Y., Ishiguro, H., Suzuki, K., Aoki, T., Maesaki, M., & Hama, M. (2019). Improvement of Japanese adults' English speaking skills via experiences speaking to a robot. *Journal of Computer Assisted Learning*, 35(2), 228–245. 10.1111/jcal.12325

Kanero, J., Oranç, C., Koskulu, S., Kumkale, G. T., Göksun, T., & Küntay, A. C. (2021). Are Tutor Robots for Everyone? The Influence of Attitudes, Anxiety, and Personality on Robot-Led Language Learning. *International Journal of Social Robotics*, 14(2), 297–312. https://api.semanticscholar.org/CorpusID:235543442. 10.1007/s12369-021-00789-3

Kennedy, J., Lemaignan, S., Montassier, C., Lavalade, P., Irfan, B., Papadopoulos, F., Senft, E., & Belpaeme, T. (2017). Child Speech Recognition in Human-Robot Interaction: Evaluations and Recommendations. *ACM/IEEE International Conference on Human-Robot Interaction, Part F1271*, (pp. 82–90). IEEE. 10.1145/2909824.3020229

Khang, A., Muthmainnah, M., Seraj, P. M. I., Al Yakin, A., & Obaid, A. J. (2023). AI-aided teaching model in education 5.0. *Handbook of Research on AI-Based Technologies and Applications in the Era of the Metaverse*. IGI Global. 10.4018/978-1-6684-8851-5.ch004

Klímová, B., & Ibna Seraj, P. M. (2023). The use of chatbots in university EFL settings: Research trends and pedagogical implications. In *Frontiers in Psychology, 14.*https://www.frontiersin.org/articles/10.3389/fpsyg.2023.1131506

Klimova, B., & Pikhart, M. (2020). Current Research on the Impact of Foreign Language Learning Among Healthy Seniors on Their Cognitive Functions From a Positive Psychology Perspective-A Systematic Review. In *Frontiers in psychology* (*Vol. 11,* p. 765). 10.3389/fpsyg.2020.00765

Konijn, E. A., Jansen, B., Mondaca Bustos, V., Hobbelink, V. L. N. F., & Preciado Vanegas, D. (2022). Social Robots for (Second) Language Learning in (Migrant) Primary School Children. *International Journal of Social Robotics*, 14(3), 827–843. 10.1007/s12369-021-00824-3

Kory Westlund, J. M., Jeong, S., Park, H. W., Ronfard, S., Adhikari, A., Harris, P. L., Desteno, D., & Breazeal, C. L. (2017). Flat vs. Expressive storytelling: Young children's learning and retention of a social robot's narrative. *Frontiers in Human Neuroscience*, 11(June), 1–20. 10.3389/fnhum.2017.0029528638330

Kouser, S., & Majid, I. (2021). Technological Tools for Enhancing Teaching and Learning Process. *Towards Excellence*, (March), 366–373. 10.37867/TE130133

Latif, E., Mai, G., Nyaaba, M., Wu, X., Liu, N., Lu, G., Li, S., Liu, T., & Zhai, X. (2023). *Artificial General Intelligence (AGI) for Education*. 1–30. http://arxiv.org/abs/2304.12479

Lin, C. C., Huang, A. Y. Q., & Yang, S. J. H. (2023). A Review of AI-Driven Conversational Chatbots Implementation Methodologies and Challenges (1999–2022). *Sustainability (Basel)*, 15(5), 4012. 10.3390/su15054012

Louie, B., Björling, E. A., & Kuo, A. C. (2021, August). The desire for social robots to support English language learners: Exploring robot perceptions of teachers, parents, and students. [). Frontiers Media SA.]. *Frontiers in Education*, 6, 566909. 10.3389/feduc.2021.566909

Lynch, C., Wahid, A., Tompson, J., Ding, T., Betker, J., Baruch, R., Armstrong, T., & Florence, P. (2023). Interactive Language: Talking to Robots in Real Time. *IEEE Robotics and Automation Letters*. 10.1109/LRA.2023.3295255

Mezzenzana, F., & Peluso, D. (2023). Conversations on Empathy. In *Conversations on Empathy*. 10.4324/9781003189978

Muthmainnah, I. S., Ibna Seraj, P. M., & Oteir, I. (2022). P. M., & Oteir, I. (2022). Playing with AI to Investigate Human-Computer Interaction Technology and Improving Critical Thinking Skills to Pursue 21st Century Age. *Education Research International*, 6468995, 1–17. 10.1155/2022/6468995

Nacher, V., Garcia-Sanjuan, F., & Jaen, J. (2016). Interactive technologies for preschool game-based instruction: Experiences and future challenges. *Entertainment Computing*, 17, 19–29. 10.1016/j.entcom.2016.07.001

Nomoto, M., Lustig, A., Cossovich, R., & Hargis, J. (2022, May). Qilin, a robot-assisted Chinese language learning bilingual chatbot. In *Proceedings of the 4th international conference on modern educational technology* (pp. 13-19). ACM. 10.1145/3543407.3543410

Pampaliari, S., Panagiotidis, P., & Sapounidis, T. (2023). Robot Assisted Language Learning: Application Of Educational Activities With Duckycode Robot In The English Classroom. In *ICERI2023 Proceedings* (pp. 2413-2421). IATED.

Pandey, D., Subedi, A., & Mishra, D. (2022, January). Improving language skills and encouraging reading habits in primary education: A Pilot Study using NAO Robot. In *2022 IEEE/SICE International Symposium on System Integration (SII)* (pp. 827-832). IEEE. 10.1109/SII52469.2022.9708843

Pellas, N. (2024). Assessing Computational Thinking, Motivation, and Grit of Undergraduate Students Using Educational Robots. *Journal of Educational Computing Research*, 62(2), 620–644. 10.1177/07356331231210946

Pennington, M. C., & Rogerson-Revell, P. (2019). Using Technology for Pronunciation Teaching, Learning, and Assessment BT. M. C. Pennington & P. Rogerson-Revell (eds.) *English Pronunciation Teaching and Research: Contemporary Perspectives*. Palgrave Macmillan UK. 10.1057/978-1-137-47677-7_5

Pentina, I., Hancock, T., & Xie, T. (2023). Exploring relationship development with social chatbots: A mixed-method study of replika. *Computers in Human Behavior, 140*. 10.1016/j.chb.2022.107600

Peura, L., Mutta, M., & Johansson, M. (2023b). Playing with Pronunciation. *Nordic Journal of Digital Literacy*, 18(2), 100–115. 10.18261/njdl.18.2.3

Psara, E., & Christodoulidou, C. (2019). ROBOTICS IN LANGUAGE LEARNING: AN EXPLORATORY STUDY USING THE BEE-BOT. *13th International Technology, Education and Development Conference*, 8675–8682.

Rosenbusch, K. (2020). Technology Intervention: Rethinking the Role of Education and Faculty in the Transformative Digital Environment. *Advances in Developing Human Resources*, 22(1), 87–101. 10.1177/1523422319886297

Rudolph, J., Tan, S., & Tan, S. (2023). War of the chatbots: Bard, Bing Chat, ChatGPT, Ernie and beyond. The new AI gold rush and its impact on higher education. *Journal of Applied Learning and Teaching*, 6(1), 364–389. 10.37074/jalt.2023.6.1.23

Saud, S., Aeni, N., & Azizah, L. (2022). Leveraging Bamboozles and Quizziz to Engage EFL Students in Online Classes. *International Journal of Language Education*, 6(2), 169–182. 10.26858/ijole.v6i2.24301

Tafazoli, D., & Gómez-Parra, M. E. (2017). Robot-Assisted Language Learning: Artificial Intelligence in Second Language Acquisition. In *Current and Future Developments in Artificial Intelligence* (Issue August). 10.2174/9781681085029117010015

Tanaka, F., Takahashi, T., Matsuzoe, S., Tazawa, N., & Morita, M. (2014). Telepresence robot helps children in communicating with teachers who speak a different language. *ACM/IEEE International Conference on Human-Robot Interaction*, (pp. 399–406). IEEE. 10.1145/2559636.2559654

Ting, S. H., Mahadhir, M., & Chang, S. L. (2010). Grammatical errors in spoken English of university students in oral communication course. *GEMA Online Journal of Language Studies*, 10(1), 53–69.

Urakami, J., & Seaborn, K. (2023). Nonverbal Cues in Human-Robot Interaction: A Communication Studies Perspective. *ACM Transactions on Human-Robot Interaction*, 12(2), 1–21. Advance online publication. 10.1145/3570169

Vân, N. T., & Hien, D. T. (2022). *DESIGN ACTIVITIES TO CORRECT PRONUNCIATION ERRORS IN /n/ SOUND AND /l/ SOUND FOR FIRST-YEAR ENGLISH MAJORS TRƯ NG Đ I H C SƯ PH M THÁI NGUYÊN*. Semantic Scholar. https://api.semanticscholar.org/CorpusID:251211852

van den Berghe, R., Oudgenoeg-Paz, O., Verhagen, J., Brouwer, S., de Haas, M., de Wit, J., Willemsen, B., Vogt, P., Krahmer, E., & Leseman, P. (2021). Individual Differences in Children's (Language) Learning Skills Moderate Effects of Robot-Assisted Second Language Learning. *Frontiers in Robotics and AI*, 8(August), 1–14. 10.3389/frobt.2021.67624834504871

van den Berghe, R., Verhagen, J., Oudgenoeg-Paz, O., van der Ven, S., & Leseman, P. (2018). Social Robots for Language Learning: A Review. *Review of Educational Research*, 89(2), 259–295. 10.3102/0034654318821286

Vashisht, V., Pandey, A. K., & Yadav, S. P. (2021). Speech recognition using machine learning. *IEIE Transactions on Smart Processing and Computing*, 10(3), 233–239. 10.5573/IEIESPC.2021.10.3.233

Wang, H. (2024). *The Design and Evaluation of Intelligent Computer-Assisted Language Learning Tools for Beginner Learners of Mandarin Chinese* [Doctoral dissertation, Trinity College, Dublin].

Wang, J., Zhang, X., & Zhang, L. J. (2022). Effects of Teacher Engagement on Students' Achievement in an Online English as a Foreign Language Classroom: The Mediating Role of Autonomous Motivation and Positive Emotions. *Frontiers in Psychology*, 13(July), 950652. 10.3389/fpsyg.2022.95065235846620

Wang, Z., Lv, J., Hou, Y., & Song, D. (2024). Enhancing experience: Investigating the impact of different personal perspectives in virtual reality with lower limb rehabilitation robots on participants' motivation, experience, and engagement. *International Journal of Industrial Ergonomics*, 99, 103496. 10.1016/j.ergon.2023.103496

Wirag, A., Li, Y., & Zhang, B. (2022). Applying cognitive linguistics to foreign language teaching and learning. *Cognitive Linguistic Studies*. https://api.semanticscholar.org/CorpusID:253870887

Woo, H., LeTendre, G. K., Pham-Shouse, T., & Xiong, Y. (2021). The use of social robots in classrooms: A review of field-based studies. *Educational Research Review*, 33, 100388. 10.1016/j.edurev.2021.100388

Wu, W.-C. V., Wang, R.-J., & Chen, N.-S. (2015). Instructional design using an in-house built teaching assistant robot to enhance elementary school English-as-a-foreign-language learning. *Interactive Learning Environments*, 23(6), 696–714. 10.1080/10494820.2013.792844

Yang, Y. (2021). The talent training mode of international service design using a human–computer interaction intelligent service robot from the perspective of cognitive psychology. *Frontiers in Psychology*, 12, 600218. 10.3389/fpsyg.2021.60021833603699

Zhang, R., & Zou, D. (2022). Types, purposes, and effectiveness of state-of-the-art technologies for second and foreign language learning. *Computer Assisted Language Learning*, 35(4), 696–742. 10.1080/09588221.2020.1744666

Zinina, A., Kotov, A., Arinkin, N., & Zaidelman, L. (2023). Learning a foreign language vocabulary with a companion robot. *Cognitive Systems Research*, 77, 110–114. 10.1016/j.cogsys.2022.10.007

Chapter 9
STEMvolution:
Mastering English Language Confidence With Blended Learning in Education

Soumya Sankar Ghosh
https://orcid.org/0000-0002-4469-4070
VIT Bhopal University, India

ABSTRACT

This research assesses the effectiveness of Blended Learning (BL) in reducing English-speaking anxiety among STEM students. Language anxiety hinders engagement and knowledge acquisition in STEM, where English proficiency is crucial. The BL program combines traditional methods with digital resources to enhance language proficiency and confidence. The study uses a mixed-methods approach, measuring anxiety and performance, followed by a tailored behavior change intervention. Results show a significant reduction in anxiety levels, and a strong link between enhanced linguistic confidence and academic success in STEM. BL is identified as a valuable tool connecting language competency to academic excellence in STEM, with implications for educators, institutions, and policymakers. Further research is needed for a comprehensive understanding of its lasting impact.

INTRODUCTION

In the context of our present-day interconnected world, the fields of Science, Technology, Engineering, and Mathematics (STEM) have assumed a crucial role in fostering innovation, facilitating economic development, and promoting general social growth. The interdependence among nations and the swift dissemination of information have heightened the importance of these fields, placing them at the forefront of creating our shared destiny. Within this particular environment, the level of expertise in the English language, often acknowledged as the global means of communication, has gained increased significance for persons involved in STEM disciplines. The aforementioned phenomenon may be attributed to the global character of research cooperation, the widespread distribution of scientific discoveries, and the

DOI: 10.4018/979-8-3693-3041-8.ch009

imperative need for efficient communication across many language contexts. English, which is widely acknowledged as the lingua franca within the global scientific community, functions as the primary means by which researchers hailing from various cultural and linguistic backgrounds disseminate their innovative discoveries, engage in the interchange of ideas, and cultivate cooperative endeavors. The presence of interconnection enables scientists and academics to collectively combine their skills, leading to expedited advancements and inventions that beyond national boundaries. The UNESCO Science Report (2021) highlights that English has the predominant position as the primary language utilized for academic publication, including a substantial share of scientific papers worldwide. The paper emphasizes the need for English proficiency for researchers to actively participate in and get advantages from the continuously developing global scientific environment. Nevertheless, in this context, a significant obstacle emerges - the occurrence of nervousness related to speaking in English. The phenomenon of experiencing psychological distress and discomfort while utilizing a language that is not one's native tongue, especially in verbal interactions, can have a profound effect on individuals, especially those who are engaged in the pursuit of education and professional endeavors in the domains of science, technology, engineering, and mathematics (STEM). Within this group, persons who do not have English as their first language frequently have this difficulty. This anxiety may present itself through a range of manifestations, including increased heart rate, cognitive disruption, avoidance tendencies, and the experience of unpleasant emotions such as self-doubt. In educational settings, where the cultivation of efficient communication, active involvement, and collaborative engagement is of utmost importance, the presence of language anxiety might pose obstacles that impede the acquisition of skills and competencies crucial for achieving success.

In the given situation, an individual who is not a native English speaker is undertaking a STEM education path, necessitating active participation in dynamic conversations, collaborative team projects, and English-language presentations within an academic setting. The apprehension experienced by individuals around potential linguistic blunders or misinterpretations might lead to their reluctance to engage in debates or express their perspectives openly. Engaging in such behavior hampers one's educational journey and deprives fellow students and teachers of valuable insights and various viewpoints that foster a comprehensive and inclusive learning atmosphere. Moreover, within a pragmatic context, such as a controlled environment like a laboratory or a collaborative research team, where effective communication and precise directives are of utmost importance, the presence of language anxiety can result in misinterpretations, mistakes, and compromised results. The consequences of anxiety related to English language proficiency extend beyond the ordinary difficulties encountered in communicating. Within the realm of STEM education, where the proficiency to communicate complex ideas, articulate hypotheses, and construct persuasive arguments has great significance, the presence of linguistic impediments created by anxiety can undermine one's self-assurance and hinder intellectual development. The study done by vHakim (2019) revealed that students who experience language anxiety tend to avoid situations that need English language skills, resulting in reduced involvement and restricted engagement with academic tasks. The aforementioned phenomenon might potentially trigger a chain reaction, since diminished levels of active participation result in a decline in understanding, hence impeding the whole process of acquiring knowledge.

As a result, the issue of reducing anxiety related to English language proficiency has emerged as a critical factor in the endeavor to enhance the effectiveness of STEM education. Equipping students with the necessary resources to address language anxiety helps cultivate an inclusive atmosphere, whereby individuals hailing from various linguistic origins can actively participate in the educational journey and harness their inherent capabilities. Blended learning approaches, characterized by the integration of conventional classroom techniques with digital materials and interactive platforms, present a potentially effective means of alleviating language anxiety. These methodologies offer students the chance to interact with the subject matter of the course at their preferred speed, obtain specific language assistance, and progressively develop their self-assurance in utilizing English for academic and professional objectives.

The main objective of this study is to:

- Evaluate the extent of English-speaking anxiety experienced by students in the STEM fields.
- This study aims to implement a blended learning intervention and assess its efficacy in mitigating anxiety levels.
- Examine the relationship between decreased anxiety levels and enhanced performance in STEM fields.

To accomplish these aims, the current work will investigate the following research inquiries:

1. What is the extent of English-speaking anxiety experienced by students in STEM fields?
2. What is the impact of the blended learning intervention on students' levels of language anxiety?
3. To what degree does the decrease in language anxiety lead to improved performance in STEM fields?

THEORETICAL FRAMEWORK AND IDENTIFYING THE GAPS: ENGLISH LANGUAGE ANXIETY IN EDUCATION

Foreign Language Anxiety (FLA) stands as a complex phenomenon, intricately woven with an individual's self-perceptions, beliefs, emotions, and behaviors within the dynamic environment of language learning in a classroom setting (Horwitz et al., 1986). In essence, FLA is not generic anxiety experienced in various situations but is uniquely tailored to the challenges posed by the language learning process (Maclntyre, 1999; Teimouri et al., 2019). At the core of FLA research is the Foreign Language Classroom Anxiety Scale (FLCAS), a pivotal instrument crafted by Horwitz et al., (1986), offering researchers a standardized approach to delve into the intricate dynamics of FLA (Horwitz et al., 1986). Numerous studies leveraging the FLCAS have consistently highlighted a negative correlation between FLA and language achievement, underscoring the profound impact of anxiety on language learning outcomes (Maclntyre & Gardner, 1991; Phillips, 1992; Aida, 1994; Saito & Samimy, 1996; Cheng et al., 1999; Liu & Xiangming, 2019). As researchers strive to understand the roots of FLA, they grapple with the intricate question of why individuals experience anxiety in language learning settings (Young, 1991; Liu, 2006; Yan & Horwitz, 2008). Furthermore, the exploration extends to the relationship between FLA and a myriad of learning variables (Oteir & Al-Otaibi, 2019). These variables encompass a vast spectrum, including willingness to communicate, learning style, self-efficacy, self-confidence, self-esteem, learning autonomy, learning strategies, motivation, learner beliefs, and personality traits. The experience of anxiety in the foreign language learning process triggers a cascade of worry and negative emotional reactions. However, the intricacies of how FLA exerts its detrimental influence on language learning and performance remain a topic of ongoing exploration. Krashen's influential affective filter hypothesis (Krashen 1982) suggests that an active affective filter might screen out input information, preventing it from reaching learners' cognitive processes. FLA, in this context, may act as the activator, impeding students' comprehension of the language input. Researchers, in their pursuit of understanding FLA's impact, have observed interference with learners' cognitive processes at various stages, spanning input, processing, and output (MacIntyre, 1995; Shao et al., 2013).

In both language classes and interpretation classes at universities, students often find themselves required to perform in a foreign language, even when their language skills are still in the developmental stages (Yan et al., 2010). Interpretation classes, in particular, present an intriguing intersection with language learning, with Simultaneous Interpretation (SI) emerging as a recognized tool for enhancing English as a Foreign Language (EFL) proficiency (Yagi, 2000; Cao, 2023). The relationship between foreign language teaching and interpretation training is dynamic and mutually beneficial (Zannirato, 2008). The significance of interpretation classes in language learning is noteworthy. Students, despite their evolving language skills, are thrust into an environment demanding performance in a foreign language (Yan et al., 2010). The intricate interplay between language learning and interpretation classes becomes evident in the utilization of simultaneous interpretation (SI) as a tool for EFL teaching (Yagi, 2000; Cao 2023). Research findings affirm that SI not only contributes significantly to oral English fluency but also effectively assesses grammar and vocabulary abilities (Yagi, 2000). This dynamic interaction between language learning and interpretation training underscores the multifaceted nature of language acquisition, where skills developed in one domain synergistically enhance performance in another.

As we navigate the intricate landscape of FLA research, it becomes evident that anxiety in language learning is not a monolithic experience but a complex interplay of individual perceptions, cognitive processes, and performance outcomes. Studies have explored this intricate web by investigating FLA's relationship with various learning variables, revealing connections with factors such as willingness to communicate, learning style, self-efficacy, and motivation (Kalsoom et al.,2020; Zhou et al., 2020). The exploration expands to encompass aspects like self-esteem, learning autonomy, learning strategies, learner beliefs, and even personality traits (Abdurahman & Rizgi, 2020; Demir & Zaimoglu 2021; Šafranj & Ziylak 2019; Cao 2023). Moreover, the acknowledgment of the symbiotic relationship between language teaching and interpretation training emphasizes the need for a holistic approach to language education, where different aspects of language learning complement and enhance one another. This multifaceted nature of language acquisition sets the stage for exploring similar challenges that students may encounter in STEM education, particularly in environments where English proficiency is crucial for comprehension and participation.

In the context of India, a country characterized by its multilingualism, the phenomenon of language anxiety assumes a unique and notable aspect. The presence of several languages inside a nation frequently overlaps with the use of English as the medium of teaching in higher education, resulting in a distinctive educational environment. The use of English as a primary language for educational purposes has the potential to intensify feelings of language anxiety, particularly among pupils whose native language is distinct from English. According to a study report (Puranik, 2015) published in the Hindustan Times, it was found that a significant majority of engineering graduates in the nation, specifically 97%, lack proficiency in the English language. The poll was performed by Aspiring Minds, which considered a sample size of over 30,000 students from 500 engineering institutions nationwide. Based on the study findings, a significant proportion of individuals, namely over 51%, are considered to have inadequate employability prospects as a result of their competence levels in spoken English. Moreover, among the annual cohort of 600,000 engineering graduates, a scant 2.9% demonstrate proficiency in spoken English. The study highlighted pronunciation and fluency as major impediments to attaining proficient oral skills in the English language. A mere 6.8% of engineers can engage in spontaneous speech or provide immediate responses. The aforementioned applicants possess the ability to communicate with fluency, exhibiting proficient pronunciation and employing appropriate sentence structure. The study conducted by Mehdi & Kumar (2019), highlights the significance of language anxiety within the context of Indian engineering students. The research conducted by the authors provides a comprehensive understanding of the impact of language anxiety on students' active engagement in classroom discussions, resulting in a reduced propensity to ask questions and contribute ideas. The inhibition in question is a result of apprehension around the potential occurrence of language faults and the subsequent unfavorable perception by both peers and teachers. The aforementioned dynamics underscore the intricate interplay between language anxiety and STEM education in the Indian set- ting, where the convergence of linguistic variety and intellectual endeavors is evident. The mentioned study rightly justifies Christopher's (2022) observation, which points out that out of the annual cohort of 10 million students doing high school final examinations in India, 65% of these students originate from educational institutions where English is not the primary medium of instruction. The inclusion of English in the higher study presents an added difficulty for students, which may prove to be insurmountable for certain individuals. As a result, this situation leads to a considerable annual attrition rate among students at prestigious educational institutions. The impact of the language barrier is most evident among underprivileged communities, when the proportion of individuals discontinuing their education may escalate to as much as 60%. In several instances, the distressing consequences of such circumstances have tragically resulted in students resorting to suicide, as evidenced by accounts published in reputable sources such as the reports of The New Indian Express (2013) and Times of India (2012).

To counter this, India is currently experiencing a notable increase in the adoption of "mother tongue" education, whereby classes are being conducted in regional languages such as Hindi, Bengali, Gujarati, and other non-English languages. Large educational technology companies that traditionally focused on serving affluent English-speaking individuals are increasingly adapting their services to meet the growing need for non-English language learning. This adaptation includes the translation of question banks and lectures, allowing these companies to capitalize on this expanding market. However, there is a prevalent belief among individuals that the provision of education, especially technical education, in local languages, leads to a lack of harmony with the global market requirements. Consequently, it is argued that graduates from higher education institutions that employ vernacular mediums of instruction may encounter difficulties in securing employment opportunities. Gupta (2021) observes that the NEP (2020) conspicuously lacks any policies about English-language education. The policy statement explicitly acknowledges that its guiding principle is centered around the profound legacy of ancient and enduring Indian knowledge and philosophy. There is a general disregard for all the advantages resulting from decades of English-language education in the nation in its endeavours to nativise the medium of instruction as well as school curriculum and resources (Zeeshan, 2020). According to Gupta (2021), students must acquire knowledge in their native languages during their early years as it enhances their comprehension of educational content. However, this approach also implies that these students will commence their English language learning at a later stage, which poses challenges in terms of their ability to assimilate the language effectively. This phenomenon has the potential to exacerbate the existing economic disparity between those who have the financial means to enroll in English-medium educational institutions and those who do not. Consequently, the latter group may face disadvantages in terms of accessing lucrative career prospects in the long run. The prevalence of language-based discrimination is expected to increase significantly in a society where the absence of English proficiency is often associated with diminished intellectual capacity and limited competence. Rai (2022) argues that the issue with English in contemporary times lies not in its foreign origins, but rather in its status as an

Indian language that is intertwined with class and caste advantages. The current status of English within the social hierarchy is expected to become increasingly complex due to the growing disparity between English-speaking, privileged segments of society and others who lack convenient access to the language, hence perpetuating economic disadvantages for the latter group.

The present study recognizes the pressing issue of language anxiety and underscores the importance of English language learning, particularly in the context of STEM fields. It seeks to investigate blended learning as an innovative approach that seamlessly combines traditional in-person teaching with digital resources, offering a promising solution to the challenges posed by language anxiety. This method aims to ease the stress associated with real-time verbal interactions by providing students with the opportunity to participate thoughtfully through written modalities. Moreover, it strives to facilitate language acquisition in both English and the student's native languages. Blended learning emerges as a potential solution to alleviate language anxiety within India's linguistically diverse educational landscape, marked by frequent transitions between languages. Keeping this in mind, the subsequent section delves into the methodological intricacies, outlining the research design, participant selection criteria, data collection methods, and the tailored implementation of blended learning strategies.

METHODOLOGY

A mixed-methods strategy that incorporates both quantitative and qualitative approaches forms the foundation of the research design for this study. Acknowledging the complex nature of the topic at hand, this methodology enables us to gather information from several perspectives, assuring a thorough and nuanced comprehension of the impact of blended learning on language anxiety and STEM education. The quantitative phase encompasses the administration of a structured survey of a heterogeneous sample of students pursuing STEM disciplines. The present study will employ standardized measures to assess the participants' degrees of language anxiety, linguistic self-efficacy, and engagement in STEM topics. We seek to identify relationships between linguistic anxiety, self-efficacy, and academic engagement through the collection of quantitative data. This phase will further facilitate the identification of distinct trends among other linguistic groupings, notably in the Indian setting, where English-medium education is prevalent. The survey data will undergo statistical analysis to identify patterns, enabling us to construct a detailed depiction of the terrain. In addition to the quantitative data, the qualitative portion of the study will entail conducting in-depth interviews with a subset of individuals selected from the survey sample. The purpose of these interviews is to provide participants with an opportunity to express their encounters with language anxiety and their perspectives on blended learning as a pedagogical approach. Through a comprehensive exploration of the intricacies inherent in their respective experiences, our objective is to unearth profound qualitative understandings that may elude quantitative assessments. The qualitative data will undergo thematic analysis, which will facilitate the identification of emergent themes and narratives in a natural manner.

Participant Selection

The study focuses on students enrolled in STEM fields who encounter English-speaking anxiety as the target group. The acquisition of exact language skills is frequently required in STEM education to facilitate the comprehension and successful communication of complex scientific topics. Within the framework of the Indian education system, where English is commonly utilized as the primary language of teaching, the convergence of linguistic variety and STEM education gives rise to a unique environment. The objective of this study is to investigate the influence of linguistic anxiety on students' experiences and outcomes in a given setting. The study will involve a sample of undergraduate and postgraduate students who are currently enrolled in STEM programs at various universities. This particular demography encompasses individuals from diverse language backgrounds, varying academic levels, and different phases of STEM education. The research's emphasis on anxiety related to English language proficiency is particularly relevant within the Indian setting, as students frequently navigate between regional languages and English. Through active involvement with this particular population, our objective is to comprehensively explore the intricate complexities of language anxiety and its influence on STEM education in a heterogeneous educational environment.

Pre-Screening Assessment

The pre-screening assessment is an essential component in the process of finding individuals who meet the criteria for participation in the study, which specifically investigates the phenomenon of English-speaking anxiety in the context of STEM education. The purpose of this evaluation is to ascertain if the persons chosen possess the appropriate attributes and experiences, hence augmenting the validity and pertinence of the study's results. The pre-screening assessment was conducted using a specialized survey that has been particularly developed to measure participants' self-reported levels of anxiety when speaking English in the context of STEM subjects. The survey will include meticulously designed inquiries that explore participants' degrees of comfort, concerns, and perceived difficulties while participating in English communication in the context of their academic endeavors. The demographic information of the survey and the average marking for each statement are shown in Tables 1 and 2, respectively:

Table 2. Average marking of the survey questionnaire

Sl no	Questionnaire for English Anxiety Surveys	Average Marking (Out of 5)
1	During English-language STEM lectures, I often feel nervous or anxious.	3.8
2	I find it challenging to express my thoughts and ideas in English during STEM discussions or group activities.	4.1
3	I frequently hesitate to ask questions or seek clarification in English during STEM classes.	3.7
4	I often worry about making grammatical errors or mispronouncing words when communicating in English with STEM subjects.	4
5	English-language STEM presentations or assignments make me feel apprehensive.	3.9
6	I feel self-conscious about my English proficiency when interacting with peers or instructors in STEM classes.	3.6
7	English-speaking anxiety has sometimes hindered my active participation in STEM-related activities.	4.3
8	I believe that improving my English communication skills within STEM would enhance my academic performance.	4.5
9	I am interested in participating in a study that explores English-speaking anxiety in STEM education and potential strategies to address it.	4

Based on the analysis of the survey data, a cohort of 100 students has been identified who exhibit a discernible propensity towards experiencing anxiety while communicating in English within the context of STEM disciplines. The selected participants will go to the subsequent stage of the research, which entails conducting qualitative interviews to further explore their experiences and opinions. The people who were chosen for this study exhibit a wide array of language origins, varying academic levels, and varied gender identities. It is anticipated that their perspectives will make a substantial contribution to our comprehension of the correlation between language anxiety and STEM education. We express our appreciation to all participants for their involvement in this initial stage, which serves as the basis of our research endeavor. As we go into the subsequent stage, we anticipate a deeper exploration of the intricacies of English-speaking anxiety and its potential impact on the efficacy of STEM learning encounters.

Table 1. Demographic characteristics of respondents

Characteristic	Static
Total Respondent	250
Average Age	21 years
Gender Distribution	Male (40%), Female (58%), Other (2%)
Academic Level	Undergraduate (65%) post-graduate (35%)

Data Collection

The subsequent stage of our research technique entails the collection of quantitative data to delve deeper into the correlation between language anxiety and STEM performance within the group of 100 students that have been chosen for this study. The objective of this phase is to measure the degrees of language anxiety expressed by participants and their opinions of their performance in the field of STEM. The collected data will yield valuable insights into the potential correlation between language anxiety and academic achievements within the STEM field. Survey Instrument: The survey instrument for this phase will encompass three main sections:

- **Assessment of Language Anxiety:** The participants were asked to answer a series of questions specifically created to evaluate their degrees of language anxiety in the context of STEM. The questions utilized in this study were derived from existing measures that assess linguistic anxiety. These scales were modified to align with the specific objectives of our research. The participants were instructed to evaluate their levels of worry, apprehension, and self-doubt while participating in English-mediated tasks as part of their STEM training.
- **STEM Performance Perception**: To assess the participants' self-perceived performance in the fields of STEM, a set of questions, was administered to enquire about their perceived accomplishments, level of confidence, and level of involvement in their STEM disciplines. The aforementioned inquiries facilitated our comprehension of how participants see their academic advancement in light of the linguistic obstacles they may encounter.
- **Analysis of Academic Records**: Along with having access to the self-reported data on STEM achievement, we have obtained consent to view the academic records of the participants. Data was collected on the student's course grades, class engagement, and general performance in STEM courses.

This methodology facilitated a comprehensive evaluation of their scholastic performance throughout the fields of science, technology, engineering, and mathematics. The Academic Performance Metrics Score will be calculated based on participants' objective academic performance, such as GPA, course grades, and attendance rates. Each metric will be assigned a score, and the overall performance score will be the sum of these scores.

Based on these three parameters the paper presents a sneak peak of the enhanced data set in Table 3:

Table 3. Sneak peak of the dataset

Participant ID	Language Anxiety Score (Out of 25)	STEM Performance Score (Out of 25)	Attendance Performance Metrics Score (Out of 15)
1	22	20	13
2	23	21	14
3	19	18	11
4	24	18	12
5	21	22	10
6	18	23	9
7	20	17	6
8	22	19	7
9	19	21	12
10	18	22	9

The information that has been gathered offers a complete perspective on the levels of language anxiety, self-assessed performance in STEM subjects, and objective academic success among the participants. The utilization of survey results in conjunction with academic performance scores allows for a more intricate examination of the correlation between language anxiety and success in STEM fields. The findings of this dataset have been analyzed and presented in the subsequent subsection.

Summary

To carry out a statistical study that centers on the Language Anxiety Survey Score and its association with other factors, a correlation analysis was conducted. This study facilitated our comprehension of the correlation between language anxiety scores and several academic indicators such as STEM performance scores, GPA, course grades, and attendance rates. The Pearson correlation coefficients were taken into consideration since they assess the magnitude and direction of linear associations between variables.

- Correlation Analysis: The present study conducted a calculation of Pearson correlation coefficients to examine the relationship between the Language Anxiety Survey Score and the subsequent variables:
    - STEM Performance Survey Score
    - GPA
    - Academic Performance Metrics Score

- Interpretation: The correlation coefficients yielded valuable information on the magnitude and orientation of the associations between linguistic anxiety scores and the aforementioned factors. A positive association signifies that there is a tendency for the other variable to grow when language anxiety scores increase. A negative correlation implies an inverse relationship between language anxiety scores and the other measure, indicating that as language anxiety scores grow, the other variable tends to decrease. Consider the result below in Table 4:

Table 4. Relation of language anxiety on STEM and academic performance

Parameters	Statistical Score	Interpretation
Language Anxiety Survey Score vs. STEM Performance Survey	r = -0.42 (negative correlation)	There is a negative correlation between language anxiety scores and self-assessed STEM performance, indicating that as language anxiety scores grow, self-assessed STEM performance tends to decline.
Language Anxiety Survey Score vs. GPA	r = -0.38 (negative correlation)	There is a moderate negative correlation between language anxiety scores and GPA. Higher language anxiety scores are associated with lower GPAs.
Language Anxiety Survey Score vs. Academic Performance Metrics Score	r = -0.45 (negative correlation)	The findings indicate a discernible inverse relationship between scores measuring language anxiety and measures assessing academic success. There exists a negative correlation between elevated levels of language anxiety and academic achievement, whereby those with higher language anxiety tend to have worse total academic performance.

The findings derived from the statistical analysis indicate the presence of a moderate inverse relationship between language anxiety scores and many indicators of academic success, including STEM performance, GPA, and other measures of academic achievement. This finding suggests that there is a positive correlation between language anxiety scores and students' perception of their STEM performance as well as their academic outcomes, including lower GPAs and total academic performance scores. The results of this study indicate that the presence of language anxiety in STEM educational environments might potentially harm students' self-perceived performance and their actual academic accomplishments. Based on the aforementioned analysis, the present study aims to provide specific blended learning strategies that might effectively improve students' academic performance by mitigating language anxiety.

BLENDED LEARNING IMPLEMENTATION

As seen in the preceding statistical study, there is a negative link between language anxiety ratings and metrics measuring academic success in the STEM fields, GPA, and overall. To effectively tackle these problems and optimize the educational experience for students experiencing language anxiety in the context of STEM education, it is imperative to adopt an effective approach. Blended learning methodologies provide a potentially effective answer. These solutions seek to address language anxiety, enhance language competency, and enhance STEM performance through the integration of both in-person and online components. Now, let us explore the intricacies of executing these strategies in the following section.

Blended Learning Strategies and Implementation

During the process of Strategy Development, our primary focus has been on the creation and refinement of blended learning techniques that will be deployed specifically in STEM courses. To accomplish this objective, a thorough strategy has been devised to effectively integrate blended learning methodologies within the realm of STEM education, with a specific emphasis on the subject matter of Chemistry. This step entails the collaborative efforts of instructional designers, language specialists, and faculty members specializing in STEM disciplines. The following, Table 5, is an analysis of the tasks and factors to be taken into account:

Table 5. Blended learning strategy planning

Time Frame	Work Distribution
Month1	• Needs Analysis • Course Mapping • Content Creation
Month 2	• Language Support • Assessment Tools
Month 3	• Pilot Testing • Feedback Analysis
Month 4	• Refinement

Having considered this approach, we have developed a comprehensive plan for the integration of blended learning methodologies inside a Chemistry curriculum. Consider the following figure (Figure 1) for better understanding.

Figure 1. Integration of blended learning in a chemistry curriculum

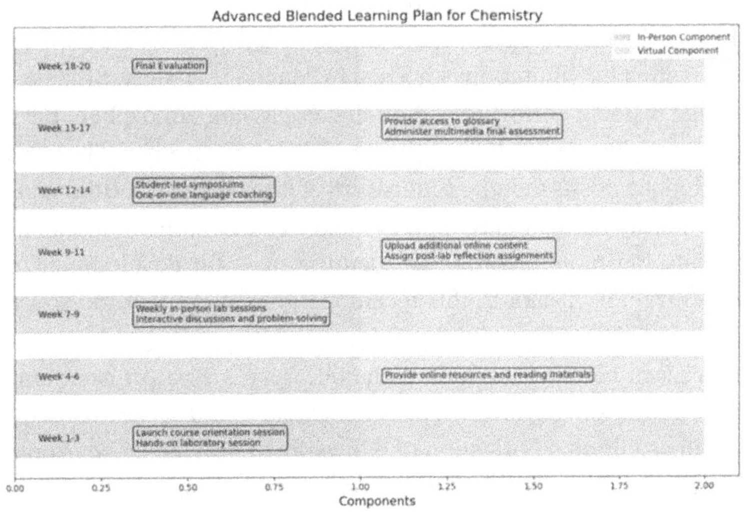

The aforementioned advanced blended learning plan exemplifies a novel strategy for STEM education, which acknowledges and actively embraces the intrinsic intricacy of the subject matter and the varied range of students it caters to. This concept surpasses conventional teaching methods since it is rooted in a comprehensive comprehension of the difficulties encountered by students who experience language anxiety. It is recognized that in the current educational context, the qualities of flexibility and inclusion are not only desirable but also essential.

Fundamentally, this method endeavors to establish a dynamic and intellectually stimulating educational encounter for each learner. By strategically integrating conventional face-to-face teaching methods with a wide range of innovative online educational tools, it effectively accommodates the numerous learning styles, preferences, and requirements of a heterogeneous student population. The use of video lectures, virtual experiments, interactive simulations, and extensive reading materials acknowledges the individualized learning paths that learners may undertake in comprehending intricate STEM subjects. The presence of a wide range of materials fosters a sense of autonomy among students, motivating them to assume responsibility for their education, engage in exploration, pose inquiries, and make discoveries. The educational platform provides a degree of adaptability that enables students to actively interact with the content in manners that align with their personal preferences and interests. One notable characteristic of this method is its intentional focus on mitigating linguistic anxiety. The incorporation of language help directly into the online platform represents a big stride in addressing a prominent obstacle encountered by students in STEM education. By using specialized language modules, students can enhance not only their scientific vocabulary but also their proficiency in academic writing and pronunciation. This approach acknowledges the importance of not just acquiring knowledge but also developing the ability to express and convey that knowledge proficiently, a critical skill essential for achieving success in STEM fields.

Nevertheless, this integrated strategy extends beyond the confines of the online element. It accords equal importance to the significance of face-to-face communication. The inclusion of weekly seminars, laboratory sessions, and peer-led discussions in the curriculum offers students a good opportunity to apply their theoretical knowledge in practical settings. Students acquire the ability to effectively utilize scientific principles within practical contexts, therefore solidifying their comprehension. The aforementioned sessions, which promote active participation and the application of critical thinking skills, serve as a crucial factor in mitigating the limitations imposed by language anxiety. Students are not only engaged in acquiring knowledge inside a nurturing and all-encompassing atmosphere but are also developing a sense of self-assurance in their aptitude to articulate intricate concepts. The underlying philosophical foundation of this technique posits that the acquisition of knowledge is a fluid and progressive phenomenon. Continuous feedback and data-gathering systems are essential components of this system. Both instructors and students can monitor progress, identify areas for development, and make immediate modifications. The utilization of data in this technique guarantees that the strategy remains dynamic and is consistently improved to cater to the changing requirements of the learners.

The proposed advanced blended learning technique serves as a prime example of the significant influence that modern education may exert. The statement recognizes the limited applicability of education and emphasizes the additional obligation of educators to provide an environment that supports the achievement of all students. The advocacy for the promotion of inclusivity, flexibility, and customized learning is widely seen as essential elements in the training of future leaders in the fields of STEM. This effort signifies a notable progression towards achieving equitable educational opportunities and fostering scholarly achievement in the mentioned domain, regardless of students' socio-economic backgrounds or individual challenges.

Result and Analysis

The use of a complete blended learning strategy in the field of STEM education demonstrates a strong dedication to fostering inclusive and transformational learning environments. Nevertheless, the genuine assessment of its effectiveness is ingrained in the perspectives and first-hand encounters of the pupils themselves. This innovative methodology effectively combines conventional face-to-face teaching with a wide range of digital resources, therefore acknowledging not only the intricate nature of STEM disciplines but also the distinct requirements and obstacles faced by each student. An essential element of this execution is the ongoing discourse it cultivates with pupils. The feedback provided by individuals is crucial in influencing the continuous improvements made to the strategy. This input is characterized by its honesty and depth, contributing significantly to the process of refining the strategy. The online platform, discussion sessions, and periodical surveys are equipped with feedback tools that offer students the opportunity to express their opinions, concerns, and suggestions. The use of two-way communication guarantees that the method is not imposed onto students, but rather fosters a collaborative environment in which students actively engage in shaping their educational trajectory.

The efficacy of student feedback resides in its capacity to elucidate the intricacies of the educational encounter. The aforementioned statement elucidates the nuanced fluctuations in self-assurance, the instances of lucidity, and the occurrences in which apprehension regarding language usage is gradually superseded by the fervor for exploration. This analysis identifies the strengths of the blended learning method and identifies areas that warrant more focus. The value of this feedback is in its ability to go beyond quantitative data, as it explores the subjective experiences of the students, providing insights into the emotional and psychological aspects of their educational progress. The implementation of a collaborative approach in education ensures the maintenance of adaptability and responsiveness within the plan. This statement encapsulates the ideology that students are not mere passive beneficiaries, but rather active participants in the process of shaping their own educational experiences. The feedback provided by individuals serves as a valuable tool for teachers, aiding them in the process of improving online resources, strengthening language assistance, and optimizing face-to-face encounters. This guarantees that the plan remains aligned with the developing demands of the learners and the dynamic landscape of STEM education.

Within this discourse-oriented educational environment, each student assumes a significant role in the continuous enhancement of the integrated learning methodology. The experiences, perspectives, and concerns of individuals are not only recognized but also recognized as essential components in the continuous pursuit of delivering fair and empowering STEM education. The monthly improvement report (represented in Figure 2) serves as evidence of the collaborative relationship between students and educators, in which feedback plays a crucial role in shaping the learning experience and promoting inclusivity and empowerment.

Figure 2. Monthly improvement report

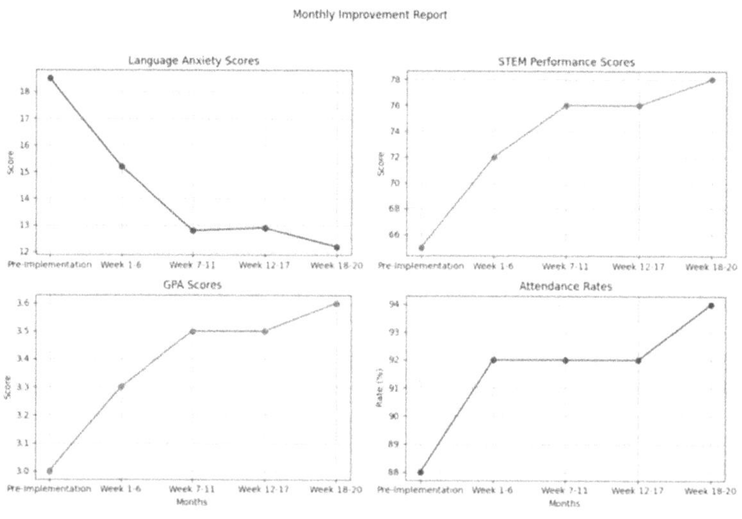

The visualized data in Figure 2 can provide insights into the month-on-month improvement of the 100 students participating in the advanced blended learning program. Let's interpret the data:

Language Anxiety Scores:

- The line plot for language anxiety scores demonstrates a consistent downward trend over the 20 weeks.
- The program initially led to a significant reduction in language anxiety during Weeks 1-6, with a 3.3-point decrease.
- Subsequent weeks showed a slight increase but remained below the baseline, indicating a stabilization of language anxiety.
- Overall, there is a substantial reduction in language anxiety by Week 18-20, i.e. in the final evaluation, with a 6.3-point decrease from the baseline.

Stem Performance Scores:

- STEM performance scores steadily increased throughout the program.
- The most notable improvement occurred during Months 1-6, with a 7-point increase in average scores.
- While there were fluctuations in subsequent months, STEM performance remained consistently above the baseline.
- Final evaluation (Week 18-20) shows, that students achieved a 13-point increase in STEM performance compared to the baseline.

GPA Scores:

- GPA scores exhibited a steady increase over the 20 weeks.

- The program led to a 0.6-point increase in average GPA by the final week, indicating academic progress and stronger performance in coursework.

Attendance Rates:

- Attendance rates remained consistently high throughout the program, with only minor fluctuations.
- The initial increase in attendance during Weeks 1-6 was sustained throughout the program.
- By Week 18-20, attendance rates reached a peak of 94%, suggesting strong student engagement and commitment to the blended learning approach.

Overall, the data analysis reveals a positive impact of the advanced blended learning program on both language anxiety and academic performance. Language anxiety scores decreased steadily, indicating that the program effectively addressed this barrier to learning. STEM performance and GPA showed continuous improvement, suggesting that the program not only reduced anxiety but also enhanced students' understanding and mastery of STEM subjects. Additionally, the consistently high attendance rates indicate that students were actively engaged in the program and motivated to participate in both online and in-person components. This engagement likely contributed to the overall success of the program.

It's important to note that while there were fluctuations in some scores, they generally remained above the baseline. These fluctuations may be attributed to individual differences among students or specific challenges encountered during certain months. Nevertheless, the overall trends demonstrate the program's positive impact on student outcomes. This analysis underscores the effectiveness of the advanced blended learning strategy in addressing language anxiety and promoting academic growth among STEM students. It highlights the importance of continuous data-driven adjustments and the value of student feedback in shaping a dynamic and inclusive educational environment.

CONCLUSION

This research not only addresses the immediate obstacles encountered by students in STEM education, but also contributes to a wider transformation in educational frameworks, highlighting inclusion, innovative teaching methods, and a nuanced comprehension of student experiences. An important aspect of this study is its acknowledgment and addressing of language anxiety, a widespread obstacle that is frequently disregarded in conventional educational frameworks. By using specific language assistance systems, the research not only addresses a barrier but also actively fosters diversity in STEM education. The concept of inclusivity in this context encompasses more than just language variety; it involves a comprehensive acceptance of students with different cultural, linguistic, and educational backgrounds. This approach acknowledges that diversity encompasses more than just language competency, creating an environment where all students feel recognized and empowered to excel in STEM fields. The study's pedagogical innovation, implemented through a blended learning method, demonstrates a deep understanding of the changing educational environment. This novel approach smoothly combines traditional face-to-face teaching with a wide range of online resources, acknowledging that modern students interact with educational material in many ways. By utilizing technology, this strategy provides a dynamic learning experience that allows students to easily access video lectures, interactive simulations, and other digital resources. This adaptability not only accommodates various learning styles but also conforms to the expectations and preferences of a technologically proficient generation, therefore contributing to the continuous development of teaching methods.

REFERENCES

Abdurahman, N. H., & Rizqi, M. A. (2020). Indonesian students' strategies to cope with foreign language anxiety. *TEFLIN Journal: A Publication on the Teaching & Learning of English, 31*(1).

Aida, Y. (1994). Examination of Horwitz, Horwitz, and Cope's construct of foreign language anxiety: The case of students of Japanese. *Modern Language Journal*, 78(2), 155–168. 10.1111/j.1540-4781.1994.tb02026.x

Cao, W. (2023). A meta-analysis of effects of blended learning on performance, attitude, achievement, and engagement across different countries. *Frontiers in Psychology*, 14, 1212056. 10.3389/fpsyg.2023.121205637502744

Cheng, Y. S., Horwitz, E. K., & Schallert, D. L. (1999). Language anxiety: Differentiating writing and speaking components. *Language Learning*, 49(3), 417–446. 10.1111/0023-8333.00095

Christopher, N. (2022). *Why Indian universities are ditching English-only education.* Rest of World. https://restofworld.org/2022/indian-universities-are-ditching-english-only-education/

Demir, A. N., & Zaimoglu, S. (2021). The relationship between foreign language anxiety and decision-making strategies among university students. *Journal of Language and Linguistic Studies*, 17(1, S1), 18–32. 10.17263/jlls.903294

Express, T. N. I. (2013). Poor English skills drive students to suicide. *New Indian Express.*https://www.newindianexpress.com/states/tamil-nadu/2013/aug/07/Poor-English-skills-drive-student-to-suicide-504655.html

Gupta, M. (2021). *The implications of 'mother tongue education': India's national education policy 2020.* Education South Asia. https://educationsouthasia.web.ox.ac.uk/article/thinkpiece11

Horwitz, E. K., Horwitz, M. B., & Cope, J. (1986). Foreign language classroom anxiety. *Modern Language Journal*, 70(2), 125–132. 10.1111/j.1540-4781.1986.tb05256.x

Kalsoom, A., Soomro, N. H., & Pathan, Z. H. (2020). How social support and foreign language anxiety impact willingness to communicate in English in an EFL classroom. *International Journal of English Linguistics*, 10(2), 80–91. 10.5539/ijel.v10n2p80

Krashen, S. (1982). *Principles and practice in second language acquisition.*

Liu, M. (2006). Anxiety in EFL classrooms: Causes and consequences. *TESL reporter, 39*, 20–20.

Liu, M., & Xiangming, L. (2019). Changes in and effects of anxiety on English test performance in Chinese postgraduate EFL classrooms. *Education Research International*, 2019, 1–11. 10.1155/2019/7213925

MacIntyre, P. D. (1995). How does anxiety affect second language learning? A reply to Sparks and Ganschow. *Modern Language Journal*, 79(1), 90–99. 10.1111/j.1540-4781.1995.tb05418.x

MacIntyre, P. D. (1999). Language anxiety: A review of the research for language teachers. *Affect in foreign language and second language learning: A practical guide to creating a low-anxiety classroom atmosphere, 24*(1).

MacIntyre, P. D., & Gardner, R. C. (1991). Language anxiety: Its relationship to other anxieties and to processing in native and second languages. *Language Learning*, 41(4), 513–534. 10.1111/j.1467-1770.1991.tb00691.x

Mehdi, Y., & Kumar, S. (2019). English language anxiety and its impact on the communicative performance of the learners with the students of B-schools in Delhi NCR, India. *International Journal of Recent Technology and Engineering (IJRTE).*

Ministry of Human Resource Development. (2020). *National Educational Policy 2020. Government of India.* Ministry of Human Resourse Development. https://www.education.gov.in/sites/upload_files/mhrd/files/NEP_Final_English_0.pdf

Oteir, I., & Al-Otaibi, A. (2019). Foreign language anxiety: A systematic review. *Arab World English Journal, 10*(3), 309–317. https://awej.org/images/Vol-ume10/Volume10Number3September2019/21.pdf

Phillips, E. M. (1992). The effects of language anxiety on students' oral test performance and attitudes. *Modern Language Journal*, 76(1), 14–26. 10.1111/j.1540-4781.1992.tb02573.x

Puranik, A. (2015). 97% of engineering graduates cannot speak English fluently: Survey. *Hindustan Times.*https://www.hindustantimes.com/education/97-engineering-graduates-cannot-speak-english-fluently-survey/story-GQEkTYwI4AX5zc7oeXkz1M.html

Rai, A. (2022). Must we dream of India in English? *Outlook India.*https://www.outlookindia.com/magazine/story/must-we-dream-of-india-in-english/266672

Sˇafranj, J., & Zivlak, J. (2019). Effects of big five personality traits and fear of negative evaluation on foreign language anxiety. *Croatian Journal Educational/Hrvatski Casopis za Odgoj I Obrazovanje, 21*(1).

Saito, Y., & Samimy, K. K. (1996). Foreign language anxiety and language performance: A study of learner anxiety in beginning, intermediate, and advanced-level college students of Japanese. *Foreign Language Annals*, 29(2), 239–249. 10.1111/j.1944-9720.1996.tb02330.x

Shao, K., Yu, W., & Ji, Z. (2013). An exploration of Chinese EFL students' emotional intelligence and foreign language anxiety. *Modern Language Journal*, 97(4), 917–929. 10.1111/j.1540-4781.2013.12042.x

Teimouri, Y., Goetze, J., & Plonsky, L. (2019). Second language anxiety and achievement: A meta-analysis. *Studies in Second Language Acquisition*, 41(2), 363–387. 10.1017/S0272263118000311

Times of India. (2012). Language barrier ups students' suicides. *Times of India.*https://timesofindia.indiatimes.com/city/madurai/language-barrier-ups-students-suicides/articleshow/16522190.cms

UNESCO. (2021). *UNESCO Science Report: The race against time for smarter development.* UNESCO. https://www.unesco.org/reports/science/2021/en/download-report

vHakim, B. M (2019). A study of language anxiety among English language learners in Saudi Arabia. *Arab World English Journal (AWEJ), 10.*

Yagi, S. M. (2000). Language labs and translation booths: Simultaneous interpretation as a learner task. *Language, Culture and Curriculum*, 13(2), 154–173. 10.1080/07908310008666596

Yan, J. X., & Horwitz, E. K. (2008). Learners' perceptions of how anxiety interacts with personal and instructional factors to influence their achievement in English: A qualitative analysis of EFL learners in China. *Language Learning*, 58(1), 151–183. 10.1111/j.1467-9922.2007.00437.x

Yan, J. X., Pan, J., & Wang, H. (2010). Learner factors, self-perceived language ability and interpreting learning: An investigation of Hong Kong tertiary interpreting classes. *The Interpreter and Translator Trainer*, 4(2), 173–196. 10.1080/13556509.2010.10798803

Young, D. J. (1991). Creating a low-anxiety classroom environment: What does language anxiety research suggest? *Modern Language Journal*, 75(4), 426–439.

Zeeshan, M. (2020). English phobia will ruin India's economic prospects. *Deccan Herald*.https://www.deccanherald.com/opinion/english-phobia-will-ruin-indias-economic-prospects-869208.html

Zhou, L., Xi, Y., & Lochtman, K. (2020). The relationship between second language competence and willingness to communicate: The moderating effect of foreign language anxiety. *Journal of Multilingual and Multicultural Development*, 44(10), 1–15.

Chapter 10
The Project-Based Learning Approach (PBL):
Enthralling Students Through Project-Based Learning Approach (PBL) in Education 5.0

Arpita Nayak
https://orcid.org/0000-0003-2911-0492
KIIT University, India

Ipseeta Satpathy
KIIT School of Management, KIIT University, India

Vishal Jain
https://orcid.org/0000-0003-1126-7424
Sharda University, India

ABSTRACT

Education is an essential component of human growth, equipping individuals with the skills and information required to tackle life's problems. Raising educational understanding is vital to providing equitable access for all. Education 5.0 aims to use modern technology to provide a more compassionate kind of education, emphasizing social and emotional development with creative solutions that improve societal well-being. Project-based learning (PBL) is a teaching strategy in which students investigate real-world challenges and topics via hands-on projects. This technique encourages the development of reasoning, problem-solving, and communication skills, all of which are crucial for success in today's professional world. PBL is an essential part of Education 5.0, a framework for personalized, collaborative, and technology-driven learning experiences. In conclusion, project-based learning systems in Education 5.0 are transforming education for the better, fostering meaningful learning experiences and practical skills that students can apply throughout their lives.

DOI: 10.4018/979-8-3693-3041-8.ch010

INTRODUCTION

Education entails studying the many strategies, facts, and information required to recognize, appreciate, and cherish our roles and obligations in society, our family, and our own country. The significance and value of coexistence as a whole is critical and comprehensive. Education acts as a bridge, allowing us to maintain a healthy relationship with the world and our civilizations. In addition to this role, it facilitates the learning process and the absorption of difficult knowledge. Project-Based Learning (PBL) plays a vital role in Education 5.0, focusing on developing essential skills required in the 21st century. This approach actively involves students in investigating real-world issues and obstacles, fostering a deeper comprehension of the subject matter. Through project work, students enhance their abilities in collaboration, communication, and problem-solving, which are crucial in a rapidly evolving, technology-oriented world. PBL also encourages student autonomy and creativity, enabling learners to take charge of their education and cultivate a lifelong passion for learning. In the context of Education 5.0, which integrates advanced technologies and emphasizes personalized learning experiences, PBL is indispensable in preparing students to navigate and excel in intricate and dynamic environments. This hands-on learning methodology not only makes education more captivating and pertinent but also equips students with the skills and mindset necessary to thrive in the future workforce (Caplan,2018). Education provides people with information and helps them become more confident in their life. It can help you find work and earn money while also improving your everyday living skills and values. Individuals who have completed their education may be citizens in an ethical society. It allows you to make the decisions you believe will give you the most power. This world operates on education, which is the wellspring of our growth in today's developed and industrialized world. To flourish in a competitive environment, we all require information to guide us. Education's stakeholders, particularly governments, organizations, and students, understand its vast significance. High-quality education, particularly higher education, is a key driver of growth in families of all socioeconomic levels. Furthermore, by combining several goals, education's value has increased, and individuals have become more aware of their environment and society, learning information that past generations lacked. The World Bank blog post "Education is Fundamental to Development and Growth" emphasizes that education may alter people's lives in a variety of ways (Shaturaev,2021). Education 5.0 integrates artificial intelligence, the Internet of Things, big data, and other sophisticated technologies to reshape the learning experience and job preparation. Integration is vital for enabling individuals to effectively navigate a complex and linked future. Education 5.0 is the implementation of new technologies to give more humanized instruction, with an emphasis on students' social and emotional growth as well as solutions that improve societal life. All social arenas, including employment, industry, and health, have recognized that technology can (and should) improve people's lives. And it couldn't be different with education, which serves as the foundation for people's upbringing (Togo & Gandidzanwa,2021). Over the previous several decades, we've seen a surge in digital change and new technologies in our daily lives. Artificial intelligence, the Internet of Things, data processing, and other technologies have become ubiquitous in our lives and businesses. With the COVID-19 epidemic, life has become increasingly digital, and educational institutions are no exception. Online classes and distance learning were no longer trends; they were the new normal, and everyone had to adjust. However, beyond technology equipment, the pandemic highlighted the importance of preparing humans for adversity, namely emotionally intelligent individuals who understand how to use digital transformation as a vehicle for social reform. This is precisely what Education 5.0 is: a chain that connects digital and technological knowledge to humans (Keshav et al.,2022). Education 5.0 can effectively incorporate Project-Based Learning (PBL) by leveraging advanced technologies and emphasizing personalized learning. An example of this integration is a project where students are tasked with designing a sustainable city. They can utilize AI-driven tools for data analysis and urban planning software to create detailed models. To cater to each student's interests and learning pace, AI-powered platforms can provide personalized resources and feedback. Collaboration tools like cloud-based platforms facilitate teamwork, while virtual reality (VR) offers immersive experiences for students to visualize their city designs in a 3D environment. Another project idea is the development of a mobile app to address a local community issue, such as waste management. Students can use coding software, IoT devices for data collection, and machine learning algorithms to optimize the app's functionality. AI can create personalized learning paths to track progress and adapt challenges based on each student's skill level, ensuring that the project not only teaches technical skills but also fosters problem-solving, creativity, and critical thinking. Through these projects, Education 5.0 utilizes technology to create engaging, relevant, and individualized learning experiences (Gunawan et al.,2023). Education 5.0 aims to provide individuals with the skills, perspective, and flexibility required to survive in a fast-changing environment. Education 5.0 helps Society 5.0 achieve its goals of sustainable development and technology integration by cultivating critical thinking, creativity, and multidisciplinary problem-solving skills. Society 5.0's emphasis on integrating technology, data, and human well-being has a direct influence on education. The availability of innovative technology, data-driven insights, and immersive learning experiences enhances the educational process, allowing Education 5.0's concepts of personalized, comprehensive, and continuous learning (Alharbi,2023). Education 5.0 focuses on developing well-rounded persons who possess cognitive talents, emotional intelligence, social awareness, and ethical principles. This comprehensive growth is consistent with Society 5.0's emphasis on human-centered solutions that encourage well-being, inclusion, and ethical considerations. The importance of the Project-Based Learning (PBL) method in Education 5.0 cannot be emphasized. It signifies a trend towards learner-centered and experiential educational approaches. Students benefit from PBL because it fosters critical thinking, problem-solving abilities, and interdisciplinary knowledge integration. PBL engages students in real-world issues or projects through inquiry-based learning, resulting in a better grasp and retention of academic knowledge. This strategy promotes intrinsic motivation and curiosity while also fostering active participation and ownership of the learning process. PBL also aligns with Education 5.0 objectives by strengthening students' ability for lifelong learning, flexibility, and teamwork, all of which are key attributes in today's rapidly expanding digital environment. Education 5.0 uses the transformational potential of PBL to develop a generation of nimble, inventive thinkers capable of excelling in complex, dynamic contexts (Lantada,2022). Governments, parents, people, and corporations continue to spend on education and training at unprecedented levels, with the total anticipated to exceed USD$10 trillion by 2030 as shown in Fig 1. By 2025, the globe will have half a billion more school and university graduates than it has today, owing mostly to population increase in emerging nations (Brothers,2019).

Figure 1. Total global education expenditures in USD trillions (https://medium.com/@patrickbrothers/ten-charts-that-explain-the-global-education-technology-market-6809fa68484c)

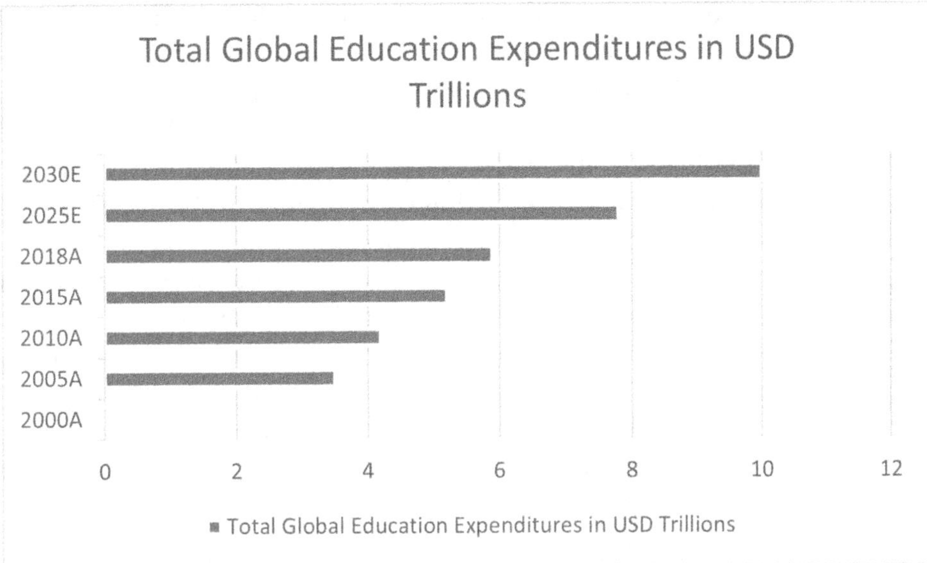

By presenting students with complicated challenges, PBL promotes a better comprehension of the subject matter while also improving critical thinking and analytical abilities. Furthermore, via collaborative projects, PBL fosters critical 21st-century skills such as communication, creativity, and flexibility. It also promotes interdisciplinary learning by combining information from numerous fields, giving students a comprehensive perspective on complicated situations and developing links between diverse concepts. By encouraging active involvement and inquiry-based investigation, PBL enables students to become self-directed learners who are excited about furthering their education and interests. As Education 5.0 advances, PBL is a critical method that not only gives students the necessary information and skills but also creates intrinsic motivation and a lifelong love of learning (Wulandani et al.,2022). Project-Based Learning (PBL) enables students to conceptualize, invent, and build practical solutions to problems. Learning PBL students not only build their creative thinking talents, but they also get the ability to solve all types of troublesome and complicated problems within collaborative teams, frequently as team leaders. This strategy flourishes when it fosters and cultivates students' creativity and collaboration within multidisciplinary teams, uses technology as a communication and project development tool, or envisions answers to global concerns provided by external bodies. Even if the assignments are basic, PBL techniques may assist pupils as well. Despite the limited scope of projects, there is still a strong opportunity to integrate learning and practical application (Sajidan et al., 2022). PBL contains numerous key procedures, and its implementation involves various stages, including (Afriansyah & Yustanti, 2021);

Defining the Problem: PBL projects should begin with students posing questions about an issue. What is the nature of the problem they are attempting to solve? What assumptions may they make regarding the problem's cause? Asking such questions will assist students in framing the problem in the proper context. If students are working on a real-world problem, they must examine how the solution will help the end user.

Generating Ideas: Next, students should be given the chance to develop and share their problem-solving strategies. The emphasis here is on generating a large number of ideas rather than necessarily good ones. In this way, brainstorming should allow students to think freely while staying focused on the issue. Setting criteria for brainstorming groups, such as allowing everyone to contribute an idea, deferring judgement of others' ideas, and creating on the ideas of others, helps ideation become a useful and creative activity.

Prototyping Solutions: Designing and prototyping a solution is often the following step in the PBL process. A prototype can take various forms, including a mock-up, a storyboard, a role-play, or even an item constructed from easily accessible materials like as pipe cleaners, popsicle sticks, and rubber bands. The goal of prototyping is to build on the ideas created during the brainstorming process and to immediately illustrate how a solution to the problem would look and feel. Prototypes may frequently expose learners' preconceptions as well as reveal unexpected obstacles that an end user of the solution may face. The emphasis on producing basic prototypes also allows students to iterate on their concepts fast and easily, incorporate input into their designs, and constantly polish their problem-solving skills.

Testing: Students can then go to the next stage of design by testing their prototypes. Ideally, testing occurs in a "live" environment. Testing helps students to determine how well their goods or services perform in a real-world situation. Testing results can give students valuable feedback on their solutions while also generating new issues to ponder. Did the solution work as expect? If not, what has to be adjusted? Testing encourages pupils to think critically and reflect on their experiences.

PBL provides a more detailed method of measuring student learning. Using project-based assessments, teachers may measure students' mastery of academic subjects, as well as how well they can apply information in real-world situations and solve actual problems. This technique not only provides a more exact assessment of students' abilities and competencies, but it also promotes a stronger feeling of engagement and motivation by linking learning to real-world applicability. Furthermore, PBL promotes constant feedback and reflection, allowing students to obtain immediate feedback on their progress and iteratively improve their work. Embracing PBL as a basic part of Education 5.0 allows educators to create learning environments that prioritize creativity, collaboration, and critical thinking, preparing students to flourish in an increasingly complex and dynamic world.

RESEARCH QUESTIONS

- What are the different implications of Education 5.0 in today's time?
- How is the project-based learning approach an innovative step in enhancing Education 5.0?

RESEARCH OBJECTIVES

- To understand the various benefits of the Project-Based Learning approach in Education 5.0.
- To understand the implication of Education 5.0 in transforming the education for better.

PROMOTING CRITICAL THINKING AND PROBLEM-SOLVING SKILLS: THE PROJECT-BASED LEARNING APPROACH

In the continually shifting environment of modern education, Project-Based Learning (PBL) stands out as an essential pedagogical method designed to suit the evolving demands of 21st-century learning settings. Based on constructivist principles, PBL emphasizes student-centered, hands-on learning experiences in which knowledge is actively created rather than passively consumed. At the heart of PBL is the development of creative thinking—a highly desired skill in a range of vocations. In education, creative thinking comprises the capacity to produce unique ideas and approach issues from several perspectives, combining features of creativity with critical analysis. (Yu, 2024). PBL, as a paradigm that emphasizes active participation in meaningful projects, has grown greatly over time, influencing students' capacity to think creatively. PBL originated in the early twentieth century and is based on John Dewey's theory of "learning by doing," which encouraged experiential learning. Dewey's disciple, William Heard Kilpatrick, expanded on this basic principle by introducing the "project method." This strategy emphasized student-led initiatives and the value of active engagement in the educational process. Gabora's description of creative thinking as the ability to switch between divergent and convergent cognitive modes dependent on task needs is consistent with PBL's approach. PBL promotes this skill by encouraging students to investigate challenges from several viewpoints, participate in critical thinking, and design novel solutions.According to the dual-process theory of creativity, PBL allows students to produce a diverse set of ideas via divergent thinking before refining these ideas to identify ideal solutions through convergent thinking (Sumarni & Kadarwati,2020). Education is a dynamic discipline that continually adapts to suit the requirements and demands of a quickly changing environment. Project-based learning (PBL) is a technique that has gained popularity in recent years. With traditional classroom techniques, PBL focuses on real-world problem-solving and active involvement, allowing students to learn via hands-on projects. Unlike traditional teaching approaches, PBL puts students at the center of their learning experience, allowing them to actively participate in real-world projects (Chen et al.,2022). Problem-solving abilities are fundamental to critical, logical, and systematic thinking. In today's globalized world, pupils must be capable of solving difficult challenges. Effective problem-solving abilities are essential for success in life. The 21st-century learning curriculum must prioritize student productivity, innovation, effectiveness, and creativity. Problem-solving represents an analytical process that generates complicated ideas while describing solutions to problems. Hybrid project-based learning (HPBL) enhances problem-solving abilities and student creativity in plant anatomy and physiology classes. The HPBL technique incorporates pretest-posttest evaluations, resulting in considerable improvements in problem-solving and creativity (Llma et al.,2023). Integrating Project Based Learning (PjBL) with the STEAM (Science, Technology, Engineering, Arts, and Mathematics) method improves creative thinking abilities through ethnomathematics-based challenges. The framework of learning activities comprises steps such as design, preparation of teaching modules, assessment tool creation, and analysis of PjBL implementation combined with STEAM (Dafik,2023). Project-based biotechnology education in high school enhances students' problem-solving and creativity, as demonstrated by high n-gain values in both categories in the experimental class. Project-based learning involves active and dynamic activities that foster communication, creativity, critical thinking, and collaboration, resulting in increased abilities and experiences. Students' enthusiastic responses to project-based learning reflect strong engagement and interest, adding to the approach's efficacy in cultivating creativity and problem-solving abilities (Amalia et al.,2022). Project-based learning has been proven to boost students' creativity and ingenuity. Project-based learning promotes critical thinking, problem-solving, and creative solutions by immersing students in hands-on, real-world projects. This approach allows students to use their knowledge and talents in a practical situation, which improves their ability to think outside the box and produce new ideas. Project-based learning promotes collaboration and teamwork, which can increase students' creativity and innovation by providing fresh perspectives and ideas. Project-based learning also enables students to take risks, explore new ideas, and learn from their failures—all of which are crucial components of the process of creativity. (Leasa et al.,2023). Project-based learning encourages student participation and creativity. Working on projects fosters critical thinking, problem-solving, and invention, resulting in enhanced creativity. Project-based learning fosters creativity by allowing students to apply theoretical knowledge to real-world situations. The interactive elements that make up project-based learning allow students to explore ideas, share perspectives, and think beyond the box, which helps to their creative growth (Illahi et al.,2022). Project-based learning involves students in real-world problem-solving projects, promoting creativity and innovation. The PjBL paradigm promotes innovative thinking by actively integrating students in projects that solve community and environmental challenges. This involves problem analysis, solution exploration, and evaluation (Pratama et al.,2023). PBL enhances students' professional knowledge and skills, including design thinking, engineering application, and creativity. It encourages students to think rapidly and produce more creative ideas based on user requirements, resulting in increased creativity in terms of adventure, curiosity, imagination, and challenge. Traditional education consists of traditional classroom lectures and rote memorization. This paradigm focuses on receiving teaching, assigning an individual's reading or task, and then evaluating a student's learning. Project-based learning allows students to work on projects across time. PBL encourages students to actively interact with the subject matter via projects. These tasks are frequently collaborative, requiring critical thinking, problem-solving, and innovation. They can commit to one week, two weeks, or the entire semester. These projects are often collaborative, allowing students to express themselves and modify project components to their specific interests. In PBL, the project serves as the vehicle for learning; teaching, learning, research, formative assessment, feedback, and modification take place during rather than after the project. PBL promotes student involvement and comprehension. For instance, imagine a semester-long project where students are assigned the task of creating renewable energy solutions for their community. They start by examining the current energy consumption and the environmental and economic consequences of non-renewable sources. This phase includes engaging in critical discussions and debates to pinpoint specific issues. Subsequently, students explore different renewable energy alternatives such as solar, wind, and hydroelectric power, evaluating their viability based on local conditions using mathematical models and data analysis. Working in teams, they develop a customized renewable energy strategy, build prototypes using simulation software and 3D modeling, and showcase their designs to peers and community stakeholders for input. If feasible, they test small-scale implementations, like setting up solar panels on the school roof and documenting the process and results. Throughout the project, students reflect on their journey, sharing achievements, obstacles, and the application of critical thinking and problem-solving abilities. This hands-on approach not only enhances their comprehension of renewable energy but also sharpens their capacity to analyze intricate problems, devise effective solutions, and adapt to challenges, embodying the core principles of PBL.

ENHANCED STUDENT ENGAGEMENT: PROJECT-BASED LEARNING HELPS STUDENTS TO SHIFT THE FOCUS FROM THE TRADITIONAL METHOD OF LEARNING

Project-based learning (PBL) is an effective catalyst for increasing student involvement and integrating education with the ideas of Education 5.0. PBL engages students in hands-on, inquiry-based projects that encourage active involvement and deeper learning. Addressing real-world problems and difficulties engages students in their learning journey, sparking innate motivation and curiosity. PBL promotes realistic learning experiences by enabling students to apply academic concepts in real-world circumstances, bridging the gap between theory and practice. PBL promotes teamwork and communication skills as students work together to solve complicated challenges and produce meaningful results. In the larger picture of Education 5.0, PBL is consistent with the trend toward learner-centered methods that prioritize personalized and immersive learning (Morais et al.,2021). Project-based learning requires students to actively participate in discussions, solve issues, teamwork, and logical thinking. Project-based learning techniques assist students get a deeper understanding of the topic, resulting in higher learning results.. Student participation in project-based learning is influenced by physiological, psychological, and response elements, as well as external ones like environment and facilities, and social factors like instructor motivation and diverse teaching approaches (Hall & Miro,2016). PBL boosts student motivation and engagement by connecting projects to their social and educational contexts. Implementing PBL increases student engagement and competency in reading, leading to better reading skills. PBL's active and inventive approach promotes student involvement, resulting in improvements in reading and comprehension abilities (Imbaquingo & Cárdenas,2023). PBL is naturally engaging. When students engage in engaging and relevant projects, they are more driven to study and devote time and effort to their studies. PBL helps students to make decisions, set objectives, and take responsibility for their education. This freedom not only enhances internal drive but also instills a sense of duty and accountability for their educational accomplishments. PBL encourages students to explore their interests and passions, which leads to greater engagement and dedication to the learning process. PBL perfectly connects with Education 5.0, which emphasizes personalized and self-directed learning, by promoting student agency and independence. Educators may create learning environments that encourage curiosity, innovation, and continuous learning in students, preparing them to succeed in the complex and ever-changing world of the twenty-first century (Imbaquingo & Cardinas,2023). Benefits of Using Project-Based Learning in Digital Signal Processing Courses Project-based learning in DSP courses enhances students' cognitive and behavioral engagement, encouraging self-learning and practical application awareness. Students improve their programming abilities and topic understanding by solving real-world signal processing issues. The PjBL framework improves student engagement, interest in studying DSP subjects, and self-learning capacity. The OBE paradigm promotes self-directed learning, leading to increased competency and self-learning capacities. The teacher's role as a facilitator in adopting student-centered learning models through active learning pedagogies is critical for developing engineering knowledge and abilities (Deshpande,2022). PBL increases student engagement and motivation by involving students in hands-on projects that address complicated issues and arouse curiosity. By providing open-ended issues and opportunities to explore particular interests, PBL fosters students' feeling of ownership and freedom in their educational journeys. Furthermore, the collaborative part of PBL encourages peer engagement and information sharing, which improves social learning and communication skills that are essential for success in today's workplace. Furthermore, by connecting academic knowledge to real-world applications, PBL promotes greater comprehension and retention of notions, bridging the gap between theory and practice. In the context of Education 5.0, which emphasizes learner-centered methods and personalized learning experiences, PBL is well aligned to increase student engagement and empowerment. Using PBL as a teaching technique allows educators to create dynamic learning environments that foster students' curiosity, critical thinking, and lifelong learning, preparing them to succeed in the ever-changing landscape of the twenty-first century (Patange et al.,2019). Even in primary school settings, project-based learning fosters 21st-century skills and provides collaborative problem-solving opportunities, which increases student engagement. According to the study, project-based learning directs students' thinking towards higher-order cognitive abilities such as analysis and assessment. Scaffolding in project-based coursework helps all students, regardless of background, construct cohesive projects. The open-ended projects in project-based learning allow students to apply ideas to real-world situations (Singer,2023). Project-Based Learning (PBL) is a pioneering educational system in which students learn by working on challenging issues or assignments over time. It is notable for its real-world relevance, emphasis on student-led research, cooperation, and public dissemination of findings. These distinguishing traits differentiate PBL from traditional teaching techniques, providing a rich and immersive learning experience. Constructivism, the pedagogical theory behind PBL, posits that learners develop knowledge via experiences and reflection. PBL enables students to lead their learning by actively engaging in inquiry and problem-solving, making it more relevant and effective. PBL fosters cooperation, metacognition, and equitable scientific education by engaging students in genuine problem-solving settings, particularly for marginalized groups (Riegel, 2023). Project-Based Learning (PBL) stimulates active involvement and improves students' grasp of subjects. Rather than passively acquiring knowledge, PBL students actively engage in the learning process. This technique brings theoretical concepts to life, allowing students to use their classroom knowledge in real-world settings. Students learn critical thinking and problem-solving abilities via project work, which are necessary for managing today's fast-changing environment. PBL fosters creativity and innovation by encouraging students to try new ideas and viewpoints while solving problems. Crucially, PBL increases student motivation and engagement by giving them control over their learning experience. Students are more intrigued and invested in their learning while they work on projects that are relevant and exciting for them (Craft et al.,2019). Project-based learning, or PBL, "is an instruction method in which pupils learn by actively participating in real-world, personally meaningful projects." PBL encourages and engages students in real-world problem-solving across a single curricular topic. Students learn and use 21st-century skills including critical thinking, problem-solving, teamwork, communication, and creativity to address real-world challenges. PBL allows students to deeply participate in writing, inquiry, teamwork, organization, and reading while also being able to apply what they have learned to their future vocations and lives in ways that traditional learning does not (Carpenter et al.,2016). Teachers all across the globe are asking the same question: how to boost student engagement in remote and hybrid learning contexts? PBL is a solution. All PBL components can be completed remotely or in hybrid learning settings. Students will work together to solve a real-world situation in which they are likely to be invested and concerned. In a day when so many kids lack a sense of connection to others and their community, PBL allows them to create, feel connected, and contribute to the solution of an issue larger than themselves. By helping students to take the title of their learning and discover topics of interest through project-based encounters, Education 5.0 supports the transformative capacity of project-based learning to cultivate critical thinking, creativity, and adaptability—the necessary skills for success in the twenty-first century.

FOSTERS SELF-DIRECTED LEARNING: THE PROJECT-BASED LEARNING APPROACH IN EDUCATION 5.0

Self-directed learning (SDL) is an academic technique in which students become autonomous learners who make their own decisions about what and how they study, with the aid of their teacher. Massive Open Online Courses, or MOOCs, might provide study route options to individual learners, however the basic concept of SDL is that the student is the primary agent of their own learning. One strategy used is Self-Directed Learning, or SDL. This technique helps students to define their learning objectives, methods, goals, and direction over a certain period of time. SDL allows students to review their progress, analyse how they are meeting their objectives, explore options objectively, and absorb material at their own speed and level (Leong, 2020). Furthermore, this unique method allows students to choose and pursue their own learning routes, allowing them to improve their education at their own speed. In this aspect, it is equally successful and adaptable as other teaching styles, providing learners with a comprehensive learning experience. It demonstrates a successful teaching that goes beyond the classroom level and requires pupils to carry out independent tasks. It does not advocate spoon-feeding; rather, it promotes and incorporates children in the learning process. Learners led and regulate their learning, accepting responsibility for their cognitive growth by encouraging them to consider what they want to learn and how they want to progress. Access to essential information has made learning significantly simpler. (Zhu et al.,2020). Self-directed learning is an important component of Education 5.0, which represents a considerable movement towards learner-centered approaches. Within this educational framework, students are accountable for directing their learning path by actively pursuing knowledge, tools, and experiences to achieve their educational goals. This technique emphasizes learners' independence, accountability, and internal motivation, giving them the freedom to pursue personal interests and adjust their learning to their own needs (Sułkowski et al.,2021). Self-directed learning encourages critical thinking and problem-solving, while continuous learning enables students to critically analyse information, make autonomous decisions, and adapt to changing situations. Furthermore, this strategy encourages cooperation through peer-to-peer learning, mentoring, and information sharing, which improves students' understanding of diverse concepts and ideas. Education 5.0 supports the ideas of individualized learning by allowing students to take control of their educational path, preparing them to flourish in a continuously changing and dynamic environment (Sukardjo & Salam,2020). Self-learning does not limit itself to specific subjects, aims, or academics. It gives students more freedom in their learning experience by allowing them to investigate and learn without being limited by resources. Self-directed learning allows you to study about a subject in depth. This type of learning is not limited by age. It gives pupils more freedom in the realm of education while minimizing teaching methods. The solutions are not supplied beforehand. Students must research solutions on their own. This improves problem-solving skills and opens up new chances for learning and growth, emphasizing the process of learning rather than the result. This prevents external variables like peer pressure, the emphasis on grades, and other distractions that impede learning (Lantada,2020). Project-based learning (PBL) promotes self-directed learning by allowing students to take responsibility for their education. PBL involves students in real-world problem-solving projects, which fosters autonomy and responsibility for their learning. PBL allows students to collaborate to solve complicated issues, which improves their self-regulated language acquisition and self-learning abilities. PBL encourages students to create goals, take an active role in their learning, and develop problem-solving abilities. By applying PBL, students develop confidence, increase their self-directed learning abilities, and get a better comprehension of the topic (Boss

& Krauss,2022). Self-directed learning is an important component of project-based learning (PBL), contributing significantly to its efficacy and influence. In PBL, students are tasked with investigating and overcoming real-world difficulties or hurdles, which requires a high level of independence and self-directed behavior. Self-directed learning allows students to take responsibility for their learning journey by actively seeking knowledge, tools, and support to help them manage the complexities of their tasks. This self-directed strategy enables students to set goals, make decisions, and successfully manage their time, fostering a feeling of responsibility and accountability for their learning outcomes. Self-directed learning encourages students to engage in critical thinking, problem-solving, and reflection as they face authentic obstacles and make autonomous decisions. Furthermore, self-directed learning promotes co-operation and peer learning within the framework of PBL, allowing students to collaborate with peers, request feedback, and exchange ideas to improve their understanding and refine their projects. By combining self-directed learning into PBL, educators may create a learning environment that promotes autonomy, inquisitiveness, and lifelong learning skills, preparing students to succeed in the complex and ever-changing 21st-century world (Sumarni & Kadarwati,2020). Self-directed project-based learning is intended to increase comprehension of topics from several disciplines. The motivating question can serve as the core of this procedure. Self-directed PBL enables students to develop critical 21st-century skills like as problem-solving, cooperation, creativity, time management, personal responsibility, and others. Self-directed project-based learning is authentic. Rather than gathering knowledge from a textbook or lecture, students interact with actual people and community experts, which fosters intrinsic drive and a passion for learning. Students, rather than the instructor, design and organize the learning experience, making it more relevant and personalized (Swart,2018). Independent thinking refers to self-motivated learning via decision-making and personal responsibility. Independent thinking in learning assumes that learners focus only on achieving learning objectives, rating abilities, developing reasoning, and building attitudes until they find themselves during the process. Learners can improve their ability to monitor their learning through exercises tailored to their own needs. It is typically defined as the ability to "stand alone, reflect critically, make judgments, and act independently." Students recognize the need to take responsibility for acquiring the necessary knowledge (Mentz et al.,2020). The project-based flipped learning paradigm combines pre-class preparation, in-depth in-class activities, and post-class additional education to improve self-directed learning, self-leadership, and learning competency. PBL program improves self-directed learning skills compared to traditional lecture-based education. Studies employing the Self-Directed Learning Readiness Scale indicate that students in PBL programs significantly improve their self-directed learning skills (Ulseth,2016). Project-based learning in engineering, particularly open-ended design projects, promotes tenacity, self-discipline, curiosity, and effective organization. Research done at the University of Calgary's Schulich School of Engineering found that project-based learning experiences improve students' self-directed learning preparedness (Eggermont et al.,2015). Learning experiences created and managed by self-directed learners are comprehensive. Experiences provide more than material or skill development alone.Self-directed learning experiences may be structured to incorporate subject-specific knowledge while also encouraging 21st-century skill development. Considering the current life as a collection of tasks you have to plan, organize, manage, and execute. Real-world projects you manage include meal planning, fitness routines, vacations, house ownership, parenting, job applications, and lesson planning. Managing such life tasks requires a variety of talents, including decision-making, organization, planning, teamwork, communication, resourcefulness, and creativity. Self-directed learning is essentially training for your pupils to develop the abilities needed to handle life's problems, organize a gazillion tasks, and manage real-world projects. Self-directed learners may simultaneously acquire information, understand concepts, and develop key life skills (Lemmetty,2023). One advantage of self-directed learning is that it is very personalised. Self-directed learning experiences appropriately represent each student's interests, needs, goals, and aspirations. Students design and conduct learning activities that they find fascinating, beneficial, or applicable to their personal lives. Personal choices drive children. When learning experiences are engaging, meaningful, and personally relevant to each pupils, they are more inclined to like them and hence learn more. Self-direction creates a desire for learning, which leads to an intrinsic drive to study. Students want to learn because the experience or topic is meaningful to them, not because they want to obtain a good grade or pass an exam (Watkins,2019). Self-directed learning shows kids how to learn. Self-directed learners understand what questions they should pose, how to ask them, and where to get the answers. Self-directed learners learn how to organize the knowledge and experiences they gain into digestible, useable chunks. Self-directed learners can view and experience learning as a continuous process rather than a fixed conclusion. Self-directed learners' experiment, try one way, trust their experience and reflect on it, make adjustments, and try again. Self-directed learning, like life, is a constant process of learning (Rashid & Ashgar,2016). PBL catalyzes the development of SDL in students, allowing them to take charge of their educational experience. While PBL's benefits in developing collaborative problem-solving, critical thinking, and creativity are well established, its function in cultivating SDL sheds fresh light on its transformational potential within educational paradigms. At its core, PBL puts students at the center of their learning experiences by immersing them in real-world, multidisciplinary projects that need active engagement and investigation. Students face difficult issues that need autonomous research and self-directed decision-making as they engage in hands-on discovery and experimentation. Students develop a sense of agency and independence in their learning process by taking on the responsibility of creating project objectives, performing research, and developing solutions (Singh et al.,2022). PBL distinguishes itself by emphasizing inquiry-based learning, in which students are urged to ask questions, seek answers, and negotiate uncertainty on their own. In contrast to traditional teaching approaches that prioritize the transmission of pre-established knowledge, PBL allows students to investigate topics that pique their interest, creating intrinsic motivation and excitement for learning. As students participate in project-based activities, they experience real-world situations that force them to build self-directed problem-solving abilities, which improves their capacity to deal with uncertainty and tackle obstacles with resilience (Brockett & Hiemstra, 2018). PBL instills in pupils a growth mentality, showing them that intellect and talents can be developed with work and determination. Through a process of investigation, reflection, and revision, students learn to see failures as opportunities for growth rather than obstacles to achievement. This cyclical method of self-assessment and growth fosters metacognitive awareness, enabling students to track their progress and alter their techniques as needed. PBL offers personalized learning opportunities that respond to each student's interests, talents, and learning styles. As students work with classmates and mentors to tackle complicated challenges, they learn about their strengths and areas for progress. Students improve their self-awareness and self-efficacy by reflecting on themselves and receiving feedback from others, resulting in a better grasp of their learning preferences and goals (Adwan et al.,2022; Usmaedi,2021). Project-based learning is an excellent strategy for improving students' self-directed learning and allowing them to take control of their educational journey. PBL instills in learners the talents and attitudes necessary to thrive in a constantly complicated and interrelated world by promoting inquiry, resilience, and reflective thinking. When educators use PBL's transformational power, they help students realise their full potential and prepare them to tackle future challenges and opportunities with confidence and skill.

CONCLUSION

Project-based learning (PBL) marks a dramatic shift in education, allowing students to take control of their learning experience and realize their full potential. PBL emphasizes active student participation via hands-on projects designed to develop fundamental skills such as creativity, critical thinking, cooperation, and problem-solving. It bridges the gap between theory and practice by incorporating real-world projects, providing students with a meaningful context for learning. This strategy guarantees that students not only learn abstract concepts, but also realize how they apply in real-world circumstances, which improves their comprehension and retention. Furthermore, PBL serves as an effective technique for developing engaged and thinking learners. By presenting students with genuine challenges and fostering inquiry-based exploration, PBL provides them with skills and knowledge that extend beyond the classroom walls. Collaborative projects also teach students the value of teamwork and cooperation, which are essential for success in a variety of professional and social settings. Despite the limitations, the advantages of PBL are considerable. PBL is an appealing alternative for educators trying to improve their teaching techniques since it increases student engagement and helps students develop critical thinking abilities. Furthermore, the emphasis on real-world application guarantees that students are active participants in their learning experience, rather than passive receivers of knowledge. As educational research investigates the complexities of PBL implementation, its positive influence on learning outcomes and personal growth becomes clearer. PBL is more than simply a teaching approach; it is a catalyst for holistic development, preparing students to negotiate the complexity of the modern world.

REFERENCES

Afriansyah, B., & Yustanti, N. V. (2021). Multiliteracy education in 5.0 era on learning entrepreneurship with the project based learning model. In *Educational Innovation in Society 5.0 Era: Challenges and Opportunities* (pp. 286-290). Routledge.

Al-Adwan, A. S., Nofal, M., Akram, H., Albelbisi, N. A., & Al-Okaily, M. (2022). Towards a Sustainable Adoption of E-Learning Systems: The Role of Self-Directed Learning. *Journal of Information Technology Education*, 21.

Alharbi, A. M. (2023). Implementation of Education 5.0 in developed and developing countries: A comparative study. *Creative Education*, 14(5), 914–942. 10.4236/ce.2023.145059

Amalia, G. R., Kurniasih, S., & Jaenudin, D. (2022). Project-Based Learning on Biotechnology Materials to Enhance High School Students' Creativity and Problem-Solving Skills. [Journal of Science Education and Practice]. *JSEP*, 6(1), 51–64. 10.33751/jsep.v6i1.5704

Boss, S., & Krauss, J. (2022). *Reinventing project-based learning: Your field guide to real-world projects in the digital age*. International Society for Technology in Education.

Brockett, R. G., & Hiemstra, R. (2018). *Self-direction in adult learning: Perspectives on theory, research and practice*. Routledge. 10.4324/9780429457319

Brothers, P. (2019, February 24). Ten charts that explain the global education technology market. *Medium*. https://medium.com/@patrickbrothers/ten-charts-that-explain-the-global-education-technology-market-6809fa68484c

Caplan, B. (2018). *The case against education: Why the education system is a waste of time and money*. Princeton University Press.

Carpenter, M. S., Yakymyshyn, C., Micher, L. E., & Locke, A. (2016, June). Improved student engagement through project-based learning in freshman engineering design. In *2016 ASEE Annual Conference & Exposition*. ASEE. 10.18260/p.25602

Chen, S. Y., Lai, C. F., Lai, Y. H., & Su, Y. S. (2022). Effect of project-based learning on development of students' creative thinking. *International Journal of Electrical Engineering Education*, 59(3), 232–250. 10.1177/0020720919846808

Craft, A. M., & Capraro, R. M. (2017). Science, technology, engineering, and mathematics project-based learning: Merging rigor and relevance to increase student engagement. *Electronic International Journal of Education, Arts, and Science (EIJEAS), 3*(6).

Dafik. (2023). The framework of project-based learning (PJBL) activities with steam approach in enhancing creative thinking skills in solving data presentation problems based on ethnomathematics. *International Journal of Multidisciplinary Research and Growth Evaluation, 4*(3), 495-504. 10.54660/.IJMRGE.2023.4.3.495-504

Deshpande, A. M. (2022). Project Based Learning Approach in Digital Signal Processing Course for Increasing Learners' Cognitive and Behavioral Engagement to Promote Self-Learning. *Journal of Engineering Education Transformations, 36*(Special Issue 1).

Eggermont, M., Brennan, R. W., & O'Neill, T. (2015). *The impact of project-based learning on self-directed learning readiness.*

Gunawan, I. G. D., & Danika, I. W. S. G. (2023). Leveraging Advanced Technologies to Enhance Learning Experiences in the Era 5.0. *International Proceeding On Religion, Culture, Law, Education, And Hindu Studies*, 1, 121–137.

Hall, A., & Miro, D. (2016). A study of student engagement in project-based learning across multiple approaches to STEM education programs. *School Science and Mathematics*, 116(6), 310–319. 10.1111/ssm.12182

Illahi, P. C., Fitri, R., & Arsih, F. (2022). The Effect of Project Based Learning Model on Creative Thinking Ability in Biology Learning. *Journal of Digital Learning and Education*, 2(3), 171–177. 10.52562/jdle.v2i3.441

Imbaquingo, A., & Cárdenas, J. (2023). Project-based learning as a methodology to improve reading and comprehension skills in the English language. *Education Sciences*, 13(6), 587. 10.3390/educsci13060587

Imbaquingo, A., & Cárdenas, J. (2023). Project-based learning as a methodology to improve reading and comprehension skills in the English language. *Education Sciences*, 13(6), 587. 10.3390/educsci13060587

Kakoty, S., Lal, M., & Sarma, S. K. (2011). E-learning as a research area: An analytical approach. *International Journal of Advanced Computer Science and Applications*, 2(9), 144–148. 10.14569/IJACSA.2011.020923

Keshav, M., Julien, L., & Miezel, J. (2022). The Role of Technology in Era 5.0 in the Development of Arabic Language in the World of Education. *JILTECH: Journal International of Lingua & Technology, 1*(2).

Lantada, A. D. (2020). Engineering education 5.0: Continuously evolving engineering education. *International Journal of Engineering Education*, 36(6), 1814–1832.

Lantada, A. D. (2022). Engineering education 5.0: Strategies for a successful transformative project-based learning. In *Insights Into Global Engineering Education After the Birth of Industry 5.0*. IntechOpen. 10.5772/intechopen.102844

Leasa, M., Papilaya, P. M., Batlolona, J. R., & Nuniary, S. (2023). Project-based learning: Changing students' scientific thinking to be creative from waste natural materials. *Jurnal Penelitian Pendidikan IPA*, 9(1), 350–359. 10.29303/jppipa.v9i1.2459

Lemmetty, S. (2023). Learning in the technology field: How to capture the benefits of self-direction? *IEEE Engineering Management Review*, 51(1), 123–128. 10.1109/EMR.2023.3237807

Loeng, S. (2020). Self-directed learning: A core concept in adult education. *Education Research International*, 2020, 1–12. 10.1155/2020/3816132

Mentz, E., Bailey, R., Bosch, C., Breed, B., Bunt, B. J., Chigona, W., & Verster, M. (2020). *Self-directed learning research and its impact on educational practice*. AOSIS. 10.4102/aosis.2020.BK206

Morais, P., Ferreira, M. J., & Veloso, B. (2021). Improving student engagement with Project-Based Learning: A case study in Software Engineering. *IEEE-RITA*, 16(1), 21–28. 10.1109/RITA.2021.3052677

Patange, A. D., Bewoor, A. K., Deshmukh, S. P., Mulik, S. S., Pardeshi, S. S., & Jegadeeshwaran, R. (2019). Improving program outcome attainments using project based learning approach for: UG course-mechatronics. *Journal of Engineering Education Transformations*, 33(1), 1–8.

Pratama, M. R., Fawaida, U., & Guarin, R. M. (2023). Project-Based Learning in Elementary School: Influence on Students' Creative Thinking Ability. *MUDARRISA: Jurnal Kajian Pendidikan Islam*, 15(1), 60–83. 10.18326/mdr.v15i1.60-83

Rashid, T., & Asghar, H. M. (2016). Technology use, self-directed learning, student engagement and academic performance: Examining the interrelations. *Computers in Human Behavior*, 63, 604–612. 10.1016/j.chb.2016.05.084

Riegel, K. A. (2023). Project based learning (PBL): Less project, more problem. *The Journal of the Acoustical Society of America*, 153(3, supplement), A272–A272. 10.1121/10.0018820

Sajidan, S., Suranto, S., Atmojo, I. R. W., Saputri, D. Y., & Etviana, R. (2022). Problem-based learning-collaboration (PBL-C) model in elementary school science learning in the industrial revolution era 4.0 and Indonesia society 5.0. *Jurnal Pendidikan IPA Indonesia*, 11(3), 477–488. 10.15294/jpii.v11i3.30631

Shaturaev, J. (2021). A Comparative Analysis of Public Education System of Indonesia and Uzbekistan. *Bioscience Biotechnology Research Communications*, 14(5), 89–92. 10.21786/bbrc/14.5/18

Singer, A. C. (2023). Project-based learning engages students at a level more directly applicable to their future careers. *The Journal of the Acoustical Society of America*, 153(3, supplement), A214–A214. 10.1121/10.0018694

Singh, H. K. B., Singh, H., Bahadin, S., Abdullah, H., Hamzah, N., Halim, K. H. K., & Abbas, M. (2022). What students say on self-directed language learning in the context of new normal: Their difficulties, coping mechanisms, and benefits. *Journal of Positive School Psychology*, 1326–1338.

Sukardjo, M., & Salam, M. (2020). Effect of Concept Attainment Models and Self-Directed Learning (SDL) on Mathematics Learning Outcomes. *International Journal of Instruction*, 13(3), 275–292. 10.29333/iji.2020.13319a

Sułkowski, Ł., Kolasińska-Morawska, K., Seliga, R., & Morawski, P. (2021). Smart learning technologization in the economy 5.0—The polish perspective. *Applied Sciences (Basel, Switzerland)*, 11(11), 5261. 10.3390/app11115261

Sumarni, W., & Kadarwati, S. (2020). Ethno-stem project-based learning: Its impact to critical and creative thinking skills. *Jurnal Pendidikan IPA Indonesia*, 9(1), 11–21. 10.15294/jpii.v9i1.21754

Sumarni, W., & Kadarwati, S. (2020). Ethno-stem project-based learning: Its impact to critical and creative thinking skills. *Jurnal Pendidikan IPA Indonesia*, 9(1), 11–21. 10.15294/jpii.v9i1.21754

Togo, M., & Gandidzanwa, C. P. (2021). The role of Education 5.0 in accelerating the implementation of SDGs and challenges encountered at the University of Zimbabwe. *International Journal of Sustainability in Higher Education*, 22(7), 1520–1535. 10.1108/IJSHE-05-2020-0158

Ulseth, R. R. (2016, June). Development of pbl students as self-directed learners. In *2016 ASEE Annual Conference & Exposition*. ASEE. 10.18260/p.26823

Usmaedi, U. (2021). Education curriculum for society 5.0 in the next decade. *Jurnal Pendidikan Dasar Setiabudhi*, 4(2), 63–79.

Watkins, S. (2019). Learners' perceptions of benefits in a self-directed teletandem course: an approach to encourage EFL learners to use English outside the classroom. *Asian EFL Journal, 23*(4.1), 4-29.

Wulandani, C., Putri, M. A., Pratiwi, R. I., & Sulong, K. (2022). Implementing project-based steam instructional approach in early childhood education in 5.0 industrial revolution era. *Indonesian Journal of Early Childhood Educational Research*, 1(1), 29–37. 10.31958/ijecer.v1i1.5819

Yu, H. (2024). Enhancing creative cognition through project-based learning: An in-depth scholarly exploration. *Heliyon*, 10(6), e27706. 10.1016/j.heliyon.2024.e2770638533042

Zhu, M., Bonk, C. J., & Doo, M. Y. (2020). Self-directed learning in MOOCs: Exploring the relationships among motivation, self-monitoring, and self-management. *Educational Technology Research and Development*, 68(5), 2073–2093. 10.1007/s11423-020-09747-8

Chapter 11
Teacher Professional Development in Education 5.0

Nhat Truong Tran Minh
Industrial University of Ho Chi Minh City, Vietnam

ABSTRACT

In the rapidly evolving landscape of education, the advent of Education 5.0 brings with it new challenges and opportunities for teachers. This chapter focuses on teacher professional development in the context of Education 5.0. It explores how teacher professional development has evolved with the integration of technology and new pedagogical approaches in education. The chapter discusses the importance of continuous professional development for teachers to keep up with the changing landscape of education and implement effective teaching practices. It also highlights the role of collaboration, personalized learning, and mentorship in enhancing teacher professional development in Education 5.0. Additionally, the chapter examines the challenges and barriers that teachers may face in adapting to the new demands of Education 5.0 and offers strategies for overcoming these challenges.

BACKGROUND

Teacher professional development is an essential component of successful education systems. In recent years, the focus has shifted from traditional models of professional development to a more dynamic and interactive approach. This shift is due to the recognition that teachers are professionals who can benefit from ongoing learning and support (Ismanto, 2019). In education 5.0, teacher professional development is designed to be personalized, collaborative, and inquiry-based. It is no longer a one-size-fits-all model but rather a process that takes into account the unique needs and interests of individual teachers. This approach allows teachers to take ownership of their learning and tailor it to their specific context and goals (Ijudin, 2022).

One of the key features of teacher professional development in education 5.0 is an emphasis on collaboration. Teachers are encouraged to work together, share ideas, and engage in reflective dialogue (Matorevhu, 2023). This collaborative approach not only promotes deeper learning but also creates a supportive and collegial learning community. Another important aspect of teacher professional development in education 5.0 is the use of technology (Kurniawan, 2022). Teachers are encouraged to use digital tools and resources to enhance their learning and instruction. This can include online courses, webinars,

DOI: 10.4018/979-8-3693-3041-8.ch011

virtual conferences, and social media platforms. Technology can also be used to facilitate collaboration and communication among teachers, allowing them to connect and learn from each other regardless of their geographical location. This chapter seeks to address the need for comprehensive teacher training programs that equip educators with the knowledge and skills required to navigate the changing landscape of Education 5.0 (Prasetya, 2023).

In the rapidly evolving landscape of education, the advent of Education 5.0 brings with it new challenges and opportunities for teachers. As the focus shifts towards personalized learning, emerging technologies, and an increasingly interconnected world, it becomes imperative for teachers to undergo continuous professional development to meet the demands of this new educational era (Skitsko, 2022). This chapter aims to explore effective strategies for implementing teacher professional development in Education 5.0, enabling educators to enhance their pedagogical practices and adapt to the changing needs of learners. We will explore the importance of teacher professional development in Education 5.0 and propose effective strategies to support educators in adapting to this new educational paradigm.

Teacher professional development in education 5.0 is important because it is essential for teachers to stay current with the latest research, technologies, and teaching strategies (Piper, 2018). This version of teacher professional development focuses on preparing educators for the rapidly changing educational landscape, which includes integrating technology into the classroom, fostering student-centered learning, and developing skills needed for the 21st-century workforce (Sukmara, 2023). By engaging in professional development opportunities, teachers can enhance their teaching practices, improve student outcomes, and stay relevant in today's dynamic education environment.

Table 1 outlines the evolution of the role of teachers in education across different eras, starting from Education 1.0, in which teachers were primarily information givers and lecturers using basic tools like blackboards and chalk. As education progressed to Education 5.0, teachers are now seen as designers of learning experiences, utilizing advanced tools and technologies such as learning analytics, interactive digital content, and simulation tools to create engaging and personalized learning environments.

Table 1. The evolving role of teachers in education 5.0

Education Era	Role of Teachers	Tools and Technologies
Education 1.0	Information giver and lecturer	Blackboard, chalk, textbooks
Education 2.0	Facilitator and guide	Overhead projectors, computers, presentation software
Education 3.0	Facilitator, mentor, and coach	Online resources, multimedia presentations, learning management systems
Education 4.0	Personalized learning facilitator	Artificial intelligence, virtual and augmented reality, adaptive learning platforms
Education 5.0	Designer of learning experiences	Learning analytics, interactive digital content, simulation tools

Key Objectives

This chapter aims to achieve the following objectives:

i. To provide an overview of Education 5.0 and its impact on teaching and learning.
ii. To highlight the importance of continuous professional development for teachers in Education 5.0.
iii. Explore innovative models of teacher professional development that align with Education 5.0.
iv. Discuss the evolving role of teachers in Education 5.0 and the skills they need to excel.

v. To propose strategies for adaptive training programs that can better prepare teachers for the challenges posed by Education 5.0.
vi. To discuss the potential benefits and challenges of implementing adaptive training in teacher professional development.

EDUCATION 5.0: UNDERSTANDING THE PARADIGM SHIFT

Definition of Education 5.0

Education 5.0 represents the next stage in the evolution of education, building upon previous models such as Education 1.0 (traditional lecture-based learning), Education 2.0 (web-based learning and collaboration), and Education 3.0 (personalized and student-centered learning) (Thomson, 2019). Education 5.0 is characterized by its focus on preparing students for the future by equipping them with 21st-century skills such as critical thinking, problem-solving, communication, collaboration, and digital literacy (Yulianto. 2021). It emphasizes the integration of technology, interdisciplinary learning, project-based approaches, and a holistic view of education that goes beyond academic content to encompass social-emotional skills and global competencies (Rusman, 2023).

Teacher professional development in Education 5.0 is designed to support educators in developing a learner-centered approach to teaching that emphasizes personalized learning experiences tailored to individual student needs and interests (Makopoulou, 2021). It encourages teachers to collaborate with colleagues, engage in reflective practice, and continuously seek opportunities for professional growth and improvement. Professional development programs in Education 5.0 also often incorporate ongoing coaching and mentoring to provide teachers with the support and feedback they need to enhance their instructional practices and maximize student learning outcomes (Leon, 2023).

In a study conducted by Early (2017), they found that teacher professional development had a significant impact on student achievement. They analyzed 35 studies that focused on the relationship between professional development programs and student outcomes and found that high-quality professional development was associated with an 11 to 40 percentile point increase in student achievement. This evidence suggests that investing in teacher professional development can lead to improved student outcomes.

Key Features and Characteristics of Education 5.0

Education 5.0 is a modern approach to education that incorporates emerging technologies, personalized learning, experiential learning, social and emotional skills development, and a focus on lifelong learning (Eliwatis, 2022). Figure 1 outlines the key features and characteristics of Education 5.0, highlighting the importance of adaptability, creativity, critical thinking, collaboration, and digital literacy in preparing students for the future.

Figure 1. Key features and characteristics of Education 5.0

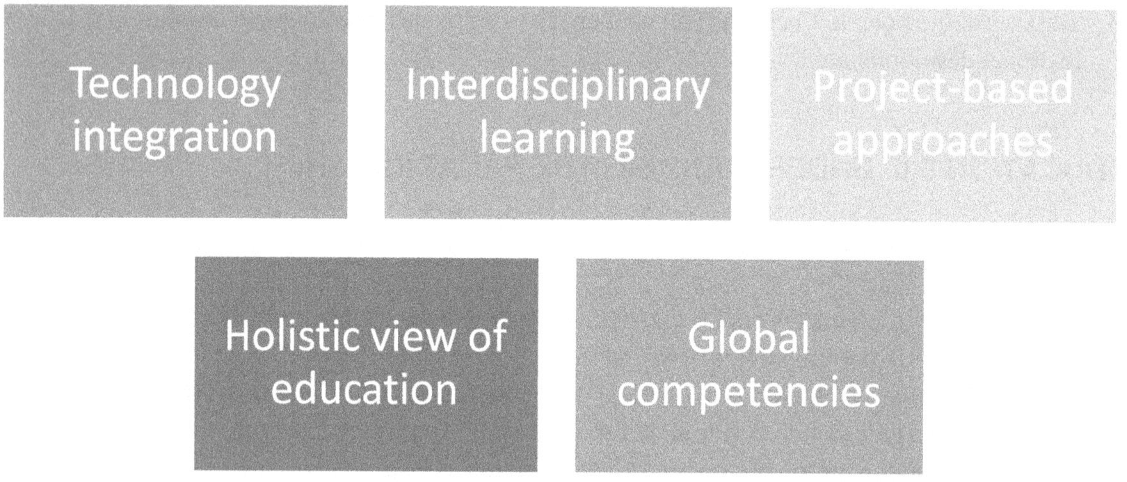

Technology integration: Education 5.0 leverages technology as a tool to enhance teaching and learning, providing opportunities for interactive, personalized, and engaging experiences for students. Virtual reality, augmented reality, artificial intelligence, and other emerging technologies are used to create immersive learning environments that support creativity, innovation, and critical thinking (Skitsko, 2022).

Interdisciplinary learning: Education 5.0 encourages the integration of various disciplines to address complex real-world problems and challenges. By connecting different subject areas and perspectives, students develop a deeper understanding of the interconnectedness of knowledge and how it applies in practical contexts (Pituła, 2021).

Project-based approaches: Education 5.0 emphasizes hands-on, experiential learning through project-based activities that allow students to apply their knowledge in authentic and meaningful ways. By working on projects collaboratively, students develop essential skills such as communication, teamwork, problem-solving, and adaptability (Mulyadi, 2019).

Holistic view of education: Education 5.0 recognizes the importance of addressing the social-emotional aspects of learning in addition to academic content. It promotes students' well-being, resilience, empathy, and cultural competence, helping them develop a strong sense of self-awareness and interpersonal skills that are essential for success in the 21st century (Kaul, 2022).

Global competencies: Education 5.0 emphasizes the development of global competencies such as intercultural understanding, environmental awareness, and ethical decision-making. By fostering a sense of global citizenship and interconnectedness, students are prepared to engage with diverse perspectives and collaborate with others on a global scale (Dahri, 2021).

Implications for Teaching and Learning

Student-centered approach: Education 5.0 shifts the focus from passive learning to active engagement, empowering students to take ownership of their learning and pursue their interests and passions (Aprilisa, 2020). Teachers serve as facilitators, mentors, and coaches, guiding students as they explore, inquire, and create meaningful learning experiences.

Lifelong learning mindset: Education 5.0 instills a lifelong learning mindset in students, encouraging them to be curious, reflective, and adaptable in an ever-changing world. Teachers model continuous learning and growth, emphasizing the importance of being flexible, resilient, and open to new ideas and perspectives (Al-Qahtani, 2015).

Collaboration and communication skills: Education 5.0 emphasizes the development of collaboration and communication skills through group projects, peer feedback, and teamwork activities (Eliwatis, 2022). Students learn how to work effectively with others, listen actively, communicate clearly, and resolve conflicts constructively, preparing them for success in a collaborative and interconnected world.

Critical thinking and problem-solving: Education 5.0 nurtures students' critical thinking and problem-solving skills by challenging them to analyze information, evaluate evidence, and generate innovative solutions to complex problems. Teachers provide opportunities for students to think critically, ask meaningful questions, and apply their knowledge in creative and practical ways (Kaul, 2022).

Embracing diversity and inclusion: Education 5.0 values diversity and inclusion as essential components of a rich learning environment. Teachers create inclusive classrooms where students feel respected, supported, and valued for their unique perspectives, backgrounds, and experiences (Komar, 2020). By celebrating diversity and promoting equity, Education 5.0 fosters empathy, understanding, and collaboration among students from different cultural and social backgrounds.

By embracing the principles of Education 5.0, educators can transform teaching and learning experiences, equip students with the skills they need to succeed in the digital age and prepare them to be lifelong learners and active participants in a rapidly changing world (Arief, 2023). In summary, Education 5.0 represents a transformative shift in education that embraces a holistic, student-centered, and future-oriented approach to teaching and learning. By integrating technology, interdisciplinary learning, project-based approaches, social-emotional skills, and global competencies, Education 5.0 prepares students to thrive in a rapidly changing and interconnected world, equipping them with the knowledge, skills, and mindsets needed to succeed in the 21st century and beyond.

Importance of Continuous Professional Development in Education 5.0

Figure 2 illustrates the importance of Continuous Professional Development in Education 5.0, highlighting the significant role it plays in shaping and improving the education sector.

Figure 2. Significance of continuous professional development in education 5.0

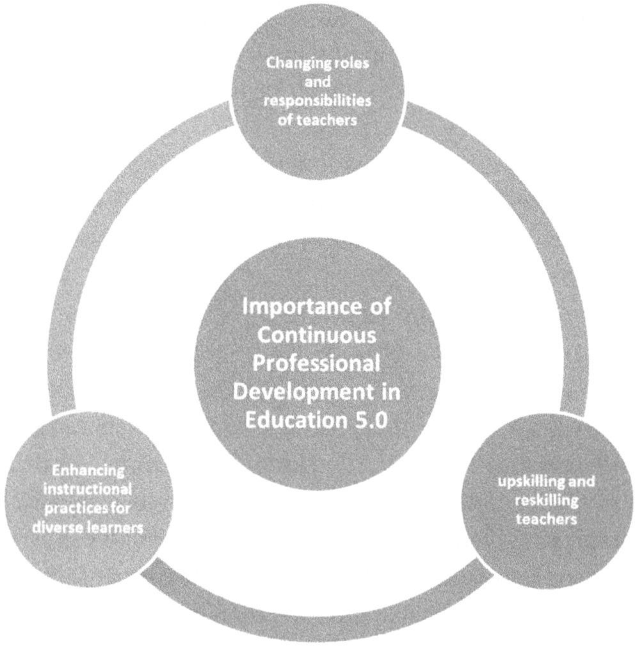

Changing Roles and Responsibilities of Teachers

In the era of Education 5.0, teachers are experiencing significant changes in their roles and responsibilities. With the integration of technology, shifting pedagogical approaches, and evolving student needs, teachers need to continuously engage in professional development to stay current and effective in their practice (Aleixo, 2023). Continuous professional development is essential in Education 5.0 as it allows teachers to adapt to the changing landscape of education, enhance their teaching skills, and ultimately improve student outcomes (Oktaviana, 2022).

One of the key reasons why continuous professional development is important in Education 5.0 is the changing roles and responsibilities of teachers. In the past, teachers were primarily seen as dispensers of knowledge, delivering content to students in a traditional classroom setting (Arief, 2023). However, in Education 5.0, teachers are expected to take on a more dynamic and multifaceted role (Rahma, 2020). They are now facilitators of learning, guiding students in inquiry-based activities, collaborative projects, and problem-solving tasks. Teachers are also becoming mentors, helping students develop 21st-century skills such as critical thinking, communication, and creativity (Erickson, 2012).

Continuous professional development plays a vital role in helping teachers navigate these changing roles and responsibilities. By engaging in ongoing training, workshops, and courses, teachers can acquire the necessary knowledge and skills to effectively facilitate student-centered learning activities (Ihsan, 2023). For example, workshops on project-based learning can help teachers design engaging and meaningful projects that promote student collaboration and critical thinking (Skitsko, 2022). Training on the use of educational technology can enable teachers to integrate digital tools into their instruction, providing students with interactive and personalized learning experiences.

Research has shown that continuous professional development leads to improved teaching practices and student learning outcomes. A study by Simonsen (2017) found that teachers who participated in high-quality professional development programs demonstrated enhanced instructional strategies, increased student engagement, and higher academic achievement among their students. This highlights the significant impact that ongoing professional development can have on both teachers and students in Education 5.0.

Moreover, continuous professional development allows teachers to stay updated on the latest research, trends, and best practices in education. In a rapidly changing world, where new technologies and teaching methods are constantly emerging, teachers need to be proactive in their professional growth to ensure they are providing a high-quality education to their students (Yulianto, 2021). By attending conferences, reading academic journals, and collaborating with fellow educators, teachers can stay informed about innovative approaches to teaching and learning (Leon, 2023).

Additionally, continuous professional development fosters a culture of lifelong learning among teachers. In Education 5.0, where the focus is on personalized and adaptive learning experiences, teachers must model a growth mindset and a commitment to ongoing improvement (Matorevhu, 2023). By engaging in continuous professional development, teachers demonstrate their dedication to their profession and their willingness to enhance their knowledge and skills. This not only benefits teachers in their own practice but also creates a culture of excellence within schools and educational institutions (Suyudi, 2021).

In general, continuous professional development is essential in Education 5.0 to support teachers in adapting to the changing roles and responsibilities of the profession. By engaging in ongoing training, workshops, and learning opportunities, teachers can enhance their teaching skills, stay updated on the latest trends in education, and ultimately improve student outcomes. Continuous professional development is not only a means for professional growth but also a reflection of teachers' commitment to providing quality education to their students in the digital age. As Education 5.0 continues to evolve, continuous professional development for teachers will become more critical in ensuring student success.

The Need for Upskilling and Reskilling Teachers

In the rapidly changing landscape of education, it is essential for teachers to engage in continuous professional development to upskill and reskill themselves. Upskilling refers to improving existing skills, while reskilling involves acquiring new skills to adapt to changing demands. The need for upskilling and reskilling teachers is driven by several factors (Skitsko, 2022).

Firstly, technological advancements have revolutionized the way education is delivered. With the integration of digital tools and platforms in teaching and learning, teachers need to acquire digital literacy skills to effectively navigate the digital world (Mäkelä, 2015). For example, teachers may need training on using learning management systems, video conferencing tools, and online assessment platforms to deliver engaging and interactive lessons in both physical and virtual classrooms (Ramadhani, 2021).

Moreover, the demands of 21st-century skills require teachers to constantly update their pedagogical practices. Skills such as critical thinking, collaboration, communication, and creativity are essential for students to thrive in the modern world (Pituła, 2021). Teachers need to incorporate these skills into their instructional strategies to prepare students for future success. Continuous professional development enables teachers to stay abreast of the latest pedagogical trends and research-based practices that can enhance student learning outcomes (Rusman, 2023).

Additionally, the diverse needs of learners in today's classrooms necessitate teachers to develop cultural competency and social-emotional skills. Teachers need to be equipped with strategies to support diverse learners, including those with special educational needs, English language learners, and students from different cultural backgrounds (Oktaviana, 2022). Professional development opportunities focused on inclusive practices, differentiation, and culturally responsive teaching can help teachers create an inclusive and supportive learning environment for all students (Sukmara, 2023).

Furthermore, the changing educational policies and curriculum frameworks often require teachers to update their knowledge and skills to align with new standards and expectations (Thomson, 2019). For example, the implementation of new assessment practices, curriculum revisions, or policy changes may necessitate training and professional development for teachers to effectively implement these changes in their teaching practice (Mulyadi, 2019).

Continuous professional development also plays a crucial role in improving teacher motivation and job satisfaction. When teachers have access to high-quality professional learning opportunities that support their growth and development, they are more likely to feel valued and motivated in their role (Kurniawan, 2022). Professional development can help teachers stay energized, engaged, and passionate about their profession, resulting in a positive impact on student learning and overall school culture.

The need for upskilling and reskilling teachers through continuous professional development is paramount in the ever-evolving field of education. By investing in teachers' ongoing growth and development, educational institutions can ensure that educators are equipped with the knowledge, skills, and tools to meet the diverse needs of students and effectively prepare them for success in the 21st century. Professional development initiatives should be personalized, relevant, and aligned with teachers' professional goals and the evolving demands of the education sector. When teachers engage in continuous professional development, they not only enhance their own practice but also contribute to creating a culture of lifelong learning and innovation within the education system. Ultimately, investing in teachers' professional development is an investment in the future of education and the success of students (Kaul, 2022).

Enhancing Instructional Practices for Diverse Learners

Continuous professional development in education 5.0 is crucial for enhancing instructional practices for diverse learners. In today's educational landscape, classrooms are becoming increasingly diverse, with students coming from various cultural, linguistic, and socioeconomic backgrounds (Satria, 2019). Teachers need to be equipped with the knowledge and skills to address the needs of these diverse learners effectively (Fahri, 2023). Continuous professional development provides teachers with ongoing opportunities to learn about new instructional strategies, technologies, and methods that can help them meet the diverse needs of their students.

One key aspect of enhancing instructional practices for diverse learners is cultural responsiveness. Teachers need to understand and appreciate the cultural backgrounds of their students to create inclusive and supportive learning environments (Piper, 2018). Continuous professional development can help teachers develop cultural competence and learn how to incorporate diverse perspectives into their lessons (Dahri, 2021). For example, a teacher participating in professional development workshops on culturally responsive teaching may learn how to integrate multicultural literature into their curriculum or use strategies to engage English language learners effectively.

Furthermore, continuous professional development can also help teachers improve their knowledge and skills in differentiated instruction. Differentiated instruction is a teaching approach that recognizes the diverse learning needs of students and provides multiple pathways for them to acquire knowledge and demonstrate understanding (Makopoulou, 2021). Through professional development opportunities, teachers can learn how to differentiate their instruction based on students' interests, abilities, and learning styles (Al-Qahtani, 2015). For example, a teacher might learn how to create tiered assignments that allow students to choose tasks based on their readiness level or provide scaffolding and support for students who struggle with complex concepts.

In addition to cultural responsiveness and differentiated instruction, continuous professional development can also support teachers in incorporating technology into their instructional practices. Technology can be a powerful tool for promoting engagement, collaboration, and personalized learning in the classroom (Meter, 2023). Through professional development workshops and training sessions, teachers can learn how to effectively integrate technology tools and resources into their lessons (Aprilisa, 2020). For instance, a teacher might learn how to use educational apps to enhance student learning or incorporate multimedia projects to allow students to demonstrate their understanding in creative ways.

Moreover, continuous professional development can help teachers stay updated on the latest research and best practices in education. The field of education is constantly evolving, with new trends, theories, and approaches emerging all the time. By engaging in ongoing professional development, teachers can stay current with the latest developments in their field and adapt their instructional practices accordingly (Alharbi, 2023). For example, a teacher participating in a conference on innovative teaching strategies may learn about the benefits of project-based learning or inquiry-based instruction and how to implement these approaches in their classroom.

In general, continuous professional development is essential for teachers in Education 5.0 to adapt to their changing roles and responsibilities, upskill and reskill in response to evolving educational practices, and enhance their instructional practices for diverse learners. By investing in ongoing training and support for teachers, schools can ensure that educators are equipped with the knowledge, skills, and mindset needed to effectively engage and support all students in the modern learning environment. Through collaborative learning experiences, personalized training, and ongoing mentorship, teachers can continue to grow and develop as professionals, ultimately leading to improved student outcomes and a more equitable and inclusive educational system.

The Evolving Role of Teachers in Education 5.0

Shift From Knowledge Transmission to Facilitation

In the traditional education system, teachers primarily played the role of knowledge transmitters, delivering information to students and assessing their understanding through exams and quizzes (Ismanto, 2019). However, with the advent of Education 5.0, there has been a significant shift in the role of teachers from being mere providers of information to facilitators of learning (Chaer, 2020). In Education 5.0, teachers are expected to create a more interactive and collaborative learning environment where students can actively engage with the content and construct their own knowledge. Figure 3 below illustrates key features in the Shift from knowledge transmission to facilitation.

Figure 3. Key features in shift from knowledge transmission to facilitation

One example of this shift can be seen in the implementation of project-based learning (PBL) in classrooms. In PBL, teachers act as guides and mentors, helping students to explore real-world problems, conduct research, and collaborate with their peers to find solutions. By taking on the role of facilitators, teachers empower students to take ownership of their learning and develop critical thinking, problem-solving, and collaboration skills (Eliwatis, 2022).

Another example of the evolving role of teachers in Education 5.0 is the use of technology to enhance teaching and learning. Teachers are now expected to integrate digital tools and resources into their lessons to provide personalized and interactive learning experiences for students (Early, 2017). For instance, teachers can use virtual reality (VR) simulations, online platforms, and educational apps to supplement their teaching and engage students in experiential learning activities. By leveraging technology, teachers can create more dynamic and engaging learning environments that cater to the diverse needs and learning styles of their students (Ijudin, 2022).

In addition to facilitating learning in the classroom, teachers in Education 5.0 are also expected to foster a culture of lifelong learning among their students. This involves instilling a growth mindset in students, encouraging them to embrace challenges, learn from their mistakes, and continually seek new knowledge and skills (Khotimah, 2022). Teachers can promote lifelong learning by modeling curiosity, adaptability, and resilience in their own professional development and demonstrating a commitment to ongoing learning and growth.

By embracing the role of facilitators, integrating technology into their teaching practices, and promoting lifelong learning among their students, teachers in Education 5.0 are well-positioned to prepare students for success in a rapidly changing and complex world (Abakah, 2022). This shift from knowledge transmission to facilitation empowers students to become active participants in their learning journey and equips them with the essential skills and competencies needed to thrive in the 21st century (Komar, 2020).

The evolving role of teachers in Education 5.0 highlights the importance of adapting to the changing educational landscape and embracing new pedagogical approaches that prioritize student-centered learning, collaboration, and the integration of technology. By redefining their role as facilitators of learning, teachers can create more engaging, personalized, and impactful learning experiences for their students, setting them up for success in an increasingly interconnected and fast-paced world.

Emphasis on Skills Development and Critical Thinking

The evolving role of teachers in Education 5.0 places a strong emphasis on skills development and critical thinking. In today's rapidly changing world, it is no longer sufficient for teachers to simply impart knowledge to their students. Instead, they must focus on equipping students with the skills they need to navigate an increasingly complex and interconnected world (Omojola, 2021).

One key aspect of this shift is a move towards a more student-centered approach to teaching and learning. In Education 5.0, teachers are no longer seen as the sole source of knowledge; rather, they act as facilitators, guiding students in their exploration of topics and encouraging them to think critically and creatively. This shift mirrors the broader trend towards personalized learning, where students' individual needs and interests are taken into account in the design of their educational experience (Prasetya, 2023). For example, in a project-based learning environment, teachers may guide students in selecting a topic of interest and then work with them to develop a project that allows them to explore that topic in depth. This approach not only encourages students to think critically and creatively but also helps them develop important skills such as collaboration, communication, and problem-solving.

Another key aspect of the evolving role of teachers in Education 5.0 is a greater emphasis on the development of 21st-century skills. These skills include critical thinking, communication, collaboration, creativity, and digital literacy (Adisendjaja, 2017). Teachers are tasked with integrating these skills into their lessons and providing opportunities for students to practice and develop them (Rahma, 2020). For example, a social studies teacher might design a unit that requires students to research and analyze historical primary sources, collaborate with their peers to develop a presentation on a specific topic and communicate their findings to the class. This project helps students develop not only their critical thinking skills by analyzing and synthesizing information but also their communication and collaboration skills as they work together to create a cohesive presentation.

The evolving role of teachers in Education 5.0 includes a focus on incorporating technology into the classroom in meaningful ways. Technology can be a powerful tool for enhancing teaching and learning, but it is important for teachers to use it thoughtfully and purposefully (Seferoğlu, 2001). Teachers must be able to integrate technology into their lessons in ways that support student learning and the development of 21st-century skills. For example, a science teacher might use virtual reality simulations to allow students to explore complex scientific concepts in a hands-on way. By providing students with immersive, interactive experiences, the teacher can help them better understand difficult concepts and develop critical thinking skills through experimentation and exploration.

Collaboration and Co-Creation in the Classroom

In Education 5.0, the role of teachers is evolving to prioritize collaboration and co-creation in the classroom. Teachers are no longer seen as the sole source of knowledge but rather as facilitators who work alongside students to co-create learning experiences (Aleixo, 2023). This shift is driven by the recognition that the rapidly changing landscape of information and communication technologies requires a new approach to education that fosters critical thinking, creativity, and collaboration (Sururi, 2020).

Collaboration in the classroom involves teachers working together with students to develop a shared understanding of learning goals and strategies. This can take many forms, such as group projects, peer learning activities, or collaborative problem-solving tasks. By involving students in the co-creation of their learning experiences, teachers empower them to take ownership of their education and develop essential 21st-century skills (Simonsen, 2017). For example, in a project-based learning scenario, students could work in groups to design and implement a community service project. The teacher's role would be to guide the process, provide resources and support, and facilitate discussions to help students reflect on their experiences and set goals for future learning. Through this collaborative approach, students not only gain academic knowledge but also develop important skills such as communication, teamwork, and problem-solving.

Research has shown that collaboration and co-creation in the classroom can lead to improved student engagement, deeper learning, and increased motivation. A study by Sururi (2020) found that collaborative learning environments where students have a voice in shaping their educational experiences positively impact academic achievement and social-emotional development. By shifting the focus from teacher-centered to student-centered learning, teachers in Education 5.0 can create meaningful and relevant learning experiences that prepare students for success in the 21st century.

Teachers in Education 5.0 are also engaging in collaborative professional development activities with their peers. This can take the form of lesson study groups, PLCs (Professional Learning Communities), or collaborative inquiry projects. By working together to explore new teaching strategies, share best practices, and reflect on their teaching practices, teachers can continuously improve their pedagogical skills and stay abreast of the latest educational research and trends (Rahma, 2020). For instance, a group of teachers could come together to explore how to integrate technology into their lessons effectively. They could collaborate on designing and implementing technology-enhanced learning activities, observe each other's classes, and provide feedback to support each other's professional growth. By engaging in collaborative professional development, teachers can strengthen their instructional practices, enhance student learning outcomes, and build a supportive network of colleagues (Abakah, 2022).

In general, the evolving role of teachers in Education 5.0 is marked by a shift from knowledge transmission to facilitation, an emphasis on skills development and critical thinking, and a focus on collaboration and co-creation in the classroom. By embracing this new role, teachers are better equipped to prepare students for success in a rapidly changing world and to foster a deeper love of learning and exploration. The examples provided illustrate how teachers can adapt their practices to meet the demands of Education 5.0 and create rich, engaging learning experiences for their students.

Essential Skills for Teachers in Education 5.0

Technological Proficiency and Digital Literacy

Technological proficiency and digital literacy are essential skills for teachers in Education 5.0. As the education landscape continues to evolve, teachers must be equipped with the knowledge and skills to effectively integrate technology into their teaching practices.

Technological proficiency refers to the ability of teachers to effectively utilize various technological tools and resources to enhance student learning. In Education 5.0, technology plays a vital role in the teaching and learning process, offering innovative ways to engage students and personalize their learning experiences (Ihsan, 2023). Teachers need to be proficient in using educational technologies such as learning management systems, interactive whiteboards, educational apps, and online resources to create interactive and engaging learning environments (Omojola, 2021).

Digital literacy, on the other hand, encompasses the ability to critically evaluate, use, and create digital content. In Education 5.0, teachers need to be digitally literate to help students navigate the vast amount of information available online, teach them how to assess the credibility of sources, and foster digital citizenship skills (Khotimah, 2022). Digital literacy also involves understanding issues related to data privacy, cyberbullying, and digital security, which are essential in today's digital world.

One relevant example of the importance of technological proficiency and digital literacy for teachers in Education 5.0 is the use of blended learning models. Blended learning combines traditional face-to-face instruction with online learning activities, providing students with a more personalized and flexible learning experience. Teachers who are technologically proficient can effectively design and deliver online content, interact with students through digital platforms, and use data analytics to monitor student progress (Eliwatis, 2022). Additionally, digitally literate teachers can help students develop the critical thinking and information literacy skills needed to navigate online resources and participate responsibly in online discussions.

Research studies have highlighted the importance of technological proficiency and digital literacy for teachers in Education 5.0. For example, a study by Alharbi (2023) emphasized the need for teachers to continually update their technological skills and digital literacy to keep pace with the rapid changes in educational technology. Another study by Chaer (2020) found that teachers who are proficient in using technology are better able to engage students, promote active learning, and enhance student achievement.

Technological proficiency and digital literacy are essential skills for teachers in Education 5.0. Teachers must be able to leverage technology to create dynamic and interactive learning experiences for students, as well as help them develop the digital literacy skills needed to succeed in today's digital world. By continuously improving their technological proficiency and digital literacy, teachers can enhance student engagement, promote critical thinking skills, and prepare students for future success in an increasingly digital society.

Adaptability and Flexibility

Adaptability and flexibility are particularly crucial in Education 5.0 as the traditional classroom model is gradually being replaced by a more personalized and technology-driven approach. Teachers need to be open to experimenting with new technologies such as virtual reality, artificial intelligence, and gamification to enhance student learning experiences (Meter, 2023). They must also be willing to adapt their curriculum and teaching methods to accommodate different learning styles and preferences among students (Ijudin, 2022). For example, in a classroom where students have access to personalized learning platforms, teachers need to be flexible in their approach to instruction. They may need to design individualized learning plans for each student, provide differentiated instruction, and offer ongoing support and feedback to ensure student success. This level of adaptability requires teachers to be responsive to student needs, open to feedback, and willing to continuously refine their teaching practices.

Moreover, the COVID-19 pandemic has highlighted the importance of adaptability and flexibility in education. With schools shifting to remote and hybrid learning models, teachers had to quickly adapt to new technologies and virtual teaching methods to continue delivering quality education to students. Those teachers who were able to quickly pivot and adjust their teaching strategies to the new learning environment were better equipped to meet the needs of their students and ensure continuity in learning (Mäkelä, 2015). Research has also shown that teachers who demonstrate adaptability and flexibility are more effective in engaging students, fostering a positive classroom environment, and promoting student achievement. A study by Komar (2020) found that teachers who were adaptable and flexible in their teaching practices were able to create a more inclusive learning environment where students felt supported and encouraged to take on new challenges. By cultivating adaptability and flexibility, teachers can create dynamic and engaging learning experiences for students, promote innovation in education, and ultimately ensure student success in the 21st century.

Data-Driven Decision Making and Assessment

Data-driven decision making involves collecting, analyzing, and interpreting data to guide instructional strategies and interventions. Teachers can use various sources of data, such as formative assessments, summative assessments, attendance records, and student work samples, to gain insights into student learning (Omojola, 2021). For example, after administering a formative assessment on a specific math concept, teachers can analyze the results to identify common misconceptions among students and adjust their teaching strategies accordingly. By analyzing data on attendance and student behavior, teachers can also identify students who may need additional support or intervention.

Teachers can also use data to monitor student progress and growth over time. By comparing assessment results from different points in the school year, teachers can track students' academic development and identify trends in learning outcomes (Rahma, 2020). For instance, teachers can use learning analytics tools to analyze student performance on digital learning platforms and identify patterns of engagement and achievement. This data can help teachers identify at-risk students and provide targeted interventions to support their learning.

Data-driven decision making and assessment also play a crucial role in personalized learning. By tailoring instruction to meet individual student needs, teachers can create a more student-centered learning environment that supports diverse learners (Sururi, 2020). For example, through the analysis of assessment data, teachers can create personalized learning plans for students with varying strengths and weaknesses. This approach allows teachers to differentiate instruction and provide targeted support to help each student reach their full potential.

Additionally, data-driven decision making can inform instructional planning and resource allocation. By analyzing data on student proficiency levels and learning progress, teachers can make informed decisions about instructional strategies, curriculum design, and resource allocation. For example, based on assessment data, teachers can identify areas where students are struggling and adjust their lesson plans to target those specific skills. Moreover, by analyzing data on student performance across different subjects, teachers can collaborate with colleagues to align instructional practices and resources to support student achievement (Yulianto, 2021).

Incorporating data-driven decision making and assessment into teacher professional development programs is essential to prepare educators for Education 5.0. Teacher training programs should provide opportunities for educators to develop skills in data analysis, interpretation, and utilization to inform instructional practices and improve student outcomes (Sururi, 2020). By integrating data literacy skills into teacher professional development programs, educators can enhance their ability to collect, analyze, and interpret data effectively to enhance their teaching practice and support student learning.

In general, technological proficiency and digital literacy, adaptability and flexibility, and data-driven decision making and assessment are essential skills for teachers in Education 5.0. By developing and honing these skills, teachers can create dynamic and engaging learning experiences, support diverse student needs, and promote academic achievement. Professional development programs that focus on building these skills can help teachers stay abreast of the latest educational trends, enhance their instructional practices, and ultimately contribute to improved student outcomes in the digital age.

Figure 4 illustrates other skills for Teachers in Education 5.0 document. It shows a representation of the different competencies that are essential for teachers in the modern educational landscape. The figure includes various skills and attributes such as digital literacy, critical thinking, adaptability, and communication, which are crucial for educators to effectively engage with students and navigate the evolving challenges in education.

Figure 4. Other skills for teachers in education 5.0

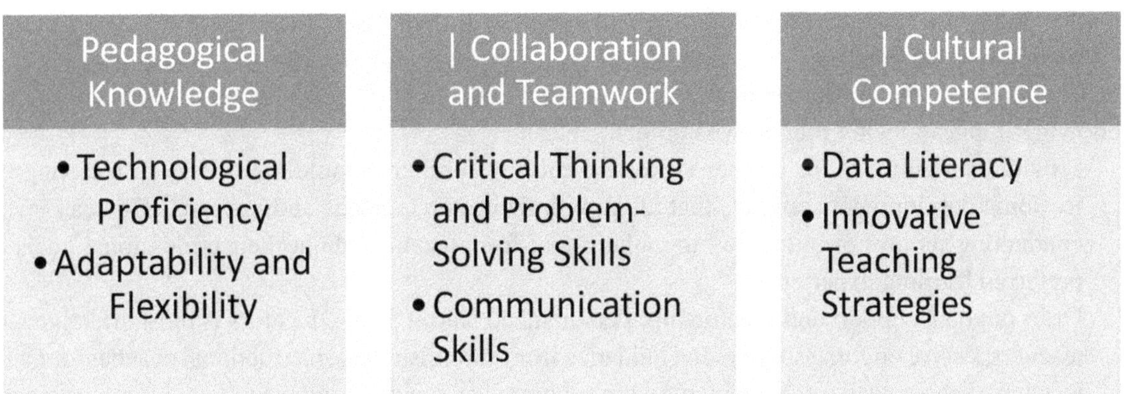

Innovative Models of Teacher Professional Develop - Ment

Personalized Learning for Educators

Personalized learning for educators is a model in which professional development is tailored to meet the individual needs, interests, and goals of teachers. This approach recognizes that each teacher has unique strengths, challenges, and areas for growth (Ramadhani, 2021). By providing personalized learning experiences, educators are empowered to take ownership of their professional development journey and engage in activities that are meaningful and relevant to their specific needs.

Another important element of personalized learning for educators is the use of mentorship and coaching. By pairing teachers with experienced mentors or coaches, educators can receive personalized feedback, guidance, and support to help them achieve their professional goals (Prasetya, 2023). This one-on-one interaction not only provides valuable insight and perspective but also creates a sense of accountability and motivation for growth.

One example of personalized learning for educators is the use of personalized learning plans. These plans are collaboratively developed between teachers and their administrators or professional development facilitators based on the teacher's goals, interests, and areas for improvement. The plans may include a mix of activities such as workshops, online courses, peer observations, mentoring, and action research projects. By customizing the professional development experience, teachers are more likely to be motivated and engaged in their learning. Another example is the use of micro-credentials or digital badges to recognize and validate teachers' skills and knowledge in specific areas (Mulyadi, 2019). Teachers can earn these credentials by completing online courses, attending workshops, or demonstrating competency through performance assessments. This personalized approach not only allows teachers to focus on areas of interest but also provides them with tangible evidence of their professional growth.

Implications for Practice:

To effectively implement personalized learning for educators, schools and districts can consider the following implications for practice (Khotimah, 2022):

1. Provide opportunities for teacher voice and choice: Teachers should have a say in selecting professional development activities that align with their unique needs and interests. This can involve conducting surveys or interviews to gather input from teachers about their professional goals and preferred learning experiences.
2. Offer ongoing support and mentorship: Personalized learning for educators is most effective when teachers receive ongoing support and guidance from administrators, instructional coaches, or mentor teachers. Schools can establish mentorship programs or coaching opportunities to support teachers in setting and achieving their professional development goals.
3. Use technology to facilitate personalized learning: Technology can play a key role in providing personalized learning opportunities for educators. Schools can use online platforms to offer self-paced courses, virtual coaching sessions, or access to learning resources tailored to individual teacher needs.
4. Promote a culture of continuous learning: Schools can create a culture that values and supports continuous learning and growth for educators. This can involve celebrating teacher achievements, providing opportunities for collaboration and peer feedback, and fostering a growth mindset among all staff members.

It is evident that personalized learning for educators leads to increased job satisfaction, improved teaching practices, and positive student outcomes. Teachers who engage in personalized professional development are more likely to implement new strategies in their classrooms, collaborate with colleagues, and reflect on their practice (Fahri, 2023). This model also promotes a culture of continuous learning and growth within schools and districts. By providing opportunities for teachers to engage in personalized learning experiences tailored to their unique needs and interests, schools and districts can support teacher growth and improve outcomes for both teachers and students. Implementing personalized learning for educators requires a commitment to teacher voice and choice, ongoing support and mentorship, the use of technology, and a culture of continuous learning.

Blended Learning Approaches

Blended learning approaches have become an increasingly popular method for teacher professional development in education. Blended learning combines traditional face-to-face instruction with online learning experiences, providing teachers with flexibility and personalized learning opportunities (Chaer, 2020). This approach allows teachers to engage in professional development at their own pace and according to their individual needs.

One example of a successful blended learning approach to teacher professional development is the Flipped Classroom model. In this model, teachers watch recorded lectures or participate in online discussions before coming to face-to-face workshops or training sessions. This allows teachers to familiarize themselves with the content and concepts before engaging in more interactive and hands-on activities during the in-person sessions (Aprilisa, 2020). The Flipped Classroom model has been shown to increase teacher engagement and retention of information, as well as provide opportunities for collaborative learning and peer feedback.

Another example of a blended learning approach to teacher professional development is the use of online learning platforms and resources. Teachers can access a wide range of resources, such as webinars, lectures, and interactive modules, to enhance their knowledge and skills in specific areas. Online learning platforms also allow teachers to connect with experts and colleagues from around the world, facilitating collaboration and the sharing of best practices (Alharbi, 2023). By combining online resources with face-to-face interactions, teachers can personalize their learning experience and address their unique professional development needs.

Blended learning approaches to teacher professional development can result in increased teacher motivation, engagement, and satisfaction. A study by Dahri (2021) found that teachers who participated in a blended learning program reported higher levels of motivation and engagement compared to those who engaged in traditional, face-to-face professional development activities. Blended learning also offers benefits in terms of cost-effectiveness and scalability, as teachers can access resources and participate in activities from anywhere, reducing the need for travel and other expenses associated with in-person training.

In addition to the Flipped Classroom model and online learning platforms, there are various other innovative blended learning approaches that can be used for teacher professional development. For example, the Rotational model involves teachers rotating between online learning activities and face-to-face workshops, allowing them to apply new knowledge and skills in real-world settings (Ijudin, 2022). The Flex model provides teachers with a flexible schedule to engage in online learning activities at their own pace while still having access to support and guidance from facilitators and peers.

Lastly, Blended learning approaches have been shown to increase access to professional development opportunities, improve engagement and retention of content, and support ongoing collaboration among educators (Kurniawan, 2022). By integrating online and face-to-face components, teachers can take advantage of a variety of learning modalities and resources to enhance their professional growth and development.

Collaborative Learning Communities and Networks

Collaborative learning communities and networks have been recognized as effective models for teacher professional development. These communities and networks bring teachers together to share ideas, resources, and best practices, ultimately fostering a culture of continuous learning and improvement.

An example of a collaborative learning community is Professional Learning Communities (PLCs). PLCs are groups of teachers who come together regularly to discuss teaching and learning, set goals, analyze student data, and collaborate on strategies to improve student outcomes. Research has shown that participation in PLCs can lead to increased teacher motivation, improved instructional practices, and better student achievement (Omojola, 2021).

Collaborative learning communities and networks also provide opportunities for teachers to engage in peer observation and feedback. Peer observation allows teachers to observe each other's classrooms, provide constructive feedback, and learn from one another. This form of professional development has been found to be particularly effective in improving teacher practice and promoting a culture of collaboration and continuous improvement (Pituła, 2021).

Collaborative learning communities and networks can also leverage technology to connect teachers who may not have the opportunity to meet in person. Online communities such as Twitter chats, Facebook groups, and virtual professional learning communities provide teachers with a platform to share resources, seek advice, and engage in discussions about teaching and learning. These online communities can be particularly useful for teachers in remote locations or those with limited access to traditional professional development opportunities (Seferoğlu, 2021). In summary, collaborative learning communities and networks offer a powerful model for teacher professional development. By bringing teachers together to share knowledge, collaborate on best practices, and engage in ongoing learning, these communities and networks can help educators improve their practice, enhance student outcomes, and foster a culture of collaboration and continuous improvement.

Figure 5 illustrates key innovative models of teacher professional development. It showcases various methods such as personalized learning, collaborative networks, inquiry-based learning, and workshops/ training programs to enhance teacher growth and skill development. The innovative models emphasize different techniques and approaches to support teachers in their professional development journey.

Figure 5. Key innovative models of teacher professional development

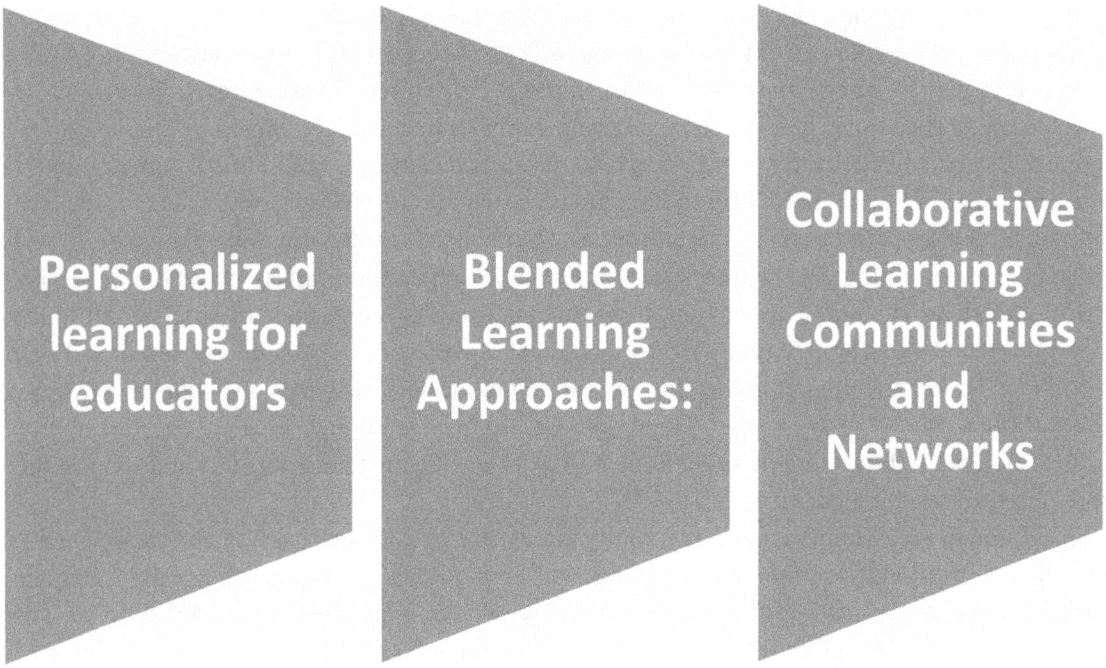

In general, personalized learning, blended learning approaches, and collaborative learning communities and networks are innovative models of teacher professional development that promote individualized growth, flexible learning opportunities, and collective expertise. By adopting these models, educators can enhance their teaching practice, improve student outcomes, and contribute to a culture of continuous learning and improvement within schools and districts. These models offer opportunities for teachers to engage in meaningful, relevant, and impactful professional development experiences that support their ongoing growth and development as educators. By incorporating these innovative approaches into teacher professional development programs, schools and districts can create a culture of collaboration, reflection, and continuous improvement that benefits teachers, students, and the entire learning community.

Key Challenges and Opportunities in Implementing Effective Professional Development

Professional development is vital for the growth and success of teachers in the ever-changing landscape of education. However, despite its importance, there are several challenges that need to be addressed to ensure that professional development efforts are effective. This sub-chapter will explore key challenges faced in implementing effective professional development: accessibility and equity issues, resistance to change and lack of motivation, and alignment with institutional goals and resources.

Accessibility and Equity Issues

One of the key challenges in addressing accessibility issues is ensuring that professional development programs are inclusive and cater to the diverse needs of all teachers. For example, teachers who work in rural areas may face barriers such as limited internet connectivity or long travel distances to attend in-person training sessions. In these cases, offering online or blended learning opportunities can help to overcome these challenges and make professional development more accessible to a wider range of educators (Suyudi, 2021). Additionally, providing financial support or stipends for teachers to participate in professional development can help mitigate the costs associated with attending workshops or conferences.

An example of a program that has successfully addressed accessibility issues is the Teach For All network, which provides professional development opportunities for teachers in underserved communities around the world. Through partnerships with local organizations and support from global funders, Teach for All offers training programs that are tailored to the specific needs and contexts of each community (Simonsen, 2017). By adapting their approach to meet the unique challenges faced by teachers in different regions, Teach for All has been able to reach a wide range of educators and support them in improving their teaching practice.

In addition to accessibility challenges, equity issues also play a significant role in shaping the effectiveness of professional development programs. Research has shown that teachers from marginalized communities or schools with high concentrations of low-income students are less likely to have access to high-quality professional development opportunities (Skitsko, 2022). This lack of equitable access can contribute to disparities in teacher effectiveness and student achievement, further widening the achievement gap.

To address equity issues in professional development, programs must prioritize diversity, equity, and inclusion in their design and implementation. This may involve actively recruiting teachers from underrepresented groups, providing culturally responsive training materials, and creating opportunities for educators to share their unique perspectives and experiences. By incorporating principles of equity and social justice into professional development programs, organizations can help to ensure that all teachers have access to the support and resources they need to be successful in the classroom (Rahma, 2020). One example of a program that has focused on equity in professional development is the National Equity Project, which works with educators to advance equity in education through leadership development and coaching. By centering issues of systemic inequity and racism in their work, the National Equity Project helps teachers and school leaders to recognize and address the structural barriers that perpetuate disparities in student outcomes. Through their programming, the National Equity Project aims to empower educators to create more inclusive and equitable learning environments that support the success of all students, regardless of their background or identity.

Resistance to Change and Lack of Motivation

Resistance to change and lack of motivation are common challenges that educators face in implementing effective professional development programs. Teachers may be hesitant to adopt new practices or strategies due to fear of the unknown, lack of confidence in their ability to change, or simply being comfortable with their current methods. Additionally, educators may not be motivated to engage in professional development if they do not see the value or relevance of the training to their daily practice (Oktaviana, 2022).

One strategy to address resistance to change is to provide teachers with ongoing support and resources to help them implement new practices. For example, in a study conducted by Komar (2020), teachers who received coaching and feedback from instructional coaches were more likely to successfully implement new teaching strategies than those who did not receive this level of support. By providing teachers with the necessary tools and guidance, educators can overcome their resistance to change and feel more confident in trying new approaches.

Another approach to addressing resistance to change is to involve teachers in the decision-making process when designing professional development programs. When educators have a say in the topics and methods of training, they are more likely to be invested in the process and feel a sense of ownership over their professional growth. A study by Kaul (2022) found that teachers who were involved in the development of a professional learning community were more likely to be engaged in professional development and implement new strategies in their classrooms.

Lack of motivation can also be a barrier to effective professional development. Educators may feel overwhelmed by their daily responsibilities and see professional development as an added burden rather than an opportunity for growth. One way to combat this lack of motivation is to make professional development relevant and meaningful to teachers' practice. For example, providing training on topics that align with teachers' interests or classroom challenges can increase their motivation to engage in professional development. Additionally, offering incentives such as continuing education credits, certifications, or financial stipends can also motivate educators to participate in training programs. A study by Eliwatis et al. (2022) found that incorporating peer collaboration into professional development programs can increase educators' motivation to participate and implement new strategies. By providing opportunities for teachers to work together, share ideas, and collaborate on projects, educators can feel supported and motivated to engage in ongoing professional development.

Furthermore, creating a culture of continuous learning within schools can help to address the challenge of lack of motivation. When professional development is seen as a regular and valued part of teachers' professional growth, educators are more likely to prioritize their own learning and seek out opportunities for development (Al-Qahtani, 2015). Schools can cultivate a culture of continuous learning by providing time and resources for professional development, recognizing and rewarding teachers for their growth and achievements, and creating a supportive environment where educators feel encouraged to take risks and try new practices.

Alignment With Institutional Goals and Resources

A third challenge in implementing effective professional development is ensuring that it aligns with institutional goals and resources. Professional development programs that are not aligned with the priorities and needs of the school or district may not have a significant impact on teacher practice or student learning outcomes (Aprilisa, 2020). Additionally, limited resources, such as funding, time, and personnel, can present barriers to implementing comprehensive professional development initiatives.

Dahri et al. (2021) found that professional development programs were more effective when they were aligned with specific school improvement goals and provided ongoing support for teachers to implement new strategies in their classrooms. Schools that lacked the necessary resources, such as funding for materials or time for collaboration, struggled to sustain meaningful professional development activities.

To address alignment with institutional goals and resources, education leaders should work collaboratively with teachers and other stakeholders to identify the most urgent needs and priorities for professional development. Resources should be allocated strategically to support ongoing professional development activities that align with school improvement goals and are sustainable in the long term (Kaul, 2022).

In general, implementing effective professional development in education faces several challenges, including accessibility and equity issues, resistance to change, lack of motivation, and alignment with institutional goals and resources. To overcome these challenges and ensure that professional development efforts are successful, education policymakers, school leaders, and teachers need to work together to provide equitable access to professional development opportunities, address resistance to change and lack of motivation, and align professional development activities with school improvement goals and available resources. By addressing these challenges proactively, educators can support the growth and development of teachers and ultimately improve student learning outcomes.

Table 2 highlights other challenges encountered in implementing effective professional development programs and provides potential solutions to address each challenge. The table offers a comprehensive overview of obstacles such as lack of funding, limited time for professional development, and difficulties in assessing the impact of training initiatives. The solutions proposed include securing additional funding sources, providing flexible scheduling options for professional development activities, and utilizing various assessment tools to measure the outcomes of professional development efforts.

Table 2. Other challenges in implementing effective professional development and how to solve them

Key Challenges	How to Address Them
Lack of time	Provide flexible and convenient options for professional development.
Lack of resources	Seek out alternative funding sources and leverage partnerships.
Resistance to change	Communicate the benefits of professional development and provide support.
Lack of buy-in from staff	Involve staff in the planning and decision-making process.
Lack of follow-up and feedback	Implement evaluation tools and mechanisms to track progress.
Inconsistency in delivery	Establish clear expectations and standards for professional development.
Lack of relevant content	Customize professional development to meet the needs of educators.
Lack of collaboration	Encourage collaboration among educators and create opportunities for sharing best practices.

Case Studies and Success Stories of Adaptive Training in Teacher Professional Development

Examples From Different Educational Contexts

In recent years, adaptive training methods have gained popularity in teacher professional development programs. These methods leverage technology to personalize learning experiences for educators, allowing them to enhance their skills and knowledge in a more targeted and efficient manner (Mulyadi, 2019). In this section, we will explore case studies and success stories of adaptive training in teacher professional development, focusing on examples from different educational contexts.

Case Study One: Implementing Flipped Classrooms in Professional Development Programs

One successful example of adaptive training in teacher professional development is the implementation of flipped classrooms. In this case study, a school district introduced flipped classrooms as a way to engage teachers in their own learning process. Teachers were provided with online resources, such as video lectures and interactive modules, to review before attending in-person training sessions. This approach allowed teachers to work at their own pace and focus on areas where they needed the most support. The in-person sessions were then used for hands-on activities, collaborative discussions, and personalized feedback, resulting in a more effective and engaging professional development experience (Rusman, 2023).

Case Study Two: Integrating Virtual Reality and Augmented Reality in Teacher Training

Another innovative approach to adaptive training in teacher professional development is the integration of virtual reality (VR) and augmented reality (AR) technologies. In this case study, a university incorporated VR and AR simulations into their teacher training programs to provide educators with immersive learning experiences. Teachers were able to practice classroom management techniques, explore different teaching strategies, and engage with diverse student populations in a safe and supportive virtual environment. This adaptive training approach allowed teachers to develop their skills in a realistic setting, receive instant feedback on their performance, and experiment with new instructional methods without the fear of failure. As a result, teachers reported increased confidence, improved teaching practices, and a deeper understanding of their students' needs (Erickson, 2012).

Case Study Three: Harnessing the Power of Data Analytics for Personalized Professional Development

One more case study that highlights the success of adaptive training in teacher professional development is the use of data analytics to tailor learning experiences to individual educators' needs. In this example, a school district implemented a data-driven approach to professional development, where teachers' performance data, feedback from supervisors, and self-assessment results were collected and analyzed to create personalized learning plans. Based on this data, teachers were recommended specific professional development opportunities, resources, and coaching support to address their unique areas for growth. This adaptive training model not only helped teachers build on their strengths but also targeted areas for improvement, ultimately leading to more impactful and sustainable professional growth (Ismanto, 2019).

These case studies demonstrate the diverse applications and benefits of adaptive training in teacher professional development across different educational contexts. By implementing innovative approaches such as flipped classrooms, virtual reality, augmented reality, and data analytics, educators can engage in personalized, interactive, and effective professional development experiences that cater to their individual learning needs. These success stories serve as examples of how adaptive training can transform traditional professional development practices and empower teachers to enhance their instructional practices, improve student outcomes, and ultimately drive positive change in education.

CONCLUSION AND FUTURE DIRECTIONS

This chapter examined the importance of adaptive training in teacher professional development in the context of Education 5.0. Adaptive training offers personalized learning experiences for teachers, allowing them to enhance their skills and knowledge in a tailored and efficient manner. By leveraging technology and data analytics, adaptive training can provide educators with targeted support and resources to effectively address their individual needs and goals.

The chapter highlighted the key elements of adaptive training, including personalized learning paths, real-time feedback, and data-driven insights. These features enable teachers to engage in self-directed learning, receive continuous support and feedback, and track their progress over time. Through adaptive training, teachers can develop a growth mindset and enhance their teaching practices to better meet the needs of diverse learners in the digital age.

Moving forward, it is recommended that educational institutions and policymakers integrate adaptive training into teacher professional development programs. This can be achieved through the design and implementation of adaptive training platforms that offer a wide range of resources and tools for teachers. Additionally, collaboration with technology providers and educational researchers can help ensure the effectiveness and scalability of adaptive training initiatives.

Furthermore, it is essential to provide ongoing support and mentorship to teachers as they engage in adaptive training. This can include access to expert guidance, peer-to-peer learning communities, and opportunities for professional growth and collaboration. By fostering a culture of continuous learning and improvement, educational institutions can empower teachers to embrace adaptive training as a valuable tool for enhancing their teaching practices in Education 5.0.

In conclusion, adaptive training holds great promise for transforming teacher professional development and promoting excellence in education. By harnessing the power of adaptive technologies and personalized learning experiences, educators can cultivate their skills and knowledge to meet the evolving needs of 21st-century learners. As we continue to navigate the challenges of Education 5.0, adaptive training offers a dynamic and innovative approach to supporting teacher growth and promoting student success. With a strategic and collaborative effort, adaptive training can play a pivotal role in shaping the future of education and empowering educators to thrive in a rapidly changing digital landscape.

Chapter Guide Study Questions

1. What are the key challenges facing teacher professional development in Education 5.0?
2. How can technology be leveraged to enhance teacher professional development in the context of Education 5.0?
3. What role does collaborative learning play in teacher professional development?
4. How can schools and educational leaders create a culture that supports ongoing professional development for teachers?
5. What are some effective strategies for measuring the impact of teacher professional development programs?
6. How can teacher professional development in Education 5.0 be aligned with current trends and best practices in pedagogy?
7. What are the benefits of personalized professional development plans for teachers?

8. How can teacher professional development programs be designed to promote equity and inclusivity in education?
9. How can teachers be supported in integrating new technologies and innovative pedagogical approaches into their practice?
10. What are the implications of Education 5.0 for the future of teacher professional development?

REFERENCES

Abakah, E., Widin, J., & Ameyaw, E. K. (2022). Continuing professional development (CPD) practices among basic school teachers in the central region of Ghana. *SAGE Open*, 12(2), 21582440221094597. 10.1177/21582440221094597

Adisendjaja, Y. H., Rustaman, N. Y., Redjeki, S., & Satori, D. (2017, February). Science teachers' understanding of scientific inquiry in teacher professional development. [). IOP Publishing.]. *Journal of Physics: Conference Series*, 812(1), 012054. 10.1088/1742-6596/812/1/012054

Al-Qahtani, H. M. (2015). Teachers' Voice: A Needs Analysis of Teachers' Needs for Professional Development with the Emergence of the Current English Textbooks. *English Language Teaching*, 8(8), 128–141. 10.5539/elt.v8n8p128

Aleixo, C., Silva, S., & Godinho, T. (2023). Education 5.0 in the Context of Teaching Accounting. In *Internet of Behaviors Implementation in Organizational Contexts* (pp. 135-152). IGI Global.

Alharbi, A. M. (2023). Implementation of Education 5.0 in developed and developing countries: A comparative study. *Creative Education*, 14(5), 914–942. 10.4236/ce.2023.145059

Aprilisa, E. (2020). Realizing society 5.0 to face the industrial revolution 4.0 and teacher education curriculum readiness in Indonesia. In *Proceeding International Conference on Science and Engineering* (Vol. 3, pp. 543-548). IEEE. 10.14421/icse.v3.559

Arief, M., & Churiyah, M. (2023, May). ArsipKita to Improve Teacher Competence in Facing the New Paradigm of Education in the Era of Society 5.0. In *BISTIC Business Innovation Sustainability and Technology International Conference (BISTIC 2022)* (pp. 327-336). Atlantis Press. 10.2991/978-94-6463-178-4_33

Chaer, M. T., Wahyuna, A. H., & Fitriana, S. (2020). Teacher Professionalism and Educational Challenges of The Industrial Revolution 5.0. *AL-MURABBI: Jurnal Studi Kependidikan dan Keislaman, 7*(1), 53-63.

Dahri, N. A., Vighio, M. S., Bather, J. D., & Arain, A. A. (2021). Factors influencing the acceptance of mobile collaborative learning for the continuous professional development of teachers. *Sustainability (Basel)*, 13(23), 13222. 10.3390/su132313222

Early, D. M., Maxwell, K. L., Ponder, B. D., & Pan, Y. (2017). Improving teacher-child interactions: A randomized controlled trial of Making the Most of Classroom Interactions and My Teaching Partner professional development models. *Early Childhood Research Quarterly*, 38, 57–70. 10.1016/j.ecresq.2016.08.005

Eliwatis, E., Aprison, W., Maimori, R., Herawati, S., & Putri, Y. M. (2022). Challenges of society era Education 5.0: Revitalization of teacher competencies and learning models. *Darussalam. Journal of Psychology and Educational*, 1(2), 1–11.

Erickson, A. S. G., Noonan, P. M., & McCall, Z. (2012). Effectiveness of online professional development for rural special educators. *Rural Special Education Quarterly*, 31(1), 22–32. 10.1177/875687051203100104

Fahri, A. F., & Azani, M. Z. (2023). Development of Islamic Religious Education Teachers in the Era of Society 5.0. *Tadrib*, 9(1), 159–166.

Ihsan, I. (2023). The challenges of elementary education in society 5.0 era. [IJSL]. *International Journal of Social Learning*, 3(3), 341–360.

Ijudin, I., Ainissyifa, H., & Wakila, Y. F. (2022). Being an Inspiring Teacher in Realizing Competitive Education in the Era of Society 5.0. *Al-Abshar: Journal of Islamic Education Management*, 1(1), 77–87. 10.58223/al-abshar.v1i1.12

Ismanto, B., & Erbianita, S. L. (2019). Determining Pedagogic And Professional Competencies Among Students In Realizing Society 5.0. *ECONOMICA Jurnal Program Studi Pendidikan Ekonomi STKIP PGRI Sumatera Barat*, 8(1), 20–27. 10.22202/economica.2019.v8.i1.3593

Kaul, V., & Kaul, A. (2022). A QFD Approach to Design a Blockchain-Based Professional Development Module in Education System for Society 5.0. In *Blockchain Technology in Supply Chain Management for Society 5.0* (pp. 157–169). CRC Press. 10.1201/9781003177432-15

Khotimah, H., & Suci, D. N. (2022). Special Competence for Preschool Teacher in 5.0 Era. *Cakrawala Dini: Jurnal Pendidikan Anak Usia Dini*, 13(2), 129–138.

Komar, O. (2020). Professional certification training model for alternative solutions for S-1 graduate teachers who do not achieve teacher professional education. In *Borderless Education as a Challenge in the 5.0 Society* (pp. 356–358). Routledge. 10.1201/9781003107279-65

Kurniawan, S. J., Situmorang, D. D. B., & Ifdil, I. (2022). Strengthening lecturer competence with the job-embedded professional development (jepd) model: A solution for dealing with education in the era of 5.0 and the metaverse. *COUNS-EDU: The International Journal of Counseling and Education*, 7(1), 21–26. 10.23916/0020210636530

Leon, R. D. (2023). Employees' reskilling and upskilling for industry 5.0: Selecting the best professional development programmes. *Technology in Society*, 75, 102393. 10.1016/j.techsoc.2023.102393

Mäkelä, K., & Whipp, P. R. (2015). Career intentions of Australian physical education teachers. *European Physical Education Review*, 21(4), 504–520. 10.1177/1356336X15584088

Makopoulou, K., Neville, R. D., Ntoumanis, N., & Thomas, G. (2021). An investigation into the effects of short-course professional development on teachers' and teaching assistants' self-efficacy. *Professional Development in Education*, 47(5), 780–795. 10.1080/19415257.2019.1665572

Matorevhu, A. (2023). Curriculum innovation implementation for industrialization: A case of education 5.0 pre-service science and mathematics teacher preparation. *Journal of Research in Instructional*, 3(1), 69–86. 10.30862/jri.v3i1.214

Meter, W., & Setiawan, B. (2023). Professional Educator in the Era of Society 5.0: Primary Education Alumni Competence. *Journal of Higher Education Theory and Practice*, 23(10).

Mulyadi, Y. (2019, December). Vocational Teacher Perception on Industry 4.0 and Society 5.0. In *International Conference on Education, Science and Technology* (pp. 62-68). Redwhite Press.

Oktaviana, D., Barizi, A., & Yaqin, M. Z. N. (2022). The Challenges of the society 5.0 era: The evaluation of learning in primary education. *Al Adzka: Jurnal Ilmiah Pendidikan Guru Madrasah Ibtidaiyah, 12*(1).

Omojola, J., Oyekan, O. A., & Zacchaeus, K. B. (2021, November). Professionalism of Educators in the Era of Society 5.0: Lessons From Society 4.0. In *1st International Conference on Continuing Education and Technology (ICCOET 2021)* (pp. 156-160). Atlantis Press.

Piper, B., Zuilkowski, S. S., Dubeck, M., Jepkemei, E., & King, S. J. (2018). Identifying the essential ingredients to literacy and numeracy improvement: Teacher professional development and coaching, student textbooks, and structured teachers' guides. *World Development*, 106, 324–336. 10.1016/j.worlddev.2018.01.018

Pituła, B. (2021). The Teacher and the Idea of Society 5.0–Initial Diagnosis of the Problem. *Polish Political Science Yearbook*, 50(2), 149–165. 10.15804/ppsy202107

Prasetya, A. D. A. (2023). Analysis of the Mobilizing Teacher Program as a Teacher's Ongoing Professional Development. *Education Challenges is The Era Disruption 5.0 in ASEAN*, 40.

Rahma, D. A., & Winarni, R., & Winarno. (2020, September). The challenges and readiness of elementary school teachers in facing society 5.0 through online learning during the Covid-19 pandemic. In *Proceedings of the 4th International Conference on Learning Innovation and Quality Education* (pp. 1-6). AM. 10.1145/3452144.3453743

Ramadhani, D., Kenedi, A. K., Helsa, Y., Handrianto, C., & Wardana, M. R. (2021). Mapping higher order thinking skills of prospective primary school teachers in facing society 5.0. *Al Ibtida: Jurnal Pendidikan Guru MI*, 8(2), 178–190. 10.24235/al.ibtida.snj.v8i2.8794

Rusman, A., Mas'udi, M. M., Hermoyo, R. P., Yarno, Y., Yunianti, S., & Rafsanjani, H. (2023, June). Education transformation in 5.0 society development era. In *AIP Conference.* ACM. 10.1063/5.0141657

Saman, A. M., & Musa, K. (2020). Instructional Coaching Through Technology Integration: Accompanying Teacher Services in the Digital Era of Education 5.0. *Education*, 3(11), 2291–2299.

Satria, R. R., Satria, R., & Mustiningsih, M. (2019, December). Supervisor in Era Industrial Revolution 4.0 and Society 5.0. In *5th International Conference on Education and Technology (ICET 2019)* (pp. 596-601). Atlantis Press.

Seferoğlu, S. S. (2001). Elementary school teachers perceptions of professional development. *Hacettepe Üniversitesi Eğitim Fakültesi Dergisi, 20*(20).

Simonsen, B., Freeman, J., Dooley, K., Maddock, E., Kern, L., & Myers, D. (2017). Effects of targeted professional development on teachers' specific praise rates. *Journal of Positive Behavior Interventions*, 19(1), 37–47. 10.1177/1098300716637192

Skitsko, V., & Osypova, O. (2022, September). Education 5.0 maturity index: concept and prospects for development. In *International Conference on Electronic Governance with Emerging Technologies* (pp. 95-108). Cham: Springer Nature Switzerland. 10.1007/978-3-031-22950-3_8

Sukmara, G., Yuliana, L., Retnowati, E., & Jannah, N. M. (2023). The Important Role of Principal in Academic Supervision to Improve Teacher Competency in Society 5.0 Era. *Cendekia: Jurnal Kependidikan dan Kemasyarakatan, 21*(2), 268-284.

Sururi, S. (2020). Teacher competency enhancement for 21st century educators and effective school management in the context of continuing professional development. In *Borderless Education as a Challenge in the 5.0 Society* (pp. 161–164). Routledge. 10.1201/9781003107279-32

Suyudi, M., & Mahmudah, U. (2021, November). Developing Indonesian Digital-Skilled Teachers for Multicultural Education Into The Society 5.0. In *Proceeding International Conference on Islam and Civilization (ICONIC)* (Vol. 1, No. 1, pp. 31-49). Research Gate.

Thomson, M. M., & Turner, J. E. (2019). The role of emotions in teachers' professional development: Attending a research experience for teachers (RET) program. *Education Research International*, 2019, 1–12. 10.1155/2019/5856793

Yulianto. (2021). The Needs of Training to Improve Teacher Competence in Preparing Society 5.0. *Technium Soc. Sci. J., 20*, 275.

ADDITIONAL READING

Karim, M., Antoni, S., & Oktarina, K. (2023). The effect of teacher professionalism in islamic religious education in the era of society 5.0 in Indonesia: A meta-analysis. *Jurnal Pendidikan dan Konseling (JPDK), 5*(2), 1710-1717.

Saman, A. M., & Musa, K. (2020). Instructional Coaching Through Technology Integration: Accompanying Teacher Services in the Digital Era of Education 5.0. *Education*, 3(11), 2291–2299.

Wahyudin, A., Zaman, N., Nisak, A. K., & Zuhriyah, I. A. (2023). Teacher Performance Assessment Development Management In Smart Society 5.0 Era. *Mudir: Jurnal Manajemen Pendidikan*, 5(1), 10–18.

KEY TERMS AND DEFINITIONS

Blended Learning: A pedagogical approach that combines traditional face-to-face instruction with online and digital learning tools to create a more dynamic and flexible learning environment.

Education 5.0: A term referring to the future-oriented paradigm of education that emphasizes personalized, adaptive, and technology-mediated learning experiences to prepare students for the demands of the 21st century.

Formative Assessment: Ongoing, informal assessment practices that provide feedback to teachers and students during the learning process to monitor progress, identify learning gaps, and guide instructional decisions.

Lifelong Learning: The idea that learning is a continuous process that extends beyond formal schooling and is essential for personal and professional growth throughout one's lifetime.

Pedagogical Content Knowledge (PCK): The specialized knowledge and skills that teachers possess about how to effectively teach specific subject matter content to students, including instructional strategies, assessment techniques, and curriculum design.

Teacher Professional Development (PD): The process of continuous learning and training that helps teachers improve their skills, knowledge, and instructional practices to enhance student learning outcomes.

Technology Integration: The strategic use of technology tools and resources in educational settings to enhance teaching and learning outcomes, promote student engagement, and facilitate the development of 21st-century skills.

Chapter 12
The Contribution of ICT in Teacher Professional Development in Education 5.0

Titus Tossy
https://orcid.org/0000-0001-8162-4656
Mzumbe University, Tanzania

ABSTRACT

This chapter addresses the relevance of ICT to teacher professional development in the changing landscape of Education 5.0. It advocates a comprehensive strategy that harnesses ICT's numerous instruments to empower teachers, foster cooperation, and cultivate the necessary competencies for navigating the fast-expanding Education 5.0. Interviews and direct observations were employed. By addressing policies, competencies, strategies, directions, and problems, the book chapter gives a holistic vision of the transformative journey education must take to satisfy the needs of the 5.0 era. The involvement of ICT in teachers' professional development results in easier content delivery, collaboration, networking, and data-driven insights." This topical and thought-provoking compendium offers essential insights for educators, policymakers, researchers, practitioners, and postgraduate students negotiating the intricacies of contemporary education

INTRODUCTION

Information and Communication Technology (ICT) refers to the vast array of tools and technologies we use to create, manage, and share information electronically; it is like a powerful toolkit that revolutionizes how we communicate, learn, work, and even entertain ourselves (Kaur, 2023). Before the internet, smartphones, and computers, Information was stored in libraries and accessed through books, and communication happened through letters, landlines, and face-to-face interactions. ICT has wholly transformed this landscape. ICT is built by various components: Information Technology (IT) and Communication Technology.

Information Technology (IT) is the backbone of ICT, encompassing everything related to computing and data processing. It includes hardware like computers, servers, storage devices, and software like operating systems, applications, and programming languages (Nowfeek & Mahrool, 2021). IT tools allow

DOI: 10.4018/979-8-3693-3041-8.ch012

us to digitally create, store, manipulate, and analyze information. Communication Technology, this part deals with the transmission of information and data over various channels. It includes wired and wireless networks, telecommunications infrastructure like phone lines and satellites, and communication protocols that ensure seamless data exchange (Nowfeek & Mahrool, 2021). Communication technology lets us instantly share information and connect, regardless of distance. Not only that but also Information and Communication Technology Convergence must be done to merge IT and communication technologies, creating robust and integrated systems. For example, the internet integrates various communication channels like email, instant messaging, and video conferencing, while smartphones combine computing capabilities with communication functions. Convergence has blurred the lines between different technologies, making them more accessible and user-friendly.

The influence of ICT is pervasive and far-reaching. It has impacted almost every aspect of our lives, including Business, where E-commerce, online communication, and data analytics have transformed how businesses operate and interact with customers (Kaur G., 2017). Electronic medical records, remote consultations, and telemedicine have improved healthcare access and delivery (Saidu et al., 2017). Agriculture enables farmers to access weather forecasts, market information, and expert advice through mobile apps (Huisinga & Martin, 2017). In industry, ICT allows for predictive maintenance, efficient supply chain management, and intelligent production techniques, enhancing productivity while reducing costs and errors (Kaur G., 2017). Social media, instant messaging, and video conferencing have made communication faster, easier, and more global. In Education, online learning platforms, digital resources, and interactive tools have revolutionized teaching and learning. Therefore, the world of ICT is constantly evolving, with new technologies always emerging. Artificial intelligence, big data, virtual reality, and the Internet of Things (IoT) are just a few examples of cutting-edge developments that promise to transform our lives further and change the education landscape.

Education 5.0 is a digitally-propelled landscape; education stands at a fascinating crossroads. The rapid evolution of Information and Communication Technologies (ICT) has irrevocably transformed how we communicate, access information, and learn and teach. However, this begs a crucial question: How can we harness the immense potential of ICT to empower teachers, the architects of tomorrow's minds, and propel their professional development to new heights? This chapter delves into this critical intersection, exploring the contribution of ICT as a catalyst for teacher growth and skill enhancement and, ultimately, creating a dynamic and adaptable teaching force capable of nurturing future generations in a technology-driven world. The chapter delves deeper through examining the impact of ICT on various aspects of Teacher Professional Development (TPD), including content delivery, assessment, and feedback mechanisms, highlighting successful case studies and best practices in ICT-integrated Teacher Professional Development (TPD) initiatives from around the world, addressing the challenges and limitations associated with ICT integration in Teacher Professional Development (TPD), offering practical strategies for overcoming them, proposing a future-oriented vision for ICT-driven Teacher Professional Development (TPD) that empowers educators to become lifelong learners and leaders in the digital age. This book chapter is geared to answer the following questions;

i. To what extent does ICT use improve teacher knowledge and skills towards professional development?
ii. How does ICT-based professional development compare to traditional methods regarding effectiveness and satisfaction?
iii. What are teachers' specific challenges in using ICT for professional development?
iv. How can ICT contribute to teachers' professional development in Education 5.0?

LITERATURE REVIEW

ICT is pivotal in enhancing teachers' professional development in Education 5.0. By leveraging ICT tools and resources, teachers can adapt to the evolving educational landscape, embrace innovative pedagogies, and ultimately contribute to the holistic development of students.

ICT in Teacher Professional Development

ICT has been widely recognized as a powerful tool for enhancing teachers' professional development (Smith, 2019). ICT enables teachers to access various professional development resources, including online courses, webinars, and educational databases (Fullan, 2017). This accessibility fosters continuous learning and skill enhancement, which is essential for adapting to the dynamic demands of Education 5.0. On the other hand, studies show that personalized Professional Development using ICT tools like online learning platforms, gamified experiences, and virtual communities can be more engaging and motivating for teachers than traditional one-size-fits-all approaches (Hall, 2019). This leads to higher completion rates and deeper learning since the personalized Professional Development programs using blended learning and flexible content choices significantly increased teachers' self-efficacy and comfort level with integrating ICT into their classrooms. On the other hand, Personalized Professional Development with ICT can provide access to a broader range of learning resources and opportunities for individualized feedback and reflection (Xiaoshu Xu, 2023). This can help teachers better understand specific topics, refine their skills, and experiment with new teaching strategies. Using a personalized online learning platform with adaptive learning features improved teachers' knowledge and skills in technology integration, leading to more effective use of technology in their classrooms (Xiaoshu Xu, 2023). Along the same lines, a study by the International Journal of Education and Development using Information and Communication Technology shows that digitally fluent teachers are more likely to create engaging and personalized learning experiences for their students (Fulgence, 2020). A study on the acquisition of digital capability by academics in Irish higher education settings found that digital fluency has become a significant concept in technology-enhanced learning and that teachers understanding how to use digital tools is no longer an option rather than it is a demand (Watts, 2018).

Impact of ICT on Teacher Professional Development and Teaching Practices

Integrating ICT in Teacher Professional Development significantly changes teaching practices (Mwalongo, 2021). Along the same line, research suggests that teachers who engage in ICT-based professional development tend to adopt innovative instructional strategies, such as blended learning and flipped classrooms, which align with the principles of Education 5.0. (Nurdiana, Effendi, Ningsih, & Abda, 2023). These strategies leverage technology to create interactive and engaging learning environments that cater to diverse student needs (Nurdiana, Effendi, Ningsih, & Abda, 2023). When teachers receive personalized Professional Development tailored to their needs and classroom context, they are more likely to implement new strategies and practices effectively, leading to improved student engagement, learning gains, and overall academic achievement (Zhang, Yang, & Carter, 2020). Another impact is enhanced pedagogical strategies; professional development empowers teachers with contemporary pedagogical methods tailored to Education 5.0, fostering student-centered learning, critical thinking, collaboration, and problem-solving skills in both learners and teachers (Mwalongo, 2021). In Education 5.0, the teacher will be required to provide tasks to learners where the learners will learn by doing, and the teacher will be required to provide a practical way of attempting the assignment provided. In the same line, research highlights another impact of ICT that enhances technology integration: effective professional development equips educators with the skills to integrate advanced technologies seamlessly into teaching practices, enabling personalized learning experiences and preparing students for the digital landscape of Education 5.0 (Reeves, 2020). Fostering lifelong learning by engaging in continuous professional development, teachers model the importance of lifelong learning and inspire students to embrace curiosity, self-directed learning, and adaptability, critical competencies in Education 5.0 (Fulgence, 2020). Not only that, but also ICT in Teacher Professional Development facilitates collaborative networks; teachers' professional development initiatives encourage collaboration, networking, and knowledge-sharing among educators, fostering communities of practice where innovative ideas, best practices, and resources are exchanged to enrich teaching and learning experiences in Education 5.0 (Guskey, 2022).

Challenges and Opportunities

While ICT offers numerous benefits for teachers' professional development, it also presents challenges, such as inadequate ICT infrastructure and digital literacy among teachers, that hinder the effective implementation of ICT-based professional development initiatives (Hall, 2019). However, proactive measures, such as targeted training programs and infrastructure investments, can mitigate these challenges and create opportunities for holistic Teacher Professional Development in Education 5.0. Research highlights the benefits of personalized Professional Development through ICT, but some challenges remain; these include ensuring equitable access to technology and support for all teachers, providing compelling online learning experiences, and integrating personalized Professional Development with existing school structures and systems (Fulgence, 2020). Not only that, but also the Digital Divide and Accessibility, As equitable access to technology and infrastructure, remains a formidable hurdle (Mishra & Koehler, 2016). Variances in internet connectivity, hardware availability, and digital literacy among teachers create chasms within the educational landscape, potentially marginalizing those on the wrong side of the digital divide (UNESCO, 2019). However, addressing this challenge demands multi-pronged solutions, including targeted investments in infrastructure, digital literacy training tailored to diverse needs, and initiatives to bridge the socioeconomic gap in technology access (Huisinga & Martin, 2017). The other research pointed out that designing engaging and effective Online Learning Experiences is another challenge. At the same time, ICT opens doors to personalized learning pathways, and creating captivating and impactful online teacher professional development experiences is not easy (Watts, 2018). Caution against the limitations of solely online learning, emphasizing the need for human interaction and practical application in Teacher Professional Development (Nowfeek & Mahrool, 2021). However, to overcome this challenge, effective online programs must incorporate interactive exercises, collaborative activities, and real-world opportunities to implement acquired knowledge (Nurdiana, Effendi, Ningsih, & Abda, 2023). Balancing individualization with standardization also presents a delicate chance, requiring flexible curriculums and adaptive technologies that cater to diverse needs while staying aligned with curriculum goals (Fullan, 2017). Integration with Existing Systems and Structures, merging personalized ICT-based teacher professional development with established school structures and cultures presents a complex puzzle (Kaur K., 2023). However, successful integration requires collaboration, building buy-in from administrators and teachers, and adapting professional development systems to accommodate individual learning pathways (Fullan, 2017). School cultures must evolve to embrace the dynamic nature of

Personalized Teacher Professional Development, fostering ongoing dialogue, reflection, and knowledge sharing among educators (Guskey, 2022). Leadership at all levels becomes crucial in this transformative journey, ensuring that personalized teacher professional development transcends individual classrooms and permeates the entire school ecosystem. On the other hand, researchers discussed the opportunities for addressing challenges experienced in teacher professional development in Education 5.0.

Personalized Learning and Empowerment, at its core, ICT-based teacher professional development holds immense potential for personalized learning and educator empowerment. The research proposes the technological pedagogical and context knowledge framework, highlighting the critical interplay between technology, pedagogy, and content knowledge in effective teaching (Mishra & Koehler, 2016). Personalized ICT-based teacher professional development can tailor learning pathways to individual strengths, weaknesses, and learning styles, fostering a deeper understanding of technological pedagogical and context knowledge and its application in specific classroom contexts. This empowers educators to take ownership of their professional development, becoming active creators of knowledge and agents of change in their classrooms. Collaboration and knowledge sharing: ICT transcends geographic boundaries, forges connections, and fosters collaboration among educators globally, envisioning online communities as powerful tools for knowledge sharing, peer-to-peer learning, and professional support (Reeves, 2020). However, online forums, social media platforms, and virtual conferences can connect educators, allowing them to share best practices, discuss challenges, and learn from each other's experiences. This collaborative learning environment empowers educators to grow professionally and continuously refine their practices in a dynamic, supportive community. Continuous Improvement and Evaluation, ICT provides powerful tools for data-driven analysis and continuous improvement of teacher professional development programs (Mishra & Koehler, 2016). Robust evaluation frameworks that assess knowledge acquisition and learning transfer into improved classroom practices are crucial (Guskey, 2022). However, ICT-based tools can track learner progress, identify areas for improvement, and inform ongoing refinement of teacher professional development programs to ensure their effectiveness and relevance. This data-driven approach allows for agile adaptation and ensures that teacher professional development programs remain responsive to the ever-evolving needs of both educators and students.

RESEARCH METHODS

Research Design

This paper used mixed-methods research where qualitative and quantitative research approaches were used together, given that all three research questions required numerical results/answers and a statement kind of discussion and conclusion. Quantitative research is a more logical and data-led approach that measures people's thoughts from statistical and numerical points of view; it can gather a large amount of data that can be easily organized and manipulated into reports for analysis. Quantitative research is predominantly used as a synonym for any data collection technique (such as questionnaires) or data analysis procedure (such as graphs or statistics) that generates or uses numerical data (Saunders et al., 2009). Qualitative research does dipper than numbers. It explores the reasons behind the phenomenon; it helps to understand what is happening and how and why it occurs, providing more prosperous and meaningful insights. Through interviews and observations, I gained a rich insight into how teachers navigate challenges, adapt to ICT's transformative potential, and ultimately redefine their roles as facilitators of personalized and collaborative learning in a digitally saturated world, especially in Education 5.0. This deeper understanding informs the design of professional development programs that foster technical proficiency, pedagogical innovation, and shift in teaching paradigms to better equip teachers for the dynamic landscape of Education 5.0.

Participants

The targeted participants are teachers, school administrators, and curriculum developers experienced in addressing potential barriers to ICT in education to gain a comprehensive understanding of the contribution of ICT to teachers' professional development. The population number is approximated to (N=50), and the sample size is (n=45). Sampling was done using the random sampling method, given that every member of the population was expected to be using ICT and participate in answering the questions about the contribution of ICT to teachers' professional development. Sam.. .e $(n) = \frac{N}{1+Ne^2}$

N=total population

N=sample size

e= margin of error

Research Instruments

The interview aimed to explore how Information and Communication Technologies (ICT) will influence and contribute to teachers' professional development in Education 5.0. By listening to the experiences and perspectives of teachers, school administrators, and curriculum developers, the interview sheds light on the benefits, challenges, and overall contribution of ICT to teachers' growth and professional practices. The interview applied open-ended questions, which were;

i. Describe a specific example of how you have used ICT tools or resources in your professional development as an education stakeholder. What impact did this experience have on your professional skills and knowledge?
ii. what are the three most significant advantages of using ICT in teacher professional development? Conversely, what are teachers' most prominent challenges when integrating ICT into their learning?
iii. Looking towards the future, how do you envision the role of ICT in shaping the landscape of teacher professional development? What specific developments or resources would you hope to see become more prevalent?

Advantages of interview in exploring the contribution of ICT in teacher professional development,

Interviews delve into the human stories behind the numbers **through open-ended questions; interviews allow teachers, school administrators, and curriculum developers** to share their personal experiences, challenges, and successes with ICT integration in Teacher Professional Development (TPD). This rich qualitative data paints a vivid picture of the lived realities of professional development in education 5.0; exploring Complexities and Nuances, interviews often simplify issues into quantifiable categories, which can overlook the intricate nuances and complexities of how teachers engage with ICT in their professional development. Interviews offer a flexible space for participants to elaborate on their perspectives, reveal unexpected connections, and share counter-narratives that challenge stereotypical assumptions. This depth enriches our understanding of the multifaceted realities of ICT contribution to Teacher Professional Development (TPD), Capturing Personal Meanings and Motivations; quantitative data tells us what but rarely explains why. Interviews provide a platform for teachers to articulate their meanings, motivations, and anxieties surrounding ICT in their professional development. We can learn what drives their willingness or reluctance to embrace technology, the underlying values and beliefs that shape their choices, and the emotional journeys they navigate during Teacher Professional Development (TPD) experiences, fostering Trust and Rapport, conducting interviews builds trust and rapport between the researcher, in this case, a book chapter writer and the participants. This creates a safe space for honest and open dialogue, allowing teachers, school administrators, and curriculum developers to share sensitive information and vulnerable experiences they might not feel comfortable disclosing in a survey. This deeper connection enhances the quality and trustworthiness of the research data, enabling Contextual Understanding; quantitative data often struggles to capture the contextual nuances of individual classrooms and schools. Interviews allow teachers, school administrators, and curriculum developers to connect their experiences with ICT in professional development to specific teaching contexts, challenges faced, and available resources. This contextual understanding helps us interpret findings meaningfully and develop recommendations tailored to local realities.

Observation was another instrument used to gather data; observation in the context of the contribution of ICT in Teacher Professional Development refers to systematically gathering information about a teacher, school administrators, and curriculum developers' use of technology in their teaching practice. Direct observation was done by watching a teacher teach a lesson using ICT tools. Student work samples, examining student work created using ICT to see how the teacher helped them use the technology. The specific contribution of ICT in teacher professional development for Education 5.0 in Tanzania is the designed focused direct observation study spanning ten schools across diverse districts and types (urban and rural, primary and secondary). The observations, with informed consent from participants, centered around;

Resources available, Technology infrastructure, access to internet and educational software, availability of ICT-trained personnel, Expert support, Presence of mentors, ICT coordinators, or dedicated professional development programs focused on ICT integration, Internet access, Reliability, speed, and limitations of internet connectivity impacting online learning and resource access, Pedagogy skills, Teachers' ability to effectively utilize ICT tools to enhance teaching and student engagement, Lifelong learning, Teachers ability to learn on their pace for their professional development.

Advantages of direct observation in Teacher Professional Development using ICT

Improves teaching effectiveness by observing how teachers, school administrators, and curriculum developers use ICT effectively, leads to precisely the effectiveness of diverse use of ICT in Education, promotes reflection and self-improvement through observation of teachers, school administrators, and curriculum developers to become aware of their strengths and weaknesses in using ICT. This can lead to a more reflective teaching practice and a commitment to continuous personalized learning for professional development. Supports collaboration and peer learning; observation can be a valuable tool for collaboration and peer learning. When teachers, school administrators, and curriculum developers are observed under study, a clear picture of ICT's usefulness and future can be determined. Provides data for decision-making; observation can provide valuable data for school leaders and professional development providers to make informed decisions about supporting teachers, school administrators, and curriculum developers in ICT for future Education 5.0. Contributes to a research-based approach to professional development; observation is used to collect data for research on the effectiveness of ICT in teacher professional development. This research can help inform best practices for professional development programs and ensure that teachers use ICT practically for their learning and student learning.

FINDING AND DISCUSSIONS

Findings and Discussion from the Interview

Table 1. Results from teachers' interview

Category	Number	Qn1	Qn2	Qn3
Teachers	25	**Diverse use of ICT Tools and Resources in TPD** - Online courses -Virtual conferences and webinars -Collaborative platforms and online communities -Interactive simulations and educational games -Digital assessment tools and data analysis platforms **Potential Impacts on Professional Skills and Knowledge** - Enhanced subject knowledge and pedagogical skills -Increased digital competence and confidence -Improved collaboration and peer learning. -More engaging and student-centered learning -Data-driven decision-making	**Advantages of ICT in Teacher Professional Development** -Enhanced Access to Resources and Learning -Improved Teaching Strategies and Innovation -Collaboration and Knowledge Sharing **Challenges of Integrating ICT into Teacher Professional Development** -Digital Divide and Accessibility -Pedagogical Integration and Skill Development -Data Privacy and Security -Resistance to change	**Optimistic Visions** -Personalized learning platforms -Immersive experiences -Global collaboration -Automated administrative tasks -Continuous feedback and self-reflection **Cautious Approaches** -Equity and access concerns -Data privacy and security -Teacher agency and workload -Focus on pedagogical value -Human connection and critical thinking **Specific developments and resources desired** -Open-source Educational Resources (OER) needs. -Interactive simulations and learning games aligned with curriculum standards. -Professional development programs focused on effective pedagogical integration of technology -Mental health and well-being support for teachers navigating the challenges of a technology-driven teaching environment.

Table 2. Statistics

Diverse Use of ICT in Teacher Professional Development	Potential impacts of professional skills and knowledge	Advantages of ICT in teacher professional development	Challenges of integrating ICT into teacher professional development	Optimistic vision	Cautious approaches	Specific development and resources desired	
Valid	25	25	25	25	25	25	25
Missing	2	2	2	2	2	2	2

Table 3. Diverse use of ICT in teacher professional development

		Frequency	Percent	Valid Percent	Cumulative Percent
Valid	Online courses	5	18.5	20.0	20.0
	Virtual conferences and webinars	3	11.1	12.0	32.0
	Corroborative platforms and online communities	5	18.5	20.0	52.0
	Interactive simulations and education games	8	29.6	32.0	84.0
	Digital assessment tools and data analysis platforms	4	14.8	16.0	100.0
	Total	25	92.6	100.0	
Missing	System	2	7.4		
Total		27	100.0		

Figure 1. Diverse use of ICT in teacher professional development

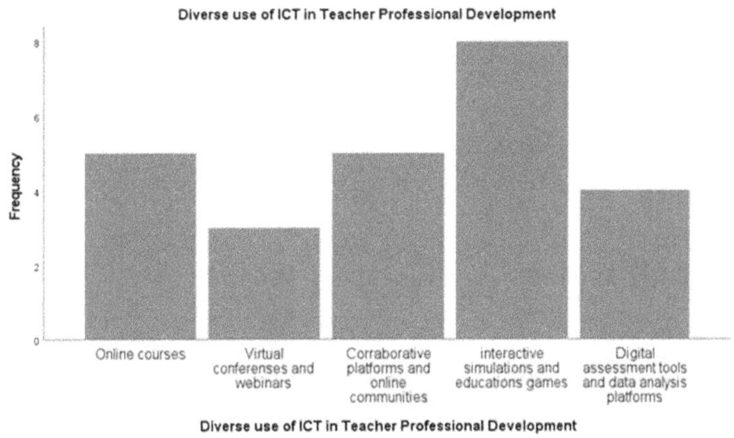

Table 4. Potential impacts of professional skills and knowledge

		Frequency	Percent	Valid Percent	Cumulative Percent
Valid	Enhances subject knowledge and pedagogical skills	3	11.1	12.0	12.0
	Improved collaboration and peer learning	7	25.9	28.0	40.0
	Increased digital competence and confidence	4	14.8	16.0	56.0
	More engaging and student-centered learning	6	22.2	24.0	80.0
	Data-driven decision making	2	7.4	8.0	88.0
	6.00	3	11.1	12.0	100.0
	Total	25	92.6	100.0	
Missing	System	2	7.4		
Total		27	100.0		

Figure 2. Potential impacts of professional skills and knowledge

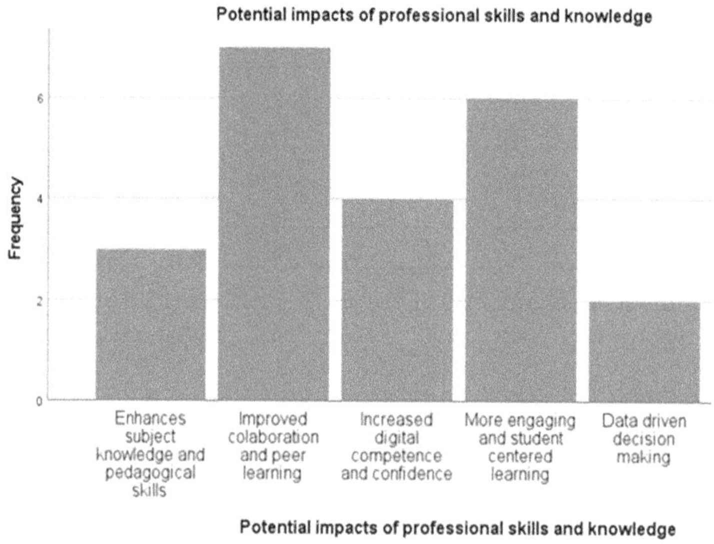

Table 5. Advantages of ICT in teacher professional development

		Frequency	Percent	Valid Percent	Cumulative Percent
Valid	Enhanced access to resources and learning	10	37.0	40.0	40.0
	Improved teaching strategies and innovations	7	25.9	28.0	68.0
	Collaboration and knowledge sharing	8	29.6	32.0	100.0
	Total	25	92.6	100.0	
Missing	System	2	7.4		
Total		27	100.0		

Figure 3. Advantages of ICT in teacher professional development

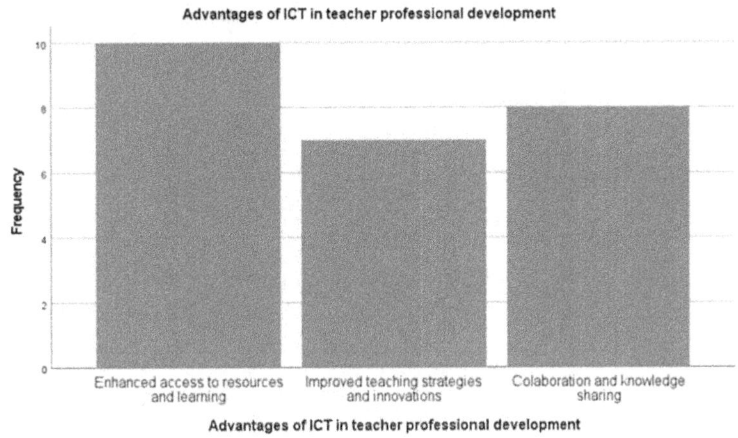

Table 6. Challenges of integrating ICT into teacher professional development

		Frequency	Percent	Valid Percent	Cumulative Percent
Valid	Digital divide and accessibility	7	25.9	28.0	28.0
	Pedagogical integration and skills development	8	29.6	32.0	60.0
	Data privacy and security	6	22.2	24.0	84.0
	Resistance to change	4	14.8	16.0	100.0
	Total	25	92.6	100.0	
Missing	System	2	7.4		
Total		27	100.0		

Figure 4. Challenges of integrating ICT into teacher professional development

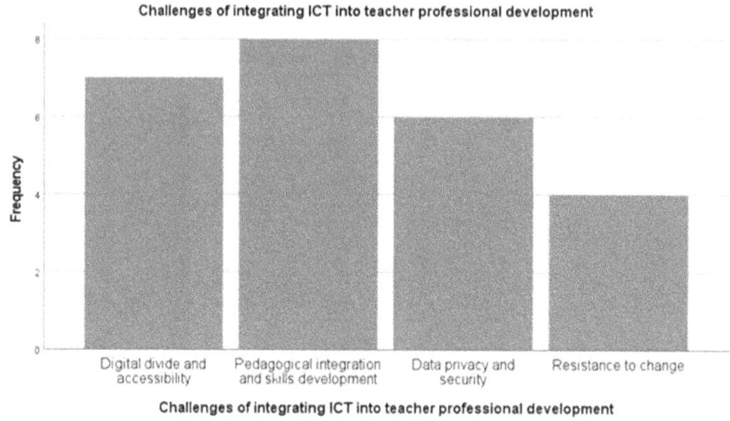

Table 7. Optimistic vision

		Frequency	Percent	Valid Percent	Cumulative Percent
Valid	Personalized learning platforms	5	18.5	20.0	20.0
	Immersive experiences	7	25.9	28.0	48.0
	Global collaboration	8	29.6	32.0	80.0
	Automated administrative tasks	5	18.5	20.0	100.0
	Total	25	92.6	100.0	
Missing	System	2	7.4		
Total		27	100.0		

Figure 5. Optimistic vision

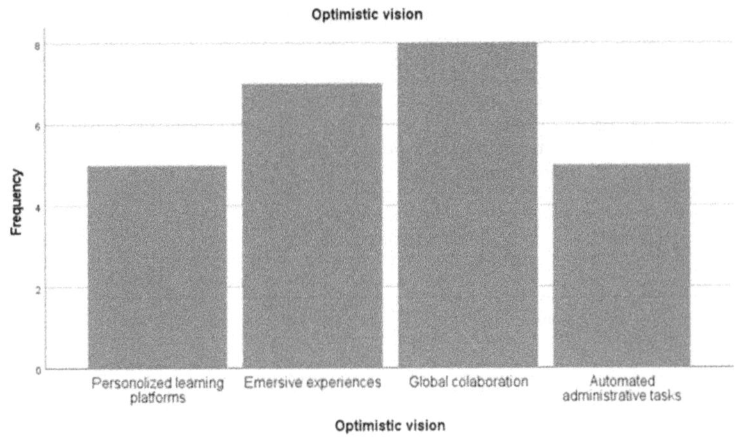

Table 8. Cautious approaches

		Frequency	Percent	Valid Percent	Cumulative Percent
Valid	Equity and access concerns	6	22.2	24.0	24.0
	Data privacy and security	4	14.8	16.0	40.0
	Teacher agency and workload	10	37.0	40.0	80.0
	Focus on pedagogical value	5	18.5	20.0	100.0
	Total	25	92.6	100.0	
Missing	System	2	7.4		
Total		27	100.0		

Figure 6. Cautious approaches

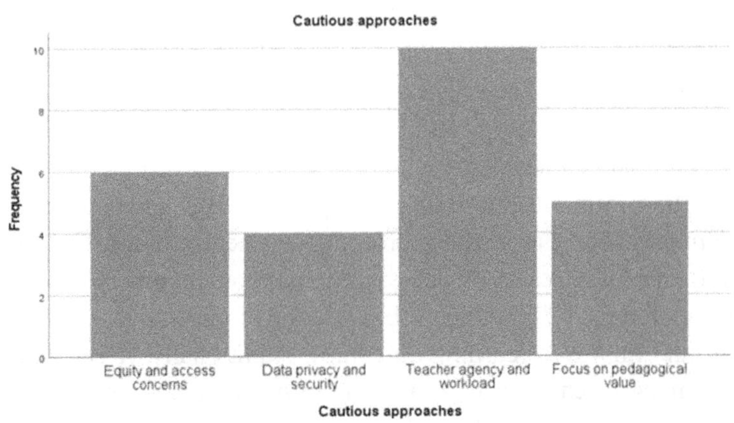

Table 9. Specific development and resources desired

		Frequency	Percent	Valid Percent	Cumulative Percent
Valid	Open-source educational resource	9	33.3	36.0	36.0
	Interactive simulation and learning games aligned with curriculum standards	8	29.6	32.0	68.0
	Professional development programs focused on effective pedagogical integration of technology	3	11.1	12.0	80.0
	mental health and well-being support for teachers navigating the challenges of a technology-driven teaching environment	5	18.5	20.0	100.0
	Total	25	92.6	100.0	
Missing	System	2	7.4		
Total		27	100.0		

Figure 7. Specific development and resources desired

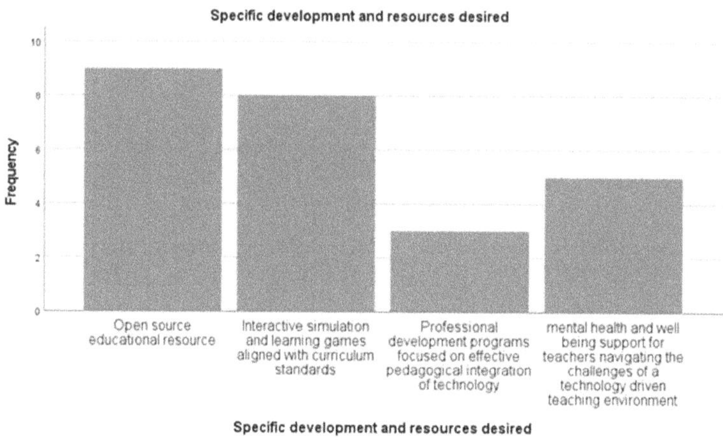

The tables and figures above show the results from teachers' interviews; it has been observed that ICT will offer a transformative potential for TPD in education 5.0 by fostering personalized learning, collaborative knowledge sharing, data-driven decision-making, and future-proof skills development. By harnessing these possibilities, we can empower teachers to become lifelong learners, adapt to the changing landscape of education, and ultimately contribute to improved learning outcomes for all students. This holistic approach to professional development aligns with the goals of Education 5.0, which seeks to leverage technology to transform education into a more personalized, interconnected, and adaptive system.

Education 5.0 demands a revolutionized approach to teacher development, and ICT stands poised as a powerful catalyst. It enables educators to access various resources and materials, fostering continuous learning and skill development. ICT facilitates the adoption of innovative teaching strategies, promoting student engagement and improved learning outcomes. Additionally, it encourages collaboration and knowledge sharing among teachers, leading to a more dynamic and enriched learning environment. However, challenges such as the digital divide, ensuring accessibility for all, integrating technology into pedagogy, and addressing data privacy and security concerns must be carefully navigated to fully harness the potential of ICT in teacher professional development within the framework of Education 5.0. By bridging these gaps and harnessing ICT responsibly, we can empower teachers to become architects of personalized learning in Education 5.0, fostering student success in a technology-driven future.

In the context of Education 5.0, which emphasizes the integration of advanced technologies into education, the contribution of Information and Communication Technology (ICT) to teachers' professional development is significant. Optimistic visions include personalized learning platforms, immersive experiences, global collaboration, automated administrative tasks, continuous feedback, and self-reflection, all of which can enhance teachers' skills and knowledge. However, cautious approaches are necessary to address equity and access concerns, data privacy and security issues, teacher agency and workload, and the need to focus on pedagogical value, human connection, and critical thinking. Specific developments and resources desired for teacher professional development in Education 5.0 include open-source educational resources (OER), interactive simulations, and learning games aligned with curriculum standards, professional development programs focusing on effective pedagogical integration of technology, and mental health and well-being support for teachers navigating the challenges of a technology-driven teaching environment. These findings highlight the complex landscape of ICT in teacher professional development, where opportunities for growth and innovation must be balanced with considerations for equity, privacy, workload, and holistic well-being.

Table 10. Results from the school administrator' interview

Category	Number	Qn1	Qn2	Qn3
School administrator	15	**Diverse use of ICT Tools and Resources in TPD** -Data-Driven -Decision Making with Online Dashboards -Collaborative Leadership with Virtual Communities -Innovative Professional Development with Virtual Mentorship -Parent Engagement with a Mobile App -Accessibility and Inclusion with Assistive Technologies **Potential Impacts on Professional Skills and Knowledge** -Innovative teaching practices -Improved student engagement and learning outcomes. -Foster a collaborative school culture, -Integration of various ICT tools in classrooms.	**Advantages of ICT in Teacher Professional Development** -Enhanced Access to Resources. -Collaboration and Knowledge Sharing -Personalized Learning -Interactive Learning and Engagement -Real-time Feedback and Assessment -Multicultural Understanding and Global Collaboration **Challenges of Integrating ICT into Teacher Learning** -Digital Divide -Pedagogical Integration -Data Privacy and Security - Lack of Infrastructure and Funding -Changing School Culture and Resistance to Change -Continuous Evaluation and Adaptation	**Optimistic Visions** -personalized instruction, -more accessible virtual reality (VR) platforms for classroom simulations and field trips. - online collaboration tools, micro-learning resources, and efficient content delivery platforms. -Secure and user-friendly platforms for peer-to-peer learning and knowledge sharing **Specific developments and resources desired** - Open-source educational resources (OER) translated into multiple languages - Learning Management Systems (LMS) will integrate seamlessly with classroom technology, creating a data-driven ecosystem for continuous improvement. -Advanced learning analytics platforms that track and analyze teacher-student interactions and effectiveness - ICT fosters a collaborative and supportive professional development environment. Social networking platforms are explicitly designed for educators.

Table 11. Statistics

		Diverse Use of ICT in Teacher Professional Development	Potential impacts of professional skills and knowledge	Advantages of ICT in teacher professional development	Challenges of integrating ICT into teacher professional development	Optimistic vision	Specific development and resources desired
N	Valid	15	15	15	15	15	15
	Missing	12	12	12	12	12	12

Table 12. Diverse use of ICT in teacher professional development

		Frequency	Percent	Valid Percent	Cumulative Percent
Valid	Data-driven decision-making with online dashboards	3	11.1	20.0	20.0
	Collaborative leadership with virtual communities	5	18.5	33.3	53.3
	Parent engagement with a mobile App	5	18.5	33.3	86.7
	Accessibility and inclusion with assistive technologies	2	7.4	13.3	100.0
	Total	15	55.6	100.0	
Missing	System	12	44.4		
Total		27	100.0		

Figure 8. Diverse use of ICT in teacher professional development

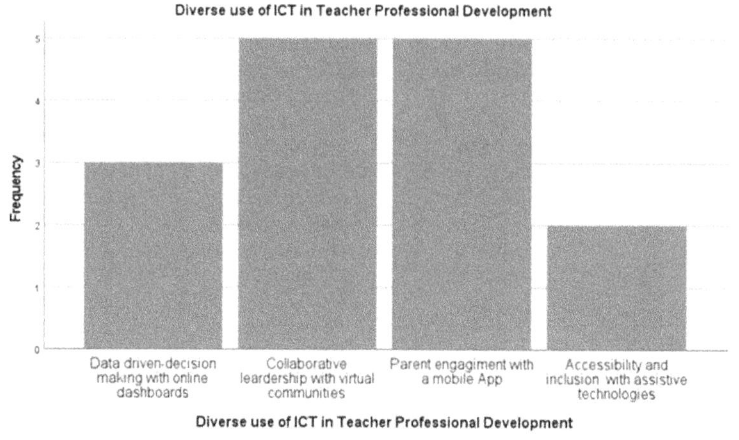

Table 13. Potential impacts of professional skills and knowledge

		Frequency	Percent	Valid Percent	Cumulative Percent
Valid	Innovative teaching practices	4	14.8	26.7	26.7
	Improved student engagement and learning outcomes	5	18.5	33.3	60.0
	Foster a collaborative school culture	5	18.5	33.3	93.3
	Integration of various ICT tools in classrooms	1	3.7	6.7	100.0
	Total	15	55.6	100.0	
Missing	System	12	44.4		
Total		27	100.0		

Figure 9. Potential impacts of professional skills and knowledge

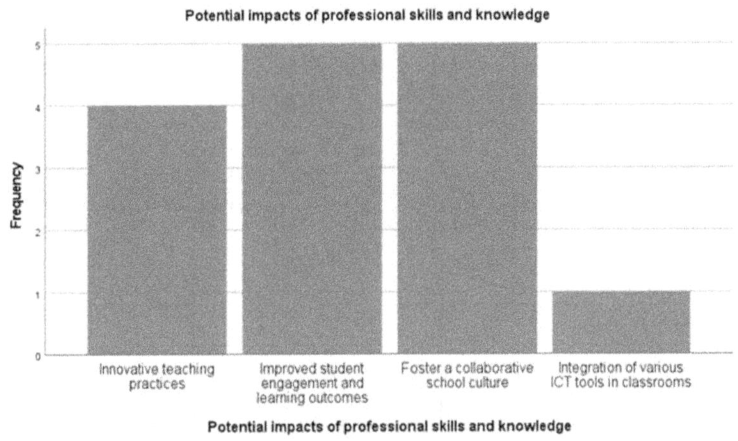

Table 14. Advantages of ICT in teacher professional development

		Frequency	Percent	Valid Percent	Cumulative Percent
Valid	Enhanced access to resources	6	22.2	40.0	40.0
	Collaboration and knowledge sharing	3	11.1	20.0	60.0
	Personalized learning	2	7.4	13.3	73.3
	Interactive learning and engagement	4	14.8	26.7	100.0
	Total	15	55.6	100.0	
Missing	System	12	44.4		
Total		27	100.0		

Figure 10. Advantages of ICT in teacher professional development

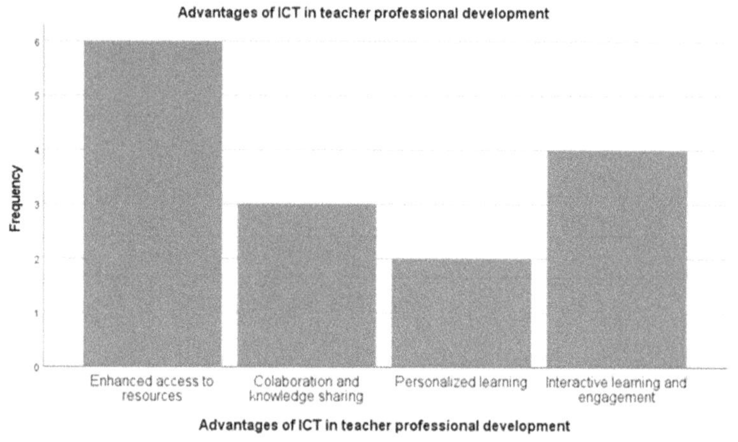

Table 15. Challenges of integrating ICT into teacher professional development

		Frequency	Percent	Valid Percent	Cumulative Percent
Valid	Digital divide	3	11.1	20.0	20.0
	Pedagogical integration	5	18.5	33.3	53.3
	Data privacy and security	4	14.8	26.7	80.0
	Lack of infrastructure and funding	3	11.1	20.0	100.0
	Total	15	55.6	100.0	
Missing	System	12	44.4		
Total		27	100.0		

Figure 11. Challenges of integrating ICT into teacher professional development

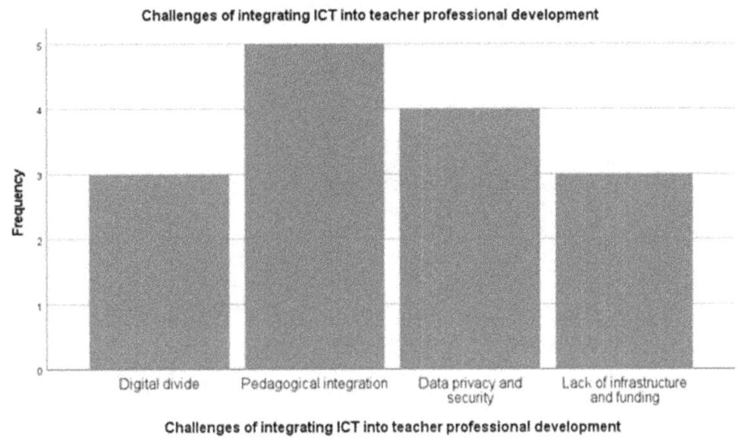

Table 16. Optimistic vision

		Frequency	Percent	Valid Percent	Cumulative Percent
Valid	Personalized instruction	4	14.8	26.7	26.7
	More accessible virtual reality platforms for classroom simulations and field trip	6	22.2	40.0	66.7
	Online collaboration tools, micro-learning resources, and efficient content delivery platforms	2	7.4	13.3	80.0
	Secure and user-friendly platforms for peer-to-peer learning and knowledge sharing	3	11.1	20.0	100.0
	Total	15	55.6	100.0	
Missing	System	12	44.4		
Total		27	100.0		

Figure 12. Optimistic vision

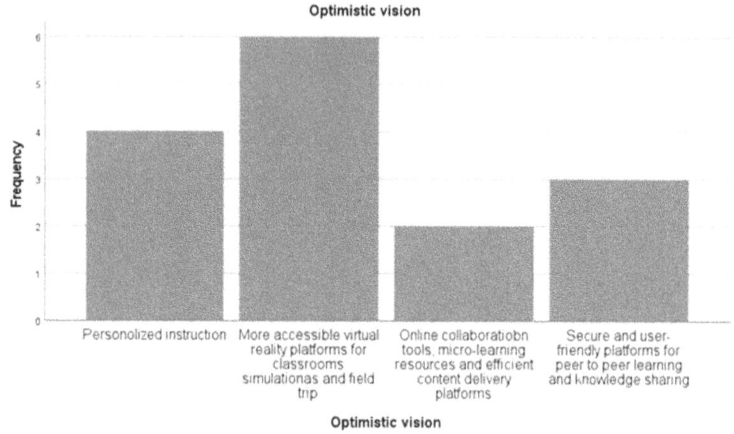

Table 17. Specific development and resources desired

		Frequency	Percent	Valid Percent	Cumulative Percent
Valid	Open-source educational resource	5	18.5	33.3	33.3
	Learning management systems integrate seamlessly with classroom technology	3	11.1	20.0	53.3
	Advanced learning platforms	5	18.5	33.3	86.7
	ICT fosters a collaborative and supportive professional development environment	2	7.4	13.3	100.0
	Total	15	55.6	100.0	
Missing	System	12	44.4		
Total		27	100.0		

Figure 13. Specific development and resources desired

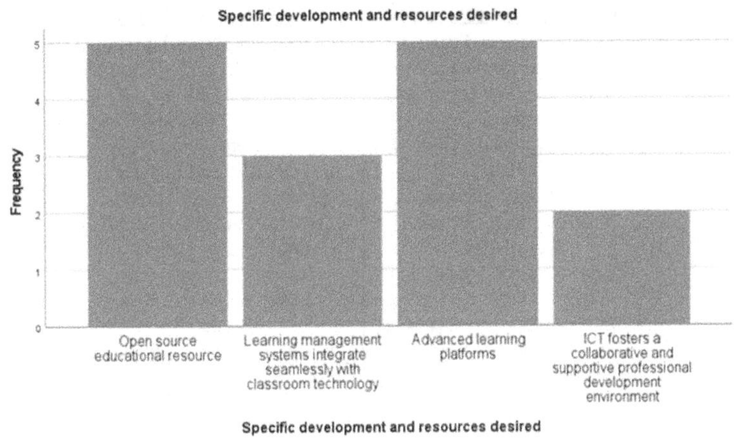

The above findings show that ICT is transformative in teachers' professional development. Diverse tools like data dashboards for informed decision-making, virtual communities for collaborative leadership, and even mobile apps for parent engagement can empower and equip our educators. Through innovative Professional Development like virtual mentorship programs and accessibility tools, we can foster a culture of continuous learning and inclusion. This translates to classrooms filled with innovative teaching practices, higher student engagement and learning outcomes, and a collaborative school environment where various ICT tools become seamlessly integrated, ultimately preparing our educators and students for the exciting future of education.

In Education 5.0, ICT offers a powerful toolkit for transformative teacher professional development. Imagine a world where teachers have effortless access to global resources, seamlessly collaborate and share knowledge, and personalize learning paths for every student. Interactive lessons with real-time feedback, enhanced engagement, and multicultural understanding through global collaboration have become the norm. However, challenges like the digital divide, pedagogical integration hurdles, and data security concerns demand our attention. To unlock ICT's full potential, we need robust infrastructure, adequate funding, and a willingness to change school cultures and embrace continuous evaluation. By navigating these challenges, we can empower teachers to harness the power of ICT in Education 5.0 for their professional development, ultimately creating a vibrant learning landscape where every student thrives.

Based on the findings from school administrators, the contribution of Information and Communication Technology (ICT) in teacher professional development in Education 5.0 is significant. Administrators are optimistic about the potential of personalized instruction, more accessible Virtual Reality (VR) platforms for classroom simulations and field trips, online collaboration tools, micro-learning resources, and efficient content delivery platforms to enhance teacher development. They desire specific developments such as open-source educational resources (OER) in multiple languages, Learning Management Systems (LMS) that integrate seamlessly with classroom technology, advanced learning analytics platforms, and social networking platforms designed for educators. These ICT advancements are expected to foster a collaborative and supportive environment for professional development, enabling teachers to improve their instructional effectiveness through data-driven insights and peer knowledge sharing.

Table 14. Results from the curriculum developer interview

Category	Number	Qn1	Qn2	Qn3
Curriculum developer	5	**Diverse use of ICT Tools and Resources in TPD** -Online collaboration platforms -Interactive webinars and simulations -Open educational resources (OERs) **Potential Impacts on Professional Skills and Knowledge** -Enhanced curriculum design skills -Developed digital competencies -Broadened knowledge base -Networking opportunities	**Advantages of ICT in Teacher Professional Development** -Enhanced Access to Resources and Learning -Improved Collaboration and Networking -Innovative and Engaging Learning Experiences **Challenges of Integrating ICT into Teacher Learning** -Access and Infrastructure -Effective Integration and Pedagogy -Ongoing Support and Evaluation	**Optimistic Visions** -Personalized and Immersive Learning -Collaborative and Connected Learning -Data-Driven Insights and Feedback **Specific developments and resources desired** -Open Educational Resources (OERs) platforms -AI-powered coaching and mentoring systems -Focus on digital citizenship and ethical considerations

Table 15. Statistics

		Diverse Use of ICT in Teacher Professional Development	Potential impacts of professional skills and knowledge	Advantages of ICT in teacher professional development	Challenges of integrating ICT into teacher professional development	Optimistic vision	Specific development and resources desired
N	Valid	5	5	5	5	5	5
	Missing	22	22	22	22	22	22

Table 16. Diverse use of ICT in teacher professional development

		Frequency	Percent	Valid Percent	Cumulative Percent
Valid	Online collaboration platforms	2	7.4	40.0	40.0
	Interactive webinars and simulations	3	11.1	60.0	100.0
	Total	5	18.5	100.0	
Missing	System	22	81.5		
Total		27	100.0		

Figure 14. Diverse use of ICT in teacher professional development

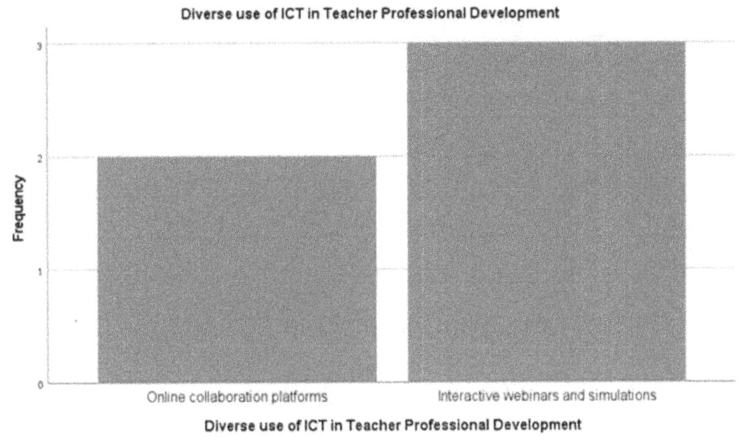

Table 17. Potential impacts of professional skills and knowledge

		Frequency	Percent	Valid Percent	Cumulative Percent
Valid	Enhanced curriculum design skills	2	7.4	40.0	40.0
	Developed digital competences	1	3.7	20.0	60.0
	Networking opportunities	2	7.4	40.0	100.0
	Total	5	18.5	100.0	
Missing	System	22	81.5		
Total		27	100.0		

Figure 15. Potential impacts of professional skills and knowledge

Table 18. Advantages of ICT in teacher professional development

		Frequency	Percent	Valid Percent	Cumulative Percent
Valid	Enhanced access to resources and learning	1	3.7	20.0	20.0
	Improved collaboration and networking	2	7.4	40.0	60.0
	Innovative and engaging learning experiences	2	7.4	40.0	100.0
	Total	5	18.5	100.0	
Missing	System	22	81.5		
Total		27	100.0		

Figure 16. Advantages of ICT in teacher professional development

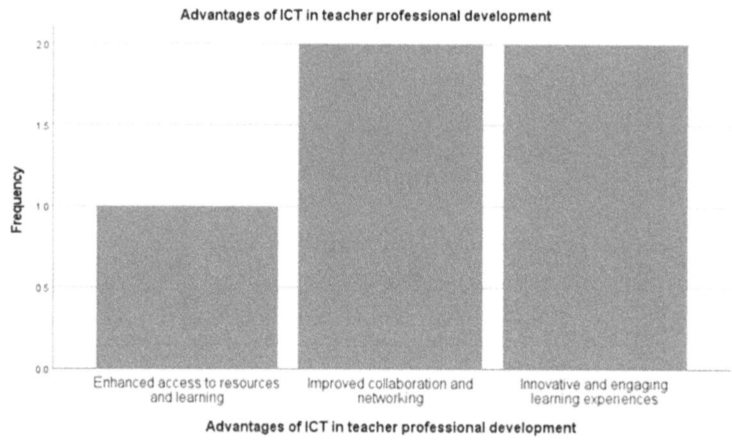

Table 19. Challenges of integrating ICT into teacher professional development

		Frequency	Percent	Valid Percent	Cumulative Percent
Valid	Access and infrastructures	2	7.4	40.0	40.0
	Effective integration and pedagogy	2	7.4	40.0	80.0
	Ongoing support and evaluation	1	3.7	20.0	100.0
	Total	5	18.5	100.0	
Missing	System	22	81.5		
Total		27	100.0		

Figure 17. Challenges of integrating ICT into teacher professional development

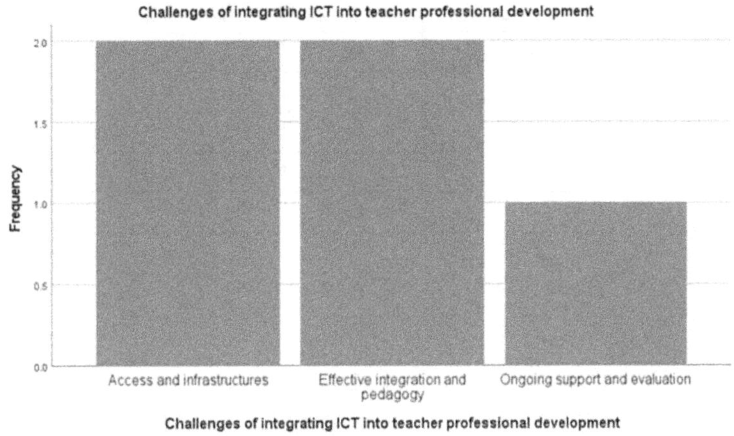

Table 20. Specific development and resources desired

		Frequency	Percent	Valid Percent	Cumulative Percent
Valid	Open-source educational resource	3	11.1	60.0	60.0
	Focus on digital citizenship and ethical considerations	2	7.4	40.0	100.0
	Total	5	18.5	100.0	
Missing	System	22	81.5		
Total		27	100.0		

Figure 18. Specific development and resources desired

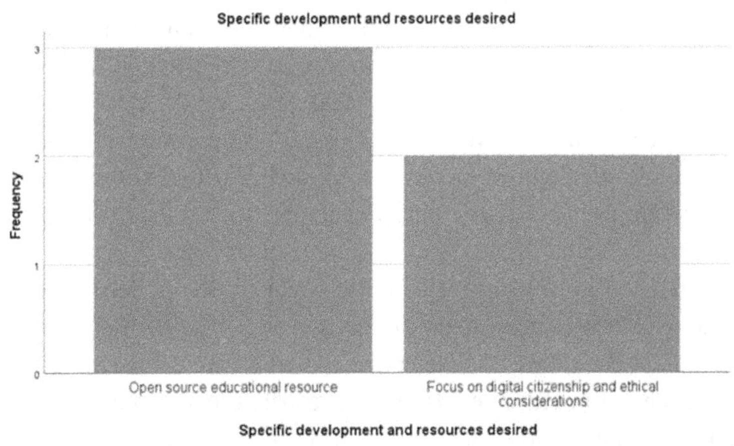

Table 21. Optimistic vision

		Frequency	Percent	Valid Percent	Cumulative Percent
Valid	Personalized and immersive learning	1	3.7	20.0	20.0
	Collaborative and connected learning	2	7.4	40.0	60.0
	Data-driven insights and feedback	2	7.4	40.0	100.0
	Total	5	18.5	100.0	
Missing	System	22	81.5		
Total		27	100.0		

Figure 19. Optimistic vision

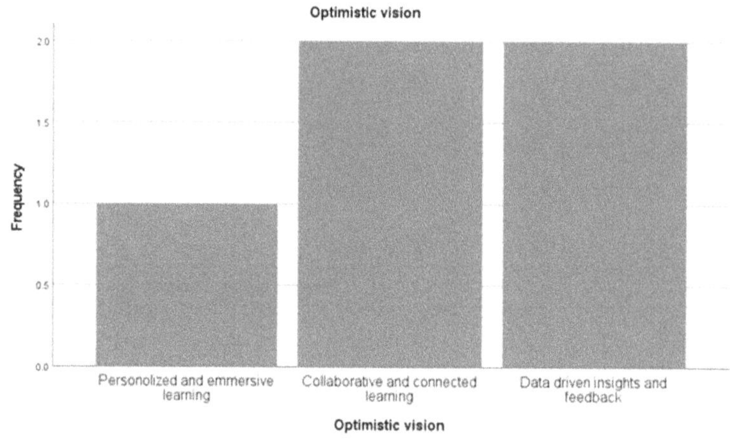

From a curriculum developer's perspective, ICT presents exciting opportunities to transform teachers' professional development in Education 5.0. Diverse tools like online collaboration platforms, interactive webinars, and readily available Open-source Education Resources (OERs) can equip teachers with enhanced curriculum design skills, empower them to develop their digital competencies and broaden their knowledge base. Collaborative learning opportunities through ICT networks further fuel this growth. This potent combination enhances individual educator development and fosters a dynamic, interconnected learning ecosystem where innovation and best practices flourish, ultimately leading to more prosperous, engaging curriculum experiences. These ICT-enabled strategies facilitate the exchange of ideas and resources. They enable curriculum developers to stay updated with the latest educational trends and practices, thus contributing to their continuous professional growth in the Education 5.0 era.

In the context of Education 5.0, integrating ICT into teacher professional development offers significant advantages and challenges. Advantages include enhanced access to learning resources, improved collaboration and networking opportunities, and the creation of innovative and engaging learning experiences. However, challenges such as limited access to ICT infrastructure, the need for effective integration with pedagogy, and ongoing support and evaluation of ICT implementation are crucial considerations for curriculum developers toward the future of Education 5.0. Balancing these advantages and challenges is vital for ensuring that ICT contributes effectively to the professional development of teachers in the Education 5.0 paradigm.

Several findings from the listed elements regarding ICT's contribution to Teacher Professional Development in Education 5.0 can be discussed. Firstly, emphasizing "Personalized and Immersive Learning" suggests that ICT can help tailor learning experiences to individual teachers' needs, making professional development more effective. Secondly, "Collaborative and Connected Learning" indicates that ICT tools can facilitate collaboration among teachers, enabling them to share knowledge and best practices. Thirdly, "Data-Driven Insights and Feedback" implies that ICT can provide valuable data on teachers' performance, which can be used to offer targeted feedback and improve their skills. Moreover, the desire for "Open Educational Resources (OERs) platforms" suggests a need for easily accessible digital resources to support professional development. The mention of "AI-powered coaching and mentoring systems" indicates an interest in leveraging Artificial Intelligence (AI) to provide personalized coaching and mentoring to teachers. Lastly, the focus on "digital citizenship and ethical considerations" highlights the importance of preparing teachers to navigate the ethical and social aspects of using ICT in their professional development. Overall, these findings suggest that ICT has the potential to significantly enhance teacher professional development in Education 5.0 through personalized, collaborative, data-driven, and ethically conscious approaches supported by advanced digital tools and resources.

Findings From Observation

Uneven Resource Distribution: Urban schools, particularly private institutions, exhibited better access to computers, projectors, and educational software than rural settings. Government schools often relied on limited resources, with some lacking essential equipment like computers. Limited Expert Support and dedicated ICT coordinators or mentors were rarely present, especially in rural schools. Teachers needed ongoing support and guidance in effectively integrating ICT into their pedagogy. Internet connectivity and reliable internet access remained significant hurdles, especially in rural areas. Slow speeds, frequent outages, and data cost limitations hampered online learning and resource utilization. Pedagogy Gaps: While some teachers showcased innovative ICT integration, others struggled beyond introductory presentations or passive screen-based learning. This highlighted the need for tailored professional development focusing on practical pedagogical approaches. The inadequacy of in-service training around the teacher's professional development makes the traditional one-fit- all approaches in professional development fall short, especially in this digitalized world and in the expected innovative society in Education 5.0, most teachers rely on government efforts for their professional development.

Discussion from Observation

The observation shows that integrating ICT into teacher professional development in Education 5.0 has various challenges. Uneven resource distribution, with urban private schools having better ICT infrastructure and software access than rural and government schools, creates disparities in teacher training and professional development opportunities. The limited presence of dedicated ICT coordinators or mentors, especially in rural areas, indicates a lack of ongoing support and guidance for teachers in effectively integrating ICT into their learning and pedagogy. Internet connectivity issues, such as unreliable access and slow speeds, hinder the implementation of online learning and resource utilization, further impacting teacher training initiatives. The observed pedagogy gaps also highlight the need for tailored professional development programs focusing on practical pedagogical approaches for ICT integration.

Addressing these challenges is crucial for ensuring equitable access to ICT resources and effective teacher professional development in Education 5.0 worldwide.

CONCLUSION

The discussion from interviews underscores the transformative potential of ICT in Teacher Professional Development (TPD) within the framework of Education 5.0. ICT offers opportunities for personalized learning, collaborative knowledge sharing, data-driven decision-making, and future-proof skills development, aligning with the goals of Education 5.0 to create a more personalized, interconnected, and adaptive educational system. However, this potential comes with challenges such as the digital divide, ensuring accessibility for all, integrating technology into pedagogy, and addressing data privacy and security concerns. Despite these challenges, ICT can empower teachers to become lifelong learners, adapt to the evolving education landscape, and improve student learning outcomes. To fully harness the potential of ICT in Teacher Professional Development (TPD), bridging these gaps and navigating ICT adoption responsibly is crucial, ensuring that it enhances pedagogical value, human connection, and critical thinking while addressing equity, privacy, workload, and holistic well-being concerns. Specific developments and resources desired for Teacher Professional Development (TPD) in Education 5.0 include open-source educational resources, interactive simulations, professional development programs focusing on effective pedagogical technology integration, and teachers' mental health and well-being support. These findings highlight the complex nature of ICT in Teacher Professional Development (TPD), where opportunities for growth and innovation must be balanced with considerations for equity, privacy, workload, and holistic well-being in the context of Education 5.0

The direct observation reveals significant challenges in integrating ICT into teacher professional development within the framework of Education 5.0 globally. The uneven distribution of resources, with urban private schools having better access to ICT infrastructure and software than rural and government schools, leads to disparities in teacher training opportunities. The lack of dedicated ICT coordinators or mentors, particularly in rural areas, indicates a need for ongoing support and guidance for teachers in effectively integrating ICT into their learning and teaching practices. Internet connectivity issues, including unreliable access and slow speeds, pose additional obstacles to online learning and resource utilization, hindering teachers' personalized learning and impacting teacher training initiatives. The observed pedagogy gaps highlight the necessity for tailored professional development programs focusing on practical pedagogical approaches for ICT integration. Addressing these challenges is crucial to ensure equitable access to ICT resources and effective teacher professional development in Education 5.0 in Tanzania.

Therefore, the journey towards transformative teacher professional development in Education 5.0 is paved with opportunities and challenges. Recognizing the duality of ICT, its potential to empower, and the obstacles it presents are crucial for navigating this complex landscape. By addressing the digital divide, designing engaging online experiences, and integrating effectively with existing systems, we can unlock the transformative potential of ICT in Education 5.0 teacher professional development. Moreover, embracing personalized learning, fostering collaboration, and employing data-driven analysis can further empower educators and drive continuous improvement in teacher professional development programs. Ultimately, harnessing the power of ICT demands a multifaceted approach that acknowledges the challenges, celebrates the opportunities, and strives towards a future where every educator has the tools and support necessary to thrive in the ever-evolving landscape of Education 5.0.

REFERENCES

Fulgence, K. (2020). Developing Digital Fluency among Teacher Educators: Evidence from Tanzanian Schools of Education. *International Journal of Education and Development Using Information and Communication Technology*, 158–175.

Fullan, M. (2017). *Rethinking professional development: Change, learning, and innovation in schools* (3 ed.). Dar es saam: John Wiley & Sons.

Guskey, T. F. (2022). *Evaluating professional development* (2 ed.). Tokyo: Evaluating professional development.

Hall, A. B., & Trespalacios, J. (2019). Personalized professional learning and teacher self-efficacy for integrated technology in K-12 classrooms. *Journal of Digital Learning in Teacher Education*, 35(4), 221–235. 10.1080/21532974.2019.1647579

Huisinga, R. N., & Martin, Y. (2017). *Indigenous Agricultural Knowledge and Gender issues in third world Agricultural Development.* India: Agricultural company.co.limited.

Kaur, G. (2017, June 6). THE IMPORTANCE OF DIGITAL MARKETING IN THE TOURISM. *International Journal of Research Granthaalayah*, 5(6), 72–77. 10.29121/granthaalayah.v5.i6.2017.1998

Kaur, K. (2023, June 3). Teaching and Learning with ICT tools: Issues and Challenges. *International Journal on Cybernetics & Informatics*, 12(3), 15–22. 10.5121/ijci.2023.120302

Mishra, P., & Koehler, J. M. (2016). Technological pedagogical and content knowledge: A framework for teacher knowledge. *Teachers College Record*, 108(6), 1017–1030. 10.1111/j.1467-9620.2006.00684.x

Mwalongo, A. (2021). Teachers' perceptions about ICT for teaching, professional. *International Journal of Education and Development Using Information and Communication Technology*, 7(3), 36–49.

Nowfeek, M. R., & Mahrool, F. (2021, May 31). The Contribution of Integrated ICT in Teaching and Learning Practice: Teacher's Perspective. *International Journal of Advanced Multidisciplinary Research, 8*(5-2021),. 78–89. doi:http://dx.doi.org/10.22192/ijamr.2021.08.05.004

Nurdiana, R., Effendi, M. N., Ningsih, K. P., & Abda, M. I. (2023). Collaborative Partnerships For Digital Education To Improve Students' Learning Achievement At The Institute Of Islamic Religion Of Sultan Muhammad Syafiuddin Sambas, Indonesia. *International Journal of Teaching and Learning*, 1, 1–15.

Reeves, T. (2020, October). Transforming learning with technology. *Perspectives on the future of education. Learning Solutions Magazine*, 6(1), 1–5.

Saidu, A., Clarkson, A. M., Adamu, S. H., Mohammed, M., & Jibo, I. (2017). Application of ICT in Agriculture:Opportunities and Challenges in Developing Countries. *International Journal of Computer Science and Mathematical Theory, pp. 3*, 8–18.

Smith, A. J. (2019). *Insights into Education: A Comprehensive Guide.* Academic Press.

UNESCO. (2019). *Global education policy report.* Corwin Press.

Watts, N. (2018). *Developing Digital Fluency in Higher Education: A study in the acquisition of digital capability by academics in Irish higher education settings. University College Dublin*. School of Education.

Xu, X., Y. S. (2023). The theoretical framework of personal learning environments: SPET model. *International Conference on Technology in Education*, (pp. 139–156). Research Gate.

Zhang, L., Yang, S., & Carter, R. A. (2020). Personalized learning and ESSA: What we know and where we go. *Journal of Research on Technology in Education*, 52(3), 253–274. 10.1080/15391523.2020.1728448

Chapter 13
Assessment and Evaluation in Education 5.0

Maida Maqsood
Government College Women University, Sialkot, Pakistan

Abeer Othman
Harbin Normal University, China

Muhammad Ilyas
University of Malakand, Pakistan

Rehan Mehmood Sabir
http://orcid.org/0009-0007-4711-8304
University of Agriculture, Faisalabad, Pakistan

Isma Urooj
Allama Iqbal Open University, Islamabad, Pakistan

Tayyaba Zahra
Allama Iqbal Open University, Islamabad, Pakistan

Obaid Muhammad Abdullah
University of Veterinary and Animal Science, Lahore, Pakistan

Hafsa Hamid Butt
Department of English Linguistics, Minhaj University Lahore, Pakistan

ABSTRACT

Education 5.0 requires a fundamental change in the way assessments are conducted. To transcend the constraints of standardized examinations, it is essential to employ inventive approaches such as portfolios, projects, and digital badges, which play a vital role in fostering personalized learning and empowering students. The utilization of technology and data-driven methodologies such as big data and AI present exciting opportunities for adaptive learning and enhanced comprehension. Nevertheless, ethical concerns, safeguarding data privacy, and guaranteeing fairness in evaluation persist as significant obstacles. To enhance the abilities of students and bring about educational transformation, it is crucial to prioritize ongoing enhancement, international cooperation, and the use of innovative technologies. These factors are vital in determining the future of assessment and evaluation in Education 5.0.

DOI: 10.4018/979-8-3693-3041-8.ch013

INTRODUCTION

Define Education 5.0 and its Key Characteristics

Education 5.0 is a proposed advancement in education that builds on past periods and focuses on integrating modern technology, individualized learning, and the development of vital skills. The objective is to equip individuals with the necessary knowledge and abilities to excel in the dynamic 21st century, specifically within the framework of Society 5.0.

Figure 1. The progression of the education system over time (Himmetoglu et al., 2020)

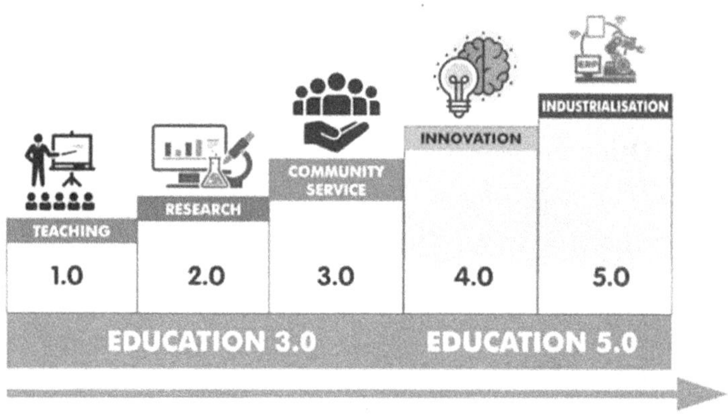

This framework prioritizes solutions that prioritize human needs, well-being, inclusion, and ethical considerations.

Key characteristics of Education 5.0:

1) Focus on Human-Centered Learning
2) Technology as an Enabler, not a Driver
3) Lifelong Learning and Skill Development
4) Global Connectedness and Collaboration
5) Sustainable and Ethical Practices

Education 5.0 is currently in its nascent phase of advancement, and its execution encounters numerous obstacles. Nevertheless, it offers a compelling outlook for the future of education that is characterized by more customization, interactivity, and alignment with the demands of individuals and society.

Role of Assessment and Evaluation in Education 5.0

Education 5.0 revolutionizes assessment and evaluation by shifting from fixed measurements to a dynamic approach that facilitates personalized learning. Assessments have transitioned from being primarily summative to being primarily formative, with a shift in emphasis from evaluating topic knowledge to evaluating skills. The learning materials are uniform yet tailored to accommodate individual learning styles and progress. The key roles encompass diagnostic, adaptive, motivating, and collaborative aspects. The tools and technologies encompass AI-driven platforms, interactive and immersive exams, as well as portfolio-based assessments. The challenges encompass guaranteeing data protection, upholding ethical standards in AI usage, creating unbiased assessments, providing training for instructors, and transitioning from a grading-focused approach to one centered on learning and feedback. The objective is to provide a feedback loop that promotes ongoing enhancement, enables learners, and equips them for a dynamic and demanding environment (Oktaviana et al., 2022).

Need for Innovative and Effective Assessment Practices

The demand for inventive evaluation methods is essential in the current fast-changing global landscape. Conventional approaches frequently prioritize rote learning and recollection, disregarding the development of critical thinking, creativity, and problem-solving skills. Additionally, they lack adaptability and adhere to strict standards, which may put certain kids at a disadvantage. The challenges of the 21st century encompass the dynamic labor market, the interdependent and intricate global landscape, and the imperative for continuous learning throughout one's life.

Innovative assessments provide individualized instruction, ongoing evaluation, practical application in real-life situations, diverse enhancement of skills, and empowerment for learners. Authentic tasks and simulations can be integrated to promote the development of metacognitive skills and a sense of ownership over the learning process. Illustrations of inventive evaluations encompass portfolios, performance-oriented assignments, self-evaluation and peer critique, open-ended projects, and digital instruments such as interactive quizzes and adaptive learning games. Effective and creative assessment techniques necessitate collaboration among educators, researchers, and policymakers. By using innovative methodologies, we may develop evaluations that genuinely facilitate and enable learners in the modern day.

RETHINKING ASSESSMENT: A PARADIGM SHIFT

Moving Beyond Traditional Assessments

The conventional method of assessment, which involves testing and assigning scores, is being challenged by the evolving learning environment of Education 5.0. Adhering to traditional pen-and-paper exams that concentrate on memorizing without considering practical application is comparable to attempting to navigate a digital ocean using a paper map. We require a fundamental change in our approach, moving away from these obsolete techniques and adopting cutting-edge assessment methodologies.

This transition necessitates a concentration on aptitudes, rather than grades. Assessments should appraise students' capacity for critical thinking, collaborative problem-solving, and effective communication, the same talents required to negotiate the intricacies of the 21st century. Envision engaging and interactive projects, realistic simulations, and individualized feedback systems that foster internal drive and enable learners to assume responsibility for their educational progress. It is not solely focused on academic performance, but rather on nurturing individuals who possess the ability to continuously learn and have the flexibility and determination to succeed in an ever-evolving society (Albritton et al., 2021).

Focus on Personalized Learning and Student Agency

The fundamental transformation in Education 5.0 requires a concentration on individualized learning and student empowerment. This entails a transition from a standardized approach to adaptable learning routes that accommodate individual aptitudes, preferences, and learning modalities. Classrooms are converted into dynamic centers of learning, where the combination of technology and human direction enables students to independently navigate their educational paths. Curriculums are flexible and cater to individual requirements by providing a variety of materials, project-based activities, and individualized instruction. The student's initiative drives this individualized experience, cultivating independent learners who inquire, investigate options, and make well-informed choices. Enacting individualized learning necessitates the utilization of inventive evaluations, encouraging educators, and adaptable curriculum. The benefits are vast, as a cohort of flexible, self-driven learners will become pioneers, troubleshooters, and trailblazers.

Formative Assessment and Feedback

Formative assessment and feedback are crucial elements of successful teaching and learning. They collaborate to consistently monitor student advancement, pinpoint strengths and weaknesses, and direct instruction to guarantee pupils reach their learning objectives.

What is Formative Assessment?

Formative assessment encompasses a range of techniques employed to collect data on student learning during the educational process. These methods are usually low-stakes and informal, serving to offer instant feedback and adapt instruction as necessary, rather than for grading purposes.

- **Examples:**
  - ✓ Exit tickets
  - ✓ Quick quizzes
  - ✓ Observations during group work
  - ✓ One-on-one discussions
  - ✓ Class discussions and open-ended questions

What is Feedback?

Feedback is the data given to students regarding their performance in a formative assessment.

- **Characteristics of Effective Feedback:**
  - ✓ Specific
  - ✓ Actionable
  - ✓ Timely
  - ✓ Goal oriented
  - ✓ Positive

Formative assessment serves as the basis for providing useful feedback. Teachers can offer precise feedback to students by consistently collecting data on their comprehension, enabling students to connect their current knowledge with the intended learning goals. The iterative process of evaluation, feedback, and adaptation results in enhanced learning, better outcomes, and heightened student involvement.

Self-Assessment and Peer Assessment

Self-evaluation and peer assessment are crucial instruments in education to improve student learning and foster independence. Self-assessment entails students assessing their work based on predetermined criteria, promoting metacognitive skills, and recognizing strengths and limitations. Peer assessment involves evaluating peers' work according to established standards, offering diverse viewpoints, and promoting collaboration. Effective strategies involve utilizing clear rubrics, implementing anonymous or formal peer assessment methods, and emphasizing improvement over criticism. Integrating self-evaluation with peer assessment can result in a more profound comprehension of strengths and limitations, inspiring students to enhance their work (Spiller, 2012).

Authentic and Performance-Based Assessments

Authentic and performance-based assessments are techniques employed to evaluate student learning by utilizing real-world tasks and activities. Authentic assessments prioritize the genuineness of assignments by simulating real-world scenarios that students may face beyond the classroom. Performance-based exams showcase students' skills and knowledge by necessitating them to use what they have learned to accomplish specific tasks actively. The advantages of these evaluations include enhanced student involvement, greater comprehension of information, and enhanced evaluation of various skills and capabilities. Challenges involve creating efficient and interesting assignments, guaranteeing fairness and impartiality, and dealing with time and resource limitations. Although challenging, authentic, and performance-based assessments provide a valuable method for assessing student learning, promoting deeper comprehension, and applying information and skills in real-world scenarios (VanTassel-Baska, 2014).

Integration of Technology and Data-Driven Approaches

Utilizing technology and data-driven methods in education can transform the learning process for pupils. Technology can be utilized for data gathering through tools like Learning Management Systems (LMS), adaptive learning platforms, educational apps, and games. Data-driven training entails examining student data to pinpoint strengths, weaknesses, and learning gaps, guide instructional choices, and monitor progress over time. The advantages of this integration comprise tailored learning, enhanced involvement, immediate feedback, and decision-making based on data. Challenges encompass access and equity, data privacy and security, and teacher training and support. Integration has great potential to revolutionize education by establishing a more customized, captivating, and efficient learning setting. Emphasizing data quality and ethical use for instructional guidance is essential, avoiding student ranking or comparison. Consistent assessment and contemplation are crucial to guarantee the efficiency of technology incorporation and data-driven strategies in attaining intended educational results. By implementing these techniques carefully and ethically, we can utilize technology and data to create a better future for education.

Big Data and Learning Analytics

Education 5.0 is a forward-looking approach to learning that focuses on customized, immersive, and technology-driven experiences. Big data and learning analytics are essential for allowing data-driven decision-making and personalized learning journeys for students. Big data is produced from a variety of sources such as Learning Management Systems (LMS), adaptive learning platforms, educational apps and games, student exams, and surveys. The information comprises academic performance data, engagement data, behavioral data, and learning analytics.

Big data and learning analytics in Education 5.0 offer advantages such as increased personalization, enhanced student engagement, timely intervention, and evidence-based decision-making. Challenges encompass data protection and security, mitigating algorithmic bias, and offering instructor training and support.

Using these tools responsibly and ethically allows us to develop customized, captivating, and efficient learning experiences that enable each student to achieve their maximum potential. It is crucial to remember that technology and data serve as tools, not solutions. Education 5.0's effectiveness depends on human-centered design, ethical considerations, and integrating these tools into a pedagogical framework that emphasizes critical thinking, creativity, and social-emotional learning, in addition to academic achievement.

Adaptive Learning and Intelligent Tutoring Systems

Education 5.0 emphasizes customized learning experiences that address individual requirements and learning preferences. Adaptive learning and intelligent tutoring systems (ITS) are essential tools that utilize technology and data to enhance learning outcomes. Adaptive learning employs algorithms and machine learning to customize content, speed, and complexity according to each student's performance and preferences. The program provides diagnostic assessments, personalized learning routes, immediate feedback, and interactive support. ITS replicates personalized human tutoring through interactive assistance and feedback customized to each student's need. These systems can be included in Learning Management Systems (LMS) and other educational technologies and can be embedded in different learning settings. Adaptive Learning and Intelligent Tutoring Systems offer advantages such as heightened engagement, enhanced learning results, optimized learning time utilization, and promotion of self-directed learning and empowerment. Challenges encompass development and implementation expenses, data privacy and security issues, and the risk of prejudice. These technologies have great promise to transform personalized learning in Education 5.0. Successful implementation necessitates cooperation among educators, technologists, and learning scientists, emphasizing pedagogical validity, ethical concerns, and ongoing enhancement (Phobun and Vicheanpanya, 2010).

Educational Games and Simulations

Educational games and simulations are advanced tools that improve learning experiences and encourage deeper comprehension in different age groups and topic areas. These interactive activities, such as serious games, instructional simulations, and gamification, aim to inspire students and enhance learning outcomes. The games offer advantages such as heightened involvement, better memory retention, advancement of critical thinking and problem-solving abilities, improved teamwork and communication, and a secure environment for practice and experimentation. Some examples of these games are language learning games that engage students in interactive settings to practice vocabulary, grammar, and conversation skills, and science simulations that enable students to explore and learn from errors without real-world repercussions. These interactive learning tools are highly effective for improving learning and promoting critical thinking.

PRINCIPLES OF ASSESSMENT AND EVALUATION IN EDUCATION 5.0

Alignment with Learning Goals and Outcomes

Educational approaches in Assessment and Evaluation 5.0 emphasize personalized learning, integrating technology and data analysis to enhance learning results. This method incorporates formative evaluation, self-assessment, and adaptive learning to provide personalized feedback and teaching. Education 5.0 highlights the incorporation of technology and data, including learning analytics and intelligent tutoring systems. It promotes critical thinking and problem-solving abilities via real-world evaluations, simulations, and games. It encourages continuous learning, providing learners with the necessary skills and knowledge to become lifelong learners. The learning objectives of the Principles of Assessment and Evaluation course may vary but often focus on understanding various assessment methodologies and their uses in education.

Continuous and Integrated Assessment

Continuous and integrated assessment is a way of evaluating student learning that occurs consistently throughout the learning process, combining several assessment methods to form a comprehensive view of student development. The approach is formative, emphasizing feedback for enhancing learning rather than just assessing performance. Assessment methods including formative, self-assessments, peer assessments, and summative assessments are used routinely during the learning process. The data from these evaluations is merged and examined to offer a thorough comprehension of student learning. Continuous and integrated assessment offers advantages such as prompt feedback, well-informed education, student empowerment, enhanced learning, and a thorough grasp of student strengths, weaknesses, and learning preferences. Continuous and integrated assessment methods include exit tickets, class discussions, and observations (Cai et al., 2012).

Emphasis on Formative Feedback and Improvement

Formative feedback is essential for optimal learning in Education 5.0 and beyond. It is an ongoing process of furnishing pupils with feedback on their performance to aid in their improvement. Effective formative feedback should be specific, practical, timely, goal-oriented, and positive. Emphasizing formative feedback benefits students by increasing engagement and motivation, fostering deeper understanding, cultivating metacognitive skills, allowing teachers to adjust their teaching methods, and resulting in enhanced learning outcomes. To highlight formative input, employ diverse assessment techniques like observations, exit tickets, brief quizzes, self-assessments, and peer evaluations. Formative feedback improves academic performance by correcting misunderstandings and offering appropriate advice.

Multiple Measures and Diverse Assessment Methods

Education 5.0 prioritizes individualized learning and in-depth comprehension rather than memorization. Educators must go beyond standardized assessments and utilize various assessment tools to accurately evaluate student learning. Individual examinations may be constrained and fail to encompass the complete spectrum of student knowledge, skills, and talents. Personalized learning necessitates varied data, as students exhibit unique learning styles and ways of demonstrating comprehension. Various evaluation methods encompass formative assessments, summative assessments, performance-based assessments, portfolios, self-assessments, peer assessments, and technology-based assessments. These strategies offer a thorough understanding of student learning, facilitate personalized learning, and encourage actions. Educators can enhance their understanding of students' development and tailor personalized learning pathways by using various measures and methodologies (Keselman et al., 2001).

Validity, Reliability, and Fairness Considerations

Education 5.0 prioritizes the significance of validity, reliability, and fairness in assessment. These criteria guarantee that exams precisely gauge the desired learning outcomes, consistently yield similar findings, and offer fair opportunities for all students to showcase their learning. Education 5.0 requires assessments tailored to students' knowledge, abilities, and attitudes, considering various learning styles and approaches. Combining formative and summative evaluations offers a thorough understanding of the validity of student learning.

Reliability guarantees consistent outcomes regardless of the administrator, timing, or other influences. Comprehensive guidelines and criteria are essential for ensuring consistency in various assessment techniques. Fairness guarantees equal opportunity for all students to showcase their learning by removing prejudice in assessment design, administration, and scoring. Varied assessments and suitable accommodations are crucial for meeting various demands.

Challenges in Education 5.0 involve reconciling various assessment techniques with standardized evaluations, mitigating bias in technology-driven assessments, and guaranteeing equity in personalized learning settings. Effective assessment strategies involve defining learning objectives clearly, utilizing various assessment methods, establishing precise rubrics for scoring, consistently evaluating, and analyzing assessment data, and offering suitable accommodations and differentiated tests. Validity, dependability, and fairness are crucial concepts for effective assessment in Education 5.0.

Ethical Use of Data and Student Privacy

Utilizing technology and data-driven methods in Education 5.0 has the potential to enhance personalized learning and boost educational results. Nevertheless, it prompts worries over the ethical utilization of data and the privacy of students. Important factors to consider are transparency, permission, minimal data collection, secure storage, access controls, data usage, prejudice and discrimination mitigation, and student privacy and ownership. Students and their families should be educated about data collection, utilization, and availability, and should have the privilege to see, rectify, and erase their data upon demand. Data sharing should be restricted to explicit consent and for genuine educational objectives. It is crucial to educate pupils about data privacy rights and appropriate online behavior. It is intricate to balance innovation and privacy, and it can be difficult to ensure compliance with changing rules.

EXAMPLES OF INNOVATIVE ASSESSMENT PRACTICES

Portfolio Assessments and E-Portfolios

Portfolio evaluations and e-portfolios are useful instruments for assessing student learning in Education 5.0. Conventional portfolios, made up of tangible compilations, display a variety of talents and development, promoting student responsibility and contemplation. They may be adjusted to accommodate different learning styles and interests. E-portfolios are digital platforms that enable students to electronically curate and showcase their work, providing accessibility, multimedia integration, and interactive features. Portfolio assessments assess student learning through the content and reflection in the portfolio. They encourage deeper learning, foster self-assessment and reflection skills, enable personalized learning, and enhance communication among students, teachers, and parents regarding learning progress. Both approaches provide advantages in encouraging profound learning, improving self-evaluation, and nurturing cooperation among students, educators, and parents (Lorenzo and Ittelson, 2005).

Projects and Problem-Based Learning

Projects and problem-based learning (PBL) are teaching methods in Education 5.0 that emphasize active learning and in-depth comprehension. Projects entail developing a final deliverable or presentation by incorporating research, planning, implementation, and reflection. They cultivate various abilities, enhance comprehension, and boost student involvement and drive. PBL begins with an open-ended challenge or scenario, encouraging critical thinking, teamwork, and self-directed learning. Both methods focus on active learning and practical application, however they possess unique variations. Projects can be done alone or with others, but PBL usually requires working together. To effectively apply a project-based learning approach, it is essential to ensure that projects and activities are in line with defined learning objectives and educational standards while offering structured guidance and assistance during the entire process.

Rubrics and Self-Reflection Tools

Rubrics and self-reflection tools are crucial for improving student learning and encouraging effective assessment practices in Education 5.0. Rubrics offer explicit assessment standards and performance levels, enhancing clarity and aiding in self-evaluation and goal establishment. They guarantee uniform and impartial evaluation, while self-reflection tools assist pupils in contemplating their learning process, strengths, limitations, and opportunities for improvement. These technologies enhance metacognitive skills, foster self-awareness, and offer useful feedback to teachers. For effective use of rubrics and self-reflection tools, introduce them early, promote self-assessment with rubrics, incorporate self-reflection post-rubric use, and utilize self-reflection data for formative assessment. By integrating these technologies, students can assume responsibility for their learning, enhance comprehension, and showcase advancement.

Digital Badges and Micro-Credentials

Digital badges and micro-credentials are components of Education 5.0 that acknowledge and confirm abilities and accomplishments. Digital badges are visual symbols obtained by showcasing proficiency in particular skills or knowledge domains, accompanied by embedded metadata. They are versatile and utilized in a range of settings, such as formal schooling, professional development, and informal learning. Micro-credentials are compact educational modules that concentrate on skills or knowledge areas, which are validated and can be combined. They are gaining awareness and are utilized to verify labor skills and professional advancement. Digital badges and micro-credentials offer advantages such as acknowledging various learning routes, encouraging continuous learning, boosting learner drive, and improving the visibility of skills. Challenges encompass standardization, accessibility, and integration with current learning ecosystems. Effective implementation should be under learning objectives and specific skills (Ifenthaler et al., 2016).

Competency-Based Assessment and Mastery Learning

Competency-based assessment (CBA) and mastery learning (ML) are educational methods designed to guarantee that all students acquire the necessary information and skills. Both methods work together effectively in Education 5.0, promoting customized learning and enhanced comprehension. CBA emphasizes showcasing proficiency in particular skills and knowledge using various assessment techniques such as projects, performance assignments, and self-evaluations. Mastery learning focuses on achieving proficiency in each learning target by employing formative evaluations to pinpoint areas requiring assistance and provide prompt feedback. Both methods advocate for a growth mentality, urging students to accept responsibility for their learning and persevere when faced with difficulties. The integrated method enhances comprehension, boosts student involvement, diminishes achievement disparities, and provides instructors with useful data.

CHALLENGES AND OPPORTUNITIES

Professional Development and Capacity Building for Educators

Education 5.0 necessitates a proficient and flexible teaching staff. Continuous professional development (PD) and capacity building are crucial for educators to enhance student learning and excel in the digital era. Important factors to consider are emphasizing 21st-century skills, including technology, supporting personalized learning, cultivating evaluation and data-driven decision-making abilities, integrating social-emotional learning, and fostering cooperation. Effective professional development methods include blended learning models, coaching and mentoring, action research and reflection, micro-learning opportunities, and professional learning communities. Challenges include time limitations, guaranteeing sufficient resources, and maintaining a harmony between technological incorporation and personalized learning opportunities. Educators may enhance student learning and succeed in the digital era by tackling these problems (Sheppard et al., 2009).

Development and Validation of New Tools and Technologies

The evolving landscape of Education 5.0 necessitates innovative assessment tools that measure deep learning, diverse skills, and personalized learning progress. To ensure the efficacy and ethical use of these tools, rigorous development and validation processes are essential. Key considerations include alignment with learning objectives, integration with diverse learning environments, accessibility and inclusivity, and ethical considerations like data privacy, security, and potential biases. The development process involves identifying specific learning objectives and skills, creating a prototype, pilot testing, field testing, data analysis and interpretation, and refinement and iteration. Validation methods include content validity, criteria-related validity, and construct validity. These processes ensure the tool's effectiveness and ethical use in the evolving educational landscape.

Addressing Equity and Access Issues in Assessment

Within Education 5.0, ensuring fair and equitable evaluation is essential for fostering an inclusive learning environment. Conventional assessment methods frequently maintain inequalities and put pupils from various origins at a disadvantage. Challenges encompass cultural bias, linguistic hurdles, socio-economic inequities, and disability considerations. Equity and access strategies encompass Universal Design for Assessment (UDL), culturally sensitive assessment, various assessment techniques, differentiation and accommodations, technology for accessibility, bias awareness and training, and student voice and involvement. UDL focuses on creating adaptable tests for a variety of learners, whereas culturally responsive assessment considers students' cultural origins, experiences, and learning preferences. Technology can improve accessibility and offer several methods for students to interact with examinations.

Data Privacy and Security Concerns

Utilizing technology and data-driven methods in Education 5.0 presents opportunities for tailored learning and enhanced educational results, while also prompting worries about data privacy and security. The extensive student data gathered, encompassing academic performance, behavioral trends, and personal details, raises worries about unauthorized entry, misuse, and potential security breaches. Utilizing data for targeted advertising or profiling may result in discrimination or manipulation. Insufficient openness and control around data gathering, use, and sharing can lead to security risks. Possible outcomes include trust erosion, privacy breaches, worsening of current disparities, and psychological damage to pupils. Robust data governance policies, transparency, communication, and data security and privacy training should be developed to address these problems.

FUTURE OF ASSESSMENT AND EVALUATION

Emerging Trends and Advancements in Assessment Technology

Assessment technology is continually progressing because of breakthroughs in artificial intelligence (AI), Big Data, and other emerging technologies. Key themes involve AI-driven exams that tailor learning experiences by adapting difficulty levels and question kinds according to student performance, automated scoring and feedback, and natural language processing (NLP) to enhance comprehension and critical thinking abilities. Utilizing gamification and immersive assessments, such as game-based and virtual reality (VR) and augmented reality (AR), enhances the engagement and interactivity of assessments. Utilizing big data and learning analytics enables educators to pinpoint individual strengths and weaknesses, forecast student risk, and offer comprehensive evaluation through the integration of data from several sources. Blockchain technology provides safe and unalterable data storage, guaranteeing the legitimacy and permanence of student evaluation data (Yadav et al., 2020).

AI-Powered Assessment and Personalized Learning Pathways

AI-driven evaluation and customized learning routes are transforming education by boosting involvement, better learning results, and enabling students to achieve their maximum capabilities. AI systems may dynamically modify difficulty levels and question kinds according to student performance, automatically score and provide feedback, and analyze student responses to pinpoint strengths, weaknesses, and learning deficiencies. Personalized learning paths utilize data-driven suggestions, tailor training to various learning styles, and encourage self-directed learning. The integrated method offers advantages such as enhanced engagement and motivation, better learning results, empowered students, and effective utilization of teacher time. Educators can use AI insights to customize lessons, accommodate various learning styles, and promote independence and responsibility in students' learning paths.

Role of Assessment in Lifelong Learning and Skill Development

Education 5.0 focuses on lifelong learning and ongoing skill enhancement for individuals. Assessment is vital in this changing environment, emphasizing competency and mastery above academic success. It employs a variety of assessment techniques to evaluate a range of abilities and knowledge, including practical application and interpersonal skills. Formative evaluation offers ongoing feedback and chances for enhancement, while self-assessment and reflection enable learners to assume responsibility for their learning. Efficient evaluation boosts motivation offers useful data for tailored learning, aids in skill enhancement, and encourages self-directed learning. Challenges involve creating assessments that have significance, guaranteeing accessibility and inclusivity for a variety of learners, finding a balance between standardized assessments and adaptable methods, and changing attitudes from conventional summative assessment strategies to a growth mindset that emphasizes ongoing learning and enhancement (Collins, 2009).

Global Collaboration and Knowledge Sharing

Education 5.0 focuses on continuous learning, customized routes, and fundamental abilities needed to navigate the difficulties of the 21st century. Global collaboration and knowledge sharing are essential for promoting innovation, and equity, and empowering learners to succeed in an interconnected society. Global collaboration offers advantages such as exposure to a variety of viewpoints, increased innovation, cross-cultural awareness, and united efforts to address worldwide issues such as climate change, poverty, and social inequality. Global cooperation examples encompass online communities, collaborative initiatives, student exchange programs, and open educational resources (OERs).

Collaborative projects and research entail cooperative efforts across schools and institutions to tackle common educational issues or explore new teaching methods. Student exchange programs offer students the chance to fully engage with various cultures and gain insights from a wide range of views. Open educational resources (OERs) distribute freely accessible educational content and resources internationally, facilitating the broader availability of high-quality education. Challenges are addressing linguistic hurdles and technological inequities.

CONCLUSION

The chapter explores the evolution of assessment and evaluation in Education 5.0, emphasizing the transition from conventional standardized examinations to personalized and flexible approaches. Technology plays a crucial role by providing tools to evaluate student learning instantly, monitor progress, and offer prompt feedback. The move towards competency-based assessment focuses on evaluating students' capacity to utilize their knowledge in practical situations. The chapter highlights the importance of educators and policymakers reassessing the role of assessment in Education 5.0 to not only gauge results but also promote critical thinking, problem-solving abilities, and creativity. It highlights the significance of ethical issues in evaluation technologies, guaranteeing fairness, equity, and openness. Assessment and evaluation in Education 5.0 signify a shift towards a comprehensive, learner-centered approach, equipping students to succeed in a dynamic environment.

REFERENCES

Albritton, K., Chen, C. I., Bauer, S. G., Johnson, A., & Mathews, R. E. (2021). Collaborating with school psychologists: Moving beyond traditional assessment practices. *Young Exceptional Children*, 24(1), 28–38. 10.1177/1096250619871951

Cai, Y., Judd, K. L., & Lontzek, T. S. (2012). *Continuous-time methods for integrated assessment models (No. w18365)*. National Bureau of Economic Research. 10.3386/w18365

Collins, J. (2009). Lifelong learning in the 21st century and beyond. *Radiographics*, 29(2), 613–622. 10.1148/rg.292085179193250 69

Himmetoglu, B., Aydug, D., & Bayrak, C. (2020). Education 4.0: Defining the teacher, the student, and the school manager aspects of the revolution. *Turkish Online Journal of Distance Education, 21*(Special Issue-IODL), 12-28.

Ifenthaler, D., Bellin-Mularski, N., & Mah, D. K. (2016). *Foundation of digital badges and micro-credentials*. Springer International Publishing. 10.1007/978-3-319-15425-1

Keselman, H. J., Algina, J., & Kowalchuk, R. K. (2001). Analysis of repeated measures designs: A review. *British Journal of Mathematical & Statistical Psychology*, 54(1), 1–20. 10.1348/000711001159357113 93894

Lorenzo, G., & Ittelson, J. (2005). An overview of e-portfolios. Educause learning initiative, 1(1), 1-27.

Oktaviana, D., Barizi, A., & Yaqin, M. Z. N. (2022). The Challenges of the society 5.0 era: The evaluation of learning in primary education. *Al Adzka: Jurnal Ilmiah Pendidikan Guru Madrasah Ibtidaiyah, 12*(1).

Phobun, P., & Vicheanpanya, J. (2010). Adaptive intelligent tutoring systems for e-learning systems. *Procedia: Social and Behavioral Sciences*, 2(2), 4064–4069. 10.1016/j.sbspro.2010.03.641

Sheppard, B., Brown, J., Dibbon, D., Sheppard, B., Brown, J., & Dibbon, D. (2009). Professional development and capacity building. School district leadership matters, 85-100.

Spiller, D. (2012). Assessment matters: Self-assessment and peer assessment. *The University of Waikato*, 13, 2–18.

VanTassel-Baska, J. (2014). Performance-based assessment: The road to authentic learning for the gifted. *Gifted Child Today*, 37(1), 41–47. 10.1177/1076217513509618

Yadav, D., Yadav, S., & Veer, K. (2020). A comprehensive assessment of Brain Computer Interfaces: Recent trends and challenges. *Journal of Neuroscience Methods*, 346, 108918. 10.1016/j.jneumeth.2020.10891832853592

Chapter 14
Ethical Considerations and Educational Constraints in 5.0 Education

Zaid Yacoub Abu-Bajeh
http://orcid.org/0000-0001-9196-7863
Independent Researcher, Jordan

ABSTRACT

The institutions which working in the educational field, are seeking to create an efficient educational process in proportion to technological changes. The success on the Educational approach, including Education 5.0, depends on the extent to which educational constraints and ethical considerations are taken into account as success requirements in the educational process such as feedback, discussions, and the teachers role, which are effects on the learners' understanding. Therefore, Institutions can work to develop the educational process without compromising educational quality through developing the ICT. So, In light of Education 5.0 endeavors achieving a smart society, and based on Perraton online education theory and other researches results, there is a need to focus on a group of necessary issues to ensure the success of the educational process and determining criteria for selecting appropriate online educational models that will overcome the educational constraints and help to keep up with the pace of acceleration and competition with other educational institutions.

INTRODUCTION

The availability of current technologies has made the globe appears to be a little town and educational technology adoption has grown in tandem with global trends in educational development, where these technologies allow learners to get knowledge and information at any time from any location (Shallal, 2017), which hastening development in all fields of education and raising the critical concerns about the nature of education and the best way to enhance it. Additionally, the use of online education is widely recognized as a vital in educational institutes' success, also a key in impact on the educational process and learners. Therefore, Developing the tools and technology methods will assist the developing countries in overcoming technological barriers and develop the educational process (Bello et al., 2014). This will also aid in the development of everyone who wishes to learn as much as possible through interactive

DOI: 10.4018/979-8-3693-3041-8.ch014

communication from any location, assisting educational institutions in accomplishing the educational process's goals without compromising educational quality.

Because of the rapidly evolving landscape of education, humanity has maintained its ambition for academic learning as it is of fundamental significance of cultures throughout humanity's evolution. Where, it is an ongoing process that equips learners with skillful practical academic knowledge that is aligned with competitive market needs and prepares graduates to play a practical role in the country's economic, medical, technical, and industrial growth by utilizing the most modern tools and techniques (Alharbi, 2023). As a result, in recent decades, education as a standard has been examined in connection to technological advancement in order to bring the innovation in the academic field. In this regard, academic authorities have coined the phrase education 5.0 to describe a new era of online education and standards that must be embraced and synced with the usage of the most contemporary technical standards. This word is frequently used to improve the academic environment in tandem with industrial standards and new technologies (Ahmad et al., 2023). As a result of this quick progress, there has been an ongoing development of the educational process as well as many research efforts have been made to understand the inner workings of the remote process for learning and teaching, as well as, to design more successful tactics to support the practices for distance education, while keeping educational ethical considerations in mind. Although many educational institutions throughout the world are still experiencing educational challenges in online education, namely inadequate teaching processes that are incompatible with the demands and expectations of the learners and do not meet the educational process's goal, However, it is essential for educational institutions who seeking for a competitive advantage (Richardson, 2018).

Clearly, most developed nations' educational infrastructures are in sync with new technology and profit from them in order to boost academic performance. The modern world places a distinct emphasis on the development of a modern education environment, which could enhance and improve the learner's academic aptitude at all levels, where education institutions have played a key role in the development of a skillful the academic environment for fostering learners by the new technology. It is especially important in developing nations where there is a significant gap between the incorporation of current technology in the education sector and IT resources (Matthew & Kazaure, 2020). Where, the educational sector suffering on bringing and creation the innovation to the educational sector, specifically, in the developing nations, where the education quality development and enhanced the acceptability in the education sector has a major priority during this era. This has become a critical and significant subject for academic professionals in poor nations, notably how to deliver and manage the online educational process while keeping educational constraints in mind.

Indeed, based on the findings of numerous studies and what has been gleaned from theories and research about educational constraints and ethical considerations that will effect on the quality of teaching and on the success of online learning. It is clear that there are many important variables to get success on the educational process. The most prominent of which are feedback, group discussions, and teachers' role, all of which directly affect and impact the level of understanding among online learners. Furthermore, and it is clear that its absence and lack of attention to them may deteriorate the learners' perception of the educational institutions and have a negative impact on the online education satisfaction level. Where, In one of the studies that conducted was highlighted the aspects on educational constraints that effects on the learning level by evaluating the differences between online education models, and its findings demonstrated by analyzed 104 questionnaires, that there are links between the remote educational model and increasing learning levels In favor of the educational model that concern and support the educational Ethical Considerations by overcome the educational constraints in distance educational

(Abu-Bajeh & Abbas, 2021a). Unfortunately, this intersects with rapid change which led many educational institutions neglect and lack focusing on the importance of interaction, discussion and feedback in the distance educational process, where the educational institutions currently facing many problems in keeping pace with technical development in information and communication technologies. So, they are working to find the solutions and creation modern ways to fulfill their educational role and overcome many of its problems, in the spot of the major and rapid changes in the provision of educational content and educational methods based on the Internet, which happened in the recent years.

Obviously, this chapter analyzes the ethical considerations, educational constraints, and acceptable learning methodologies that must be considered in the Education 5.0 process. Whereas the educational constraints are the requirements that necessitate reformulation of the educational process based on online education requirements and seek to specify and explain the importance of focusing on these necessary elements by educational institutions to ensure success in education 5.0 and to keep up with the pace of acceleration and competition with other educational institutions. This chapter attempts to validate the impact of face-to-face education on the distance education process by focusing on parts of Perraton's Theory of Distance Education (Perraton, 1988) and Holmberg's Theory of Online Learning (Holmberg, 1995), where there are believes that there are necessary issues that must be taken into account for the success of implementing education 5.0 in educational institutions, and it also discusses some aspects on educational constraints (group discussion, feedback, and teacher roles) and its relationship with learners level understanding, which will assist educational institutions in selecting distance educational models that will overcome distance educational limits and improve learning levels.

ETHICAL CONSIDERATIONS

The teaching profession, by definition, sets an ethical standard for teachers, not confining them only to the topics of syllabuses that we expect them to cover within a specified time frame, but also requiring them to go beyond their in-built narrow boundaries to perform other responsibilities, where quality teaching necessitates some additional services that teachers voluntarily supplement to the teaching-learning activities. On the other hand, with the increased use of new communication technologies, the need to assess ethical concerns becomes more pressing, particularly in light of recent advancements, such as the increased use of e-learning for the formation of models to determine ethical dilemmas in distant and open learning. For this reason, UNESCO has advocated ethics in its educational programs and has initiated deep instilling of ethical values in the cultural, legal, philosophical, and religious heritage of various human communities (UNESCO, 2008), because it is believed that the culture in which one works has a significant impact on an individual's behavior (Raiborn & Payne, 1990).

Ethics in education in general, and remote education in particular, takes many forms, including those relevant to the student-teacher relationship, dedication to the student, commitment to the distance education system, and commitment to the profession. Six fundamental components of distant education were recognized by (Keegan, 2013): Separation of the instructor and learner, Influence of an educational organization, Use of media to link teacher and learner, Two-way exchange of communication, Learners as individuals rather than groups, Education as an industrialized form.

In order to develop a moral atmosphere and fill the gap in online education in light of recent developments, an ethical relationship between the learner, teacher, and institution in online learning is required to emphasize the public duties and moral commitment of education. 5.0. Numerous factors of educational ethics were covered in a research paper by (Farahani, 2012) to govern professionals' behaviors in everyday practice, especially ethical principles in distant education. These moral standards are as follows:

1. Commitment to the Student:

   Respecting the autonomy of the student and maintaining a healthy atmosphere, as well as keeping a suitable interaction with distance education students in all settings, is a part of this principle. The teacher shall work to foster an inquisitive spirit, the acquisition of knowledge and understanding, and the thoughtful formulation of worthy goals, and shall conduct activities for professional educational groups in accordance with sound educational practices that are in the best interests of the student.

2. Commitment to the online education system

   Using available tools (email, teleconference, mobile, and online) to enhance learning to the greatest degree feasible while not abandoning professional tasks without a compelling cause.

3. Commitment to the Profession and to Professional Education:

   In the belief that the quality of services to the education profession has a direct influence on the educational process, institutions shall make every effort to improve service, to promote a climate in which the teacher can practice his role professionally, and to enable growth and development in the profession practice, in order to use that knowledge in improving students' educational opportunities, experiences, and performance.

4. Instructional designers' ethical commitment in the online education System by delivering efficiently, effective and practicable, with lower cost-effective solutions to client problems.

Because the experience of grappling with challenging moral issues increases moral judgment, debates integrated within the educational process improve educational moral maturity (Pascarella & Terenzini, 2005). Educational institutions must work to eliminate Technical constraints that make it difficult to enable a dynamic conversation (Chachra, 2005), as well as use suitable technology to empower and deepen the human relationships that are essential for individual and social wellbeing.

THEORIES IN ONLINE EDUCATION

1. Perraton's Theory

Perraton's theory for distance education (Perraton, 1988) is a collection and consolidation of some theories in the field of communication and proliferation, particularly those related to educational philosophies, where it is composed of elements from communication theories that deal with the ways in which distance teaching can be used to enhance education, through providing Distance education supported by group discussion and feedback, and using all available resources, as well as, online education may assist learners to accomplish educational gains by highlighting the benefits of face-to-face contact, group discussion and feedback and incorporating these features into the online education system (Figure 1).

When we look more into this theory, we see that it has addressed a number of issues in the educational process, which are as follows:

a. You can teach anything using any way.

b. Online education can address the issue of faculty member-to-student ratio, which has been a barrier to the expansion of conventional education since it has been difficult to get the necessary number of professors to achieve a balanced ratio.
c. In certain cases, online education is less expensive than traditional education, both in terms of the number of students enrolled and the type of education provided.
d. The economics of online education is determined by the following variables: the level of learning, the number of students enrolled, the media used, and the complexity of the decision-making processes.
e. Online education can reach students who are unable to attend regular educational institutions.
f. Online education may be structured in ways that encourage dialogue, discussion, and interaction.
g. When the instructor sees his pupil in person via an online education system, his purpose shifts from the information supplier to facilitator.
h. When online learning is used to find relevant information for this group, group discussion is a good learning approach.
i. Most institutions and organizations have educational resources that may be used to support and promote online education in order to generate educational and economic benefits for these institutions.
j. Feedback is an essential component of an online educational system.

Figure 1. A Theory for Distance Education for Perraton (1988)

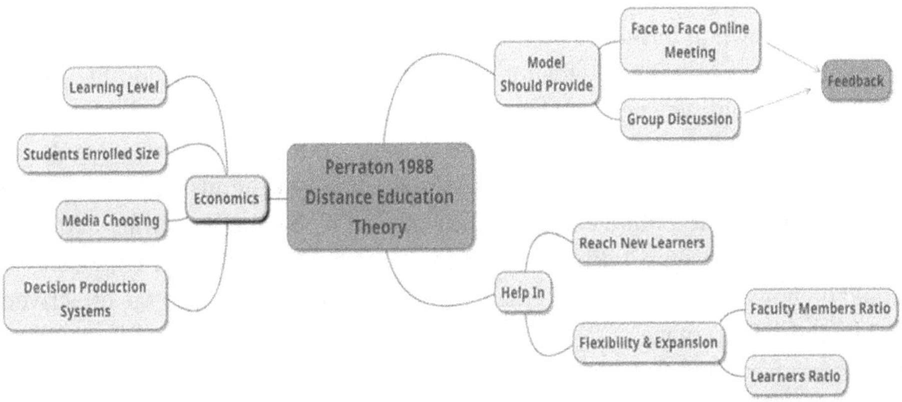

In Particular, The focus in this theory is on a part related to education 5.0 as a new age of online education and how it should be provided, where theory mentioned that online education should be organized in ways that support discussion and interactive, where group discussion is an effective method to searching for appropriate information for learner groups and where group discussion is an effective method to searching for appropriate information for learner groups. Feedback is an essential component of an online educational system. The sort of feedback and interaction that occurs is influenced by the connection utilized (Schlosser & Simonson, 2009). All of this may be used to achieve educational benefits and serving the ethical considerations for the educational process by utilizing all educational resources accessible.

2. Holmberg's Theory

The guided didactic discussion online learning theory proposed by (Holmberg, 1995) falls under the category of communication theories. Holmberg asserted that his theory could explain the effects of belonging and collaboration on teaching efficacy, as well as the actual interchange of questions, replies, and arguments in mediated communication. The researcher established his theory of distant learning in 1995, and part of this enlarged theory centered on the emotional involvement in study and sentiments about personal interactions between the two sides of education and learning, which contributes to boosting the joy of learning. Indeed, the theory states that teaching efficiency is related to feelings of belonging and cooperation, as well as the actual exchange of questions, responses, and debates, and it explains the impact of feelings of belonging and cooperation on teaching effectiveness, in addition, how the relationships between the two sides of education and learning can impact and contribute to increasing the fun of learning, as well as the actual exchange of questions, responses, and debates.

EDUCATIONAL CONSTRAINTS

According to Hornby (1998) defines constraints as "things that limit or restrict". The constraints that must be recognized as "given" in a planning environment; that is, restrictions that are feasible in the current situation. Designing effective feedback in online education is a significant challenge given time and resource constraints (Pearson, 2016). The amount and type of feedback and engagement that occurs is governed by the connection utilized (Schlosser & Simonson, 2009). Interaction between professors and classmates has been shown to influence satisfaction with online education (Taghizadeh & Hajhosseini, 2021). The social context of online education environments contributes, as do the limited opportunities to interact directly with teachers, which characterize teachers as disengaged and disinterested in their roles, and this has a negative effect on how learners respond to teachers, impacts online learners' success, and can lead to a deterioration in learners' perception of the institution (Clifford, 2018). The most important contributor to online education satisfaction is the quality of instruction, indicating the importance of instructors' responsibilities in boosting learners' knowledge (Taghizadeh & Hajhosseini, 2021). It should be noted that the instructor has a considerable influence on the effectiveness of online education (Choudhuri & Kumar, 2022). The teacher's methodology and practice do have a significant effect in student satisfaction with online learning (Bhatia et al., 2022). Constraints are objects that limit or restrict movement (Figure 2).

Figure 2. Educational Constraints

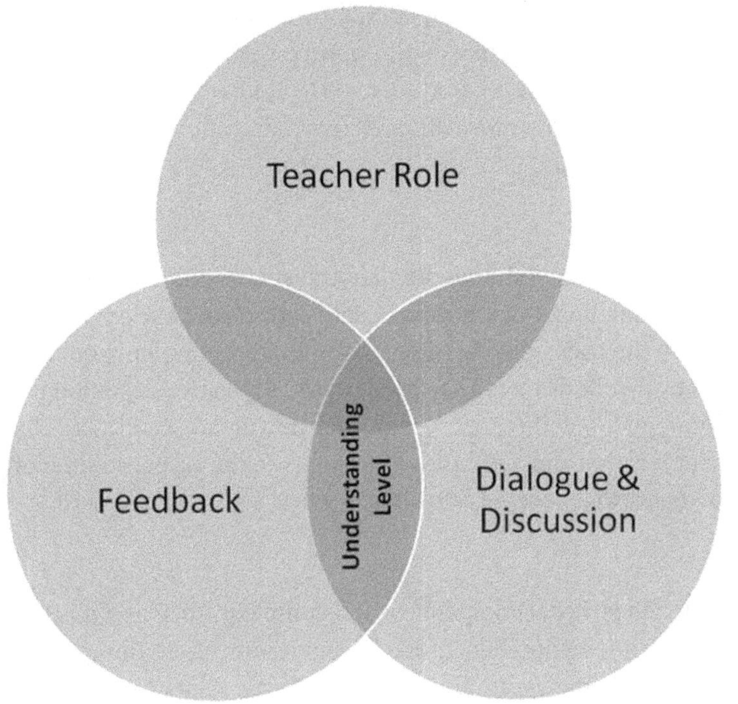

Back to the theory of online education (Perraton, 1988), the educational constraints are the requirements and constraints that necessitate reformulation of the educational process based on online education requirements (Abu-Bajeh & Abbas), so there is a need to focus on some of the educational constraints that limit, restrict and affect the educational process and the level of learning. This chapter seeks to focus on a group of elements in this field of it and specify how the supports being implemented which are: group discussion, feedback, teacher roles and its impact on level of understanding. In reality, the extent of educational constraints varies depending on the education 5.0 models.

1. ICT Resources

Today's ICT Resources must keep up with the expansion of any company, and projects frequently need unique methods to fulfilling business objectives by boosting flexibility in order to catapult organizations to new heights. In general, the information & communication technology is made up of two major components: hardware, which consists of hard devices that serve as input, output, and processing units, also communications, which connect stations in different locations in an environment that allows beneficiaries to send and receive data and information. This advancement in information technology has influenced the area of education, resulting in the creation of a new vision in the teaching and learning arena through the use of new technological applications in the educational system.

Obviously, schools have been investing in information, and communications technology (ICT) infrastructure to increase educational quality, raise the performance of the education 5.0 process, and deploy new eLearning system models to accomplish this. Nonetheless, several challenges remain, such as high initial costs and the human resources required managing them in order to implement these types of systems. As a result, many schools have begun to adopt cloud computing as a solution in which they can host all ICT infrastructures, software and online education services in cloud provider servers. Due to considerations related to infrastructure capabilities, the performance of online educational systems implemented in cloud-based infrastructures will improve with better performance metrics than online educational systems on traditional web-based servers (Mwakisole et al., 2019).

To shed light on the concept of information & communication technology infrastructure, various associated terms must be clarified:

a. Internet service

The number of bytes per second, that are data travels from the user's device to the internet (upload), representing how quickly data is delivered from your device to the internet, and from the internet to the user's device (download), representing how quickly you can extract data from a server to your device. The speed drastically varies depending on the connection type (DSL, Fibre optic, Satellite...etc.), and your download speed may change greatly based on your present location and activities. Ping refers to the response time of your connection and how soon your device receives a response when you send a request.

b. Hardware

Hardware refers to the physical components of a computer, such as a machine and wiring, or tools and manufacturing equipment. In the IT environment, equipment is represented by input, output, and processing units. Computer hardware refers to the physical components of a computer and associated devices (Microsoft, 2013). Hardware is often utilized in combination with software to perform any instruction or command. A usable computer system consists of a combination of hardware and software, although there are other systems that are exclusively composed of hardware.

The online education 5.0 model's success It is dependent on the internet speed available on both sides (teacher and learner) as well as the availability of hardware components, where appropriate communication speed and the availability of hardware components support the establishment of an interactive educational process in which discussion and feedback can be ensured without interruptions. It also guarantees that the instructor performs his instructional function appropriately, all of which will have a favorable influence on the learner's degree of understanding. This is a barrier, particularly in underdeveloped nations, and restricts their reliance on contemporary technology in the educational process. Students in remote locations and those from low-income households encounter challenges due to a lack of sufficient digital gadgets (Coman et al., 2020). It should be noted that internet connectivity is an important factor in influencing the effectiveness of online learning (Choudhuri & Kumar, 2022). Universities that provide online education services should provide high-speed networks to compensate for service quality issues (Bello et al., 2014).

As a result, continuing to build on educational successes, maximizing learning, providing new teaching models in virtual learning environments, collaborative and management learning systems, implement, and assess online learning processes are challenges that can be overcome by implementing a non-geographically infrastructure.

2. Feedback

Feedback is described as information about one's performance or knowledge provided by an agent (e.g., a teacher, a peer, a book, a parent, oneself, or experience) (Hattie & Timperley, 2007). A teacher or parent can supply correcting information; a colleague can provide an alternate technique and a book can help to explain ideas. A parent may offer encouragement, and a student can check up the solution to assess the accuracy of a response, and a book can offer information to clarify concepts, and a parent can offer encouragement, and a learner can look up the answer to assess the correctness of a response. Feedback is a "consequence" of performance; as a result, the response contributes to the activation of the discussion and has the potential to shift the dialogue's direction to explore a previously unexplored element of the subject, as well as to clear up misunderstandings about educational content. Because analyzing learners' "body language" via audio connection or video recording is highly difficult, the connection used determines the quantity and kind of interaction and feedback between the teacher and the learners.

Perraton's theory for online education advocates the importance of feedback as an aspect of communication, diffusion, and an essential part of the educational process in order to gain educational advantages and optimize education (Perraton, 1988). Where the feedback encourages and activates the groups' debate and has an influence on the possibilities of adjusting the path of the discussions to study a previously unconsidered aspect of the subject and clear up misunderstandings. Face-to-face contact is crucial to feedback effectiveness, and this should be considered in the remote education model to clear up topic ambiguities and give an effective online education. Feedback assists teachers in determining the degree of comprehension of their students by identifying their faults and strengths (Nasir et al., 2019). Feedback is an essential component of the online education system (Perraton, 1988). The educational process should provide for feedback in order to determine the degree of knowledge and comprehension of learners (Picciano, 2017). Whereas this is not provided in the same way in all distance educational models, it will have an effect on the learners' level of comprehension, either adversely or favorably, because it is tied to feedback. Data (feedback) is supplied to a student and teacher to show how much the learner has learned (Schlosser & Simonson, 2009). Feedback from teachers teaches pupils how to improve their work and how to deal with failure when it comes. It also provides new networking possibilities, which ultimately improves student achievement (Kennette & Chapman, 2021). Feedback helps professors or lecturers communicate the outcome to students (Edwards, 2003).

Based on the foregoing, it is obvious how an essential Ethical Considerations in the educational process linked to the level of mastery of learning goals can be ensured via the influence of the feedback process on the efficacy of teaching strategies and activities, whereas face-to-face communication is critical to the effectiveness of the feedback process.

3. Group Discussion

According to Perraton's Theory for online education, group discussion is a continual process centered on capturing knowledge, structuring it and republishing it (Perraton, 1988). Furthermore, according to Holmberg's online learning theory, teaching efficiency is tied to the genuine exchange of questions, replies, and discussions (Holmberg, 1995).

Group discussions are crucial in the educational process because they have the greatest influence on the level of learning and aid in the acquisition of more diverse information and its processing, as well as learning processes that require group work to complete a task or the confidence to engage in more challenging tasks. There are two types of academic involvement: agentic engagement and social engagement (Salem et al., 2022). When there is a discrepancy between what is understood and what is aimed to be understood, group talks in the educational process help learners receive information about comprehension, knowledge, and skills from others in the process, as well as increase their learning level.

The discussions show how successful the teaching method and learning activities are in assisting learners in achieving the goals of the learning process. Students consider the discussions to be a significant component of their online education (Vonderwell et al., 2007). Group conversations in the educational process are most effective and vital when they lead to increased effort and involvement in the educational process, as well as achievement of goals, and they aid in the creation of ideas and information about hypotheses and concepts, and this will not be done correctly and effectively in the distance educational process unless the education 5.0 is provided in a model that ensures interaction, feedback, and support group discussion. As a result, online courses should be constructed in such a manner that students are encouraged to participate in meaningful conversations, for as by using a discussion rubric (Vonderwell et al., 2007).

One thing that must be considered, particularly by online learning lecturers, is how lectures and discussions should be presented to our learners using a learning management system (Pane et al., 2020), so education 5.0 is a strategy for teaching and imparting data to students that relies on the new computer and global information network technologies and interactive media such as integrated plates, learning software, email, dialogue and discussion. The discussions have the potential to alter learning levels, self-proficiencies, and opinions.

4. Teacher Roles

Traditionally, a teacher's personal features, beliefs, and techniques of teaching have the greatest influence on a classroom atmosphere and learning activities; also, a teacher is assumed to have the supreme authority in a class. He may be either authoritarian or quite forgiving in granting autonomy to pupils in order to enable them accept responsibility for their learning.

Exceptional instructors have a long-term influence on students and society by instilling a love of learning, igniting curiosity, instilling confidence, and promoting a sense of belonging. Holmberg relates teaching efficiency to sentiments of belonging and collaboration, which contribute to increasing the joy of learning (Holmberg, 1995). They also foster the skills and attribute required for success in an ever-changing world: critical thinking, flexibility, resilience, and a desire to learn.

Every teacher assists their pupils in making career decisions and teaches them to respect elders. They teach their students the distinction between respect and disrespect, among other things. The three core characteristics that help create an active learning environment are respect (a positive and nonjudgmental regard for another person), empathy (being able to see things from the other person's perspective as if looking through their eyes), and authenticity (being oneself without hiding behind job titles, roles and masks) (Scrivener, 2011). These characteristics of instructors may be key variables in structuring their duties in classrooms, and they can assist them in creating a learning atmosphere in which learners feel calm and comfortable participating in something meaningful. Furthermore, these Teachers can increase students' excitement and confidence, resulting in students being independent and expressive in their demands and interests (Parker, 2002). As a result, teachers should focus on inspiring learners to learn and working according to their interests to attain their full potential, as well as concern for fostering problem-solving, reasoning abilities, and creating a learning environment to support learners' development.

According to Murdoch (1997) asserts that the teacher is no longer required to organize and dominate all activities in the classroom. He suggests that a teacher's role is better defined as a facilitator who creates conditions and activities that allow pupils to operate with language because they have a genuine interest in the completion of the assignments. Teachers play the function of facilitators. They define and revise the curriculum (Siddiqui & Ahamed, 2020), as well as interpret and modify it to make learning more manageable for learners. In other words, what instructors believe and do in the classroom ultimately influences what students learn in class. The curriculum and learning outcomes include an emphasis on sophisticated 21st-century abilities such as problem-solving, critical thinking, creativity, people management, teamwork and cooperation, emotional intelligence, judgment, and decision-making.

In look closely at educational institutions; we can see that many still use the traditional classroom structure; also the basic duty of a teacher has not altered over time. Also, changing the structure of the institutes requires changing the job of the teacher, which confirms and increases the importance and utility of this profession, and its emphasis that understanding technology and psychology has become necessary in the teaching profession to make change in the institutes and educational process. Where, teachers continue to guide students toward new information, and a teacher's responsibility today extends beyond expecting students to follow as they lead (A., 2023), because learning is no longer confined to the classroom setting; it occurs at home, in the community, and throughout the digital and physical world. Furthermore, knowledge sources are no longer limited to books and traditional instructional materials; information may be found anywhere, and from conventional education systems to interacting mode using basic mediums where the teacher is more a facilitator than an instructor, and where the learning can happen at any place or time with students' evaluated based on projects and involvement.

In particular with the Education 5.0 version, now we poised at a point of achieving a smart society woven with critical thinking, problem solving and value creation aided by technology in a purposeful approach to learning that lines up with the futuristic curriculum and pedagogy aligned with the concepts of the sustainable development, through educational sectors that can adapt to the digitalization of the growing education system in a spot of rapid and massive development of technology. As a result, instructors are expected to provide rich, distinctive, and individualized learning experiences to their pupils in a manner consistent with huge advances in information technology and knowledge availability.

Based on the Norms and Standards for Educators (Asmd, 2000), the key duties of a teacher are as follows:

a. Assessor:

The teachers are responsible for designing and managing assessment techniques, as well as keeping records of each learner's abilities, achievements and progress. They should also be able to provide feedback, identify "problem areas," and understand how to use assessment results to improve learning.

b. Citizenship and Community Role:

Demonstrate and cultivate a sense of belonging, as well as respect and responsibility for others and the environment. Cultivate supportive partnerships with parents and other organizations to address social and environmental challenges, as well as to create an empowering atmosphere for learning and growth.

c. Lifelong Learner and Researcher:

Strive for continuous professional development by conducting research, reading, attending courses and seminars, and remaining open to new ideas and information.

d. Administrator and leader:

Many teachers have sole control of the classroom assigned to them, and they must therefore be able to carry out the necessary administrative duties efficiently, as well as manage groups and individuals, as well as understand school legislation and establish a learning-friendly classroom environment.

e. Designer of Learning Programs:

The teacher must have ability and skill to create and implement learning programs that support creativity and can be combined with media to understand the curriculum correctly and effectively.

f. Facilitator of Learning:

A teacher is responsible for creating an inspiring learning environment that is appropriate for his class's age and ability. Also, he must have a strong communication and linguistic abilities, as well as a solid knowledge and grasp of subject content and methodologies, as well as the ability to make the most use of available resources.

g. Specialist Educator:

It should be able to recognize the unique talents and emphasis of giving education in that specific sector and provide the learners with the required knowledge and acceptable resources.

5. Level of Understanding

The outcome of the educational process which is represented as a set of procedures and activities that work together to meet educational technologies and practices to provide learners with the information and knowledge they need to raise their level of understanding (Bruner, 2009). The teacher can refine learners' understanding through ongoing feedback and identify learners' strengths and weaknesses (Nasir et al., 2019), so Feedback leads to effective education and informs the teacher how is the level of learners' understanding. In order to check the learners' knowledge and content understanding, the educational process should enable discussions (Picciano, 2017). Where, the level of understanding is closely related to feedback, dialogue and discussion, where these matters are not available in the same way in all online educational models, so this will affect either negatively or positively the learners' level of understanding. The interaction with their peer during live broadcasts is an important element regarding their sense of educational community, and it help in increasing the level of learning and understanding (Kocdar et al., 2018).

It became clear that There is a possibility to improving the learning levels in Education 5.0 by using educational model that supports activates discussions, interaction and feedback processes, and this will be reflected in the adoption of online education as an official education way.

INTERACTIVE EDUCATION

Teachers are being challenged to design content and learning models to help learners engage with the educational process in deep and rich textual interactive ways as a result of recent educational developments (Ibiloye, 2021), so it recommends migration strategies from the traditional education model to a more efficient, flexible, and interactive education model as shown in the table 1. As a result, there is a necessity to adopt the use of interactive online education as an online education method, to overcome all of these obstacles and issues, and to allow direct connection between the instructor and student, cannot be overstated. The main purpose of interactive online education is to help educators create online courses that allow teachers and students to cooperate and communicate online, hence speeding up the learning process and enhancing students' learning performance (Ayuyang, 2019).

All strategies for interacting with students in the course of creative teaching by the instructor to the class as a whole or a subgroup are referred to as interactive teaching (Vonderwell et al., 2007). The interaction in interactive online education is a direct connection system between the teacher and learners in the same session using one of the many videos conferencing techniques with the ability to include conversations, discussions, and Q&A based presentations (Abu-Bajeh & Abbas, 2021b). This type of teaching and learning may include any of the mode combinations ranging from simple direct one-to-one all the way up to many-to-many. This type of online education is easily classified as synchronous online education approaches, which can significantly limit the problems in online education, specifically in feedback, interaction, dialogues and discussions. As a result, the educational process simulates its corresponding process in the physical classroom, with the only difference being that it is conducted online using information technology tools. Furthermore, this allows learners to exchange input regarding aspects of their learning that are not offered and cannot be accomplished on their own.

Table 1. Differences between Online and Traditional Education

Comparison of	Traditional Education	Online Education
Teacher	The teacher is a carrier of knowledge and the basis for the education process	The teacher is a participant, and the learner is the basis for the education process
Learner	Receiver	Interactive and participatory
Content	Long fixed	Constantly renewing
Knowledge	Memorisation - Remember - Accumulation of Facts	Inquiry - Innovation
Focusing	Focus on the amount of the material	Focus on the quality of the material
Globality	Limited	Not limit
Cost	High	Medium / Low

Synchronous online education interaction is directly connected by connecting the teacher and learners together via live video conference with the ability to exchange immediate files and messages (Abu-Bajeh & Abbas, 2021c), and this mode can be represented by live online broadcast (many-to-many), so the teacher must be present on the network with the learners at the same time during the educational process to entice them. Online synchronous classrooms are classes that allow students to study and interact with their lecturers and classmates in real time (Delgado, 2020). It can be considered one of the synchronous online education models that can reduce the ethics issues in education 5.0, particularly with regard to taking educational constraints into account in order to maintain educational quality; it can also help in meeting the challenges in the new educational environments.

FUTURE VISION OF EDUCATION

Education standards have progressed to the point where both old and new tools are being used. Also, old education systems are being transformed into more contemporary and sophisticated technology-based systems. This evolution relied on digital transformation to equip academic sectors to fulfill the demands and requirements of the rapidly expanding academic requirements worldwide, beginning with 1.0 and continuing until it recently reached level 5.0, to contribute in the development of future education that is more beneficial to both students and instructors as shown in Table 2.

Table 2. Education Development Stages Based on Digital Transformation

Era	Feature	Author
Education 1.0	The initial attempt in this regard to acquiring knowledge through education	Maria et al., 2018
Education 2.0	Supply additional recommended techniques for learners by providing developed ideas to optimize and increase the education output and quality.	Tan et al., 2018
Education 3.0	By connecting the telecom industry, it made it simpler for	Mustafa Kamal et al., 2019
Education 4.0	Using the modern technologies like artificial intelligence, machine learning and data analytics in an immersive and interactive learning environment.	Alharbi, 2023
Education 5.0	A very inventive strategy that can take teaching staff, students, and administration to the next level of technology usage in the learning environment.	Alharbi, 2023

To realize and understand the inclusivity and quality of modern learning, as well as to gain a clear vision of education in the future, educational sectors should collaborate to form and develop the most appropriate and suitable learning environment for the betterment of the education infrastructure, while focusing on the innovative requirements for the overall education sector, resolving the challenges and obstacles encountered, and restructuring the entire academe through the following:

1. Determined the general goals and key performance indicators in accordance with the Education 5.0 transformations.
2. Create an improved learning environment that fosters creativity, skills and operational success by using cost-effective approaches and maximizing people talents and resources.
3. Ensure equitable quality educational opportunities for all by enhancing educational practice, engaging in activities, and attending forums.
4. Improving operational performance efficiency by increasing financial resources for education and training systems to satisfy the criteria of an effective educational process.
5. Focusing on the modern technologies and strategies in education sectors.
6. Futuristic curriculum and pedagogy aligned with the concepts of sustainable development and aided by advanced technology and automation.

Summary of Previous Research

Numerous studies published during the previous period by the author emphasised that there is a relation between the educational models and the educational constraints that related to the ethical considerations:

Study 1: under the title "The Impact of Interactive Distance Education on Learning Level Enhancement" (Abu-Bajeh & Abbas, 2021a) focused on a group of elements that restrict and affect the educational process which are: Group Discussion and feedback as educational constraints and its impact on learning level. The study used data collected directly from two distance learners groups, who attended the same distance educational program through different educational model to find the impact of educational models on educational constraints that related to the ethical considerations, and the findings demonstrated that there are links between educational models and learning levels in favor of the interactive model.

Study 2 (Abu-Bajeh & Abbas, 2021b): A conference paper intends to see if there is a relation between students' Knowledge Amplifying and the online educational models. The study gathered data from 126 parents who have children in two schools: Public schools and another private school; to measure the students' knowledge life cycle based on the educational model. The study concluded that they were relations between students' knowledge life cycle and online educational models in favor of the interactive model.

These studies demonstrate the extent of the impact of educational models on the educational process, specifically on educational obstacles, which will inevitably affect ethical considerations by virtue of the relationship that was proven in the theoretical review. This is due to the fact that some online educational models can't support in achieving the involvement between the teacher and learners, and limits the mastery level of learning objectives.

CONCLUSION

It should be noted the education is witnessing major changes in the organizational method of teaching recently. Accordingly the educational institutions must seek to build a smart society using advanced technology and automation, taking into account the necessity of determining and using the appropriate learning tools, techniques and educational models that can overcome the educational constraints that related to the ethical considerations, especially that regarding to achieving the educational process goals. Where, education model is being critical to educational institutions' competitive advantage, as well as, to being a major influence on the educational process and learners, in terms of support the educational process in achieving its goals in line with established expectations about the impact of automation and technology on the type of jobs in the future, and this will require that educational institutions work to modernize educational systems and their contents and prepare students to take on the challenges directly and to become professional workers and leaders. Therefore, institutions have to reimagine traditional educational paradigms with a futuristic approach that takes into account the educational constraints to transforms the future of education using advanced technology and automation, to take the educational process according to its goals. Restructuring the educational environment, integrating operational excellence into the education sector, and using ICT resources in education through the application of Education 5.0, will not be sufficient procedures to revolutionize the academic process in order to improve the overall academic environment and raise the level of education, unless educational models are adopted and used that supports processes for feedback, interaction and empowerment of teachers' roles to bridge the gap between the vision of the educational process and its implementation, and to ensure the educational process goes according to its goals.

REFERENCES

A., N. (2023). *The 7 Roles of a Teacher in the 21st Century*. Eton Institute. https://www.etoninstitute.com/blog/the-7-roles-of-a-teacher-in-the-21st-century

Abu-Bajeh, Z. Y., & Abbas, R. A. (2021a). The Impact of Interactive Distance Education on Learning Level Enhancement. *Review Of International Geographical Education, 11*(10).

Abu-Bajeh, Z. Y., & Abbas, R. A. (2021b). *The Impact of Interactive Online Learning on Students Knowledge Amplifying by Parents Perspective.* Paper presented at the 2021 International Conference of Women in Data Science, Taif University. 10.1109/WiDSTaif52235.2021.9430235

Abu-Bajeh, Z. Y., & Abbas, R. A. (2021c). Justifications for using interactive online education. *IACSIT International Journal of Engineering and Technology*, 10(1), 8–13.

Ahmad, S., Umirzakova, S., Mujtaba, G., Amin, M., & Whangbo, T. (2023). *Education 5.0: Requirements, Enabling Technologies, and Future Directions.*

Alharbi, A. M. (2023). Implementation of Education 5.0 in Developed and Developing Countries: A Comparative Study. *Creative Education*, 14(5), 914–942. 10.4236/ce.2023.145059

Asmd, K. (2000). *Norms and Standards for Educators* South African Minister of Education Retrieved from https://www.gov.za/sites/default/files/gcis_document/201409/20844.pdf

Ayuyang, R. R. (2019). Interactive Learning (iLEARN) Tool: An eLearning Portal Designed Using MOODLE for Cagayan State University in the Philippines.*Paper presented at theProceedings of the 2019 5th International Conference on Computing and Artificial Intelligence*. Research Gate. 10.1145/3330482.3330507

Bello, O. W., Ehira, D. N., Ayeni, J. K., Faruk, N., & Balogun, N. A. (2014). Towards the design of a synchronous virtual learning system. *Covenant Journal of Informatics and Communication Technology, 2*(2).

Bhatia, V., Nasser, S., & Bhansali, R. (2022). Impact of Online Education on Student Satisfaction. *International Journal Of Advance Research And Innovative Ideas In Education*, 8, 1331–1341.

Bruner, J. S. (2009). *The process of education*. Harvard University Press. 10.2307/j.ctvk12qst

Chachra, D. (2005). Beyond course-based engineering ethics instruction: Commentary on "topics and cases for online education in engineering. *Science and Engineering Ethics*, 11(3), 459–461. 10.1007/s11948-005-0015-216190286

Choudhuri, S., & Kumar, D. (2022). Online Education and Its Viability during Pandemic. *Journal of Pharmaceutical Negative Results*, 13, 1308.

Clifford, B. (2018). *Understanding Disinterest: How Online Undergraduate Students Perceive And Respond To Disengaged Faculty Members*.

Coman, C., îru, L. G., Mese an-Schmitz, L., Stanciu, C., & Bularca, M. C. J. S. (2020). Online teaching and learning in higher education during the coronavirus pandemic: students' perspective. *12*(24), 10367.

Delgado, P. (2020). *Synchronous and asynchronous learning: definition, advantages, and disadvantages.* TEC. https://observatory.tec.mx/edu-news/synchronous-and-asynchronous-learning-definitions

Edwards, S. H. (2003). *Rethinking computer science education from a test-first perspective.* Paper presented at the Companion of the 18th annual ACM SIGPLAN conference on Object-oriented programming, systems, languages, and applications, Anaheim, CA, USA. 10.1145/949344.949390

Farahani, M. F. (2012). Ethics principles in distance education. *Procedia: Social and Behavioral Sciences*, 46, 890–894. 10.1016/j.sbspro.2012.05.218

Hattie, J., & Timperley, H. (2007). The power of feedback. *Review of Educational Research*, 77(1), 81–112. 10.3102/003465430298487

Holmberg, B. (1995). Theory of Interaction and Communication. In Sewart, D., Keegan, D., & Holmberg, B. (Eds.), *Distance education: International perspectives* (pp. 34–45). Routledge.

Hornby, S. A. (1998). *Oxford Advanced Learner's Dictionary* (Edition, S. P., Ed.). Oxford University Press.

Ibiloye, A. (2021). Perspectives on Blended Learning Models and Recommendations on Instructional Applications. Academia Letters. *Distributed under CC BY 4.0.*

Keegan, D. (2013). *Foundations of distance education.* Routledge. 10.4324/9781315004822

Kennette, L., & Chapman, M. (2021). Providing positive student feedback in an online environment. *Academia Letters*, 1-3.

Kocdar, S., Karadeniz, A., & Goksel, N. (2018). Using Facebook for Leveraging Sense of Community in Self-Paced Open and Distance Learning Courses. *International Journal of Emerging Technologies in Learning*, 13(5), 100. 10.3991/ijet.v13i05.8192

Maria, M., Shahbodin, F., & Pee, N. C. (2018). Malaysian higher education system towards industry 4.0–current trends overview.*Paper presented at theAIP Conference Proceedings.* ACM. 10.1063/1.5055483

Matthew, U. O., & Kazaure, J. S. (2020). Multimedia E-Learning Education in Nigeria and Developing Countries of Africa for Achieving SDG4. *International Journal of Information Communication Technologies and Human Development*, 12(1), 40–62. 10.4018/IJICTHD.2020010103

Microsoft. (2013). *Parts of computer.* Microsoft.

Murdoch, G. (1997). Practicing what we preach-a trainee-centered approach to in-service education. *Paper presented at the Teacher development: Making the right moves.* Washington, D.C.: English Language Programs Divison.: United States Information Agency.

Mustafa Kamal, N. N., Mohd Adnan, A. H., Yusof, A. A., Ahmad, M. K., & Mohd Kamal, M. A. (2019). Immersive interactive educational experiences–adopting Education 5.0, Industry 4.0 learning technologies for Malaysian Universities.*Paper presented at the Proceedings of the International Invention, Innovative & Creative (InIIC) Conference, Series.* Research Gate.

Mwakisole, K. F., & Mussa, M., & Mtebe PhD, J. S. (2019). Cloud Computing Architecture for eLearning Systems in Secondary Schools in Tanzania. *The African Journal of Information Systems*, 11(4), 3.

Nasir, S., Wan Yaacob, W. F., & Ismail, N. (2019). The nature of online students' feedback in higher education. *International Journal of Innovation and Learning*, 25(4), 377. 10.1504/IJIL.2019.099982

Pane, M. M., Siregar, C., & Rumeser, J. A. (2020). The Role of Big Data for Interactive Online Learning: A Case Study in Students' Participations and Perceptions. Paper presented at the *Proceedings of the 2020 2nd International Conference on Big Data Engineering and Technology*. Research Gate. 10.1145/3378904.3378923

Parker, B. (2002). *Roles and responsibilities, institutional landscapes and curriculum mindscapes: A partial view of teacher education policy in South Africa, 1990-2000*. Centre for International Education, University of Sussex.

Pascarella, E. T., & Terenzini, P. T. (2005). *How College Affects Students: A Third Decade of Research* (Vol. 2). ERIC.

Pearson. (2016). *Providing Educational Feedback (White Paper)*. Pearson. https://www.pearson.com

Perraton, H. (1988). A theory for distance education. In Sewart, D., Keegan, D., & Holmberg, B. (Eds.), *Distance education: International perspectives* (pp. 34–45). Routledge.

Picciano, A. G. (2017). Theories and frameworks for online education: Seeking an integrated model. *Online Learning : the Official Journal of the Online Learning Consortium*, 21(3), 166–190. 10.24059/olj.v21i3.1225

Raiborn, C. A., & Payne, D. (1990). Corporate codes of conduct: A collective conscience and continuum. *Journal of Business Ethics*, 9(11), 879–889. 10.1007/BF00382911

Richardson, C. (2018). The Next Revolution In Global eLearning. *Forbes*.https://www.forbes.com

Salem, S. F., Al-Jubari, I., Aldholay, A., Jalal, A. N., & Mutahar, A. M. (2022). Covid-19 and Online Learning Engagement: Effects of Internal Crisis Communication, Technology and Social Responsibility. *Paper presented at theProceedings of International Conference on Emerging Technologies and Intelligent Systems: ICETIS 2021* (Volume 1). Springer. 10.1007/978-3-030-82616-1_25

Schlosser, L. A., & Simonson, M. R. (2009). *Distance Education: Definition and Glossary of Terms* (3rd Edition ed.). USA: Association for Educational Communications and Technology.

Scrivener, J. (2011). *The essential guide to English language teaching* (3rd ed.). MacMillan.

Shallal, A. H. (2017). *Design and implement an educational model by using cloud computing technologies*. Alnilain University.

Siddiqui, S., & Ahamed, M. M. J. A. W. E. J. V. (2020). Teachers' Roles Beyond and Within the Context: An Ever-Changing Concept. *11*.

Taghizadeh, M., & Hajhosseini, F. (2021). Investigating a blended learning environment: Contribution of Attitude, interaction, and quality of teaching to satisfaction of graduate students of TEFL. *The Asia-Pacific Education Researcher*, 30(5), 459–469. 10.1007/s40299-020-00531-z

Tan, S., Al-Jumeily, D., Mustafina, J., Hussain, A., Broderick, A., & Forsyth, H. (2018). Rethinking our education to face the new industry era. EDULEARN18 Proceedings.

UNESCO. (2008). *Learning to live together: an intercultural and interfaith programme for ethics education*. UNESDOC Digital Library: Incl. bibl. Pub. with the assistance of UNESCO.

Vonderwell, S., Liang, X., & Alderman, K. J. J. o. R. o. T. i. E. (2007). *Asynchronous discussions and assessment in online learning*. Research Gate.

KEY TERMS AND DEFINITIONS

Educational Constraints: The educational constraints are a collection of restrictions and requirements that necessitate the reformulation of the educational process based on the education needs, and it aims to calibration the implemented of the educational process and critically assesses the area of it, as well as any other concerns worthy of research.

Educational Institutions: The educational institution is the specific space for conducting the learning process. It is a place where individuals and their teachers come together to learn, share knowledge, empower and hone skills. So it's a complete environment consisting of facilities, teachers, students, rules and administrative bodies, and it can be called a learning environment.

Educational Process: The term educational process refers to a series of activities and procedures carried out in a classroom or training facility with the goal of providing learners with theoretical knowledge or practical skills as well as new knowledge in order to move their minds from one reality to another.

Ethical Considerations: These are issues that arise as a result of disagreement with the rules of conduct that should govern how manner. In the educational process, are the rules that govern the educational process and methods of providing scientific content in a way that ensures that students obtain their educational right and raise their knowledge level, in a manner that is consistent with the goals of the educational process.

Interactive Education: A new type of synchronous online education with an appropriate level of ability to manage learners, in whom the teacher or trainer is able to watch the students and communicate with them instantly via video, and can also receive the feedback at the same time, which will contribute to making the online educational process very similar to the Traditional classroom, but via Internet.

Knowledge Level: The knowledge level rationalizes the people behavior, and it's explaining the level of understanding about an issue or subject. From an educational perspective, knowledge is shared in order to move learners' understanding to a higher level, as a major goal in the educational process.

Online Education: Online education is systematic educational activities that uses instructional telematics resources which help in reduce the study constraints such as access, time, location, pace, study technique, or any combination of these.

Chapter 15
Education 5.0:
Navigating the Future of Learning

Froilan Delute Mobo
https://orcid.org/0000-0002-4531-8106
Philippine Merchant Marine Academy, Philippines

ABSTRACT

"Steering Through Tomorrow's Educational Wave" provides a deep understanding of the areas of impact Education 5.0 is going to have within the learning environment of the future. This part is linked to the new technologies and evermore developing methods of educating, as well as newly appearing needs in society. Hence, this chapter concentrates on the changes the transformation of traditional educational strategies and tactics by Schooling 5.0 entails. Crucial topics include education that is customized to the relevant person, learning for life, the usage implementation of cutting-edge educational technology tools, the skills needed for the 21st-century skills, cooperation partnership cultures, equality and inclusion, and being able to change and adapt. As presented throughout the article in a complex form; this chapter is going to provide information based on sailing medical pills through the mazes of education as a student to get acquainted.

BACKGROUND

The era of digital technology is currently undergoing a significant revolution in the field of education, which has given birth to the concept of Education 5.0, an innovative paradigm that redefines our perception and experience in learning. This chapter of the book highlights the intricacies of Education 5.0 through the analysis of its significance, the challenges encountered, and its transformative potential while charting a course for future learning. Considering this context, it becomes evident that traditional educational models are no longer adequate to meet the demands of a rapidly changing world, (Salinas-Navarro et al., 2023). As a result of technological disruptions brought about by globalization

DOI: 10.4018/979-8-3693-3041-8.ch015

and socio-economic changes in our societies, there is an increasing demand for us to rethink education as a dynamic adaptive ecosystem that allows learners to thrive in various contexts.

First and foremost, unlike past paradigms, Education 5.0 is not a one-size-fits-all solution but rather fosters a tailored, lifelong learning experience that considers the individual needs, and choices, including learning models, of every individual. It does so using entirely new ways of using big data analytics and immersive simulations based on AI.

Moreover, as a result, the above skills must develop and be taught from day one. As a result, learners are required to solve tons of complex issues that the world faces today.

Education 5.0 is a phenomenon of great consequence for the future of education and the underlying principles will be covered in this chapter. This chapter is about giving insight by looking at some examples, cases of success, and recent trends on what educators, policymakers, and stakeholders can do to harness Education 5.0 to build learning ecosystems that are inclusive, equitable, and future-oriented.

OVERALL APPROACH

Education plays a role, in shaping the future, and Education 5.0 revolutionizes the core of learning in today's age through advancements in technology teaching methods, student empowerment, and societal impacts. Essentially Education 5.0 embraces a human-centered approach, by leveraging technology to offer education and nurture thinking skills. This discussion offers an overview of Education 5.0 exploring its foundations, practical implementations, obstacles, and opportunities to enhance our understanding of how education evolves in an increasingly complex and interconnected world.

The cornerstone of Education 5.0 rests on the realization that most of the established academic trends will not equip the new crop of learners in the dawn of the digital era. Products of the fast-paced world's technology trends and socio-cultural dynamics demand radical changes in the way things are done in the educational arena. The paradigm shift from Education 4.0 means transcending the erstwhile 'one-size-fits-most' learning escapade to a truly student-centered learning pathway that could harness their unique strength, interest, and learning style while deploying artificial intelligence, data analytics, augmented reality, and other emergent technological tools to create an immersive learning experience.

A second major feature of Education 5.0 is the empowerment of the learner. Instead of being passively taught answers, novices become active learners by asking questions, offering hypotheses, finding counterexamples, and engaging in crowdsourced argumentation. This is learning where neophytes get to drive the car, literally - deciding where to go, setting the learning goals, seeking out alternative perspectives, and even collaborating on building pathways of their own. In this shift, the educator becomes less of an oracle and more mentor and coach: a respected companion who persistently encourages novices to move beyond their comfort zones, critically assesses alternative sources to determine whether they are reliable or not, and cultivates the habits of a lifelong learner; in other words, learn to learn.

Above all, the pedagogical envisioning of Education 5.0 is represented by a shift towards competency-based education, challenge-based learning, experiential learning, and interdisciplinary education that emphasizes students learning to think, listen, and learn creatively, communicate and collaborate, and become digitally fluent. Education 5.0 is also characterized by a high sensitivity to holistic education: not just cognitive ability but also to social-emotional learning, well-being, and global citizenship.

The path to Education5.0 is very tough. There are several challenges that we need to collectively like required infrastructure, teacher professional development, curriculum redesign, digital resources, student data privacy, unprivileged students' equitable access to digital technologies, ethical use of technology, zero role of technology in replacing the teaching profession through automation, etc. We need policymakers, educators, technology experts, parents, and even students to put together their brains to overcome these challenges of Education 5.0. In conclusion, the future of Education5.0 is very promising and is going to lead to personalized learning and inclusive education, self-paced learning and lifelong learning, global collaboration, teacher-led and master-led instruction and learning, and transformation in teaching and learning practices. These future study criteria will explore emerging technologies, pedagogical best practices, assessment methodologies, policy frameworks, the changing role of educators in the digital era, and an endless possibility of academic research in the field of Education5.0, etc. With foresight thinking and utilizing the transformative potential of Education5.0, we are ready to face the future of learning.

CHALLENGES AND OPPORTUNITIES

A conceptual shift within the paradigm of mastering, Education 5.0 offers both troubles and possibilities to training systems worldwide. First and most important, the redefinition of conventional educational fashions to satisfy the ever-altering wishes of the digital age. This includes adjustments or shifts in the position of educators and students, as well as the seamless integration of technology into mastering areas. Additionally, the virtual divide wishes to be addressed, and efforts to make certain equitable get entry to education resources for all novices. The complexity of huge data management and studying procedures in Education 5.0 may make it tough to govern data privacy, safety, and social use (Information burstiness). However, in its warfare are considerable possibilities. Education 5.0 affords the potential to customize and customize studying reviews. Big statistics and AI (Artificial Intelligence) may be utilized to tailor mastering to the desires of male or woman learners (Information Precision). Moreover, Education 5.0 presents possibilities for collaborative and interactive gaining knowledge. It can spoil bodily limitations and broaden worldwide networking among freshmen. Education 5.0 additionally fosters the advancement of crucial thinking, creativity, and hassle-solving competencies, which can be quintessential inside the contemporary staff demands. A proactive effort is wanted from educators, policymakers, and stakeholders to capitalize on the potential of Education 5.0 in shaping the destiny of mastering.

Expanding on those issues, the demand-driven context inscribed in Education 5.0 leads to organizational and structural changes in academic institutions. Deploying new technology and new pedagogies also results in the need for huge investments in the infrastructure and teacher training, as well as their continuous support. Another challenge is the education 5.0 inclusiveness issue, as social-economic disparities, language barriers, and many learning needs must be met. Improving education for the future means making tests match new ways of measuring skills. Education 5.0 brings both good and hard things. Using AI and the latest tech like VR/AR makes learning more practical through simulations, virtual labs, and immersive experiences. This changes old teaching ways and helps more people access knowledge worldwide through open online resources, digital libraries, and internet platforms. Social media, forums, and project-based learning create interactive places that encourage innovation, teamwork, and learning from peers.

ILLUSTRATIVE EXAMPLE

In Education 5.0, think about this: using personalized learning tools in a diverse academic institution. This brings both challenges and chances. One problem is making sure all students have the same access to tech and digital stuff. This means dealing with issues like the cost of devices and internet access and giving the right training and help. Another issue is handling and examining the vast amount of data from personalized learning. This calls for strong data systems and plans to keep data safe and used in the right way. On the other side of the situation, personalized learning tools offer big chances to shape schooling to meet each student's needs. For instance, smart learning programs can study how students learn and make paths that fit each student's way of learning. This not only makes learning better but also gets students more into it by giving them stuff that's useful and means something to them.

In addition, the collaborative technological tools that can support peer-to-peer learning, group projects, and online collaboration, eliminating geographical barriers and promoting global connections among students can strengthen the navigation of future learnings. In addition to enhancing learning, the collaborative factor helps students develop vital twenty-first-century skills such as relationships, cooperation, and innovation, which are critical for achieving success in a digital age.

Education 5.0, by addressing difficult and difficult situations inclusive of equitable access, data control, and ensuring inclusive studying environments, at the same time as patronizing personalized schooling, collaboration, and facts-driven insights, can remodel the records of mastering, making schooling extra adaptive, participating, and effective for all college students. In sum, Education 5.0 represents a transformative approach to studying, incorporating superior technology and modern methodologies to maximize academic outcomes in philology.

One of the best implementations of personalized learning pathways using artificial intelligence online platforms. In this framework the students' learning styles, preferences, and progress data are analyzed to tailor educational content and experiences. For example, other technological platforms like universities abroad use adaptive algorithms to provide personalized learning journeys, adjusting difficulty levels and content based on individual performance. Immersive and interactive technologies like Virtual Reality (VR) / Augmented Reality (AR) were also deployed for learning purposes during the pandemic. VR Simulation for Experiential Learning: Institutions are using VR simulations for experiential learning where students can explore historical events, conduct scientific experiments, or practice real-world skills in a safe, controlled environment (Almuqati, 2019) and to make them more aware of real-life scenarios.

Similarly, AR and VR applications like Google Expeditions bring interactive learning experiences into classrooms, enabling students to visualize complex concepts or interact with digital content overlaid on the physical world.

Collaborative approaches are also centralized to Education 5.0 which can foster peer-to-peer learning and global collaboration. One notable example is the use of online collaboration platforms like Google Workspace and Microsoft Teams in education. These platforms facilitate synchronous and asynchronous communication, document sharing, and collaborative project work among students and educators across geographical boundaries. Additionally, social learning networks such as Edmodo, Schoology, and Moodle provide virtual spaces for communities of learners to connect, share resources, and engage in discussions. These platforms promote collaborative problem-solving, knowledge co-creation, and cultural exchange, enriching the learning experience beyond traditional classroom settings.

Furthermore, Education 5.0 and other game-based learning (GBL) strategies enhance student engagement and motivation. Gamification elements such as points, badges, leaderboards, and interactive challenges are incorporated into educational platforms and curricula, (Editor, 2024). For instance, platforms like Kahoot!, Quizlet, and other gamified quizzes and assessments, make learning more interactive and enjoyable for students. Moreover, educational games like Minecraft Education Edition and Code Combat offer immersive learning environments where students can develop problem-solving skills, computational thinking, and creativity through gameplay. These gamified approaches not only increase student participation and retention but also foster a growth mindset and a passion for lifelong learning.

In the context of professional education, Education 5.0 emphasizes skills development for the future workforce. Competency-based education (CBE) frameworks are implemented to align curriculum with industry demands and job market trends. For example, platforms like LinkedIn Learning and Coursera offer skill-based courses and micro-credentials recognized by employers, enabling learners to acquire and showcase relevant competencies. Additionally, work-integrated learning (WIL) programs, such as internships, apprenticeships, and industry collaborations, provide hands-on experience and bridge the gap between academic knowledge and practical skills. These initiatives prepare learners for career pathways, entrepreneurship, and lifelong employability in dynamic and evolving industries.

Moreover, Education 5.0 encompasses the concept of lifelong and personalized learning ecosystems. Online learning marketplaces like Udemy and Skillshare empower individuals to pursue continuous learning and professional development at their own pace and convenience. Micro-learning modules, podcasts, and interactive tutorials offer bite-sized content for on-the-go learning and just-in-time skill acquisition. Furthermore, open educational resources (OER) and Massive Open Online Courses (MOOCs) democratize access to high-quality education globally, promoting inclusivity, diversity, and lifelong learning opportunities for learners of all ages and backgrounds.

In summary, Education 5.0 represents a paradigm shift in education, leveraging technology, collaboration, gamification, industry alignment, and lifelong learning to navigate the future of learning effectively. These illustrative examples showcase the diverse applications and benefits of Education 5.0 in fostering personalized, engaging, and impactful learning experiences for learners worldwide.

FUTURE DIRECTIONS

The trajectory in which learning will shape in the years to come will contain a huge pool of challenges and opportunities in the form of future guidelines in Education 5.0. A major hurdle is to keep pace with rapidly moving technology and integrate it into education in a way that works. This extends to the use of new technology such as artificial intelligence, digital and augmented reality, blockchain, and big data analytics to improve the learning experience, customize education, and promote innovation in pedagogy.

And the return to equity in access to digital sources and opportunities poses an important challenge in Education With these changes, Education 5.0 has been seen as a new reconfiguration of the processes and practices that new technologies draft on educational spaces and the new trends we are living. That manner bridging divides in net connectivity; furnishing cheap, trustworthy right of entry to devices; and growing a virtual literacy curriculum for all, to empower newcomers of all backgrounds.

Conversely, new directions in Education 5.0 future investigations also offer promise for transformational change. We are transferring away from the one-size-suits-all entry to getting to know the development of smart mastering structures, driven by way of AI, able to convey customized mastering pathways that recognize the individual desires, gaining knowledge of styles, and preferences of each learner. Even though the aim is to deepen the learning, it also helps students incorporate deeper engagement and motivation in them.

Additionally, the incorporation of an immersive era inclusive of digital and augmented facts extends the horizons of experiential schooling, simulations, and digital labs, allowing students to interact with hard ideas in a tactile and interactive environment. Collaborative learning systems and social knowledge of networks also create possibilities for worldwide collaboration, cultural diversity, and peer-to-peer gaining knowledge, breaking down geographical barriers and peer-to-peer learning, breaking down geographical barriers, and promoting pass-cultural understanding.

Additionally, the developing emphasis on lifelong studying and non-stop upskilling in a hastily converting task market offers opportunities for developing bendy and adaptive mastering ecosystems. Education 5.0 can guide people in obtaining new skills, retraining for new professional pathways, and staying competitive in an evolving virtual economy.

By embracing these possibilities and addressing the associated demanding situations proactively, Education 5.0 can navigate the future of getting to know using fostering innovation, inclusivity, and lifelong learning possibilities for all novices.

CONCLUSION

Finally, Education 5.0 reflects a lively landscape of demanding situations and opportunities to doubtlessly lead the future of learning. Encompassing the above with imbibing innovative technologies combating the digital divide and ensuring data privacy and ethical use is a challenge that requires concerted effort by educators, policymakers, and stakeholders alike, to overcome (Iordanishvili, 2019). Nevertheless, with those demanding situations come gigantic opportunities for transformative change in education.

The opportunities in Education 5.0 include customized studying experiences, using AI and data analytics to customize education to character needs, constructing collaboration and global connections via digital platforms, and developing vital twenty-first-century skills like vital thinking, creativity, and problem-solving, (Herodotou et al., 2019).

Also, Education 5.0 supports lifelong learning ecosystems, non-stop upskilling, and modern pedagogical strategies that educate learners to succeed in an ever-changing digital age.

Through strategic navigation of these demanding situations and seizing the possibilities furnished by using Education 5.0, stakeholders can construct a more inclusive, adaptable, and destiny-equipped schooling device that empowers newcomers to reach a complex and interconnected global. Unleashing the full potential of Education 5.0 requires a commitment to innovation, equity, and lifelong learning to ensure that education remains a catalyst for individual growth, collective advancement, and global prosperity.

REFERENCES

Иорданишвили, А. К. (2019). Фториды: их значение для здоровья человека в современных условиях и перспективы использования. *Čelovek I Ego Zdorov e, 2*, 66–73. 10.21626/vestnik/2019-2/07

Almuqati, A. A. (2019). *An Exploratory Study of Science, Technology, Engineering, and Mathematics (STEM) Teachers' Understanding and Practices Using Problem-Based Learning for Middle and High School Students* [Dissertation, Concordia University Chicago]. https://www.proquest.com/docview/2454635815

(Ed.). (2024, May 31). 6 Ways Technology Transformed the Educational Landscape - Antigua News Room. *Antigua News Room*. https://antiguanewsroom.com/6-ways-technology-transformed-the-educational-landscape/

Herodotou, C., Sharples, M., Gaved, M., Kukulska-Hulme, A., Rienties, B., Scanlon, E., & Whitelock, D. (2019). Innovative Pedagogies of the Future: An Evidence-Based Selection. *Frontiers in Education*, 4, 113. Advance online publication. 10.3389/feduc.2019.00113

Salinas-Navarro, D. E., Garay-Rondero, C. L., & Arana-Solares, I. A. (2023). Digitally enabled Experiential Learning spaces for Engineering Education 4.0. *Education Sciences, 13*(1), 63. https://doi.org/.10.3390/educsci13010063

Wagner, T. (2008). *The Global Achievement Gap: Why Even Our Best Schools Don't Teach the New Survival Skills Our Children Need—and What We Can Do About It.* Basic Books.

Chapter 16
Freedom and Responsibility in Education 5.0

Mohammad Ali Al-Saggaf
http://orcid.org/0000-0001-7401-0509
Xiamen University Malaysia, Malaysia

ABSTRACT

This chapter attempts to address the issue of freedom-responsibility nexus in the era of Education 5.0, defining and establishing the rationale between freedom and responsibility and their resilience in the educational realm through reviewing relevant literature from various respects steering towards education and particularly Education 5.0. This chapter also discusses the space of freedom anticipated and the extent of responsibility it places. It also discusses the opportunities and challenges that freedom-responsibility nexus in the era of Education 5.0 is prone to offer. The intersection between freedom, responsibility and education is further demonstrated with reference to historical and philosophical perspectives, and through analyzing three relevant case studies from different contexts to recommend a three-pillar method for introducing the change into education. Bearing in mind the impact of conceptualizing and reconceptualizing the nexus across freedom, responsibility and education alongside the massive new possibilities Education 5.0 offers.

INTRODUCTION

Freedom is neither a simple word that is enchanted nor a mere fancy concept that is sought for. We learned from history how nations, and even every single human being, have fought for their existence by fighting for their right to freedom. However, we also learned that the brightest side that freedom entails is responsibility. Responsibility on its own is not more than a mere reflection of the amount of freedom human beings enjoyed.

Many definitions can be found for these two concepts. So, why is Freedom highly valued and why responsibility is called for whenever the former is mentioned?! This would be understood when clearer conceptualisation of the two terms is forwarded. In Sheldon, K. M., Gordeeva, T., Leontiev, D., Lynch, M. F., Osin, E., Rasskazova, E., & Dementiy, L. (2018), the term “Freedom” is defined as “… a personal and/or social good that can be conceptualized in political, philosophical, scientific, ethical, and psychological terms, and/or in terms of liberty, autonomy, free will, individualism, and more.” While

DOI: 10.4018/979-8-3693-3041-8.ch016

"Responsibility" is defined as "a personal and social good that can be conceptualized in many different ways, i.e., in terms of moral, legal, collective, social, professional or personal responsibilities, and/or in terms of duties, obligations, liabilities, and more." (pp. 63-64).

In a clearer view, the nexus of freedom and responsibility is perceived in the underlying nexus of person and situation, in which the society as a system or part(s) thereof claim the power through a dichotomic matrix that can be approximately displayed as follows:

Figure 1. Freedom-responsibility nexus

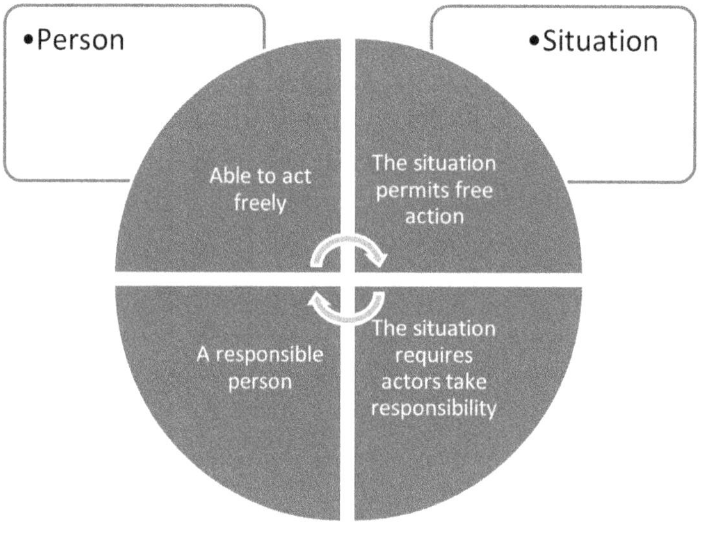

RATIONALE OF FREEDOM-RESPONSIBILITY NEXUS

Freedom and responsibility are two concepts that are viewed in literature as two historically contradicting concepts where the presence of one would mean the absence of the other. Another perspective assumes that more freedom entails less responsibility. While a third view emphasises that freedom entails responsibility. Despite the instinctive tendency towards Freedom, the question is what is the rationale of these terms? Well, that depends on one's stance. In other words; while freedom semantically carries positive connotation, many others may disagree. Specially those running institutions would view freedom as a threat to the structure of their institution, and therefore would rationalize the priority of responsibility over freedom. This dichotomy of freedom and responsibility nexus is seen as an analogy of that nexus between instinct and reason as narrated and fossilized throughout history. And from that point one can understand why there is a call for responsibility whenever freedom is called for. As a result, it is an uneasy task to rationalize freedom apart from the concept of responsibility, which in its turn, also, requires a rationale that is inseparable from freedom.

Evidence for such integrated relationship is well established theoretically in famous quotes attributed to great philosopher and outstanding figures, as cited in Sheldon, K. M. et.al. (2018, p. 63), "*Freedom means responsibility.*" By George Bernard Shaw; "*Freedom makes a huge requirement of every human being. With freedom comes responsibility.*" By Eleanor Roosevelt; "*Freedom of will is the ability to do gladly that which I must do.*" By Carl Jung; and "*The price of freedom is responsibility, but it is a bargain, because freedom is priceless.*" By Hugh Downs. However, empirical evidence show more tendency towards giving up freedom to avoid responsibility. In other words, the burden of responsibility that freedom necessitates has, almost always been the turning point and the major cause for turning down the right to freedom. Allow me to share my personal experience briefly in a few lines below before we go into the philosophical debate of the matter.

Freedom-Responsibility on a Side Note

The most frequent phrase I heard from my father since I was a little child was "*bos-rek*", an indefinable phrase in local Hadrami-Arabi dialect, but let me to take a moment telling you a bit more about it and its meaning. I remember whenever my father took me with him, he would never tell me to select this over that, rather, he would, in the best-case scenario, tell me the pros and cons of the choices at hand, and would utter his typical phrase "*bosrek*". I guess you should be able now to sense the phrase; yes, "Bos-rek" approximately means "you see, you decide". What is really interesting about it is that all people surrounding us accused my father of spoiling me by neither deciding on my behalf nor for me as per our local societal expectation of parenting. I did not know then why he was doing so, but I enjoyed the privilege. Growing up, I could slowly conceptualise and interpret how scary that phrase is in reality, because it simply means it is your own choice; it is your own responsibility. Precisely, my father was educating me to bear my own responsibility independently through freedom of choice; end of story.

At a philosophical debate, existentialists advocacy for freedom is seen through Jean-Jacques Rousseau's *Emile*, Plato's Republic, Sartre's *Notebooks for an Ethics*, and many more. One can trace these linking elements of freedom to education with much evidence in Sartre's particular narrative of freedom and responsibility; that linkage which promotes for the educational process itself to be approached in a more active and critical way of responsibility as "the consciousness (of) being the incontestable author of an event or of an object" (Sartre, 1992, p.707). Yet, the systemic formal traditional educational platform was closely connected to the industrial revolution, and the need for workers who can run the industry in its earlier stages has laid the foundations for the educational platforms to tailoring learners as per the industry's need and demand. Hence, the educational systems turned into merely factories producing workers, or at their very best were vehicles for regimes in passing their policies, which in both scenarios advocated for structured learning process that is controversial when freedom and responsibility came into debate.

In education, the nexus of freedom and responsibility was misunderstood. Not in theory, but in practice. What we see in traditional and classical education is that almost everything is designed and pre-selected for the learners, leaving little, if any, space of freedom of choice to be practiced, experienced or exercised by the learners themselves; Learn this, not that; here, not there; now, not then; this way not that way, in an endless series of dos and don'ts. Thinking that by giving more tasks and deciding for them what they should do and what they should not, we are educating them on taking responsibility. Enaya, B. P.

(2021) advocates that "There is certainly freedom in education, and there is education in freedom." (p. 124). Nonetheless, we are depriving learners of their right to freedom, and if we try to transparently and sincerely examine such practise, we are spoiling learners and are contributing to producing solemnly dependant members of the society lacking the sense of responsibility towards themselves in the first place and towards society, second. I know at this very point you would have already developed some queries to my argument, if not objections.

FREEDOM-RESPONSIBILITY IN EDUCATION 5.0

Academic discussion of freedom and responsibility and their relation to education is not new in itself (See Albornoz (1991); Winch (2002); Glenn, C. L., De Groof, J., & Candal, C. S. (2005); Che Noraini Hashima, et. al. (2014); Gibbs (2016); and Sheldon, K. M., Gordeeva, T., Leontiev, D., Lynch, M. F., Osin, E., Rasskazova, E., & Dementiy, L. (2018)) to name but a few. However, what is new in this discussion is the new era of Education 5.0 and the space of freedom and responsibility it is prone to offer. The term Education 5.0 has been thoroughly explicated in the other chapters of this book, but what really matters here are three new features that will change our perception towards freedom and responsibility in education.

First, the integration of advanced technologies, such as AI, VR & AVR and other advanced technologies into education, which means opening new temporal and spatial platforms for education (Zhou, C. (2023); Saputra, I. et.al. (2023); Aggarwal, D. (2023); Amado-Salvatierra, H. R. et.al. (2024). Second, accessibility to knowledge of any type at any level, which leads to the third feature, and that is the departure from structured learning where classical education system enjoyed the privilege of authority and control over the entire process.

The first characteristic of integrating advanced technology poses a major challenge to the current classical curriculums and the dependency on text-book-style for sourcing and referencing information. Nur, N., Goh, S. J., Patel, J., & Mizrahi, M. (2024) insist that "The accelerated integration of Artificial Intelligence (AI) into education has led to transformative changes, enhancing various educational processes and experiences" (p. 7654). The new technologies offer way much better mechanisms for sourcing information that surpasses the best structuralized educational systems could offer to the extent that intelligent tutoring systems are being implemented for personalized learning (ibid).

It opens new temporal and spatial platforms for learners surpassing limitations that classical education could not go beyond (Celik, I. 2023). With these new platforms of technology enhanced learning environment, accessibility to knowledge and information is a lot easier, faster and even cheaper than before (Zhou, C. 2023). All credit goes to the advanced technologies in Education 5.0 where learners can get what they need whenever they need it, by just a click or a prompt, as is the case with ChatGPT (Chen, L., Chen, P., & Lin, Z. 2020).

OPPORTUNITIES AND CHALLENGES IN EDUCATION 5.0

Such an ease in accessibility offers a wider space of freedom for the learners to have more control over, not only their convenient time and place of education, but also what to learn and what not to (Olatunde-Aiyedun, T. G. 2024). The biggest challenge here comes from the departure from the structuralized educational system which means no more control for the educational authorities over education itself; in other words, educationalist will have lesser and lesser control over education due to learners' departure from classical education. Freedom that Education 5.0 offer, therefore, is seen as a threat, in the best attribution, to the future of the learners themselves as it could be seen as a departure from responsibility, and thus leading to a huge paradigm shift in Education arguably controversial in so many respects. (Mariappan, J., & Krishnan, C. 2022)

Unlike any other precedented development to the scale of freedom and responsibility does Education 5.0 bring forward, the amount of controversy it brings along is unprecedented as well. Between advocates, critics and opponents, the opportunities and challenges, threats and obstacles associated with Education 5.0 are enticing the attention of researchers up. In Saputra, I. et.al. (2023) the opportunities AI bring into education would be linked to "the delivery of learning materials, evaluation, management systems, and educational policy making." (p.1095). But when it comes to challenges and threats, integration of AI triggers issues like "the security of personal data, character building and educational ethics." Yet the most important point they highlight is the obstacles of "high costs required, … and slow changes in curriculum structure and structural level of education." (ibid)

Not only is there a need to consider challenges associated with Education 5.0, but there is an urgent need to consider some ethical issues associated with the integration of AI in this new platform of education. Nur, N. et.al. (2024) highlight a number of these ethical considerations including "unequal access to AI-driven analytics, privacy breaches, discriminatory outcomes, harmful content generation compromising individuals' learning experience, and learning stagnation" (p. 7654). These ethical issues require a serious abrupt intervention by introducing new wise policies that cater for all stakeholders into the educational system across all levels, associated with carefully balanced planned reconceptualization of the freedom-responsibility nexus.

So, the question here is as we are heading radically towards education 5.0, What would be the space of freedom and responsibility? In an attempt to answering this crucial question, let us jump onto the realm of freedom-responsibility nexus at institutionalized bodies.

SPACE OF FREEDOM AND RESPONSIBILITY IN EDUCATION 5.0

The conflicting nexus between freedom and responsibility appears vividly within institutionalised bodies. Starting from the smallest institute of family; where parents advocate responsibilities over freedom when it comes to their children, and vice a versa. One can easily make an observation that it all depends on who defines which. Hence, moving towards upper institutionalized bodies, authorities would revolt freedom or at least would prefer to give its subjects its minimum space.

Education is no exception. Educational authorities, including teachers, have always advocated responsibilities over freedom, and this is not to judge if it is right or wrong, rather, it shows that freedom in educational systems has been associated with lack of discipline and commitment, which are deemed necessary props for a learner to succeed and excel in his/her education.

Surprisingly, in almost all types of institutionalized education systems, learners are not given enough space of freedom. That was feasible then, as all sources and resources were in the hands of the authorities, exclusively. Yet, with the rapid advancement in human civilization under the undeniable impact of massive technological progress, education has the lion's share of this jump (Aggarwal, D. 2023). We are not talking about Education 4.0 anymore, rather, it is Education 5.0 now, which is characterized mainly by the space of freedom it is anticipated to provide for the learners, where authorities would have lesser control over it. So, to better understand the new era of education, it would be highly commendable to visit some case studies that highlight introducing more freedom to education during the past eras of education.

FREEDOM AND RESPONSIBILITY IN EDUCATION: EARLIER CASE STUDIES

In Olssen's *The neo-liberal appropriation of tertiary education policy: Accountability, research and academic freedom* (2000), there were new changes introduced to the educational system pushed by "the New Right" after 1984. For such an initiative, New-Zealand's policy making was motivated by the "Fourth Labour Government, the New Zealand Treasury, and the New Zealand State Services Commission". The interesting part of this study is that the new changes entailed a replacement for the government's controlling role of direction and authority in directing and regulating, not only economy but also education, with an array of novel standpoints that can be seen to have accumulated through a series of liberal thoughts weighing heavily on freedom and refuting that dominating role of the state. This shows the importance of governmental support for any change in education and that new policies are needed to accommodate the new level freedom entailed within education 5.0, along with a well-studied set of responsibilities for all parties involved.

Another interesting case study relevant to the discussion here is "*Academic freedom in international higher education: right or responsibility?*" Conducted in the USA by Gibbs (2016). It investigates how academic freedom was conceptualized historically and how it developed such a practical right that applies to academia and universities in the USA. This study reveals that conceptualization and reconceptualization in the first place caused by contingent circumstance could be the reason for the shift in considering academic freedom as a mean of protection for the academic staff right for teaching and researching autonomously, but not as a responsibility. This comes with a huge implication of the significant role conceptualization and reconceptualizing for freedom-responsibility nexus during the so-called contingent circumstance, which applies exactly to the current era of education 5.0, urging for a careful and serious consideration for the reconceptualization of freedom-responsibility nexus in a way that parties involved in the educational process hold the two balanced. (Glenn, C. L., De Groof, J., & Candal, C. S. (2005)

Talking about balance, an interesting case study about academic freedom and responsibility in Malaysian higher institutions by Hashim, C. N., Azman, S. M. M. S., & Azman, S. N. A. S. was conducted in 2014, in which they interviewed senior academics who have been attached to universities for over two decades and the study reveals a sense of urgency to restore balance between freedom and responsibility to academia for both students and learners. This is a vigorous indicator coming from senior academics for the need to balancing freedom and responsibility at universities. The question remains; what about primary and secondary education? Is there a need for freedom-responsibility balance as well?!

It is, therefore, crucial for embracing Education 5.0 to cater for a three-pillar method of change. The first pillar is the role of the governing state to introduce new policies into the educational system in order to cope with the new realm of education. The second pillar is seriously observing balanced reconceptualization of freedom-responsibility nexus at earlier possible stages of contingent educational circumstance. The third pillar is for the former two pillars need to be circulated across all levels of institutions from nurseries to higher education and academies.

CONCLUSION

Education 5.0 in a clearer sense means integrating the most advanced technology in teaching and learning, namely Artificial Intelligence (AI) and Augmented Virtual Reality. In this regard, for classical institutional educations to survive, they have to cope, not only with transformation into the digital realm, but also, absorbing, tolerating and acknowledging the fact that they will have lesser and lesser controlling authorities over education. Having said so, this does not mean that they will not be needed anymore, on the contrary, their role shall be even more significant should they understand what their new role in education 5.0 really is. On top of all, accepting the new reality and learning it and about it to build the necessary skills & capabilities of both feeding and prompting AI machines to help transfer credible, authentic and verifiable knowledge.

REFERENCES

Aggarwal, D. (2023). Integration of innovative technological developments and AI with education for an adaptive learning pedagogy. *China Petroleum Processing and Petrochemical Technology*, 23(2).

Amado-Salvatierra, H. R., Morales-Chan, M., Hernandez-Rizzardini, R., & Rosales, M. (2024, March). Exploring Educators' Perceptions: Artificial Intelligence Integration in Higher Education. In *2024 IEEE World Engineering Education Conference (EDUNINE)* (pp. 1-5). IEEE. 10.1109/EDUNINE60625.2024.10500578

Celik, I. (2023). Towards Intelligent-TPACK: An empirical study on teachers' professional knowledge to ethically integrate artificial intelligence (AI)-based tools into education. *Computers in Human Behavior*, 138, 107468. 10.1016/j.chb.2022.107468

Chen, L., Chen, P., & Lin, Z. (2020). Artificial intelligence in education: A review. *IEEE Access : Practical Innovations, Open Solutions*, 8, 75264–75278. 10.1109/ACCESS.2020.2988510

Enaya, B. P., & Villaroya, A. F. (2021). Sartrean Freedom and Responsibility in Rousseau's Emile. *Philippine Social Science Journal*, 4(1), 117–126. 10.52006/main.v4i1.320

Gibbs, A. (2016). Academic freedom in international higher education: Right or responsibility? *Ethics and Education*, 11(2), 175–185. 10.1080/17449642.2016.1181844

Glenn, C. L., De Groof, J., & Candal, C. S. (2005). *Balancing Freedom, Autonomy and Accountability in Education* (Vol. I). Wolf Legal Publishers.

Hashim, C. N., Azman, S. M. M. S., & Azman, S. N. A. S. (2014). Academic Freedom and Educational Responsibility in Malaysian Higher Institutions of Learning. *IIUM Journal of Educational Studies*, 2(1), 1–11. 10.31436/ijes.v2i1.30

Mariappan, J., & Krishnan, C. (2022). Integration of AI in Learning: A Paradigm Shift in Education. In *Technology Training for Educators From Past to Present* (pp. 263–275). IGI Global. 10.4018/978-1-6684-4083-4.ch014

Nur, N., Goh, S. J., Patel, J., & Mizrahi, M. (2024). Navigating the ethical landscape of ai integration in educational settings. In *INTED2024 Proceedings* (pp. 7654-7663). IATED.

Olatunde-Aiyedun, T. G. (2024). Artificial Intelligence (AI) in Education: Integration of AI Into Science Education Curriculum in Nigerian Universities. *International Journal of Artificial Intelligence for Digital*, 1(1).

Olssen, M. (2000). The neo-liberal appropriation of tertiary education policy: Accountability, research and academic freedom. *Access: Critical Perspectives on Cultural & Policy Studies in Education*, 19(2), 9–70.

Saputra, I., Astuti, M., Sayuti, M., & Kusumastuti, D. (2023). Integration of Artificial Intelligence in Education: Opportunities, Challenges, Threats and Obstacles. A Literature Review. *Indonesian Journal of Computer Science*, 12(4). 10.33022/ijcs.v12i4.3266

Sartre, J. P. (1992). *Notebooks for an Ethics*. University of Chicago Press.

Sheldon, K. M., Gordeeva, T., Leontiev, D., Lynch, M. F., Osin, E., Rasskazova, E., & Dementiy, L. (2018). Freedom and responsibility go together: Personality, experimental, and cultural demonstrations. *Journal of Research in Personality*, 73, 63–74. 10.1016/j.jrp.2017.11.007

Sheldon, K. M., Gordeeva, T., Leontiev, D., Lynch, M. F., Osin, E., Rasskazova, E., & Dementiy, L. (2018). Freedom and responsibility go together: Personality, experimental, and cultural demonstrations. *Journal of Research in Personality*, 73, 63–74. 10.1016/j.jrp.2017.11.007

Zhou, C. (2023). Integration of modern technologies in higher education on the example of artificial intelligence use. *Education and Information Technologies*, 28(4), 3893–3910. 10.1007/s10639-022-11309-9

Compilation of References

A., N. (2023). *The 7 Roles of a Teacher in the 21st Century*. Eton Institute. https://www.etoninstitute.com/blog/the-7-roles-of-a-teacher-in-the-21st-century

Abakah, E., Widin, J., & Ameyaw, E. K. (2022). Continuing professional development (CPD) practices among basic school teachers in the central region of Ghana. *SAGE Open*, 12(2), 21582440221094597. 10.1177/21582440221094597

Abdurahman, N. H., & Rizqi, M. A. (2020). Indonesian students' strategies to cope with foreign language anxiety. *TEFLIN Journal: A Publication on the Teaching & Learning of English, 31*(1).

Abu-Bajeh, Z. Y., & Abbas, R. A. (2021a). The Impact of Interactive Distance Education on Learning Level Enhancement. *Review Of International Geographical Education, 11*(10).

Abu-Bajeh, Z. Y., & Abbas, R. A. (2021b). *The Impact of Interactive Online Learning on Students Knowledge Amplifying by Parents Perspective*. Paper presented at the 2021 International Conference of Women in Data Science, Taif University. 10.1109/WiDSTaif52235.2021.9430235

Abu-Bajeh, Z. Y., & Abbas, R. A. (2021c). Justifications for using interactive online education. *IACSIT International Journal of Engineering and Technology*, 10(1), 8–13.

Abumalloh, R. A., Asadi, S., Nilashi, M., Minaei-Bidgoli, B., Nayer, F. K., Samad, S., Mohd, S., & Ibrahim, O. (2021). The impact of coronavirus pandemic (COVID-19) on education: The role of virtual and remote laboratories in education. *Technology in Society*, 67, 101728. 10.1016/j.techsoc.2021.10172834538984

Abuzhuri, N. M., & Hashim, N. B. (2017). Impact of entrepreneurship education on entrepreneurial opportunity recognition. *IOSR Journal of Business and Management*, 19(11), 74–79.

Ačimović, S., Jovanović, M., & Jovanović, V. (2021). Critical thinking skills in the age of artificial intelligence. In *International Conference on New Trends in Education and Their Impact* (pp. 45-52). Springer, Cham.

Adıgüzel, A. (2010). The Status of Instructional Technologies in Primary Schools and Classroom Teachers' Levels of Using These Technologies. *Dicle University Ziya Gökalp Education Faculty Journal*, (15), 1–17.

Adisendjaja, Y. H., Rustaman, N. Y., Redjeki, S., & Satori, D. (2017, February). Science teachers' understanding of scientific inquiry in teacher professional development. [). IOP Publishing.]. *Journal of Physics: Conference Series*, 812(1), 012054. 10.1088/1742-6596/812/1/012054

Aeni, N., & Nadya Nurhidayah, N. Hasriani, Ammade, S., & Dewi, A. C. (2023). How online learning materials developed: Need analysis in developing online materials for zoom platform teaching. *AIP Conference Proceedings, 2510*(1), 30043. 10.1063/5.0128844

Afriansyah, B., & Yustanti, N. V. (2021). Multiliteracy education in 5.0 era on learning entrepreneurship with the project based learning model. In *Educational Innovation in Society 5.0 Era: Challenges and Opportunities* (pp. 286-290). Routledge.

Agarwal, N. (2018). A study of innovations in instructional strategies and designs for quality enrichment in Higher Education. *Cosmos: An International Journal of Art & Higher Education*, 7(2), 1–12.

Aggarwal, D. (2023). Integration of innovative technological developments and AI with education for an adaptive learning pedagogy. *China Petroleum Processing and Petrochemical Technology*, 23(2).

Aggarwal, L., Chahal, D., & Kharb, L. (2020). Pruning deficiency of big data analytics using cognitive computing. *2020 International Conference on Emerging Trends in Communication, Control and Computing (ICONC3)*, (pp. 1–4). 10.1109/ICONC345789.2020.9117504

Aghav-Palwe, S., & Gunjal, A. (2021). Introduction to cognitive computing and its various applications. In *Cognitive Computing for Human-Robot Interaction* (pp. 1–18). Elsevier. 10.1016/B978-0-323-85769-7.00009-4

Ahmad, S., Umirzakova, S., Mujtaba, G., Amin, M., & Whangbo, T. (2023). *Education 5.0: Requirements, Enabling Technologies, and Future Directions.*

Ahmed, H., & Popova, N. (2023). Globalization and Its Socioeconomic Consequences: A Comprehensive Review. *The Critical Review of Social Sciences Studies*, 1(02), 87–97.

Ahtinen, A., & Kaipainen, K. (2020). Learning and Teaching Experiences with a Persuasive Social Robot in Primary School – Findings and Implications from a 4-Month Field Study. *Lecture Notes in Computer Science (Including Subseries Lecture Notes in Artificial Intelligence and Lecture Notes in Bioinformatics), 12064 LNCS*, 73–84. Springer. 10.1007/978-3-030-45712-9_6

Aida, Y. (1994). Examination of Horwitz, Horwitz, and Cope's construct of foreign language anxiety: The case of students of Japanese. *Modern Language Journal*, 78(2), 155–168. 10.1111/j.1540-4781.1994.tb02026.x

Akbulut, Y., & Ozcelik, M. (2020). Information literacy in the digital age. *International Journal of Technology and Learning*, 16(2), 145–158.

Akinci, M., Burak, M., Kasal, F. Z., Özaslan, E. A., Huri, M., & Kurtaran, Z. A. (2024). The Effects of Combined Virtual Reality Exercises and Robot Assisted Gait Training on Cognitive Functions, Daily Living Activities, and Quality of Life in High Functioning Individuals With Subacute Stroke. *Perceptual and Motor Skills*, 131(3), 00315125241235420. 10.1177/0031512524123542038418444

Akkoyunlu, B., & Yılmaz, M. (2005). Derivativist Multimedia Learning Theory. *Hacettepe University Journal of Faculty of Education*, 28, 9–18.

Aktürk, A. O., & Şahin, İ. (2011). Üstbiliş Ve Bilgisayar Öğretimi. *Selçuk Üniversitesi Ahmet Keleşoğlu Eğitim Fakültesi Dergisi*, 31, 383–407.

Al Hakim, V. G., Yang, S.-H., Liyanawatta, M., Wang, J.-H., & Chen, G.-D. (2022). Robots in situated learning classrooms with immediate feedback mechanisms to improve students' learning performance. *Computers & Education*, 182, 104483. 10.1016/j.compedu.2022.104483

Al Omoush, M. H., & Mehigan, T. (2023). Leveraging Robotics to Enhance Accessibility and Engagement in Mathematics Education for Vision-Impaired Students. *HORA 2023 - 2023 5th International Congress on Human-Computer Interaction, Optimization and Robotic Applications, Proceedings*. IEEE. 10.1109/HORA58378.2023.10156748

Al Yakin, A., Khang, A., & Mukit, A. (2023). Personalized social-collaborative iot-symbiotic platforms in smart education ecosystem. In *Smart Cities* (pp. 204–230). CRC Press.

Al-Adwan, A. S., Nofal, M., Akram, H., Albelbisi, N. A., & Al-Okaily, M. (2022). Towards a Sustainable Adoption of E-Learning Systems: The Role of Self-Directed Learning. *Journal of Information Technology Education*, 21.

Alam, S. (2023). The conceptual relevance of English as lingua franca in non-English speaking countries: Revisiting history, policies and praxis. *Theory and Practice in Language Studies*, 13(9), 2398–2405. 10.17507/tpls.1309.28

Albritton, K., Chen, C. I., Bauer, S. G., Johnson, A., & Mathews, R. E. (2021). Collaborating with school psychologists: Moving beyond traditional assessment practices. *Young Exceptional Children*, 24(1), 28–38. 10.1177/1096250619871951

AlDaajeh, S., Saleous, H., Alrabaee, S., Barka, E., Breitinger, F., & Raymond Choo, K.-K. (2022). The role of national cybersecurity strategies on the improvement of cybersecurity education. *Computers & Security*, 119, 102754. 10.1016/j.cose.2022.102754

Aldağ, H.& Sezgin E. (2003). Dual Coding Theory and Cognitive Model in Multimedia Learning. *Çukurova University Journal of Institute of Social Sciences*, *11*(11).

Aleixo, C., Silva, S., & Godinho, T. (2023). Education 5.0 in the Context of Teaching Accounting. In *Internet of Behaviors Implementation in Organizational Contexts* (pp. 135-152). IGI Global.

Alemi, M., Meghdari, A., & Ghazisaedy, M. (2015). The impact of social robotics on L2 learners' anxiety and attitude in English vocabulary acquisition. *International Journal of Social Robotics*, 7(4), 523–535. 10.1007/s12369-015-0286-y

Alexander, J. O. (1999). Colloborative design, constructivist learning, infor- mation technology immersion & electronic communities: A case study. *Interpersonal Computing and Technology: An Electronic Journal for the 21st Century*, *7*(1-2).

Alharbi, A. M. (2023). Implementation of Education 5.0 in Developed and Developing Countries: A Comparative Study. *Creative Education*, 14(5), 914–942. 10.4236/ce.2023.145059

Alharbi, J., Almahdi, H., & Mosbah, A. (2018). The impact of entrepreneurship education programs (EEPs) on the entrepreneurial attitudes among higher education students. *International Journal of Management, Economics and Social Sciences*, 7(3), 245–271. 10.32327/IJMESS.7.3.2018.16

Al-Issa, A., & Mirhosseini, S. A. (2019). *Worldwide English Language Education Today*. Routledge. 10.4324/9780429485879

Al-Jubari, I., Mosbah, A., Talib, Z., Khalid, M. A., & Azman, N. (2019). How do entrepreneurship education and self-efficacy influence entrepreneurship intention. *International Journal of Innovation. Creativity and Change*, 5(2), 949–966.

Alkan, F. & Altundağ (Koçak), C. (2015). the role of technology in science teaching activities: Web based teaching applications. *Journal for the Education of Gifted Young Scientists*, *3*(2),1-7.

Allodi, L., Cremonini, M., Massacci, F., & Shim, W. (2018). The Effect of Security Education and Expertise on Security Assessments: The Case of Software Vulnerabilities. *Workshop of Economics of Information Security (WEIS'2018), May*.

Almaiah, M. A., Alfaisal, R., Salloum, S. A., Hajjej, F., Thabit, S., El-Qirem, F. A., Lutfi, A., Alrawad, M., Al Mulhem, A., Alkhdour, T., Awad, A. B., & Al-Maroof, R. S. (2022). Examining the Impact of Artificial Intelligence and Social and Computer Anxiety in E-Learning Settings: Students' Perceptions at the University Level. *Electronics (Basel)*, 11(22), 1–22. 10.3390/electronics11223662

Almuqati, A. A. (2019). *An Exploratory Study of Science, Technology, Engineering, and Mathematics (STEM) Teachers' Understanding and Practices Using Problem-Based Learning for Middle and High School Students* [Dissertation, Concordia University Chicago]. https://www.proquest.com/docview/2454635815

Alnwairan, M., Al Harthy, S. R., Darwish, A. S., & Yacoub, M. A. (2023). To Correct or Not to Correct: The Impact of Written Corrective Feedback on Improving Students' Writing about Literature. *World Journal of English Language*. https://api.semanticscholar.org/CorpusID:260999444

Al-Qahtani, H. M. (2015). Teachers' Voice: A Needs Analysis of Teachers' Needs for Professional Development with the Emergence of the Current English Textbooks. *English Language Teaching*, 8(8), 128–141. 10.5539/elt.v8n8p128

Alrobaian, S., Alshahrani, S., & Almaleh, A. (2023). *Cybersecurity Awareness Assessment among Trainees of the Technical and Vocational Training Corporation*. Big Data and Cognitive Computing., 10.3390/bdcc7020073

Alshebami, A., Al-Jubari, I., Alyoussef, I., & Raza, M. (2020). Entrepreneurial education as a predicator of community college of Abqaiq students' entrepreneurial intention. *Management Science Letters*, 10(15), 3605–3612. 10.5267/j.msl.2020.6.033

Altundağ, C. (2023). *Teaching profession in the 100th year of the Republic, yesterday, today and tomorrow. Teacher training from the perspective of teaching 21st century skills in the 100th year of the Republic*. Nobel.

Amado-Salvatierra, H. R., Morales-Chan, M., Hernandez-Rizzardini, R., & Rosales, M. (2024, March). Exploring Educators' Perceptions: Artificial Intelligence Integration in Higher Education. In *2024 IEEE World Engineering Education Conference (EDUNINE)* (pp. 1-5). IEEE. 10.1109/EDUNINE60625.2024.10500578

Amalia, G. R., Kurniasih, S., & Jaenudin, D. (2022). Project-Based Learning on Biotechnology Materials to Enhance High School Students' Creativity and Problem-Solving Skills. [Journal of Science Education and Practice]. *JSEP*, 6(1), 51–64. 10.33751/jsep.v6i1.5704

Amankwa, E. (2023). Relevance of Cybersecurity Education at Pedagogy Levels in Schools. In *Research Highlights in Mathematics and Computer Science* (*Vol. 7*, pp. 21–37). 10.9734/bpi/rhmcs/v7/4624B

Andrews, T., Sayer, P., & Cameron, C. (2020). Developing a growth mindset in students: A review of growth mindset interventions in school settings. *Educational Research Review*, 31, 100322.

Aprilisa, E. (2020). Realizing society 5.0 to face the industrial revolution 4.0 and teacher education curriculum readiness in Indonesia. In *Proceeding International Conference on Science and Engineering* (Vol. 3, pp. 543-548). IEEE. 10.14421/icse.v3.559

Arief, M., & Churiyah, M. (2023, May). ArsipKita to Improve Teacher Competence in Facing the New Paradigm of Education in the Era of Society 5.0. In *BISTIC Business Innovation Sustainability and Technology International Conference (BISTIC 2022)* (pp. 327-336). Atlantis Press. 10.2991/978-94-6463-178-4_33

Asmawi, A., Zakaria, S., & Wei, C. C. (2013). Understanding transformational leadership and R&D culture in Malaysian universities. *Innovation (North Sydney, N.S.W.)*, 15(3), 287–304. 10.5172/impp.2013.15.3.287

Asmd, K. (2000). *Norms and Standards for Educators* South African Minister of Education Retrieved from https://www.gov.za/sites/default/files/gcis_document/201409/20844.pdf

Avgousti, M. I. (2018). Intercultural communicative competence and online exchanges: A systematic review. *Computer Assisted Language Learning*, 31(8), 819–853. 10.1080/09588221.2018.1455713

Awodiran, M. A., Ogundele, A. T., Idem, U. J., & Anwana, E. O. (2023). Cybercrime Consciousness Among Undergraduate Students. *2023 International Conference on Cyber Management and Engineering, CyMaEn 2023*, (pp. 301–306). IEEE. 10.1109/CyMaEn57228.2023.10050982

Ayuyang, R. R. (2019). Interactive Learning (iLEARN) Tool: An eLearning Portal Designed Using MOODLE for Cagayan State University in the Philippines.*Paper presented at theProceedings of the 2019 5th International Conference on Computing and Artificial Intelligence*. Research Gate. 10.1145/3330482.3330507

Bager, T. (2011). Entrepreneurship Education and new venture creation: a comprehensive approach. In Hindle, K., & Klyver, K. (Eds.), *Handbook of Research on New Venture Creation*. Edward Elgar. 10.4337/9780857933065.00024

Baker, L., & Brown, A. L. (1980). Metacognitive skills and reading. In Pearson, P. D. (Ed.), *Handbook of Reading Research* (pp. 1–74). Longman.

Baker, R. S. J. D., & Yacef, K. (2009). The state of Educational Data Mining in 2009: A review and future visions. *Journal of Educational Data Mining*, 1(1), 3–16. https://files.eric.ed.gov/fulltext/EJ1115366.pdf

Baker, R. S., Corbett, A. T., & Koedinger, K. R. (2004). Detecting student misuse of intelligent tutoring systems. In *Intelligent Tutoring Systems* (pp. 531–540). Springer Berlin Heidelberg. 10.1007/978-3-540-30139-4_50

Barenholz, H., & Tamir, P. (1992). A comprehensive use of concept mapping in design instruction and assesment. *Research in Science & Technological Education*, 10(1), 37–52. 10.1080/0263514920100104

Barik, S. (2023). Embracing the transformative dynamics of English teaching and technology in higher education: A posthumanist perspective. *Smart Moves Journal IJELLH*, 17-31.

Barrett, M. (2018). How schools can promote the intercultural competence of young people. *European Psychologist*, 23(1), 93–104. 10.1027/1016-9040/a000308

Barrot, J. (2022). Language education. *International Encyclopedia of Education*, 216-223.

Bates. Robert, H. (2019; Vol. 1). Modernization, Ethnic Competition, and the Rationality of Politics in Contemporary Africa. In State Versus Ethnic Claims.

Becker, H. J. (1994). How Exemplary Computer-Using Teachers Differ From Other Teachers: Implications For Realizing The Potential of Computers in Schools. *Journal of Research on Computing in Education*, 26(3), 291–321. 10.1080/08886504.1994.10782093

Beevevino, M. M., Dengel, J., & Adams, K. (1999). Costructivist Theory in The Classroom: Internalizing Concepts Through Inquiry Learning. *The Clearing House: A Journal of Educational Strategies, Issues and Ideas*, 72(5), 275–278. 10.1080/00098659909599406

Behrens, A. W., Jones, M. H., & Lowery, R. S. (2018). Pediatric ocular injury secondary to a Burmese python bite. *Journal of AAPOS*, 22(5), 399–400.e1. 10.1016/j.jaapos.2018.03.00229574138

Bello, O. W., Ehira, D. N., Ayeni, J. K., Faruk, N., & Balogun, N. A. (2014). Towards the design of a synchronous virtual learning system. *Covenant Journal of Informatics and Communication Technology, 2*(2).

Belpaeme, T., Vogt, P., van den Berghe, R., Bergmann, K., Göksun, T., de Haas, M., Kanero, J., Kennedy, J., Küntay, A. C., Oudgenoeg-Paz, O., Papadopoulos, F., Schodde, T., Verhagen, J., Wallbridge, C. D., Willemsen, B., de Wit, J., Geçkin, V., Hoffmann, L., Kopp, S., & Pandey, A. K. (2018). Guidelines for Designing Social Robots as Second Language Tutors. *International Journal of Social Robotics*, 10(3), 325–341. 10.1007/s12369-018-0467-630996752

Benito-Osorio, D., Peris-Ortiz, M., Armengot, C. R., & Colino, A. (2013). Web 5.0: The future of emotional competences in higher education. *Global Business Perspectives*, 1(3), 274–287. 10.1007/s40196-013-0016-5

Berry, H. S. (2023). Survey of the Challenges and Solutions in Cybersecurity Awareness Among College Students. *ISDFS 2023 - 11th International Symposium on Digital Forensics and Security*. IEEE. 10.1109/ISDFS58141.2023.10131851

Bhatia, V., Nasser, S., & Bhansali, R. (2022). Impact of Online Education on Student Satisfaction. *International Journal Of Advance Research And Innovative Ideas In Education*, 8, 1331–1341.

Bingham, G. A., Southee, D. J., & Page, T. (2015). Meeting the expectation of industry: An integrated approach for the teaching of mechanics and electronics to design students. *European Journal of Engineering Education*, 40(4), 410–431. 10.1080/03043797.2014.1001813

Blakey, E., & Spence, S. (1990). *Developing metacognition.* Clearinghouse on Information Resources (ERIC Document Reproduction Service No. ED 327 218).

Blenker, P., Elmholdt, S. T., Frederiksen, S. H., Korsgaard, S., & Wagner, K. (2014). Methods in entrepreneurship education research: A review and integrative framework. *Education + Training*, 56(8/9), 697–715. 10.1108/ET-06-2014-0066

Boehm, S., & Kopec, D. (2016). Interior design as a post-disaster team partner. *International Journal of Disaster Resilience in the Built Environment*, 7(3), 276–289. 10.1108/IJDRBE-10-2014-0075

Bogdan, B., & Bilken, S. K. (1992). Quality research for education: An introduction to theory and methods. *Qualitative Research For Education An Introduction to Theory and Methods : Allyn and Bacon.*, 106–156.

Boss, S., & Krauss, J. (2022). *Reinventing project-based learning: Your field guide to real-world projects in the digital age.* International Society for Technology in Education.

Brockett, R. G., & Hiemstra, R. (2018). *Self-direction in adult learning: Perspectives on theory, research and practice.* Routledge. 10.4324/9780429457319

Broo, D. G., Kaynak, O., & Sait, S. M. (2022). Rethinking engineering education at the age of industry 5.0. *Journal of Industrial Information Integration*, 25, 100311. 10.1016/j.jii.2021.100311

Brooks, G., & Books, M. G. (1993). *The case for constructivist classrooms.* ASCD Alexandria.

Brothers, P. (2019, February 24). Ten charts that explain the global education technology market. *Medium.* https://medium.com/@patrickbrothers/ten-charts-that-explain-the-global-education-technology-market-6809fa68484c

Brown, A. L. (1980). Metacognitive development and reading. In Spiro, R. J., Bruce, B. C., & Brewer, W. F. (Eds.), *Theoretical issues in reading comprehension* (pp. 453–481). Routledge.

Bruner, J. S. (2009). *The process of education.* Harvard University Press. 10.2307/j.ctvk12qst

Bülbül, A. H. (2019). *The Effect of Emotional Design in Multimedia Applications on Cognitive Load, Motivation, Subject Interest and Learning.* Anadolu University Graduate School of Educational Sciences.

Butler, D., Leahy, M., Twining, P., Akoh, B., Chtouki, Y., Farshadnia, S., Moore, K., Nikolov, R., Pascual, C., Sherman, B., & Valtonen, T. (2018). Education systems in the digital age: The need for alignment. *Technology. Knowledge and Learning*, 23(3), 473–494. 10.1007/s10758-018-9388-6

Cai, Y., Judd, K. L., & Lontzek, T. S. (2012). *Continuous-time methods for integrated assessment models (No. w18365).* National Bureau of Economic Research. 10.3386/w18365

Cakmak, E. K. (2007). Bottleneck in Multiple Environments: Cognitive Overload. *Gazi University Gazi Faculty of Education Journal*, 27(2), 1–24.

Calderón, A., Boubeta-Puig, J., & Ruiz, M. (2018). MEdit4CEP-Gam: A model driven approach for user-friendly gamification design, monitoring and code generation in CEP-based systems. *Information and Software Technology*, 95, 238–264. 10.1016/j.infsof.2017.11.009

Callan, G. L., Marchant, G. J., Finch, W. H., & German, R. L. (2016). Metacognition, strategies, achievement, and demographics: Relationships across countries. *Educational Sciences: Theory & Practice*, 16, 1485–1502.

Cao, W. (2023). A meta-analysis of effects of blended learning on performance, attitude, achievement, and engagement across different countries. *Frontiers in Psychology*, 14, 1212056. 10.3389/fpsyg.2023.121205637502744

Caplan, B. (2018). *The case against education: Why the education system is a waste of time and money.* Princeton University Press.

Carayannis, E. G., & Morawska-Jancelewicz, J. (2022). The Futures of Europe: Society 5.0 and Industry 5.0 as Driving Forces of Future Universities. *Journal of the Knowledge Economy*, 13(4), 3445–3471. 10.1007/s13132-021-00854-2

Carmona Marques, P. (2017). Comparing Freshman and doctoral engineering students in design: Mapping with a descriptive framework. *European Journal of Engineering Education*, 42(6), 1097–1112. 10.1080/03043797.2016.1263277

Carpenter, M. S., Yakymyshyn, C., Micher, L. E., & Locke, A. (2016, June). Improved student engagement through project-based learning in freshman engineering design. In *2016 ASEE Annual Conference & Exposition*. ASEE. 10.18260/p.25602

Celik, I. (2023). Towards Intelligent-TPACK: An empirical study on teachers' professional knowledge to ethically integrate artificial intelligence (AI)-based tools into education. *Computers in Human Behavior*, 138, 107468. 10.1016/j.chb.2022.107468

Chachra, D. (2005). Beyond course-based engineering ethics instruction: Commentary on "topics and cases for online education in engineering. *Science and Engineering Ethics*, 11(3), 459–461. 10.1007/s11948-005-0015-216190286

Chaer, M. T., Wahyuna, A. H., & Fitriana, S. (2020). Teacher Professionalism and Educational Challenges of The Industrial Revolution 5.0. *AL-MURABBI: Jurnal Studi Kependidikan dan Keislaman, 7*(1), 53-63.

Chang, Y., Chen, Y., & Lin, Y. (2021). The importance of social and emotional learning (SEL) in Education 5.0. *International Journal of Learning and Development*, 11(2), 213–222.

Chen Hsieh, J., & Lee, J. S. (2023). Digital storytelling outcomes, emotions, grit, and perceptions among EFL middle school learners: Robot-assisted versus PowerPoint-assisted presentations. *Computer Assisted Language Learning*, 36(5–6), 1088–1115. 10.1080/09588221.2021.1969410

Cheng, M. Y., Chan, W. S., & Mahmood, A. (2009). The effectiveness of entrepreneurship education in Malaysia. *Education + Training*, 51(7), 555–566. 10.1108/00400910910992754

Cheng, Y. S., Horwitz, E. K., & Schallert, D. L. (1999). Language anxiety: Differentiating writing and speaking components. *Language Learning*, 49(3), 417–446. 10.1111/0023-8333.00095

Chen, L., Chen, P., & Lin, Z. (2020). Artificial intelligence in education: A review. *IEEE Access : Practical Innovations, Open Solutions*, 8, 75264–75278. 10.1109/ACCESS.2020.2988510

Chen, M., Herrera, F., & Hwang, K. (2018). Cognitive Computing: Architecture, Technologies and Intelligent Applications. *IEEE Access : Practical Innovations, Open Solutions*, 6, 19774–19783. 10.1109/ACCESS.2018.2791469

Chen, P., Liu, X., & Li, Y. (2021). Promoting metacognition in the era of Education 5.0: A review of literature. *Studies in Educational Sciences*, 11(12), 1183–1192.

Chen, S. Y., Lai, C. F., Lai, Y. H., & Su, Y. S. (2022). Effect of project-based learning on development of students' creative thinking. *International Journal of Electrical Engineering Education*, 59(3), 232–250. 10.1177/0020720919846808

Chetty, K., Qigui, L., Gcora, N., Josie, J., Wenwei, L., & Fang, C. (2018). Bridging the digital divide: Measuring digital literacy. *Economics*, 12(1), 20180023. 10.5018/economics-ejournal.ja.2018-23

Chiang, Y. hui V., Cheng, Y. W., & Chen, N. S. (2023). Improving Language Learning Activity Design through Identifying Learning Difficulties in a Platform Using Educational Robots and IoTbased Tangible Objects. *Journal of Educational Technology & Society*, 26(3), 84–100. 10.30191/ETS.202307_26(3).0007

Chin, A., Jones, B., & Little, P. (2021). A Comparative Analysis of Smartphone Security Behaviors and Practices. [IJEDICT]. *International Journal of Education and Development Using Information and Communication Technology*, 17, 57–80.

Chiva, R., & Alegre, J. (2009). Investment in Design and Firm Performance: The Mediating Role of Design Management. *Journal of Product Innovation Management*, 26(4), 424–440. 10.1111/j.1540-5885.2009.00669.x

Choudhuri, S., & Kumar, D. (2022). Online Education and Its Viability during Pandemic. *Journal of Pharmaceutical Negative Results*, 13, 1308.

Christiensen, R. (2002). Effects of Technology Integration Education on the Attitudes of Teachers and Students. *Journal of Research on Technology in Education*, 34(4), 411–433. 10.1080/15391523.2002.10782359

Christopher, N. (2022). *Why Indian universities are ditching English-only education.* Rest of World. https://restofworld.org/2022/indian-universities-are-ditching-english-only-education/

Clifford, B. (2018). *Understanding Disinterest: How Online Undergraduate Students Perceive And Respond To Disengaged Faculty Members.*

Coccoli, M., Maresca, P., & Stanganelli, L. (2016). Cognitive computing in education. *Journal of E-Learning and Knowledge Society*, 12(2), 55–69. 10.20368/1971-8829/1185

Collins, J. (2009). Lifelong learning in the 21st century and beyond. *Radiographics*, 29(2), 613–622. 10.1148/rg.292085179 19325069

Coman, C., îru, L. G., Mese an-Schmitz, L., Stanciu, C., & Bularca, M. C. J. S. (2020). Online teaching and learning in higher education during the coronavirus pandemic: students' perspective. *12*(24), 10367.

Craft, A. M., & Capraro, R. M. (2017). Science, technology, engineering, and mathematics project-based learning: Merging rigor and relevance to increase student engagement. *Electronic International Journal of Education, Arts, and Science (EIJEAS), 3*(6).

Cruz, N. M., Rodriguez Escudero, A. I., Hernangomez Barahona, J., & Saboia Leitao, F. (2009). The effect of entrepreneurship education programmes on satisfaction with innovation behaviour and performance. *Journal of European Industrial Training*, 33(3), 198–214. 10.1108/03090590910950578

Dafik. (2023). The framework of project-based learning (PJBL) activities with steam approach in enhancing creative thinking skills in solving data presentation problems based on ethnomathematics. *International Journal of Multidisciplinary Research and Growth Evaluation, 4*(3), 495-504. 10.54660/.IJMRGE.2023.4.3.495-504

Dahri, N. A., Vighio, M. S., Bather, J. D., & Arain, A. A. (2021). Factors influencing the acceptance of mobile collaborative learning for the continuous professional development of teachers. *Sustainability (Basel)*, 13(23), 13222. 10.3390/su132313222

Davidsen, H. M., & Sørensen, K. B. (2017). A holistic design perspective on entrepreneurship education. *Universal Journal of Educational Research*, 5(10), 1818–1826. 10.13189/ujer.2017.051020

De Jager, B., Jansen, M., & Reezigt, G. (2005). The development of metacognition in primary school learning environments. *School Effectiveness and School Improvement*, 16(2), 179–196. 10.1080/09243450500114181

Delgado, P. (2020). *Synchronous and asynchronous learning: definition, advantages, and disadvantages.* TEC. https://observatory.tec.mx/edu-news/synchronous-and-asynchronous-learning-definitions

Delil, A., & Güleş, S. (2007). Evaluation of Geometry and Measurement Learning Areas in the New Primary 6th Grade Mathematics Programme in terms of Constructivist Learning Approach. *Journal of Uludağ University Faculty of Education*, 20(1), 35.

Demir, A. N., & Zaimoglu, S. (2021). The relationship between foreign language anxiety and decision-making strategies among university students. *Journal of Language and Linguistic Studies*, 17(1, S1), 18–32. 10.17263/jlls.903294

Deshpande, A. M. (2022). Project Based Learning Approach in Digital Signal Processing Course for Increasing Learners' Cognitive and Behavioral Engagement to Promote Self-Learning. *Journal of Engineering Education Transformations, 36*(Special Issue 1).

Deterding, S., Dixon, D., Khaled, R., & Nacke, L. (2011). From game design elements to gamefulness: Defining "gamification". In *Proceedings of the 15th International Academic MindTrek Conference: Envisioning Future Media Environments* (pp. 9-15). ACM. 10.1145/2181037.2181040

Dimulescu, C., & Nechifor, A. (2022). Accommodating English for Specific Purposes to Computer Assisted Language Learning. *Bulletin of the Transilvania University of Brasov. Series IV: Philology and Cultural Studies, 14*(2), 5–18. 10.31926/but.pcs.2021.63.14.2.1

Du, X., Yang, J., Hung, J.-L., & Shelton, B. (2020). Educational data mining: A systematic review of research and emerging trends. *Information Discovery and Delivery*, 48(4), 225–236. 10.1108/IDD-09-2019-0070

Early, D. M., Maxwell, K. L., Ponder, B. D., & Pan, Y. (2017). Improving teacher-child interactions: A randomized controlled trial of Making the Most of Classroom Interactions and My Teaching Partner professional development models. *Early Childhood Research Quarterly*, 38, 57–70. 10.1016/j.ecresq.2016.08.005

Eden, C. A., Chisom, O. N., & Adeniyi, I. S. (2024). Cultural competence in education: Strategies for fostering inclusivity and diversity awareness. *International Journal of Applied Research in Social Sciences*, 6(3), 383–392. 10.51594/ijarss.v6i3.895

Edwards, S. H. (2003). *Rethinking computer science education from a test-first perspective*. Paper presented at the Companion of the 18th annual ACM SIGPLAN conference on Object-oriented programming, systems, languages, and applications, Anaheim, CA, USA. 10.1145/949344.949390

Eggermont, M., Brennan, R. W., & O'Neill, T. (2015). *The impact of project-based learning on self-directed learning readiness.*

Eliwatis, E., Aprison, W., Maimori, R., Herawati, S., & Putri, Y. M. (2022). Challenges of society era Education 5.0: Revitalization of teacher competencies and learning models. *Darussalam. Journal of Psychology and Educational*, 1(2), 1–11.

Ellis, R. D., & Kurniawan, S. H. (2000). Increasing the usability of online information for older users: A case study in participatory design. *International Journal of Human-Computer Interaction*, 12(2), 263–276. 10.1207/S15327590IJHC1202_6

Ely, D. P. (1993). *The Field of Educational Technology: A Dozen Frequently Asked Questions*. ERIC Digest # ED366330.

Enaya, B. P., & Villaroya, A. F. (2021). Sartrean Freedom and Responsibility in Rousseau's Emile. *Philippine Social Science Journal*, 4(1), 117–126. 10.52006/main.v4i1.320

Erdem, E., & Demirel, Ö. (2002). Constructivism Approach in Programme Development. *Hacettepe University Journal of Faculty of Education*, 23, 81–87.

Erickson, A. S. G., Noonan, P. M., & McCall, Z. (2012). Effectiveness of online professional development for rural special educators. *Rural Special Education Quarterly*, 31(1), 22–32. 10.1177/875687051203100104

Ersoy, M., & Güneyli, A. (2016). Social networking as a tool for lifelong learning with orthopedically impaired learners. *Journal of Educational Technology & Society*, 19(1), 41–52.

ESET. (2017). *2015 ESET Asia Cyber Savviness Report*. ESET.

Evmenova, A. (2018). Preparing teachers to use universal design for learning to support diverse learners. *Journal of Online Learning Research*, 4(2), 147–171.

Express, T. N. I. (2013). Poor English skills drive students to suicide. *New Indian Express*.https://www.newindianexpress.com/states/tamil-nadu/2013/aug/07/Poor-English-skills-drive-student-to-suicide-504655.html

Fahri, A. F., & Azani, M. Z. (2023). Development of Islamic Religious Education Teachers in the Era of Society 5.0. *Tadrib*, 9(1), 159–166.

Fakaruddin, F. J., Shahali, E. H. M., & Saat, R. M. (2024). Creative thinking patterns in primary school students' hands-on science activities involving robotic as learning tools. *Asia Pacific Education Review*, 25(1), 171–186. 10.1007/s12564-023-09825-5

Farahani, M. F. (2012). Ethics principles in distance education. *Procedia: Social and Behavioral Sciences*, 46, 890–894. 10.1016/j.sbspro.2012.05.218

Faridi, A. (2020). The importance of communication skills in the digital age. *Journal of Applied Communication Research*, 48(3), 232–248.

Fayolle, A. (2013). Personal views on the future of entrepreneurship education. *Entrepreneurship and Regional Development*, 25(7–8), 692–701. 10.1080/08985626.2013.821318

Fayolle, A. (2018). Personal views on the future of entrepreneurship education. In *A research agenda for entrepreneurship education* (pp. 127–138). Edward Elgar Publishing. 10.4337/9781786432919.00013

Feigin, V. L., Nichols, E., Alam, T., Bannick, M. S., Beghi, E., Blake, N., Culpepper, W. J., Dorsey, E. R., Elbaz, A., Ellenbogen, R. G., Fisher, J. L., Fitzmaurice, C., Giussani, G., Glennie, L., James, S. L., Johnson, C. O., Kassebaum, N. J., Logroscino, G., Marin, B., & Vos, T. (2019). Global, regional, and national burden of neurological disorders, 1990–2016: A systematic analysis for the Global Burden of Disease Study 2016. *Lancet Neurology*, 18(5), 459–480. 10.1016/S1474-4422(18)30499-X30879893

Fernandes, V. (2019). Investigating the role of data-driven decision-making within school improvement processes. In *Evidence-based initiatives for organizational change and development* (pp. 201–219). IGI Global. 10.4018/978-1-5225-6155-2.ch010

Ferry, B., Herberg, S., & Harper, B. (1996). How Do Preserves Teachers Use Concept Maps to Organize Their Curriculum Concept Knowledge, *Research in Science Education. Cilt*, 26, 205–209.

Feser, M. S., Haak, I., & Rabe, T. (2023). *VeSP-Be – Vergleich von Studieneingangsphasen in Physik hinsichtlich des Sense of Belonging von Studierenden. Dokumentation der Erhebungsinstrumente und deren deskriptive, quantitative Ergebnisse. 9*. https://doi.org/10.25656/01

Fischer, L., Nistor, A., & Morar, A. (2020). Problem-solving skills in the digital age: A theoretical framework. *Journal of Information Technology Education*, 19(1), 187–202.

Fisher, R. (1998). Thinking about thinking: Developing metacognition in children. *Early Child Development and Care*, 141(1), 1–15. 10.1080/0300443981410101

Flavell, J. H. (1976). Metacognitive aspects of problem solving. In Resnick, L. (Ed.), *The Nature of Intelligence* (pp. 231–236). Erlbaum.

Flavell, J. H. (1979). Metacognition and cognitive monitoring: A new area of cognitive–developmental inquiry. *The American Psychologist*, 34(10), 906–911. 10.1037/0003-066X.34.10.906

Forcier, C. R., & Descy, E. D. (2002). *The computer as an educational tool: productivity and problem solving*. Merrill Prentice Hall.

Fox, J., & Gambino, A. (2021). Relationship Development with Humanoid Social Robots: Applying Interpersonal Theories to Human-Robot Interaction. *Cyberpsychology, Behavior, and Social Networking*, 24(5), 294–299. 10.1089/cyber.2020.018133434097

Fulgence, K. (2020). Developing Digital Fluency among Teacher Educators: Evidence from Tanzanian Schools of Education. *International Journal of Education and Development Using Information and Communication Technology*, 158–175.

Fullan, M. (2017). *Rethinking professional development: Change, learning, and innovation in schools* (3 ed.). Dar es saam: John Wiley & Sons.

Furrer, O., Sudharshan, D., Tsiotsou, R., & Liu, B. S. (2016). A framework for innovative service design. *Service Industries Journal*, 36(9-10), 452–471. 10.1080/02642069.2016.1248420

García, O., & Kleifgen, J. A. (2018). *Educating emergent bilinguals: Policies, programs, and practices for English learners*. Teachers College Press.

Gay, G. (2018). *Culturally responsive teaching: Theory, research, and practice*. teachers college press.

Geçkin, V. (2023). Assessing the Learning Outcomes of Robot-Assisted Second Language Learning. In *Handbook of Research on Perspectives in Foreign Language Assessment* (p. 18). IGI Global. 10.4018/978-1-6684-5660-6.ch005

Gee, J. P. (2003). What video games have to teach us about learning and literacy. [CIE]. *Computers in Entertainment*, 1(1), 20–20. 10.1145/950566.950595

Gibbs, A. (2016). Academic freedom in international higher education: Right or responsibility? *Ethics and Education*, 11(2), 175–185. 10.1080/17449642.2016.1181844

Glenn, C. L., De Groof, J., & Candal, C. S. (2005). *Balancing Freedom, Autonomy and Accountability in Education* (Vol. I). Wolf Legal Publishers.

Goertz, M. E. (1996). *Studies of education reform: Systemic reform* (Vol. 1). Department of Education.

Gómez Puente, S. M., van Eijck, M., & Jochems, V. (2015). Professional development for design-based learning in engineering education: A case study. *European Journal of Engineering Education*, 40(1), 14–31. 10.1080/03043797.2014.903228

González-Pérez, L. I., & Ramírez-Montoya, M. S. (2022). Components of Education 4.0 in 21st century skills frameworks: Systematic review. *Sustainability (Basel)*, 14(3), 1493. 10.3390/su14031493

Green, L. W., & Glasgow, R. E. (2006). Evaluating the relevance, generalization, and applicability of research: Issues in external validation and translation methodology. *Evaluation & the Health Professions*, 29(1), 126–153. 10.1177/0163278705284445165 10882

Greenlaw, R., & Hepp, E. (1999). *In-line / On-line: Fundamentals of the Internet and The World Wide Web*. McGraw-Hill.

Gunawan, I. G. D., & Danika, I. W. S. G. (2023). Leveraging Advanced Technologies to Enhance Learning Experiences in the Era 5.0. *International Proceeding On Religion, Culture, Law, Education, And Hindu Studies*, 1, 121–137.

Guo, Y., Xu, J., & Chen, C. (2022). Measurement of engagement in the foreign language classroom and its effect on language achievement: the case of Chinese college EFL students. *International Review of Applied Linguistics in Language Teaching, 0*. https://api.semanticscholar.org/CorpusID:246362278

Gupta, M. (2021). *The implications of 'mother tongue education': India's national education policy 2020.* Education South Asia. https://educationsouthasia.web.ox.ac.uk/article/thinkpiece11

Guskey, T. F. (2022). *Evaluating professional development* (2 ed.). Tokyo: Evaluating professional development.

Hadi, S. A. (2022). Foreign Language Learning in Light of Cognitive Learning Theory. *Journal of English Language Teaching and Applied Linguistics*. https://api.semanticscholar.org/CorpusID:253755264

Hägg, G., & Kurczewska, A. (2022). *Entrepreneurship education: Scholarly progress and future challenges*. Taylor & Francis.

Halder, S. (2023). *Global Economic Integration-Challenges and Prospects.*

Hall, A. B., & Trespalacios, J. (2019). Personalized professional learning and teacher self-efficacy for integrated technology in K-12 classrooms. *Journal of Digital Learning in Teacher Education*, 35(4), 221–235. 10.1080/21532974.2019.1647579

Hall, A., & Miro, D. (2016). A study of student engagement in project-based learning across multiple approaches to STEM education programs. *School Science and Mathematics*, 116(6), 310–319. 10.1111/ssm.12182

Halverson, A. C., & Collins, R. (2009). *Rethinking education in the age of technology*. Teachers College, Columbia University.

Hands, C. M., Armstrong, D. E., & Mitchell, C. (2020). Collaborative Learning and Knowledge-Sharing: The Potential of New Administrator Networks and Mentoring Programs. *The Wiley International Handbook of Mentoring: Paradigms, Practices, Programs, and Possibilities*, 205-222. Wiley.

Hantoobi, S., Wahdan, A., Al-Emran, M., & Shaalan, K. (2021). A Review of Learning Analytics Studies. In Al-Emran, M., & Shaalan, K. (Eds.), *Recent advances in technology acceptance models and theories* (pp. 119–134). Springer Nature. 10.1007/978-3-030-64987-6_8

Harison, E., & Warshavski, T. (2014). Exploring the links between design and innovation: evidence from Israeli firms, *UNU-MERIT Innovation & Governance in Development Conference*. Maastricht.

Hartanto, B. (2022). Grammatical Errors in English Study Made by UIB Students. *Issues in Applied Linguistics & Language Teaching*. https://api.semanticscholar.org/CorpusID:258850624

Hashim, C. N., Azman, S. M. M. S., & Azman, S. N. A. S. (2014). Academic Freedom and Educational Responsibility in Malaysian Higher Institutions of Learning. *IIUM Journal of Educational Studies*, 2(1), 1–11. 10.31436/ijes.v2i1.30

Hattie, J., & Timperley, H. (2007). The power of feedback. *Review of Educational Research*, 77(1), 81–112. 10.3102/003465430298487

Hennen, L., & Van Est, R. (2023). Globalisation as Reflexive Modernisation—Implications for S&T Governance. In *Technology Assessment in a Globalized World: Facing the Challenges of Transnational Technology Governance* (pp. 53–73). Springer International Publishing. 10.1007/978-3-031-10617-0_4

Herodotou, C., Sharples, M., Gaved, M., Kukulska-Hulme, A., Rienties, B., Scanlon, E., & Whitelock, D. (2019). Innovative Pedagogies of the Future: An Evidence-Based Selection. *Frontiers in Education*, 4, 113. Advance online publication. 10.3389/feduc.2019.00113

Himmetoglu, B., Aydug, D., & Bayrak, C. (2020). Education 4.0: Defining the teacher, the student, and the school manager aspects of the revolution. *Turkish Online Journal of Distance Education, 21*(Special Issue-IODL), 12-28.

Hodges, C., Smith, M., Hayes, D., & Watson, J. (2021). Lifelong learning and the future of higher education. *Teaching & Learning Inquiry*, 10(1), 104–121.

Holmberg, B. (1995). Theory of Interaction and Communication. In Sewart, D., Keegan, D., & Holmberg, B. (Eds.), *Distance education: International perspectives* (pp. 34–45). Routledge.

Hong, Z.-W., Chen, Y.-L., & Lan, C.-H. (2014). A courseware to script animated pedagogical agents in instructional material for elementary students in English education. *Computer Assisted Language Learning*, 27(5), 379–394. 10.1080/09588221.2012.733712

Hong, Z.-W., Huang, Y.-M., Hsu, M., & Shen, W.-W. (2016). Authoring Robot-Assisted Instructional Materials for Improving Learning Performance and Motivation in EFL Classrooms. *Journal of Educational Technology & Society*, 19, 337–349. https://api.semanticscholar.org/CorpusID:17667686

Hornby, S. A. (1998). *Oxford Advanced Learner's Dictionary* (Edition, S. P., Ed.). Oxford University Press.

Horwitz, E. K., Horwitz, M. B., & Cope, J. (1986). Foreign language classroom anxiety. *Modern Language Journal*, 70(2), 125–132. 10.1111/j.1540-4781.1986.tb05256.x

Hrastinski, S., Olofsson, A. D., Arkenback, C., Ekström, S., Ericsson, E., Fransson, G., Jaldemark, J., Ryberg, T., Öberg, L.-M., Fuentes, A., Gustafsson, U., Humble, N., Mozelius, P., Sundgren, M., & Utterberg, M. (2019). Critical Imaginaries and Reflections on Artificial Intelligence and Robots in Postdigital K-12 Education. *Postdigital Science and Education*, 1(2), 427–445. 10.1007/s42438-019-00046-x

Hsu, T.-C., Chang, C., & Liang, Y. S. (2023). Sequential Behavior Analysis of Interdisciplinary Activities in Computational Thinking and EFL Learning With Game-Based Learning. *IEEE Transactions on Learning Technologies*, 16(2), 256–265. https://api.semanticscholar.org/CorpusID:257320094. 10.1109/TLT.2023.3249749

Huang, G., & Moore, R. K. (2023). Using social robots for language learning: Are we there yet? *Journal of China Computer-Assisted Language Learning*, 3(1), 208–230. 10.1515/jccall-2023-001338013743

Huang, Y.-T., Chen, M. C., & Sun, Y. S. (2018). *Development and Evaluation of a Personalized Computer-aided Question Generation for English Learners to Improve Proficiency and Correct Mistakes*. http://arxiv.org/abs/1808.09732

Huisinga, R. N., & Martin, Y. (2017). *Indigenous Agricultural Knowledge and Gender issues in third world Agricultural Development.* India: Agricultural company.co.limited.

Hwang, G., & Lim, S. (2022). Data analysis skills in the era of Education 5.0: A review of literature. [JETDE]. *Journal of Educational Technology Development and Exchange*, 16(3), 221–234.

Hymel, S., & Katz, J. (2019). Designing classrooms for diversity: Fostering social inclusion. *Educational Psychologist*, 54(4), 331–339. 10.1080/00461520.2019.1652098

Ibiloye, A. (2021). Perspectives on Blended Learning Models and Recommendations on Instructional Applications. Academia Letters. *Distributed under CC BY 4.0.*

Ifenthaler, D., Bellin-Mularski, N., & Mah, D. K. (2016). *Foundation of digital badges and micro-credentials*. Springer International Publishing. 10.1007/978-3-319-15425-1

Ihsan, I. (2023). The challenges of elementary education in society 5.0 era. [IJSL]. *International Journal of Social Learning*, 3(3), 341–360.

Iio, T., Maeda, R., Ogawa, K., Yoshikawa, Y., Ishiguro, H., Suzuki, K., Aoki, T., Maesaki, M., & Hama, M. (2019). Improvement of Japanese adults' English speaking skills via experiences speaking to a robot. *Journal of Computer Assisted Learning*, 35(2), 228–245. 10.1111/jcal.12325

Ijudin, I., Ainissyifa, H., & Wakila, Y. F. (2022). Being an Inspiring Teacher in Realizing Competitive Education in the Era of Society 5.0. *Al-Abshar: Journal of Islamic Education Management*, 1(1), 77–87. 10.58223/al-abshar.v1i1.12

Illahi, P. C., Fitri, R., & Arsih, F. (2022). The Effect of Project Based Learning Model on Creative Thinking Ability in Biology Learning. *Journal of Digital Learning and Education*, 2(3), 171–177. 10.52562/jdle.v2i3.441

Imbaquingo, A., & Cárdenas, J. (2023). Project-based learning as a methodology to improve reading and comprehension skills in the English language. *Education Sciences*, 13(6), 587. 10.3390/educsci13060587

Irfan, A., Rasli, A., Sulaiman, Z., Sami, A., & Qureshi, M. I. (2018). Use of Social Media Sites by Malaysian Universities and its Impact on University Ranking. *International Journal of Engineering & Technology*. www.sciencepubco.com/index.php/IJET

Irfan, M. T., & Gudivada, V. N. (2016). Cognitive computing applications in education and learning. In *Handbook of Statistics* (pp. 283–300). Elsevier.

Ismail, A. R., Nguyen, B., & Melewar, T. C. (2018). Impact of perceived social media marketing activities on brand and value consciousness: Roles of usage, materialism and conspicuous consumption. *International Journal of Internet Marketing and Advertising*, 12(3), 233. 10.1504/IJIMA.2018.093387

Ismanto, B., & Erbianita, S. L. (2019). Determining Pedagogic And Professional Competencies Among Students In Realizing Society 5.0. *ECONOMICA Jurnal Program Studi Pendidikan Ekonomi STKIP PGRI Sumatera Barat*, 8(1), 20–27. 10.22202/economica.2019.v8.i1.3593

Ivie, S. D. (1998). Ausubel's Learning Theory: An Approach To Teaching Higher Order Thinking Skills.(educational psychologist David Paul Ausubel). *High School Journal*, 82(1), 35.

Jackson, J. (2019). *Introducing language and intercultural communication*. Routledge. 10.4324/9781351059275

Jantan, H., Hamdan, Gatautis, R., Dagiene, V., & Futschek, G. (2016). Gamification and education: A literature review. In Proceedings of the 11th European Conference on Game Based Learning (pp. 230-238). Academic Conferences International Limited.

Jayashanka, R., Hettiarachchi, E., & Hewagamage, K. P. (2022). Technology enhanced learning analytics dashboard in higher education. *Electronic Journal of e-Learning*, 20(2), 151–170. 10.34190/ejel.20.2.2189

Jensen, T. L. (2014). A holistic person perspective in measuring entrepreneurship education impact–Social entrepreneurship education at the Humanities. *International Journal of Management Education*, 12(3), 349–364. 10.1016/j.ijme.2014.07.002

Jimenez-Aleixandre, M. P. (2007). Designing argumentation learning enviroments. In Erduran, S., & Jimenez-Aleixandre, M. P. (Eds.), *Argumentation in Science Education: Perstectives from Classroom-Based Research* (pp. 3–27). Springer. 10.1007/978-1-4020-6670-2_5

Jiménez-Guerrero, J. F., Gázquez-Abad, J. C., & Ceballos-Santamaría, G.Jiménez-Guerrero. (2015). Innovation in eco-packaging in private labels. *Innovation (North Sydney, N.S.W.)*, 17(1), 81–90. 10.1080/14479338.2015.1011055

Jonassen, D. H. (1994). Towards a Constructivist Design Model. *Educational Technology*, 34(4), 34–37.

Jyothi, A. P., Badiger, V. N., & Shivakumar, V. (2023). Security in Social Networks and Media. *IEEE International Conference on Advances in Electronics, Communication, Computing and Intelligent Information Systems, ICAECIS 2023 - Proceedings*. IEEE. 10.1109/ICAECIS58353.2023.10170002

Kakoty, S., Lal, M., & Sarma, S. K. (2011). E-learning as a research area: An analytical approach. *International Journal of Advanced Computer Science and Applications*, 2(9), 144–148. 10.14569/IJACSA.2011.020923

Kalaycı, N., & Çakmak, M. (2000). Using Concept Maps in the Teaching Process. *Journal of Educational Administration in Theory and Practice.*, 24, 571–580.

Kalemkuş, J. (2021). Bilmeyi Bilme: Üstbiliş. *Atatürk Üniversitesi Kazım Karabekir Eğitim Fakültesi Dergisi*, (42), 471–495.

Kalsoom, A., Soomro, N. H., & Pathan, Z. H. (2020). How social support and foreign language anxiety impact willingness to communicate in English in an EFL classroom. *International Journal of English Linguistics*, 10(2), 80–91. 10.5539/ijel.v10n2p80

Kanero, J., Oranç, C., Koskulu, S., Kumkale, G. T., Göksun, T., & Küntay, A. C. (2021). Are Tutor Robots for Everyone? The Influence of Attitudes, Anxiety, and Personality on Robot-Led Language Learning. *International Journal of Social Robotics*, 14(2), 297–312. https://api.semanticscholar.org/CorpusID:235543442. 10.1007/s12369-021-00789-3

Kantipudi, M. V. V. P., Aluvalu, R., Maheswari, U. V., & Raisinghani, M. S. (2022). Insights on implications of cognitive computing in leveraging online education systems. *International Journal of Online Pedagogy and Course Design*, 12(1), 1–16. 10.4018/IJOPCD.302082

Kapp, K. M. (2012). *The gamification of learning and instruction: Game-based methods and strategies for training and education*. John Wiley & Sons.

Kaptan, F. (1998). Using Concept Map Method in Science Teaching. *Hacettepe University Journal of Faculty of Education*, 14, 95–99.

Karadağ, E., Deniz, S., Korkmaz, T., & Deniz, G. (2008). Constructivist Learning Approach: A Research within the Scope of Classroom Teachers' Opinions. *Journal of Uludağ University Faculty of Education*, 21(2), 383–402.

Karataş, S., & Yapıcı, M. (2006). Öğretim Teknolojileri ve Materyal Geliştirme Dersinin İşlenişi ve Uygulama Örnekleri. *Afyon Kocatepe Üniversitesi Sosyal Bilimler Dergisi*, 8(2), 311–325.

Karimi, S., Biemans, H. J., Lans, T., Aazami, M., & Mulder, M. (2016). Fostering students' competence in identifying business opportunities in entrepreneurship education. *Innovations in Education and Teaching International*, 53(2), 215–229. 10.1080/14703297.2014.993419

Katz, J. A. (2003). The chronology and intellectual trajectory of American entrepreneurship education: 1876–1999. *Journal of Business Venturing*, 18(2), 283–300. 10.1016/S0883-9026(02)00098-8

Kaul, V., & Kaul, A. (2022). A QFD Approach to Design a Blockchain-Based Professional Development Module in Education System for Society 5.0. In *Blockchain Technology in Supply Chain Management for Society 5.0* (pp. 157–169). CRC Press. 10.1201/9781003177432-15

Kaur, G. (2017, June 6). THE IMPORTANCE OF DIGITAL MARKETING IN THE TOURISM. *International Journal of Research Granthaalayah*, 5(6), 72–77. 10.29121/granthaalayah.v5.i6.2017.1998

Kaur, K. (2023, June 3). Teaching and Learning with ICT tools: Issues and Challenges. *International Journal on Cybernetics & Informatics*, 12(3), 15–22. 10.5121/ijci.2023.120302

Kauthamy, K., Ashrafi, N., & Kuilboer, J. P. (2017). Mobile Devices and Cyber Security: An Exploratory Study on User's Response to Cyber Security Challenges. *WEBIST 2017 - Proceedings of the 13th International Conference on Web Information Systems and Technologies*, (pp. 306–311). Research Gate. 10.5220/0006298803060311

Kaya, O. N. (2003). Concept Maps in Science Education. *Pamukkale University Journal of Faculty of Education*, 13, 70–79.

Kaymak, H. (2005). *The Effect of Concept Map Method on Students' Understanding of Periodic Table*. Pamukkale University Graduate School of Natural and Applied Sciences.

Keegan, D. (2013). *Foundations of distance education*. Routledge. 10.4324/9781315004822

Kennedy, J., Lemaignan, S., Montassier, C., Lavalade, P., Irfan, B., Papadopoulos, F., Senft, E., & Belpaeme, T. (2017). Child Speech Recognition in Human-Robot Interaction: Evaluations and Recommendations. *ACM/IEEE International Conference on Human-Robot Interaction, Part F1271*, (pp. 82–90). IEEE. 10.1145/2909824.3020229

Kennette, L., & Chapman, M. (2021). Providing positive student feedback in an online environment. *Academia Letters*, 1-3.

Keselman, H. J., Algina, J., & Kowalchuk, R. K. (2001). Analysis of repeated measures designs: A review. *British Journal of Mathematical & Statistical Psychology*, 54(1), 1–20. 10.1348/000711001159357113938 94

Keshav, M., Julien, L., & Miezel, J. (2022). The Role of Technology in Era 5.0 in the Development of Arabic Language in the World of Education. *JILTECH: Journal International of Lingua & Technology, 1*(2).

Khang, A., Muthmainnah, M., Seraj, P. M. I., Al Yakin, A., & Obaid, A. J. (2023). AI-aided teaching model in education 5.0. *Handbook of Research on AI-Based Technologies and Applications in the Era of the Metaverse*. IGI Global. 10.4018/978-1-6684-8851-5.ch004

Khotimah, H., & Suci, D. N. (2022). Special Competence for Preschool Teacher in 5.0 Era. *Cakrawala Dini: Jurnal Pendidikan Anak Usia Dini*, 13(2), 129–138.

Khribi, M. K. Jemni, M., Nasraoui, O., Graf, S., & Kinshuk. (2013). Toward a fully automatic learner modeling based on web usage mining with respect to educational preferences and learning styles. *2013 IEEE 13th International Conference on Advanced Learning Technologies*, 403–407.

Khribi, M. K., Jemni, M., & Nasraoui, O. (2008). Automatic recommendations for E-learning personalization based on web usage mining techniques and information retrieval. *2008 Eighth IEEE International Conference on Advanced Learning Technologies*, (pp. 241–245). IEEE. 10.1109/ICALT.2008.198

Kitto, K., Whitmer, J., Silvers, A. E., & Webb, M. (2020). *Creating data for learning analytics ecosystems*. The Society for Learning Analytics Research (SoLAR). https://www.solaresearch.org/wp-content/uploads/2020/09/SoLAR_Position-Paper_2020_09.pdf

Kleine, K., Giones, F., & Tegtmeier, S. (2019). The learning process in technology entrepreneurship education—Insights from an Engineering Degree. *Journal of Small Business Management*, 57(sup1), 94–110. 10.1111/jsbm.12514

Klett, F. (2002). Visual communication in web-based learning environments. *Journal of Educational Technology & Society*, 5(4), 38–48.

Klímová, B., & Ibna Seraj, P. M. (2023). The use of chatbots in university EFL settings: Research trends and pedagogical implications. In *Frontiers in Psychology, 14*.https://www.frontiersin.org/articles/10.3389/fpsyg.2023.1131506

Klimova, B., & Pikhart, M. (2020). Current Research on the Impact of Foreign Language Learning Among Healthy Seniors on Their Cognitive Functions From a Positive Psychology Perspective-A Systematic Review. In *Frontiers in psychology* (*Vol. 11,* p. 765). 10.3389/fpsyg.2020.00765

Knauf, R., Sakurai, Y., Tsuruta, S., Takada, K., & Dohi, S. (2009). Personalized curriculum composition by learner profile-driven data mining. *2009 IEEE International Conference on Systems, Man and Cybernetics*, (pp. 2068–2073). IEEE. 10.1109/ICSMC.2009.5346317

Kocdar, S., Karadeniz, A., & Goksel, N. (2018). Using Facebook for Leveraging Sense of Community in Self-Paced Open and Distance Learning Courses. *International Journal of Emerging Technologies in Learning*, 13(5), 100. 10.3991/ijet.v13i05.8192

Kohnke, L. (2024). *Navigating the digital turn: recent books on technological integration in ELT.*

Komar, O. (2020). Professional certification training model for alternative solutions for S-1 graduate teachers who do not achieve teacher professional education. In *Borderless Education as a Challenge in the 5.0 Society* (pp. 356–358). Routledge. 10.1201/9781003107279-65

Konijn, E. A., Jansen, B., Mondaca Bustos, V., Hobbelink, V. L. N. F., & Preciado Vanegas, D. (2022). Social Robots for (Second) Language Learning in (Migrant) Primary School Children. *International Journal of Social Robotics*, 14(3), 827–843. 10.1007/s12369-021-00824-3

Kory Westlund, J. M., Jeong, S., Park, H. W., Ronfard, S., Adhikari, A., Harris, P. L., Desteno, D., & Breazeal, C. L. (2017). Flat vs. Expressive storytelling: Young children's learning and retention of a social robot's narrative. *Frontiers in Human Neuroscience*, 11(June), 1–20. 10.3389/fnhum.2017.0029528638330

Kouser, S., & Majid, I. (2021). Technological Tools for Enhancing Teaching and Learning Process. *Towards Excellence*, (March), 366–373. 10.37867/TE130133

Krashen, S. (1982). *Principles and practice in second language acquisition.*

Kumbo, L., Mero, R. F., & Hayuma, B. J. (2023). Navigating The Digital Frontier: Innovative Pedagogies for Effective Technology Integration in Education. *Journal of Informetrics*, 3(1).

Kuratko, D. F. (2005). The emergence of entrepreneurship education: Development, trends, and challenges. *Entrepreneurship Theory and Practice*, 29(5), 577–597. 10.1111/j.1540-6520.2005.00099.x

Kurniawan, S. J., Situmorang, D. D. B., & Ifdil, I. (2022). Strengthening lecturer competence with the job-embedded professional development (jepd) model: A solution for dealing with education in the era of 5.0 and the metaverse. *COUNS-EDU: The International Journal of Counseling and Education*, 7(1), 21–26. 10.23916/0020210636530

Kyza, E. A., Varda, C., Panos, D., Karageorgiou, M., Komendantova, N., Perfumi, S. C., Shah, S. I. H., & Hosseini, A. S. (2020). Combating misinformation online: Re-imagining social media for policy-making. *Internet Policy Review*, 9(4). Advance online publication. 10.14763/2020.4.1514

Lackéus, M. (2015). *Entrepreneurship in education: What, why, when, how.* (OECD Working paper). OECD. https://www.vcplist.com/wp-content/uploads/2014/10/Lackeus-2014_WP_Entrepreneurship-in-Education-FINAL-for-OECD-141023.pdf

Landers, R. N., & Landers, A. K. (2014). An empirical test of the theory of gamified learning: The effect of leaderboards on time-on-task and academic performance. *Simulation & Gaming*, 45(6), 769–785. 10.1177/1046878114563662

Lang, C., Wise, A. F., Merceron, A., Gašević, D., & Siemens, G. (2022). What is learning analytics? In C. Lang, G. Siemens, A. F. Wise, D. Gašević, & A. Merceron (Eds.) *Handbook of Learning Analytics* (2nd. ed.) (pp. 8-18). SoLAR.

Lantada, A. D. (2020). Engineering education 5.0: Continuously evolving engineering education. *International Journal of Engineering Education*, 36(6), 1814–1832.

Lantada, A. D. (2022). Engineering education 5.0: Strategies for a successful transformative project-based learning. In *Insights Into Global Engineering Education After the Birth of Industry 5.0.* IntechOpen. 10.5772/intechopen.102844

Latif, E., Mai, G., Nyaaba, M., Wu, X., Liu, N., Lu, G., Li, S., Liu, T., & Zhai, X. (2023). *Artificial General Intelligence (AGI) for Education.* 1–30. http://arxiv.org/abs/2304.12479

Lau, W. S., & Shea, M. (2022). Empowering English learners in the classroom through culturally responsive social-emotional teaching practices. *Journal of Multilingual and Multicultural Development*, 1–18. 10.1080/01434632.2022.2078337

Leasa, M., Papilaya, P. M., Batlolona, J. R., & Nuniary, S. (2023). Project-based learning: Changing students' scientific thinking to be creative from waste natural materials. *Jurnal Penelitian Pendidikan IPA*, 9(1), 350–359. 10.29303/jppipa.v9i1.2459

Lee, J., Lim, C., & Kim, H. (2017). Development of an instructional design model for flipped learning in higher education. *Educational Technology Research and Development*, 65(2), 427–453. 10.1007/s11423-016-9502-1

Lemmetty, S. (2023). Learning in the technology field: How to capture the benefits of self-direction? *IEEE Engineering Management Review*, 51(1), 123–128. 10.1109/EMR.2023.3237807

Leon, R. D. (2023). Employees' reskilling and upskilling for industry 5.0: Selecting the best professional development programmes. *Technology in Society*, 75, 102393. 10.1016/j.techsoc.2023.102393

Lever-Duffy, J., & McDonald, J. B. ve Mizell, A. P. (2003). *Teaching and Learning with Technology.* New York, USA: Allyn and Bacon.

Liem, A., Oritsland, T. A., & Norstebo, C. A. (2006). Introducing Form and User Sensitivity to Mechanical Engineering Students through Industrial Design Projects. In: Rodgers, P., Brodhurst, L. & Hepburn, D. (Eds.), *Crossing Design Boundaries:Proceedings of the 3rd Engineering & Product Design Education International Conference*, London: CRC Press.

Lima, E., Lopes, R. M., Nassif, V., & Silva, D. (2015). Opportunities to improve entrepreneurship education: Contributions considering Brazilian challenges. *Journal of Small Business Management*, 53(4), 1033–1051. 10.1111/jsbm.12110

Lin, C. C., Huang, A. Y. Q., & Yang, S. J. H. (2023). A Review of AI-Driven Conversational Chatbots Implementation Methodologies and Challenges (1999–2022). *Sustainability (Basel)*, 15(5), 4012. 10.3390/su15054012

Lindner, J. (2018). Entrepreneurship education for a sustainable future. *Discourse and Communication for Sustainable Education*, 9(1), 115–127. 10.2478/dcse-2018-0009

Lindsey, R. B., Nuri-Robins, K., Terrell, R. D., & Lindsey, D. B. (2018). *Cultural proficiency: A manual for school leaders.* Corwin Press.

Liu, M. (2006). Anxiety in EFL classrooms: Causes and consequences. *TESL reporter, 39*, 20–20.

Liu, H., Kulturel-Konak, S., & Konak, A. (2021). A measurement model of entrepreneurship education effectiveness based on methodological triangulation. *Studies in Educational Evaluation*, 70, 100987. 10.1016/j.stueduc.2021.100987

Liu, M., & Xiangming, L. (2019). Changes in and effects of anxiety on English test performance in Chinese postgraduate EFL classrooms. *Education Research International*, 2019, 1–11. 10.1155/2019/7213925

Li, Y., Schoenfeld, A. H., diSessa, A. A., Graesser, A. C., Benson, L. C., English, L. D., & Duschl, R. A. (2019). Design and design thinking in STEM education. *Journal for STEM Education Research*, 2(2), 93–104. 10.1007/s41979-019-00020-z

Loeng, S. (2020). Self-directed learning: A core concept in adult education. *Education Research International*, 2020, 1–12. 10.1155/2020/3816132

Lorenzo, G., & Ittelson, J. (2005). An overview of e-portfolios. Educause learning initiative, 1(1), 1-27.

Louie, B., Björling, E. A., & Kuo, A. C. (2021, August). The desire for social robots to support English language learners: Exploring robot perceptions of teachers, parents, and students. []). Frontiers Media SA.]. *Frontiers in Education*, 6, 566909. 10.3389/feduc.2021.566909

Luo, Y., Liu, Y., & Liu, X. (2023). Self-directed learning in the era of Education 5.0: A literature review. [IJETL]. *International Journal of Emerging Technologies in Learning*, 18(1), 52–65.

Lykourentzou, I., Giannoukos, I., Nikolopoulos, V., Mpardis, G., & Loumos, V. (2009). Dropout prediction in e-learning courses through the combination of machine learning techniques. *Computers & Education*, 53(3), 950–965. 10.1016/j.compedu.2009.05.010

Lynch, C., Wahid, A., Tompson, J., Ding, T., Betker, J., Baruch, R., Armstrong, T., & Florence, P. (2023). Interactive Language: Talking to Robots in Real Time. *IEEE Robotics and Automation Letters*. 10.1109/LRA.2023.3295255

MacIntyre, P. D. (1999). Language anxiety: A review of the research for language teachers. *Affect in foreign language and second language learning: A practical guide to creating a low-anxiety classroom atmosphere, 24*(1).

MacIntyre, P. D. (1995). How does anxiety affect second language learning? A reply to Sparks and Ganschow. *Modern Language Journal*, 79(1), 90–99. 10.1111/j.1540-4781.1995.tb05418.x

MacIntyre, P. D., & Gardner, R. C. (1991). Language anxiety: Its relationship to other anxieties and to processing in native and second languages. *Language Learning*, 41(4), 513–534. 10.1111/j.1467-1770.1991.tb00691.x

Madani, R. A. (2019). Analysis of educational quality, a goal of education for all policy. *Higher Education Studies*, 9(1), 100–109. 10.5539/hes.v9n1p100

Magee, C. L., Leong, P. K., Jin, C., Luo, J., & Frey, D. D. (2012). Beyond R&D: What design adds to a modern research university. *International Journal of Engineering Education*, 28(2).

Maistry, S. M., & Ramdhani, J. (2010). Integrating Social Responsibility into an Entrepreneurship Education Program: A Case Study. *Online Submission*, 7(4), 23–29.

Mäkelä, K., & Whipp, P. R. (2015). Career intentions of Australian physical education teachers. *European Physical Education Review*, 21(4), 504–520. 10.1177/1356336X15584088

Makopoulou, K., Neville, R. D., Ntoumanis, N., & Thomas, G. (2021). An investigation into the effects of short-course professional development on teachers' and teaching assistants' self-efficacy. *Professional Development in Education*, 47(5), 780–795. 10.1080/19415257.2019.1665572

Manjaly, Z.-M., & Iglesias, S. (2020). A computational theory of mindfulness based cognitive therapy from the "Bayesian brain" perspective. *Frontiers in Psychiatry*, 11, 1–16. 10.3389/fpsyt.2020.0040432499726

Maqsood, M., Sheikh, S., Shah, S. A., Haider, Z., Gul, S., & Gul, A. (2023). Sociolinguistic implications of online efl learning: an empirical study of language use and interaction in teacher education. *PalArch's Journal of Archaeology of Egypt/Egyptology, 20*(2), 1960-1980.

Maria, M., Shahbodin, F., & Pee, N. C. (2018). Malaysian higher education system towards industry 4.0–current trends overview.*Paper presented at theAIP Conference Proceedings*. ACM. 10.1063/1.5055483

Mariappan, J., & Krishnan, C. (2022). Integration of AI in Learning: A Paradigm Shift in Education. In *Technology Training for Educators From Past to Present* (pp. 263–275). IGI Global. 10.4018/978-1-6684-4083-4.ch014

Marquardson, J., & Gomillion, L., D. (2018). Cyber Security Curriculum Development: Protecting Students and Institutions While Providing Hands-On Experience. [ISEDJ]. *Information Systems Education Journal*, 16(5).

Matoori, S. S., & Nourafza, N. (2021). Big data analytics and cognitive computing: A review study. *Journal of Business Data Science Research*, 1(01), 23–32. http://jbdsr.com/index.php/home/article/view/4

Matorevhu, A. (2023). Curriculum innovation implementation for industrialization: A case of education 5.0 pre-service science and mathematics teacher preparation. *Journal of Research in Instructional*, 3(1), 69–86. 10.30862/jri.v3i1.214

Matthew, U. O., & Kazaure, J. S. (2020). Multimedia E-Learning Education in Nigeria and Developing Countries of Africa for Achieving SDG4. *International Journal of Information Communication Technologies and Human Development*, 12(1), 40–62. 10.4018/IJICTHD.2020010103

Mayer, R. E. (2001). *Multimedia learning*. Cambridge University Press. 10.1017/CBO9781139164603

Mayer, R. E. (2009). *Multimedia Learning* (2nd ed.). Cambridge University Press. 10.1017/CBO9780511811678

Mehdi, Y., & Kumar, S. (2019). English language anxiety and its impact on the communicative performance of the learners with the students of B-schools in Delhi NCR, India. *International Journal of Recent Technology and Engineering (IJRTE)*.

Meixian, S., Ruiyang, Z., & Zhe, S. (2021). Research of Cognitive Computing and Educational Application from the Perspective of "Intelligence +" Education. *Journal of Distance Education*, 39(2), 21–33.

Melluso, D., Pappano, L., & Anelli, F. (2020). *Implementation of Education 5.0 in Developed and Developing Countries: A Comparative Study*. Scientific Research Publishing. https://www.sydle.com/blog/education-5-0-61e71a99edf3b9259714e25a

Mene, J. M., & Mene, J. W. (1972). The relative efficiency of bimodal presentation as an aid to learning. *AV Communication Review*, 20(2), 170–180. 10.1007/BF02768415

Mentz, E., Bailey, R., Bosch, C., Breed, B., Bunt, B. J., Chigona, W., & Verster, M. (2020). *Self-directed learning research and its impact on educational practice*. AOSIS. 10.4102/aosis.2020.BK206

Meter, W., & Setiawan, B. (2023). Professional Educator in the Era of Society 5.0: Primary Education Alumni Competence. *Journal of Higher Education Theory and Practice*, 23(10).

Mezzenzana, F., & Peluso, D. (2023). Conversations on Empathy. In *Conversations on Empathy*. 10.4324/9781003189978

Micheli, P., Wilner, S. J., Bhatti, S. H., Mura, M., & Beverland, M. B. (2019). Doing design thinking: Conceptual review, synthesis, and research agenda. *Journal of Product Innovation Management*, 36(2), 124–148. 10.1111/jpim.12466

Microsoft. (2013). *Parts of computer*. Microsoft.

Minaei-Bidgoli, B., Kashy, D. A., Kortemeyer, G., & Punch, W. F. (2003). Predicting student performance: An application of data mining methods with an educational web-based system. *33rd Annual Frontiers in Education, 2003.FIE*, 2003, T2A_13–T2A_18. 10.1109/FIE.2003.1263284

Ministry of Human Resource Development. (2020). *National Educational Policy 2020. Government of India*. Ministry of Human Resourse Development. https://www.education.gov.in/sites/upload_files/mhrd/files/NEP_Final_English_0.pdf

Mishra, P., & Koehler, J. M. (2016). Technological pedagogical and content knowledge: A framework for teacher knowledge. *Teachers College Record*, 108(6), 1017–1030. 10.1111/j.1467-9620.2006.00684.x

Mitchell, J., & Guile, D. (2022). Fusion skills and industry 5.0: conceptions and challenges. In Bouezzeddine, M. (Ed.), *Insights into Global Engineering Education After the Birth of Industry 5.0*. IntechOpen. 10.5772/intechopen.100096

Mohammed, S., Larsen-Reindorf, R. E., & Awal, I. (2020). Menstrual Hygiene Management and School Absenteeism among Adolescents in Ghana: Results from a School-Based Cross-Sectional Study in a Rural Community. *International Journal of Reproductive Medicine*, 2020, 1–9. 10.1155/2020/687249132411782

Mohd Yusof, S. B., Huda Sheikh Abdullah, S. N., Mohd, M., Adnan, N., Raja Yusof, R. J., Mokhtar, U. A., Norman, A. A., & Paizi Fauzi, W. F. (2022). The effectiveness of Women 4IR Cyber 3A #Aware, Avoid, Act Program in Malaysia. *International Conference on Cyber Resilience, ICCR 2022*. IEEE. 10.1109/ICCR56254.2022.9995864

Mokhtar, S., Alshboul, J. A., & Shahin, G. O. (2019, December). Towards data-driven education with learning analytics for educator 4.0. []. IOP Publishing.]. *Journal of Physics: Conference Series*, 1339(1), 012079. 10.1088/1742-6596/1339/1/012079

Morais, P., Ferreira, M. J., & Veloso, B. (2021). Improving student engagement with Project-Based Learning: A case study in Software Engineering. *IEEE-RITA*, 16(1), 21–28. 10.1109/RITA.2021.3052677

Moreira, M., Murphy, E., & McAra-McWilliam, I. (2016). The Emergence of an Amplified Mindset of Design: Implications for Postgraduate Design Education. *International Journal of Art & Design Education*, 35(3), 356–368. 10.1111/jade.12118

Mougiakou, S., Vinatsella, D., Sampson, D., Papamitsiou, Z., Giannakos, M., & Ifenthaler, D. (2023). *Educational data analytics for teachers and school leaders*. Springer. 10.1007/978-3-031-15266-5

Mulyadi, Y. (2019, December). Vocational Teacher Perception on Industry 4.0 and Society 5.0. In *International Conference on Education, Science and Technology* (pp. 62-68). Redwhite Press.

Murdoch, G. (1997). Practicing what we preach-a trainee-centered approach to in-service education. *Paper presented at the Teacher development: Making the right moves*. Washington, D.C.: English Language Programs Divison.: United States Information Agency.

Murray, D. E. (2020). The world of English language teaching: Creating equity or inequity? *Language Teaching Research*, 24(1), 60–70. 10.1177/1362168818777529

Mustafa Kamal, N. N., Mohd Adnan, A. H., Yusof, A. A., Ahmad, M. K., & Mohd Kamal, M. A. (2019). Immersive interactive educational experiences–adopting Education 5.0, Industry 4.0 learning technologies for Malaysian Universities.*Paper presented at the Proceedings of the International Invention, Innovative & Creative (InIIC) Conference, Series*. Research Gate.

Muthmainnah, I. S., Ibna Seraj, P. M., & Oteir, I. (2022). P. M., & Oteir, I. (2022). Playing with AI to Investigate Human-Computer Interaction Technology and Improving Critical Thinking Skills to Pursue 21st Century Age. *Education Research International*, 6468995, 1–17. 10.1155/2022/6468995

Mwakisole, K. F., & Mussa, M., & Mtebe PhD, J. S. (2019). Cloud Computing Architecture for eLearning Systems in Secondary Schools in Tanzania. *The African Journal of Information Systems*, 11(4), 3.

Mwalongo, A. (2021). Teachers' perceptions about ICT for teaching, professional. *International Journal of Education and Development Using Information and Communication Technology*, 7(3), 36–49.

Nabi, G., Liñán, F., Fayolle, A., Krueger, N., & Walmsley, A. (2017). The impact of entrepreneurship education in higher education: A systematic review and research agenda. *Academy of Management Learning & Education*, 16(2), 277–299. 10.5465/amle.2015.0026

Nacher, V., Garcia-Sanjuan, F., & Jaen, J. (2016). Interactive technologies for preschool game-based instruction: Experiences and future challenges. *Entertainment Computing*, 17, 19–29. 10.1016/j.entcom.2016.07.001

Nair, M. M., Tyagi, A. K., & Sreenath, N. (2021). The Future with Industry 4.0 at the Core of Society 5.0: Open Issues, Future Opportunities and Challenges. *2021 International Conference on Computer Communication and Informatics (ICCCI)*, (pp. 1–7). IEEE. 10.1109/ICCCI50826.2021.9402498

Najjar, L. J. (1996). Multimedia information and learning. *Journal of Educational Multimedia and Hypermedia*, 5, 129–150.

Nasir, S., Wan Yaacob, W. F., & Ismail, N. (2019). The nature of online students' feedback in higher education. *International Journal of Innovation and Learning*, 25(4), 377. 10.1504/IJIL.2019.099982

Nazari, M., Karimpour, S., & De Costa, P. (2023). English language teachers' emotion-bearing situations in a professional development course: A critical-ecological perspective. *Journal of Multilingual and Multicultural Development*, 1–15. 10.1080/01434632.2023.2240750

Neck, H. M., & Greene, P. G. (2011). Entrepreneurship education: Known worlds and new frontiers. *Journal of Small Business Management*, 49(1), 55–70. 10.1111/j.1540-627X.2010.00314.x

Newby, T. J., Stepich, D. A., Lehman, J. D., & Rusell, J. D. (2000). *Instructional technology for teaching and learning desinging instruction, integrating computers and using media* (2nd ed.). Prentice-Hall Inc.

Nietfeld, J. L., Cao, L., & Osborne, J. W. (2005). Metacognitive motitoring accuracy and student performance in the postsecondary classroom. *Journal of Experimental Education*, 74(1), 7–28.

Nomoto, M., Lustig, A., Cossovich, R., & Hargis, J. (2022, May). Qilin, a robot-assisted Chinese language learning bilingual chatbot. In *Proceedings of the 4th international conference on modern educational technology* (pp. 13-19). ACM. 10.1145/3543407.3543410

Novak, J. D. & ve Gowin, D. B. (1984). *Learning how to learn.* Newyork: Cambridge University Press.

Novak, J.D. (2010). Learning, creating, and using knowledge: Concept maps as facilitative tools in schools and corporations. *Journal of e-Learning and Knowledge Society*, *6*(3), 21-30.

Nowfeek, M. R., & Mahrool, F. (2021, May 31). The Contribution of Integrated ICT in Teaching and Learning Practice: Teacher's Perspective. *International Journal of Advanced Multidisciplinary Research, 8*(5-2021),. 78–89. doi:http://dx .doi.org/10.22192/ijamr.2021.08.05.004

Numanoğlu, G., & Şen, B. (2007). Learning Styles of Computer Education and Instructional Technology Department Students. *Journal of Ahi Evran University Kırşehir Faculty of Education*, 8(2), 129–148.

Nur, N., Goh, S. J., Patel, J., & Mizrahi, M. (2024). Navigating the ethical landscape of ai integration in educational settings. In *INTED2024 Proceedings* (pp. 7654-7663). IATED.

Nurdiana, R., Effendi, M. N., Ningsih, K. P., & Abda, M. I. (2023). Collaborative Partnerships For Digital Education To Improve Students' Learning Achievement At The Institute Of Islamic Religion Of Sultan Muhammad Syafiuddin Sambas, Indonesia. *International Journal of Teaching and Learning*, 1, 1–15.

Oktaviana, D., Barizi, A., & Yaqin, M. Z. N. (2022). The Challenges of the society 5.0 era: The evaluation of learning in primary education. *Al Adzka: Jurnal Ilmiah Pendidikan Guru Madrasah Ibtidaiyah, 12*(1).

Olatunde-Aiyedun, T. G. (2024). Artificial Intelligence (AI) in Education: Integration of AI Into Science Education Curriculum in Nigerian Universities. *International Journal of Artificial Intelligence for Digital*, 1(1).

Olssen, M. (2000). The neo-liberal appropriation of tertiary education policy: Accountability, research and academic freedom. *Access: Critical Perspectives on Cultural & Policy Studies in Education*, 19(2), 9–70.

Omojola, J., Oyekan, O. A., & Zacchaeus, K. B. (2021, November). Professionalism of Educators in the Era of Society 5.0: Lessons From Society 4.0. In *1st International Conference on Continuing Education and Technology (ICCOET 2021)* (pp. 156-160). Atlantis Press.

Oteir, I., & Al-Otaibi, A. (2019). Foreign language anxiety: A systematic review. *Arab World English Journal, 10*(3), 309–317. https://awej.org/images/Vol-ume10/Volume10Number3September2019/21.pdf

Özsoy, G. (2008). Üstbiliş. *Türk Eğitim Bilimleri Dergisi*, 6(4), 713–740.

Paas, F., Renkl, A., & Sweller, J. (2004). Cognitive load theory: Instructional implications of the interaction between information structures and cognitive architecture. *Instructional Science*, 32(1/2), 1–8. 10.1023/B:TRUC.0000021806.17516.d0

Pahl, G., & Beitz, W. (2013). *Engineering Design: A Systematic Approach* (2nd ed.). Springer Verlag.

Pampaliari, S., Panagiotidis, P., & Sapounidis, T. (2023). Robot Assisted Language Learning: Application Of Educational Activities With Duckycode Robot In The English Classroom. In *ICERI2023 Proceedings* (pp. 2413-2421). IATED.

Pandey, D., Subedi, A., & Mishra, D. (2022, January). Improving language skills and encouraging reading habits in primary education: A Pilot Study using NAO Robot. In *2022 IEEE/SICE International Symposium on System Integration (SII)* (pp. 827-832). IEEE. 10.1109/SII52469.2022.9708843

Pane, M. M., Siregar, C., & Rumeser, J. A. (2020). The Role of Big Data for Interactive Online Learning: A Case Study in Students' Participations and Perceptions. Paper presented at the *Proceedings of the 2020 2nd International Conference on Big Data Engineering and Technology*. Research Gate. 10.1145/3378904.3378923

Parker, B. (2002). *Roles and responsibilities, institutional landscapes and curriculum mindscapes: A partial view of teacher education policy in South Africa, 1990-2000.* Centre for International Education, University of Sussex.

Pascarella, E. T., & Terenzini, P. T. (2005). *How College Affects Students: A Third Decade of Research* (Vol. 2). ERIC.

Patange, A. D., Bewoor, A. K., Deshmukh, S. P., Mulik, S. S., Pardeshi, S. S., & Jegadeeshwaran, R. (2019). Improving program outcome attainments using project based learning approach for: UG course-mechatronics. *Journal of Engineering Education Transformations*, 33(1), 1–8.

Paulsen, L., & Lindsay, E. (2024). Learning analytics dashboards are increasingly becoming about learning and not just analytics: A systematic review. *Education and Information Technologies*. Advance online publication. 10.1007/s10639-023-12401-4

Pearson. (2016). *Providing Educational Feedback (White Paper)*. Pearson. https://www.pearson.com

Pei, E., Campbell, I., & Evans, M. (2011). A taxonomic classification of visual design representations used by industrial designers and engineering designers. *Design Journal*, 14(1), 64–91. 10.2752/175630610X12877385838803

Pellas, N. (2024). Assessing Computational Thinking, Motivation, and Grit of Undergraduate Students Using Educational Robots. *Journal of Educational Computing Research*, 62(2), 620–644. 10.1177/07356331231210946

Pennington, M. C., & Rogerson-Revell, P. (2019). Using Technology for Pronunciation Teaching, Learning, and Assessment BT. M. C. Pennington & P. Rogerson-Revell (eds.) *English Pronunciation Teaching and Research: Contemporary Perspectives*. Palgrave Macmillan UK. 10.1057/978-1-137-47677-7_5

Pentina, I., Hancock, T., & Xie, T. (2023). Exploring relationship development with social chatbots: A mixed-method study of replika. *Computers in Human Behavior, 140.* 10.1016/j.chb.2022.107600

Pessôa, M. P., & Becker, J. J. (2020). Smart design engineering: A literature review of the impact of the 4th industrial revolution on product design and development. *Research in Engineering Design*, 31(2), 175–195. 10.1007/s00163-020-00330-z

Peura, L., Mutta, M., & Johansson, M. (2023b). Playing with Pronunciation. *Nordic Journal of Digital Literacy*, 18(2), 100–115. 10.18261/njdl.18.2.3

Phillips, E. M. (1992). The effects of language anxiety on students' oral test performance and attitudes. *Modern Language Journal*, 76(1), 14–26. 10.1111/j.1540-4781.1992.tb02573.x

Phobun, P., & Vicheanpanya, J. (2010). Adaptive intelligent tutoring systems for e-learning systems. *Procedia: Social and Behavioral Sciences*, 2(2), 4064–4069. 10.1016/j.sbspro.2010.03.641

Picciano, A. G. (2017). Theories and frameworks for online education: Seeking an integrated model. *Online Learning : the Official Journal of the Online Learning Consortium*, 21(3), 166–190. 10.24059/olj.v21i3.1225

Pieterse, J. N. (2019). *Globalization and culture: Global mélange*. Rowman & Littlefield.

Pintrich, P. R. (2002). The role of metacognitive knowledge in learning, teaching and assessing. *Theory into Practice*, 41(4), 219–225. 10.1207/s15430421tip4104_3

Piper, B., Zuilkowski, S. S., Dubeck, M., Jepkemei, E., & King, S. J. (2018). Identifying the essential ingredients to literacy and numeracy improvement: Teacher professional development and coaching, student textbooks, and structured teachers' guides. *World Development*, 106, 324–336. 10.1016/j.worlddev.2018.01.018

Pituła, B. (2021). The Teacher and the Idea of Society 5.0–Initial Diagnosis of the Problem. *Polish Political Science Yearbook*, 50(2), 149–165. 10.15804/ppsy202107

Polit, D. F., Beck, C. T., & Owen, S. V. (2007). Focus on Research Methods: Is the CVI an Acceptable Indicator of Content Validity? Appraisal and Recommendations. *Research in Nursing & Health*, 30(4), 459–467. 10.1002/nur.2019917654487

Prasetya, A. D. A. (2023). Analysis of the Mobilizing Teacher Program as a Teacher's Ongoing Professional Development. *Education Challenges is The Era Disruption 5.0 in ASEAN*, 40.

Pratama, M. R., Fawaida, U., & Guarin, R. M. (2023). Project-Based Learning in Elementary School: Influence on Students' Creative Thinking Ability. *MUDARRISA: Jurnal Kajian Pendidikan Islam*, 15(1), 60–83. 10.18326/mdr.v15i1.60-83

Psara, E., & Christodoulidou, C. (2019). ROBOTICS IN LANGUAGE LEARNING: AN EXPLORATORY STUDY USING THE BEE-BOT. *13th International Technology, Education and Development Conference*, 8675–8682.

Puranik, A. (2015). 97% of engineering graduates cannot speak English fluently: Survey. *Hindustan Times*. https://www.hindustantimes.com/education/97-engineering-graduates-cannot-speak-english-fluently-survey/story-GQEkTYwI4AX5zc7oeXkz1M.html

Rahim, M. N. (2021). Post-pandemic of Covid-19 and the need for transforming education 5.0 in Afghanistan higher education. *Utamax: Journal of Ultimate Research and Trends in Education*, 3(1), 29–39. 10.31849/utamax.v3i1.6166

Rahma, D. A., & Winarni, R., & Winarno. (2020, September). The challenges and readiness of elementary school teachers in facing society 5.0 through online learning during the Covid-19 pandemic. In *Proceedings of the 4th International Conference on Learning Innovation and Quality Education* (pp. 1-6). AM. 10.1145/3452144.3453743

Rahman, L. (2022). Cognitive Computing and Education and Learning. [IJASRD]. *International Journal of Advanced Scientific Research & Development*, 6(3), 1628–1632.

Rahman, S. F. A., Yunus, M. M., & Hashim, H. (2020). The uniqueness of flipped learning approach. *International Journal of Education and Practice*, 8(3), 394–404. 10.18488/journal.61.2020.83.394.404

Rai, A. (2022). Must we dream of India in English? *Outlook India*. https://www.outlookindia.com/magazine/story/must-we-dream-of-india-in-english/266672

Raiborn, C. A., & Payne, D. (1990). Corporate codes of conduct: A collective conscience and continuum. *Journal of Business Ethics*, 9(11), 879–889. 10.1007/BF00382911

Rajasekharaiah, K., Dule, C. S., & Sudarshan, E. (2020). Cyber security challenges and its emerging trends on latest technologies. *Paper presented at the IOP Conference Series: Materials Science and Engineering*. IOP Science. 10.1088/1757-899X/981/2/022062

Ramadhani, D., Kenedi, A. K., Helsa, Y., Handrianto, C., & Wardana, M. R. (2021). Mapping higher order thinking skills of prospective primary school teachers in facing society 5.0. *Al Ibtida: Jurnal Pendidikan Guru MI*, 8(2), 178–190. 10.24235/al.ibtida.snj.v8i2.8794

Ramakrishnan, K., Yasin, N. M., & Periasamy, J. (2022). Digital divide on cybersecurity awareness among the Malaysian higher learning institution students. *AIP Conference Proceedings*, 040022. 10.1063/5.0092796

Rao, P. S. (2019). The role of English as a global language. *Research journal of English, 4*(1), 65-79.

Rashid, T., & Asghar, H. M. (2016). Technology use, self-directed learning, student engagement and academic performance: Examining the interrelations. *Computers in Human Behavior*, 63, 604–612. 10.1016/j.chb.2016.05.084

Rasmussen, E. A., & Sørheim, R. (2006). Action-based entrepreneurship education. *Technovation*, 26(2), 185–194. 10.1016/j.technovation.2005.06.012

Rathakrishnan, B., Singh, S. S. B., Yahaya, A., Kamaluddin, M. R., Mohamed, N. H., Krishnan, A. R., & Rahman, Z. A. (2023). *The Influence of Social Media Use on Social Connectedness Among University Students*., 10.1007/978-3-031-16865-9_37

Raupers, P. M. (2000). Effects of accommodating learning- style preferences on long-term retention of technology training content [Electronic Version]. *National Forum of Special Education Journal, 9E.*

Reeve, R. A., & Brown, A. L. (1985). Metacognition reconsidered: Implications for intervention research. *Journal of Abnormal Child Psychology*, 13(3), 343–356. 10.1007/BF009127214045006

Reeves, T. (2020, October). Transforming learning with technology. *Perspectives on the future of education. Learning Solutions Magazine*, 6(1), 1–5.

Retna, K. S. (2019). Thinking about "design thinking": A study of teacher experiences. In *Teachers' perceptions, experience and learning* (pp. 4–18). Routledge. 10.4324/9781351173285-1

Richardson, C. (2018). The Next Revolution In Global eLearning. *Forbes.*https://www.forbes.com

Rideout, E. C., & Gray, D. O. (2013). Does entrepreneurship education really work? A review and methodological critique of the empirical literature on the effects of university-based entrepreneurship education. *Journal of Small Business Management*, 51(3), 329–351. 10.1111/jsbm.12021

Riegel, K. A. (2023). Project based learning (PBL): Less project, more problem. *The Journal of the Acoustical Society of America*, 153(3, supplement), A272–A272. 10.1121/10.0018820

Romero, D., Stahre, J., & Taisch, M. (2020). The Operator 4.0: Towards socially sustainable factories of the future. *Computers & Industrial Engineering*, 139(106128), 106128. 10.1016/j.cie.2019.106128

Rompelman, O., & De Graaff, E. (2007). The engineering of engineering education: Curriculum development from a designer's point of view. *European Journal of Engineering Education*, 31(2), 215–226. 10.1080/03043790600567936

Rosenbusch, K. (2020). Technology Intervention: Rethinking the Role of Education and Faculty in the Transformative Digital Environment. *Advances in Developing Human Resources*, 22(1), 87–101. 10.1177/1523422319886297

Ruane, C. (2022). *Global English, Global Identities, and the Global World: perceptions of a group of Korean English language users* [Doctoral dissertation, Macquarie University].

Rudolph, J., Tan, S., & Tan, S. (2023). War of the chatbots: Bard, Bing Chat, ChatGPT, Ernie and beyond. The new AI gold rush and its impact on higher education. *Journal of Applied Learning and Teaching*, 6(1), 364–389. 10.37074/jalt.2023.6.1.23

Rusman, A., Mas'udi, M. M., Hermoyo, R. P., Yarno, Y., Yunianti, S., & Rafsanjani, H. (2023, June). Education transformation in 5.0 society development era. In *AIP Conference Proceedings* (*Vol. 2727*, No. 1). AIP Publishing.

Rusman, A., Mas'udi, M. M., Hermoyo, R. P., Yarno, Y., Yunianti, S., & Rafsanjani, H. (2023, June). Education transformation in 5.0 society development era. In *AIP Conference.* ACM. 10.1063/5.0141657

Sˇafranj, J., & Zivlak, J. (2019). Effects of big five personality traits and fear of negative evaluation on foreign language anxiety. *Croatian Journal Educational/Hrvatski Casopis za Odgoj I Obrazovanje, 21*(1).

Şahin, F. (2001). Prospective Teachers' Opinions on Making and Applying Concept Maps. *Pamukkale University Journal of Faculty of Education*, 10, 12–25.

Saidu, A., Clarkson, A. M., Adamu, S. H., Mohammed, M., & Jibo, I. (2017). Application of ICT in Agriculture:Opportunities and Challenges in Developing Countries. *International Journal of Computer Science and Mathematical Theory, pp. 3*, 8–18.

Saito, Y., & Samimy, K. K. (1996). Foreign language anxiety and language performance: A study of learner anxiety in beginning, intermediate, and advanced-level college students of Japanese. *Foreign Language Annals*, 29(2), 239–249. 10.1111/j.1944-9720.1996.tb02330.x

Sajidan, S., Suranto, S., Atmojo, I. R. W., Saputri, D. Y., & Etviana, R. (2022). Problem-based learning-collaboration (PBL-C) model in elementary school science learning in the industrial revolution era 4.0 and Indonesia society 5.0. *Jurnal Pendidikan IPA Indonesia*, 11(3), 477–488. 10.15294/jpii.v11i3.30631

Salem, S. F., Al-Jubari, I., Aldholay, A., Jalal, A. N., & Mutahar, A. M. (2022). Covid-19 and Online Learning Engagement: Effects of Internal Crisis Communication, Technology and Social Responsibility. *Paper presented at the Proceedings of International Conference on Emerging Technologies and Intelligent Systems: ICETIS 2021* (Volume 1). Springer. 10.1007/978-3-030-82616-1_25

Salimovna, S. X. (2024). Enhancing the Pedagogical System for the Development of Professional Culture in General Urban Education Teachers. *Science Promotion*, 7(1), 210–216.

Salinas-Navarro, D. E., Garay-Rondero, C. L., & Arana-Solares, I. A. (2023). Digitally enabled Experiential Learning spaces for Engineering Education 4.0. *Education Sciences, 13*(1), 63. https://doi.org/.10.3390/educsci13010063

Saman, A. M., & Musa, K. (2020). Instructional Coaching Through Technology Integration: Accompanying Teacher Services in the Digital Era of Education 5.0. *Education*, 3(11), 2291–2299.

Sánchez-Hernández, M. I., & Maldonado-Briegas, J. J. (2019). Sustainable entrepreneurial culture programs promoting social responsibility: A European regional experience. *Sustainability (Basel)*, 11(13), 3625. 10.3390/su11133625

Saputra, I., Astuti, M., Sayuti, M., & Kusumastuti, D. (2023). Integration of Artificial Intelligence in Education: Opportunities, Challenges, Threats and Obstacles. A Literature Review. *Indonesian Journal of Computer Science*, 12(4). 10.33022/ijcs.v12i4.3266

Saputro, S., Perdana, R., Atmojo, I., & Nugraha, D. (2020). Development of Science Learning Model towards Society 5.0: A Conceptual Model. *Journal of Physics: Conference Series*, 1511(1), 012124. Advance online publication. 10.1088/1742-6596/1511/1/012124

Sarıca, R., & Çetin, B. (2012). The Effect of Using Concept Maps in Teaching on Students' Academic Achievement and Retention. *Primary Education Online Journal*, 11(2), 306–318.

Sartre, J. P. (1992). *Notebooks for an Ethics*. University of Chicago Press.

Satria, R. R., Satria, R., & Mustiningsih, M. (2019, December). Supervisor in Era Industrial Revolution 4.0 and Society 5.0. In *5th International Conference on Education and Technology (ICET 2019)* (pp. 596-601). Atlantis Press.

Saud, S., Aeni, N., & Azizah, L. (2022). Leveraging Bamboozles and Quizziz to Engage EFL Students in Online Classes. *International Journal of Language Education*, 6(2), 169–182. 10.26858/ijole.v6i2.24301

Scharmer, C.O. (2007). *Theory U: Leading from the Future as It Emerges*. soL Press

Schlosser, L. A., & Simonson, M. R. (2009). *Distance Education: Definition and Glossary of Terms* (3rd Edition ed.). USA: Association for Educational Communications and Technology.

Schoenfeld, A. H. (2016). Learning to think mathematically: Problem solving, metacognition, and sense-making in mathematics. *Journal of Education*, 196(2), 1–38. 10.1177/002205741619600202

Schraw, G., & Dennison, R. S. (1994). Assessing metacognitive awareness. Contemporary Educational Psychology, 19, 460-475.Schraw, G., & Moshman, D. (1995*). Metacognitive theories.Educational Psychology*, 7(4), 351–371.

Schwier, R. A. ve Misanchuk, E. R. (1994). *Interactive Multimedia Instruction*. Englewood Cliffs, New Jersey: Educational Technology Publications.

Scott, J. M., Penaluna, A., & Thompson, J. L. (2016). A critical perspective on learning outcomes and the effectiveness of experiential approaches in entrepreneurship education: Do we innovate or implement? *Education + Training*, 58(1), 82–93. 10.1108/ET-06-2014-0063

Scrivener, J. (2011). *The essential guide to English language teaching* (3rd ed.). MacMillan.

Seaborn, K., & Fels, D. I. (2015). Gamification in theory and action: A survey. *International Journal of Human-Computer Studies*, 74, 14–31. 10.1016/j.ijhcs.2014.09.006

Seferoğlu, S. S. (2001). Elementary school teachers perceptions of professional development. *Hacettepe Üniversitesi Eğitim Fakültesi Dergisi, 20*(20).

Seidel, V. P., & Fixson, S. K. (2013). Adopting Design Thinking in Novice Multidisciplinary Teams: The Application and Limits of Design Methods and Reflexive Practices. *Journal of Product Innovation Management*, 30(S1, No. S1), 19–33. 10.1111/jpim.12061

Selwyn, N., & Aagaard, J. (2021). Banning mobile phones from classrooms—An opportunity to advance understandings of technology addiction, distraction and cyberbullying. *British Journal of Educational Technology*, 52(1), 8–19. 10.1111/bjet.12943

Serrano, D. R., Dea-Ayuela, M. A., Gonzalez-Burgos, E., Serrano-Gil, A., & Lalatsa, A. (2019). Technology-enhanced learning in higher education: How to enhance student engagement through blended learning. *European Journal of Education*, 54(2), 273–286. 10.1111/ejed.12330

Shah, M., Nair, C. S., & Richardson, J. T. E. (2017). *Measuring and enhancing the student experience*. Elsevier.

Shahri, A., Asadollahi, A., & Khoshraftar, E. (2019). Understanding the concept of gamification in education: A systematic literature review. *Computers & Education*, 142, 103641. 10.1016/j.compedu.2019.103641

Shallal, A. H. (2017). *Design and implement an educational model by using cloud computing technologies.* Al-nilain University.

Shao, K., Yu, W., & Ji, Z. (2013). An exploration of Chinese EFL students' emotional intelligence and foreign language anxiety. *Modern Language Journal*, 97(4), 917–929. 10.1111/j.1540-4781.2013.12042.x

Shaturaev, J. (2021). A Comparative Analysis of Public Education System of Indonesia and Uzbekistan. *Bioscience Biotechnology Research Communications*, 14(5), 89–92. 10.21786/bbrc/14.5/18

Sheldon, K. M., Gordeeva, T., Leontiev, D., Lynch, M. F., Osin, E., Rasskazova, E., & Dementiy, L. (2018). Freedom and responsibility go together: Personality, experimental, and cultural demonstrations. *Journal of Research in Personality*, 73, 63–74. 10.1016/j.jrp.2017.11.007

Shepherdson, E. (2001). *Teaching concepts utilizing active learning computer environments* [Doctoral dissertation, Massachusetts Institute of Technology].

Sheppard, B., Brown, J., Dibbon, D., Sheppard, B., Brown, J., & Dibbon, D. (2009). Professional development and capacity building. School district leadership matters, 85-100.

Shih, T., & Huang, Y. Y. (2017). A case study on technology entrepreneurship education at a Taiwanese research university. *Asia pacific management review, 22*(4), 202-211.

Siddiqui, S., & Ahamed, M. M. J. A. W. E. J. V. (2020). Teachers' Roles Beyond and Within the Context: An Ever-Changing Concept. *11*.

Siemens, G., Gasevic, D., Haythornthwaite, C., Dawson, S., Shum, S. B., Ferguson, R., Duval, E., Verbert, K., & Baker, R. (2011). *Open Learning Analytics: an integrated & modularized platform.* The Society for Learning Analytics Research (SoLAR). https://solaresearch.org/wp-content/uploads/2011/12/OpenLearningAnalytics.pdf

Siemens, G. (2013). Learning analytics: The emergence of a discipline. *The American Behavioral Scientist*, 57(10), 1380–1400. 10.1177/0002764213498851

Siemens, G., & Gasevic, D. (2012). Guest Editorial - Learning and Knowledge Analytics. *Journal of Educational Technology & Society*, 15(3), 1–2. https://www.jstor.org/stable/jeductechsoci.15.3.1

Simon, N., Jiménez, J. L., & Strocchia, D. (2023). Reimaging Cybersecurity in Educational Practices: An International Case Study. In *Handbook of Research on Current Trends in Cybersecurity and Educational Technology.* 10.4018/978-1-6684-6092-4.ch001

Simonsen, B., Freeman, J., Dooley, K., Maddock, E., Kern, L., & Myers, D. (2017). Effects of targeted professional development on teachers' specific praise rates. *Journal of Positive Behavior Interventions*, 19(1), 37–47. 10.1177/1098300716637192

Singer, A. C. (2023). Project-based learning engages students at a level more directly applicable to their future careers. *The Journal of the Acoustical Society of America*, 153(3, supplement), A214–A214. 10.1121/10.0018694

Singh, H. K. B., Singh, H., Bahadin, S., Abdullah, H., Hamzah, N., Halim, K. H. K., & Abbas, M. (2022). What students say on self-directed language learning in the context of new normal: Their difficulties, coping mechanisms, and benefits. *Journal of Positive School Psychology*, 1326–1338.

Skitsko, V., & Osypova, O. (2022, September). Education 5.0 Maturity Index: Concept and Prospects for Development. In *International Conference on Electronic Governance with Emerging Technologies* (pp. 95-108). Cham: Springer Nature Switzerland. 10.1007/978-3-031-22950-3_8

Smith, A. J. (2019). *Insights into Education: A Comprehensive Guide*. Academic Press.

Smith, A. J., Collins, L. A., & Hannon, P. D. (2006). Embedding new entrepreneurship programmes in UK higher education institutions: Challenges and considerations. *Education + Training*, 48(8/9), 555–567. 10.1108/00400910610710001

Smith, A., & Johnson, B. (2019). The role of gamification in teacher development: Engaging educators through interactive learning experiences. *Journal of Educational Technology*, 42(3), 365–378.

Solomon, G. T., Weaver, K. M., & Fernald, L. W.Jr. (1994). A historical examination of small business management and entrepreneurship pedagogy. *Simulation & Gaming*, 25(3), 338–352. 10.1177/1046878194253003

Sousa, E. B. G., Alexandre, B., Mello, R. F., Falcão, T. P., Vesin, B., & Gašević, D. (2021). Applications of learning analytics in high schools: A systematic literature review. *Frontiers in Artificial Intelligence*, 4, 1–14. 10.3389/frai.2021.73789134647016

Spiller, D. (2012). Assessment matters: Self-assessment and peer assessment. *The University of Waikato*, 13, 2–18.

Stewart, J., & Claeys, L. (2011). Problems and Opportunities of Interdisciplinary Work Involving Users in Speculative Research for Innovation of Novel ICT Applications. In Pierson, J., Mante-Meijer, E., & Loos, E. (Eds.), *New Media Technologies and User Empowerment* (pp. 101–122). Peter Lang.

Sukardjo, M., & Salam, M. (2020). Effect of Concept Attainment Models and Self-Directed Learning (SDL) on Mathematics Learning Outcomes. *International Journal of Instruction*, 13(3), 275–292. 10.29333/iji.2020.13319a

Sukmara, G., Yuliana, L., Retnowati, E., & Jannah, N. M. (2023). The Important Role of Principal in Academic Supervision to Improve Teacher Competency in Society 5.0 Era. *Cendekia: Jurnal Kependidikan dan Kemasyarakatan, 21*(2), 268-284.

Sułkowski, Ł., Kolasińska-Morawska, K., Seliga, R., & Morawski, P. (2021). Smart Learning Technologization in the Economy 5.0—The Polish Perspective. *Applied Sciences (Basel, Switzerland)*, 11(11), 5261. 10.3390/app11115261

Sumarni, W., & Kadarwati, S. (2020). Ethno-stem project-based learning: Its impact to critical and creative thinking skills. *Jurnal Pendidikan IPA Indonesia*, 9(1), 11–21. 10.15294/jpii.v9i1.21754

Summit Consulting, L. L. C. (2009). *Toward Effective Education of Innovative Entrepreneurs in Small Business: Initial Results from A Survey of College Students and Graduates*. SBA Office of Advocacy.

Sung, Y., Zheng, K., & Shao, A. (2022). Collaborative learning in the era of Education 5.0: A review of literature and a conceptual framework. [IJETL]. *International Journal of Emerging Technologies in Learning*, 17(2), 18–31.

Sun, P., & Liu, X. (2020). Fostering emotional intelligence in students for success in Education 5.0. *Journal of Educational Psychology*, 62(4), 521–532.

Susnjak, T., Ramaswami, G. S., & Mathrani, A. (2022). Learning analytics dashboard: A tool for providing actionable insights to learners. *International Journal of Educational Technology in Higher Education*, 19(12), 1–23. 10.1186/s41239-021-00313-735194560

Suyudi, M., & Mahmudah, U. (2021, November). Developing Indonesian Digital-Skilled Teachers for Multicultural Education Into The Society 5.0. In *Proceeding International Conference on Islam and Civilization (ICONIC)* (Vol. 1, No. 1, pp. 31-49). Research Gate.

Tafazoli, D., & Gómez-Parra, M. E. (2017). Robot-Assisted Language Learning: Artificial Intelligence in Second Language Acquisition. In *Current and Future Developments in Artificial Intelligence* (Issue August). 10.2174/9781681085029117010015

Taghizadeh, M., & Hajhosseini, F. (2021). Investigating a blended learning environment: Contribution of Attitude, interaction, and quality of teaching to satisfaction of graduate students of TEFL. *The Asia-Pacific Education Researcher*, 30(5), 459–469. 10.1007/s40299-020-00531-z

Tan, S., Al-Jumeily, D., Mustafina, J., Hussain, A., Broderick, A., & Forsyth, H. (2018). Rethinking our education to face the new industry era. EDULEARN18 Proceedings.

Tanaka, F., Takahashi, T., Matsuzoe, S., Tazawa, N., & Morita, M. (2014). Telepresence robot helps children in communicating with teachers who speak a different language. *ACM/IEEE International Conference on Human-Robot Interaction*, (pp. 399–406). IEEE. 10.1145/2559636.2559654

Tan, Z., Beuran, R., Hasegawa, S., Jiang, W., Zhao, M., & Tan, Y. (2020). Adaptive security awareness training using linked open data datasets. *Education and Information Technologies*, 25(6), 5235–5259. 10.1007/s10639-020-10155-x

Tavakoli, M., Tixier, J., Baur, P., & Vincent-Lancrin, S. (2019). Hopes and challenges of entrepreneurship education: Dialogue between public civil servants and academics. *Entreprendre & innover*, (3), 12-21.

Teimouri, Y., Goetze, J., & Plonsky, L. (2019). Second language anxiety and achievement: A meta-analysis. *Studies in Second Language Acquisition*, 41(2), 363–387. 10.1017/S0272263118000311

Tenenbaum, G., Naidu, S., Jegede, O., & Austin, J. (2001). Constructivist pedagogy in conventional on-campus and distance learning practice: An exploratory investigation. *Learning and Instruction*, 11(2), 87–111. 10.1016/S0959-4752(00)00017-7

Thomas, C., & Jayagopi, D. B. (2017). Predicting student engagement in classrooms using facial behavioral cues. *Proceedings of the 1st ACM SIGCHI International Workshop on Multimodal Interaction for Education*, (pp. 33–40). ACM. 10.1145/3139513.3139514

Thomson, M. M., & Turner, J. E. (2019). The role of emotions in teachers' professional development: Attending a research experience for teachers (RET) program. *Education Research International*, 2019, 1–12. 10.1155/2019/5856793

Times of India. (2012). Language barrier ups students' suicides. *Times of India*. https://timesofindia.indiatimes.com/city/madurai/language-barrier-ups-students-suicides/articleshow/16522190.cms

Ting, S. H., Mahadhir, M., & Chang, S. L. (2010). Grammatical errors in spoken English of university students in oral communication course. *GEMA Online Journal of Language Studies*, 10(1), 53–69.

Togo, M., & Gandidzanwa, C. P. (2021). The role of Education 5.0 in accelerating the implementation of SDGs and challenges encountered at the University of Zimbabwe. *International Journal of Sustainability in Higher Education*, 22(7), 1520–1535. 10.1108/IJSHE-05-2020-0158

Trowbidge, J., & Ve Wandesee, J. (1994). Identifying Citical Junctures in Learning in a College Course on Evolution. *Journal of Research in Science Teaching*, 31(5), 459–473. 10.1002/tea.3660310504

Trung, B. D., Son, N. T., Tung, N. D., Son, K. A., Anh, B. N., & Lam, P. T. (2023). Educational data mining: A systematic review on the applications of classical methods and deep learning until 2022. *2023 IEEE Symposium on Industrial Electronics & Applications (ISIEA)*, (pp. 1–15). ACM. 10.1109/ISIEA58478.2023.10212273

Tsai, Y. (2019, August 18). *Learning analytics in a nutshell* [Video]. YouTube. https://www.youtube.com/watch?v=XscUZ8dIa-8

Tsou, W., Wang, W., & Tzeng, Y. (2004). Applying a multimedia storytelling website in foreign language learning. *Computers & Education*, 47(1), 17–28. 10.1016/j.compedu.2004.08.013

Uğurlu, C. T. (2009). Primary School First Grade Teachers' Opinions on Constructivist Learning Approach and First Literacy Teaching. *Electronic Journal of Social Sciences*, 8(30), 103–114.

Ulseth, R. R. (2016, June). Development of pbl students as self-directed learners. In *2016 ASEE Annual Conference & Exposition*. ASEE. 10.18260/p.26823

UNESCO. (2008). *Learning to live together: an intercultural and interfaith programme for ethics education*. UNESDOC Digital Library: Incl. bibl. Pub. with the assistance of UNESCO.

UNESCO. (2019). *Global education policy report*. Corwin Press.

UNESCO. (2021). *UNESCO Science Report: The race against time for smarter development*. UNESCO. https://www.unesco.org/reports/science/2021/en/download-report

Urakami, J., & Seaborn, K. (2023). Nonverbal Cues in Human-Robot Interaction: A Communication Studies Perspective. *ACM Transactions on Human-Robot Interaction*, 12(2), 1–21. Advance online publication. 10.1145/3570169

Usmaedi, U. (2021). Education curriculum for society 5.0 in the next decade. *Jurnal Pendidikan Dasar Setiabudhi*, 4(2), 63–79.

van den Berghe, R., Oudgenoeg-Paz, O., Verhagen, J., Brouwer, S., de Haas, M., de Wit, J., Willemsen, B., Vogt, P., Krahmer, E., & Leseman, P. (2021). Individual Differences in Children's (Language) Learning Skills Moderate Effects of Robot-Assisted Second Language Learning. *Frontiers in Robotics and AI*, 8(August), 1–14. 10.3389/frobt.2021.67624834504871

van den Berghe, R., Verhagen, J., Oudgenoeg-Paz, O., van der Ven, S., & Leseman, P. (2018). Social Robots for Language Learning: A Review. *Review of Educational Research*, 89(2), 259–295. 10.3102/0034654318821286

Vân, N. T., & Hien, D. T. (2022). *DESIGN ACTIVITIES TO CORRECT PRONUNCIATION ERRORS IN /n/ SOUND AND /l/ SOUND FOR FIRST-YEAR ENGLISH MAJORS TRƯ NG Đ I H C SƯ PH M THÁI NGUYÊN*. Semantic Scholar. https://api.semanticscholar.org/CorpusID:251211852

VanTassel-Baska, J. (2014). Performance-based assessment: The road to authentic learning for the gifted. *Gifted Child Today*, 37(1), 41–47. 10.1177/1076217513509618

Vashisht, V., Pandey, A. K., & Yadav, S. P. (2021). Speech recognition using machine learning. *IEIE Transactions on Smart Processing and Computing*, 10(3), 233–239. 10.5573/IEIESPC.2021.10.3.233

Vázquez-Parra, J. C., García-González, A., & Ramírez-Montoya, M. S. (2022). Ethical education and its impact on the perceived development of social entrepreneurship competency. *Higher Education. Skills and Work-Based Learning*, 12(2), 369–383. 10.1108/HESWBL-01-2021-0012

Ventura, S., Romero, C., & Hervás, C. (2008). *Analyzing rule evaluation measures with educational datasets: A framework to help the teacher*. Educational Data Mining 2008.

vHakim, B. M (2019). A study of language anxiety among English language learners in Saudi Arabia. *Arab World English Journal (AWEJ), 10*.

Villa, R., & Thousand, J. (2021). *The Inclusive Education Checklist: A Checklist of Best Practices*. National Professional Resources, Inc.

Vonderwell, S., Liang, X., & Alderman, K. J. J. o. R. o. T. i. E. (2007). *Asynchronous discussions and assessment in online learning*. Research Gate.

Vo, T. N. C., & Nguyen, H. P. (2012). A knowledge-driven educational decision support system. *2012 IEEE RIVF International Conference on Computing & Communication Technologies, Research, Innovation, and Vision for the Future*, (pp. 1–6). IEEE.

Vrugt, A., & Oort, F. J. (2008). Metacognition, achievement goals, study strategies and academic achievement: Pathways to achievement. *Metacognition and Learning*, 30(2), 123–146. 10.1007/s11409-008-9022-4

Wagner, T. (2008). *The Global Achievement Gap: Why Even Our Best Schools Don't Teach the New Survival Skills Our Children Need—and What We Can Do About It*. Basic Books.

Wang, H. (2024). *The Design and Evaluation of Intelligent Computer-Assisted Language Learning Tools for Beginner Learners of Mandarin Chinese* [Doctoral dissertation, Trinity College, Dublin].

Wang, J., Zhang, X., & Zhang, L. J. (2022). Effects of Teacher Engagement on Students' Achievement in an Online English as a Foreign Language Classroom: The Mediating Role of Autonomous Motivation and Positive Emotions. *Frontiers in Psychology*, 13(July), 950652. 10.3389/fpsyg.2022.95065235846620

Wang, Z., Lv, J., Hou, Y., & Song, D. (2024). Enhancing experience: Investigating the impact of different personal perspectives in virtual reality with lower limb rehabilitation robots on participants' motivation, experience, and engagement. *International Journal of Industrial Ergonomics*, 99, 103496. 10.1016/j.ergon.2023.103496

Warren, C. A. (2018). Empathy, teacher dispositions, and preparation for culturally responsive pedagogy. *Journal of Teacher Education*, 69(2), 169–183. 10.1177/0022487117712487

Watkins, S. (2019). Learners' perceptions of benefits in a self-directed teletandem course: an approach to encourage EFL learners to use English outside the classroom. *Asian EFL Journal, 23*(4.1), 4-29.

Watts, N. (2018). *Developing Digital Fluency in Higher Education: A study in the acquisition of digital capability by academics in Irish higher education settings. University College Dublin.* School of Education.

Werbach, K., & Hunter, D. (2012). *For the win: How game thinking can revolutionize your business*. Wharton Digital Press.

Wilson, B. G. (1995). *Maintaining the ties between learning theory and instructional design.*

Wilson, E. W., & Zamberlan, L. (2017). Design Pedagogy for an Unknown Future: A View from the Expanding Field of Design Scholarship and Professional Practice. *International Journal of Art & Design Education*, 36(1), 106–117. 10.1111/jade.12076

Winberg, C., Bramhall, M., Greenfield, D., Johnson, P., Rowlett, P., Lewis, O., & Wolff, K. (2020). Developing employability in engineering education: A systematic review of the literature. *European Journal of Engineering Education*, 45(2), 165–180. 10.1080/03043797.2018.1534086

Wirag, A., Li, Y., & Zhang, B. (2022). Applying cognitive linguistics to foreign language teaching and learning. *Cognitive Linguistic Studies*. https://api.semanticscholar.org/CorpusID:253870887

Woo, H., LeTendre, G. K., Pham-Shouse, T., & Xiong, Y. (2021). The use of social robots in classrooms: A review of field-based studies. *Educational Research Review*, 33, 100388. 10.1016/j.edurev.2021.100388

Wulandani, C., Putri, M. A., Pratiwi, R. I., & Sulong, K. (2022). Implementing project-based steam instructional approach in early childhood education in 5.0 industrial revolution era. *Indonesian Journal of Early Childhood Educational Research*, 1(1), 29–37. 10.31958/ijecer.v1i1.5819

Wu, W.-C. V., Wang, R.-J., & Chen, N.-S. (2015). Instructional design using an in-house built teaching assistant robot to enhance elementary school English-as-a-foreign-language learning. *Interactive Learning Environments*, 23(6), 696–714. 10.1080/10494820.2013.792844

Xiang, C. S., & Hasbullah, M. (2023). Cybersecurity Awareness, Cyber Human Values and Cyberbullying Among University Students in Selangor, Malaysia. *International Journal of Advanced Research in Technology and Innovation*. 10.55057/ijarti.2023.5.2.1

Xu, X., Y. S. (2023). The theoretical framework of personal learning environments: SPET model. *International Conference on Technology in Education*, (pp. 139–156). Research Gate.

Yadav, D., Yadav, S., & Veer, K. (2020). A comprehensive assessment of Brain Computer Interfaces: Recent trends and challenges. *Journal of Neuroscience Methods*, 346, 108918. 10.1016/j.jneumeth.2020.10891832853592

Yagi, S. M. (2000). Language labs and translation booths: Simultaneous interpretation as a learner task. *Language, Culture and Curriculum*, 13(2), 154–173. 10.1080/07908310008666596

Yang, Z., Fan, G., Pan, W., & Ren, Z. (2023). Research on educational cognitive computing model based on problem solving. *2023 IEEE 12th International Conference on Educational and Information Technology (ICEIT)*, (pp. 125–131). IEEE.

Yang, P., Xiong, N., & Ren, J. (2020). Data security and privacy protection for cloud storage: A survey. *IEEE Access : Practical Innovations, Open Solutions*, 8, 131723–131740. 10.1109/ACCESS.2020.3009876

Yang, Y. (2021). The talent training mode of international service design using a human–computer interaction intelligent service robot from the perspective of cognitive psychology. *Frontiers in Psychology*, 12, 600218. 10.3389/fpsyg.2021.60021833603699

Yan, J. X., & Horwitz, E. K. (2008). Learners' perceptions of how anxiety interacts with personal and instructional factors to influence their achievement in English: A qualitative analysis of EFL learners in China. *Language Learning*, 58(1), 151–183. 10.1111/j.1467-9922.2007.00437.x

Yan, J. X., Pan, J., & Wang, H. (2010). Learner factors, self-perceived language ability and interpreting learning: An investigation of Hong Kong tertiary interpreting classes. *The Interpreter and Translator Trainer*, 4(2), 173–196. 10.1080/13556509.2010.10798803

Yasin, F. M., Rahman, M. S., & Hassan, A. (2022). Digital literacy in the era of Education 5.0: A conceptual framework for educators. *International Journal of Instruction*, 15(2), 133–152.

Yildirim, I. (2017). The effects of gamification-based teaching practices on student achievement and students' attitudes toward lessons. *The Internet and Higher Education*, 33, 86–92. 10.1016/j.iheduc.2017.02.002

Yoon, B. (2022). *Effective teacher collaboration for English language learners*. Routledge.

Young, D. J. (1991). Creating a low-anxiety classroom environment: What does language anxiety research suggest? *Modern Language Journal*, 75(4), 426–439.

Yucel, A. S. (2006). E-learning approach in teacher training. *Turkish Online Journal of Distance Education*, 7(4), 123–131.

Yücel, A. S., & Koçak, C. (2010). *Evaluation of the basic technology competency of the teacher's candidate according to the various variables. 2nd World Conference on Educational Sciences (WCES-2010)*, İstanbul, Turkey.

Yu, H. (2024). Enhancing creative cognition through project-based learning: An in-depth scholarly exploration. *Heliyon*, 10(6), e27706. 10.1016/j.heliyon.2024.e2770638533042

Yulianto. (2021). The Needs of Training to Improve Teacher Competence in Preparing Society 5.0. *Technium Soc. Sci. J., 20*, 275.

Yünkül, E. (2018). Learner Opinions on Multimedia Learning. *Balıkesir University Journal of Institute of Social Sciences*, 21(40), 255–269.

Yünkül, E. (2019). The Effect of Multimedia Learning Material on Academic Achievement and Retention Level. *Kastamonu Journal of Education*, 27(2), 727–736.

Zalli, E. (2024). Globalization and Education: Exploring the Exchange of Ideas, Values, and Traditions in Promoting Cultural Understanding and Global Citizenship. *Interdisciplinary Journal of Research and Development, 11*(1 S1), 55-55.

Zeeshan, M. (2020). English phobia will ruin India's economic prospects. *Deccan Herald.*https://www.deccanherald.com/opinion/english-phobia-will-ruin-indias-economic-prospects-869208.html

Zepeda, S. J. (2019). *Professional development: What works*. Routledge.

Zhang, L., Yang, S., & Carter, R. A. (2020). Personalized learning and ESSA: What we know and where we go. *Journal of Research on Technology in Education*, 52(3), 253–274. 10.1080/15391523.2020.1728448

Zhang, R., & Zou, D. (2022). Types, purposes, and effectiveness of state-of-the-art technologies for second and foreign language learning. *Computer Assisted Language Learning*, 35(4), 696–742. 10.1080/09588221.2020.1744666

Zhou, C. (2023). Integration of modern technologies in higher education on the example of artificial intelligence use. *Education and Information Technologies*, 28(4), 3893–3910. 10.1007/s10639-022-11309-9

Zhou, L., Xi, Y., & Lochtman, K. (2020). The relationship between second language competence and willingness to communicate: The moderating effect of foreign language anxiety. *Journal of Multilingual and Multicultural Development*, 44(10), 1–15.

Zhu, M., Bonk, C. J., & Doo, M. Y. (2020). Self-directed learning in MOOCs: Exploring the relationships among motivation, self-monitoring, and self-management. *Educational Technology Research and Development*, 68(5), 2073–2093. 10.1007/s11423-020-09747-8

Zinina, A., Kotov, A., Arinkin, N., & Zaidelman, L. (2023). Learning a foreign language vocabulary with a companion robot. *Cognitive Systems Research*, 77, 110–114. 10.1016/j.cogsys.2022.10.007

Zohuri, B. (2023). Navigating the Global Energy Landscape Balancing Growth, Demand, and Sustainability. *J Mat Sci Apl Eng 2*(4).

Zwilling, M., Klien, G., Lesjak, D., Wiechetek, Ł., Cetin, F., & Basim, H. N. (2022). Cyber security awareness, knowledge and behavior: A comparative study. *Journal of Computer Information Systems*, 62(1), 82–97. 10.1080/08874417.2020.1712269

Ван, Ш. (2022). Students' Cognitive And Cognitive Activity In The Process Of Learning A Foreign Language Using Learning Robots. *Вестник Тверского Государственного Университета. Серия: Педагогика и Психология*. https://api.semanticscholar.org/CorpusID:253616374

Иорданишвили, А. К. (2019). Фториды: их значение для здоровья человека в современных условиях и перспективы использования. *Čelovek I Ego Zdorov e, 2*, 66–73. 10.21626/vestnik/2019-2/07

About the Contributors

Ali Sorayyaei Azar is a senior lecturer at the Department of Education, School of Education and Social Sciences, Management & Science University (MSU). He got his Ph.D. (in Applied Linguistics) from Faculty of Languages and Linguistics, University of Malaya, Malaysia in 2017. In a career spanning 26 years, he has worked as an EFL/ESL senior lecturer, researcher, and curriculum developer in Iran, Turkey, Qatar, and Malaysia. He has published and presented research papers on his topic of interest namely TESL, Academic Discourse Analysis, Genre Analysis, Corpus Linguistics, Educational Technology, and English Language Teaching Strategies in several prestigious journals including GEMA Online@ Journal of Language Studies (UKM, Malaysia), Asian ESP Journal, Asian EFL Journal, Studies in English Language and Education, World Journal of English Language, and Education and Information Technologies (Springer). He is the Editor of three books, including 'Reconceptions of Policies, Strategies, and Challenges in Education 5.0.', 'Innovations in Educational Robotics: Advancing AI for Sustainable Development', and 'Smart Education and Sustainable Learning Environments in Smart Cities'. The books will be published by IGI Global- Publisher, USA. Besides, Dr. Azar has been appointed as a member of the Editorial Board for several journals, including the *Asian Journal of University Education* (AJUE), established by Universiti Teknologi MARA, Shah Alam, Malaysia; the *International Journal of Modern Languages and Applied Linguistics* (IJMAL), established by Akademi Pengajian Bahasa (APB), Universiti Teknologi MARA, Shah Alam, Malaysia; *Education Quarterly Reviews*, established by the Asian Institute of Research; and the *Pegem Journal of Education and Instruction* (PEGEGOG), established by PEGAGOG Academy Yayıncılık Eğitim Danışmanlık Hizmetleri Editörlük Hizmetleri, Turkey.

Ahmad Albattat is an Associate Professor in Graduate School of Management, Post Graduate Centre, Management and Science University, Shah Alam, Selangor, Malaysia. He is a Visiting Professor and External Examiner in Medan Academy of Tourism (Akpar Medan). He received a PhD in Hospitality Management "Disaster and Emergency Planning and Preparedness" from University Sains Malaysia (USM), Malaysia. He worked as an Assistant Professor, Ammon Applied University College in Amman, Jordan. Senior Lecturer and Research Coordinator in School of Hospitality & Creative Arts, Management and Science University, Shah Alam, Selangor, Malaysia, and Researcher at Sustainable Tourism Research Cluster (STRC), Pulau Pinang, Malaysia. He had been working for the Jordanian hospitality industry for 17 years. His teaching and consulting fields include hospitality management, events management, research methodology, strategic management and final research projects. His research areas include hospitality management, hotel, tourism, events, emergency planning, disaster management, sustainable development goals and human resource. He is an active member of several Scientific and Editorial Board of International journals, reviewer, author and editor for book projects. His latest works have been published in the refereed international journals, conference proceedings, books and book chapters.

Marco Valeri is Associate Professor of Organizational Behavior, Faculty of Economics, Niccolã Cusano University, Italy. He is Lecture in Applied Organizational Behaviour, Xenophon College, UK. He is a Visiting Professor at University of Information Science and Technology (UIST). Paul The Apostle, Macedonia. He is Adjunct Professor at Faculty of Social Sciences and Leisure Management, School of Hospitality, Tourism and Events, Taylor's University, Malaysia. He is Adjunct Professor at Faculty of Economics, Lovely Professional University (LPU), Phagwara, India. He is Associate Researcher in Strategy, Magellan Research Center, School of Management, Iaelyon Business School, Jean Monet University, France. He is Honorary Associate Professor, University of Pannonia, Hungary. Ranked #7 worldwide the most productive family economics scholars according to the ranking published by Texas State University. Teaching and consultancy fields include strategic management, leadership development, cross-cultural management, international hospitality management. He is member of several Editorial Boards of international tourism journals, reviewer and editor of several handbooks on entrepreneurship, tourism and hospitality management (Emerald Publishing, Springer Publishing, Routledge Publishing, Edward Publishing and IGI Global Publishing).

About the Contributors

Viana Hassan is actively involved in academic and research work in Tourism & Cultural Management in Lebanon and Malta. She got her Ph.D. in Tourism Management and Cultural from Saint Joseph University, Beirut. Her Thesis was entitled "Medical Tourism in Lebanon". She has more than 19 years of tourism experience in many related Travel and Tourism Fields, varying from airline sales experience (MEA), to Co-management several Lebanese Travel agencies. She is an Experienced Lecturer with more than 18 years' experience at several universities in Lebanon (Lebanese University, A.U. L, Lebanese International University, Islamic University), the Institute of Tourism Studies, STC higher education partner of Wolver Hampton and University of Malta (Malta, GBS Malta partner of Spa bath university UK with a demonstrated history of working in the Higher education industry, Skilled in Tourism Management, Customer service, Branding, Event Management, Airline Business Management, Niche Tourism, Business operations management, Customer acquisition and Medical Tourism. Dr. Viana has participated in international conferences (Expo Dubai 2020, 7th Medical Tourism World Summit, etc...) including Athens, Paris, Vienna, Dubai, Beirut, Valencia, Amman, Lisbon, Istanbul, India and has published papers in peer review journals.

***

Nur Aeni, S.Pd.,M.Pd is a lecturer of English Education Department at Universitas Negeri Makassar. She attended some International Conference as the Presenter. Namely: Brown Bag Seminar at Northern Illinois University, DeKalb, USA, Closing Ceremony of PKPI in 2016 at Northern Illinois University, DeKalb, IL, USA. International Conference on language education, TEFLIN International Conference in 2018, International Conference on Education. Science, Art and Technology in 2018: AsiaTEFL 2020 International Conference (Kintex. Goyang South Korea, virtually) . Asia TEFL in Dajeon, South Korea, 2023. She is a member of TEFLIN, ASIA TEFL, TEFL Kuwait. Institute of Global Professional member (ISO certified 2021-now). She is the Assessor for BKD, she pursed from the Indonesian Minister of Education and Culture. She is the reviewer and editor in Elsevier, Taylor and Francis, Web of Science. She has got several awards, namely: The Best Presenter at PKPT Research Report hosted by Higher Education of Indonesia (2018).The Best Report Design for Basic Training for Civil Servant Hosted by The Ministry of Education and Culture of Indonesia & PUSLATBANG LAN (2020); Global Educator of The Decade Award given by Leadership in Education Academy Development in Philippines (2020) International Ambassador of Peace given by World Literary Forum for Peace and Human Rights (2021); Certificate of Appreciation in World Teachers' Day given by LEAD (Leadership in Education Academy and Development) Philippines 2022; International Most Outstanding Educator 2022 by Academic Development for Global Leadership In Education-Greece (ADGLE Philippines); SPSC UK Ambassador (2023) Her research interests are Teaching English as Foreign language (TEFL), Teaching English Oral Communication, English Oral Communication Apprehension, & ELT Material Development and Evaluation, ICT, Emerging Trends in ELT.

Canan Koçak Altundağ is currently an Associate Professor in the Department of Mathematics and Science Education at Hacettepe University, Ankara, Turkey. Dr. Altundağ received B.Sc., M.Sc., and Ph.D. degree from the Faculty of Education at Hacettepe Univer-sity. Her research interests include daily life chemistry, context based learning and chemistry education. She has teaching experience of more than 10 years in the area of chemistry education. Dr. Altundağ published a number of papers in preferred Journals and participated in a range of conferences.

Eka Apriani, M.Pd. is an English Lecturer at English Tadris Study Program of the Faculty of Tarbiyah in Islamic State Institute of Curup. She is a Editor in Chief in Journal of English Franca and International Journal of Education Research and Development. She is also the secretary of Corolla Education Centre Foundation, Indonesia. She Received her Master Degree (Master of Language Education) from Sriwijaya University in 2013 and Doctor of Education in Bengkulu University 2022. She has published some researchs in international journal and national journal. She has Scopus Id and WOS Id. She is a member of profession organisation: ADRI, TEFLIN, PDPI and ELITE. She is treasurer of ADRI in Bengkulu Province. Her research interest is in Writing skill and ICT in learning English. She write some books: The beauty of Rejang Lebong, Semantics Crossword, Metode Pengajaran BIPA, Drama Manuscript: The Marriage of Siti Zubaidah. She has also some Intelektual Property Right: Semantics Crossword, The beauty of Rejang Lebong, The Marriage of Siti Zubaidah, Metode Pengajaran BIPA.

Hapini Awang is the Director of the Institute for Advanced and Smart Digital Opportunities (IASDO), a part of the School of Computing at the College of Arts and Sciences, Universiti Utara Malaysia. His research interests center around Information Systems, E-Government, E-Learning, Educational Technology, ICT in Education, and Instructional Technology. He has made significant contributions to academic research, with numerous publications in reputable journals. Moreover, he has actively participated in various research and consultancy projects, including Information Systems, E-Government, E-Learning, Educational Technology, and ICT in Education. Additionally, he possesses professional qualifications as a member of the lifetime/ technical exco of the Association of Information Systems, Malaysian Chapter (MyAIS).

Abderrahmane Benlahcene is an assistant professor at the department of management, College of Commerce and Business Administration, Dhofar University, Oman. He also worked as an international lecturer at the School of Government at Universiti Utara, Malaysia. He holds master's and PhD degrees in public management from Universiti Utara Malaysia. His current research interests fall under the umbrella of public management, leadership, and organizational behavior in public organizations. Dr. Abderrahmane has extensive experience with qualitative research approaches and expertise in exploring and scrutinizing social and organizational issues. In his research, Dr. Abderrahmane has focused primarily on the application of qualitative methods to understand the complex dynamics of social and organizational issues, resulting in numerous publications in top-tier academic journals.

Elad Harison is the head of Industrial Engineering and Management Department at the Shenkar College of Engineering and Design (Israel) and an affiliated researcher at the United Nations University-MERIT (The Netherlands). He holds a PhD from the Maastricht University (The Netherlands). His research interests are in the areas of innovation, services and ICT. He has written a book on the economics and policy of software intellectual property rights and has published in international journals including: Research Policy, the International Journal of Information Management, Economics of Innovation and New Technology and the Journal of Air Transport Management. He has been a policy expert on Israeli innovation and on the patentability of computer implemented inventions in EC projects and a member of the EC's Expert Group on Intellectual Property Rights in Internet Collaborations.

Haida Umiera Hashim, PhD is a lecturer in the English Language Department, Academy of Language Studies in Universiti Teknologi Mara (UiTM) Shah Alam, Malaysia. She earned her bachelor's degree and masters degree at the University of Malaya and Universiti Kebangsaan Malaysia (UKM) in the field of education (Teaching English as Secondary Language) respectively. She graduated from Universiti Kebangsaan Malaysia and received her doctorate in the same area. Her fields of interest are English as Secondary Language (ESL) Learning, Teaching English as Secondary Language Learning (TESL), and Technology-Enhanced Language Learning (TELL). She has published an array of research articles in indexed journals and have become a jury for international innovation competitions also a reviewer for indexed journals. She, currently is the Chief Editor of home grown university journal, the International Journal of Modern Languages and Applied Linguistics (IJMAL).

Muhammad Ilyas is a dedicated and passionate research student in the field of education. Born and raised in a small town, his early experiences as a student sparked his interest in understanding and improving the educational system. He pursued his undergraduate studies in Education Sciences, where he excelled academically and demonstrated a keen curiosity for exploring innovative teaching methodologies. Motivated by a desire to make a meaningful impact, Muhammad Ilyas continued his education journey by enrolling in a master's program in Educational Research. During this time, he actively engaged in various research projects, focusing on topics such as inclusive education, technology integration, and student motivation. His commitment to advancing knowledge in the field led him to present his research findings at national and international conferences. Muhammad Ilyas is known for his collaborative spirit, often working with educators, policymakers, and fellow researchers to address pressing issues in education. His research work reflects a commitment to bridging the gap between theory and practice, aiming to create evidence-based solutions that positively influence educational outcomes. With a firm belief in lifelong learning, Muhammad Ilyas is currently pursuing a Ph.D. in Education, where he is delving deeper into the intersection of educational psychology and instructional design. His research aspirations include developing interventions that cater to diverse learning styles and promoting equity in education. In addition to his academic pursuits, Muhammad Ilyas is actively involved in community outreach programs, where he shares his knowledge and experiences to inspire the next generation of educators. His holistic approach to education research showcases a genuine dedication to creating a positive impact on the educational landscape.

Vishal Jain is presently working as an Associate Professor at Department of Computer Science and Engineering, School of Engineering and Technology, Sharda University, Greater Noida, U. P. India. Before that, he has worked for several years as an Associate Professor at Bharati Vidyapeeth's Institute of Computer Applications and Management (BVICAM), New Delhi. He has more than 14 years of experience in the academics. He obtained Ph.D (CSE), M.Tech (CSE), MBA (HR), MCA, MCP and CCNA. He has authored more than 90 research papers in reputed conferences and journals, including Web of Science and Scopus. He has authored and edited more than 30 books with various reputed publishers, including Elsevier, Springer, Apple Academic Press, CRC, Taylor and Francis Group, Scrivener, Wiley, Emerald, NOVA Science and IGI-Global. His research areas include information retrieval, semantic web, ontology engineering, data mining, ad hoc networks, and sensor networks. He received a Young Active Member Award for the year 2012–13 from the Computer Society of India, Best Faculty Award for the year 2017 and Best Researcher Award for the year 2019 from BVICAM, New Delhi.

Nur Suhaili Binti Manso is a deputy director at the Institute for Advanced and Smart Digital Opportunities (IASDO), School of Computing, the College of Arts and Sciences, Universiti Utara Malaysia. Her research interests currently revolve around GIS network analysis, GIS, Remote Sensing, and Artificial Intelligence. She has made significant contributions to academic research, boasting numerous publications in reputable journals. In addition to this, she has been actively involved in various research and consultancy projects, such as those focusing on land suitability evaluation, national unity, and agricultural land management. Furthermore, she possesses professional qualifications as an Associate Professional Member of the Institution of Geospatial and Remote Sensing Malaysia (IGRSM) and is a member of the Association of Information Systems, Malaysian Chapter (MyAIS).

About the Contributors

Abdul Gafur Marzuki is a lecturer at the State Islamic University of Datokarama Palu, completed his Bachelor's and Master's degrees in English Education at Tadulako University, a Doctorate in Instructional Technology at Malang State University, and a Short course at Leiden University Netherlands in 2016. Aside from being an academician, he is also active as a Writer and researcher in Education and Learning, ELT, Linguistics, and Literature, he is also becoming a Reviewer of more than 30 National and International journals, school accreditation assessor in Central Sulawesi Province, a research reviewer in Ministry of Religious Affairs, Facilitators of Sekolah Penggerak, and a core administrator of several professional and social community organizations.

Aissa Mosbah is an assistant professor of entrepreneurship and the Department of Marketing and Entrepreneurship, Dhofar University, Oman. He obtained a master's degree in international business and a PhD in Management from Malaysian universities. His PhD research dealt with the immigrant entrepreneurship phenomenon. Aissa is expert in both qualitative and quantitative research, and his research areas include entrepreneurship, family business, firm internationalization, and organizational behavior.

Jahirul Mullick is an Assistant Professor of Educational Leadership at the College of Education and also serves as Director of the LEAD Research Institute at Wenzhou-Kean University, China. With nearly two decades of experience, Dr. Mullick has made significant contributions to the field of education through teaching and research studies in Australia, Bangladesh and China. His primary areas of expertise include educational leadership and management, inclusive education, behavior analysis, positive behavior support, and teacher development. Currently, Dr. Mullick is engaged in international studies focusing on inclusive school leadership, distributed leadership practices, parental perspectives on educating children with additional needs, and inclusive STEAM pedagogy.

Rehan Mehmood Sabir is a P.hD. Scholar Agricultural Engineering My career objectives is to expand skills and experience in Climate change impacts on Agriculture, precision agriculture, Remote sensing and GIS. I want to develop novel techniques on climate change. Based on my findings I would like to introduce new tools and techniques for the farmer's community to boost crop yield.

Rabia Elmas completed her undergraduate education at Marmara University Science Teaching Department and was appointed as a Science teacher in Gaziantep province in 2018. In 2023, Hacettepe University Department of Mathematics and Science Education. She completed her master's degree without thesis in the department of Technology and Environmental Education in Chemistry Education and graduated in February 2024. Today, he is still working as a Science Teacher at Gaziantep Oğuzeli Atatürk Secondary School.

Qiusu Wang is a doctoral student and Graduate Research Assistant at Wenzhou-Kean University's LEAD Research Institute, focusing her research on inclusive education and educational leadership practices. She holds a Bachelor of Science in Economics and Statistics and a Master of Science in Applied Economics and Predictive Analysis, both from Southern Methodist University in the United States. In addition, she expanded her academic qualifications with a Master of Science in Education from Johns Hopkins University. Prior to commencing her EdD studies, Ms. Wang acquired valuable teaching experience in mathematics at a primary school in the United States.

Muthmainnah Yakin, Ph.D., an accomplished Assistant Professor at Universitas Al Asyariah Mandar in West Sulawesi, Indonesia, stands as a distinguished academician with a diverse and impactful professional portfolio. Her multifaceted career spans roles such as Chairman of the Indonesian Language Department, Public Relations Officer, Director of Women's Centre Studies, Deputy Director of Quality Assurance Unit, and her current position as Deputy Director of the Language and Character Development Institute. In addition to her administrative roles, Muthmainnah is a prolific author, contributing to the scholarly landscape with 58 national and international books. Her publications, hosted by prestigious publishers such as Springer, Emerald, IGI Global, Wiley, Routledge, and Taylor and Francis, underscore her commitment to advancing knowledge in various domains. Her profile of authored books is accessible via the Science and Technology Index (SINTA) portal: https://sinta.kemdikbud.go.id/profile/books. Muthmainnah's global influence extends beyond her academic achievements. As an international board member for several scientific innovation research groups and a member of the United Nations Volunteers roster, she actively contributes to international research collaborations and initiatives. Her exceptional contributions have earned her over 100 international awards, including recognitions as Outstanding Professor, Outstanding Leadership, Best International Influencer, Best Emerging Professor of the Year, and the International Award for Working Women and SDGs Warrior. Notably, she holds an honorary doctorate degree from Layahe University and has been honored with the Doctor of Excellence award from the Philippines. Muthmainnah's dedication to education is further evidenced by her membership in the United Nations Volunteers' roster and her advisory role in the Indonesian Education Share to Care Volunteers. Her research interests encompass a broad spectrum, including the development of literary works, instructional teaching materials, Assurance of Learning (Assure), Teaching English to Speakers of Other Languages (TESOL), ICT in education, digital education, and cybergogy. Muthmainnah's scholarly impact is quantified by her Sinta score of 2052, h-index of 18, and her role as an External Examiner for Ph.D. students at three A+ accredited campuses in India and Australia. Her commitment to international collaboration and teamwork positions her as an ideal candidate for various academic and leadership roles.

Midya Yousefi is an assistant professor in the Doctorate of Educational Leadership & Master of Educational Administrative programs at Wenzhou Kean University. She earned her Ph.D. in Educational Leadership & Management and MEd in Educational Administration & Management from the Research University of Science Malaysia. She has over nine years of experience teaching educational leadership, management, and administration courses. She has taught students from different countries. Her educational leadership roles include being the program leader of the MSc. in Education Management & head of the Centre for Leadership & Development in Malaysia. She is experienced in quantitative research methodology and facilitating statistical software workshops, including SPSS, AMOS & SmartPLS in Malaysia, the Middle East, and China. She is also an academic Academy of Management (AOM) member.

Index

F

G

H

I

L

M

N

O

P

R

S

T

V

www.ingramcontent.com/pod-product-compliance
Lightning Source LLC
LaVergne TN
LVHW081251011026
849162LV00006BA/1482

* 9 7 9 8 3 6 9 3 3 0 4 1 8 *